PRAISE FOR *WHY NOTHING WORKS*

"*Why Nothing Works* is the best book to date on the biggest political issue that nobody is talking about, but everyone feels—a palpable and basically accurate sense that American society has lost the capacity to plan and execute large projects in the physical world. How can it be that the richest country on earth and the home to so many globe-straddling companies is saddled with second-rate infrastructure and endemic housing shortages?"
—Matthew Yglesias

"For progressive politics to work, the public must have an affirmative view of government and its effectiveness. This book is essential reading to appreciate how sometimes we can be our own worst enemy."
—Rahm Emanuel

"Anyone who has been frustrated with the inefficiency of government must read this book. Dunkelman takes us on a sweeping investigation of how, over the course of the twentieth century, the public sector has been increasingly paralyzed from exercising authority, demonstrating convincingly that the Progressive Left has been as much at fault in undermining popular trust as the Conservative Right. This beautifully written book cuts to the central dilemma of our day: how to empower a strong central government that works while still respecting the will of the people and inviting democratic participation. Dunkelman has confidence that we can do better—and he shows us how."
—Lizabeth Cohen, Howard Mumford Jones Professor of American Studies, Harvard University, and author of *Saving America's Cities*

"America is living the truth of the old saying: Any old jackass can kick down a barn, but it takes a carpenter to build one. Today, it feels like anyone can stop progress, but nobody's capable of starting it. I got into politics because when I was a kid, government delivered big things for my little corner of Louisiana—roads, and canals, and electricity. If you want to know why that happened back then, why it's not happening now, and how we can start doing and building big things again, then this is the book for you."

—James Carville

"Friends of democracy typically hold two honorable impulses in tension: Power should be widely dispersed, and citizens should control the decisions affecting their lives; and democratic government should be able to accomplish big things and undertake big projects. Dunkelman's provocative, well-argued thesis is that errors made in the name of the first objective have prevented democracy from achieving the second. *Why Nothing Works* is a spirited and thoughtful intervention in the debate progressives need to have."

—E.J. Dionne Jr., author of *Why Americans Hate Politics*

"Why America can't build is the central economic and political question of our time. In *Why Nothing Works* Marc Dunkelman asks progressives to reflect on how their own ideas have stymied the nation's ability to address the housing and climate crises and slashed national ambition in public works projects. A fantastic thinker, Dunkelman has written an essential book for anyone seeking to understand how Americans have lost faith in democratic institutions that over-promise and under-deliver."

—Jerusalem Demsas, *The Atlantic*

"Why can't the United States do big things anymore? Dunkelman tackles that question in this brilliant book, which takes a deep dive into why the well-meaning ideals of progressivism became unexpected obstacles to progress. Through a series of illuminating case studies, Dunkelman presents a thorough examination of what went wrong and offers ideas for a path forward."

—Jonathan Lemire, cohost, MSNBC's *Morning Joe*, and author of *The Big Lie*

"Dunkelman has written a terrific book that both illustrates the extent of America's public sector dysfunction and explains how that dysfunction emerged. From housing to public transportation to energy infrastructure, Dunkelman explains what went wrong and what to do about it. This book is a crucial addition to the national discussion of how to make our country more productive and affordable."
—Edward Glaeser, Fred and Eleanor Glimp Professor of Economics, Harvard University, and author of *Triumph of the City*

"Politicians debate policy but ignore that America's governing framework is often 'authentically incompetent.' With vivid stories laced with historical feuds and fears, Dunkelman shows how democracy descended into a state of rigor mortis. The cure is clear but bold—to largely abandon the procedural framework and put humans in charge again."
—Philip K. Howard, author of *The Death of Common Sense*

"So much hinges on understanding what Dunkelman so clearly explains in this book—why we got stuck in a pattern of blocking everything from housing, to transportation, to green energy infrastructure and the price we're paying for it now. Getting unstuck must become the most urgent priority of the left if we value our democracy. Everyone who reads this engaging, revealing book will want to be part of this much-needed change."
—Jennifer Pahlka, author of *Recoding America*

"In this richly researched, compellingly argued, and sparklingly entertaining book, Dunkelman shows how American liberals—once builders and innovators par excellence—lost touch with their own mission and forgot how to build. This is a book for anyone who cares about putting *progress* back into progressivism and restoring government's capacity to solve problems. In other words, it's urgent reading for everyone."
—Jonathan Rauch, senior fellow, Brookings Institution, and author of *Government's End*

"A powerfully argued book that ably clarifies and takes on America's deep cultural aversion to power."
—Gordon Wood, Pulitzer Prize–winning author of *The Radicalism of the American Revolution*

WHY
NOTHING
WORKS

ALSO BY MARC J. DUNKELMAN

The Vanishing Neighbor:
The Transformation of American Community

WHY NOTHING WORKS

WHO KILLED PROGRESS—AND
HOW TO BRING IT BACK

MARC J. DUNKELMAN

PUBLICAFFAIRS

New York

PublicAffairs
Hachette Book Group
1290 Avenue of the Americas, New York, NY 10104
www.publicaffairsbooks.com
@Public_Affairs

Printed in the United States of America

First Edition: February 2025

Published by PublicAffairs, an imprint of Hachette Book Group, Inc. The PublicAffairs name and logo is a registered trademark of the Hachette Book Group.

The Hachette Speakers Bureau provides a wide range of authors for speaking events. To find out more, go to hachettespeakersbureau.com or email HachetteSpeakers@hbgusa.com.

PublicAffairs books may be purchased in bulk for business, educational, or promotional use. For information, please contact your local bookseller or Hachette Book Group Special Markets Department at special.markets@hbgusa.com.

The publisher is not responsible for websites (or their content) that are not owned by the publisher.

Print book interior design by Sheryl Kober.

Library of Congress Cataloging-in-Publication Data
Names: Dunkelman, Marc J., author.
Title: Why nothing works : who killed progress—and how to bring it back / Marc J. Dunkelman.
Description: First edition. | New York : PublicAffairs, 2025. | Includes bibliographical references and index.
Identifiers: LCCN 2024031101 | ISBN 9781541700215 (hardcover) | ISBN 9781541700246 (ebook)
Subjects: LCSH: Progressivism (United States politics) | Progress. | Public administration—United States. | United States—Politics and government.
Classification: LCC JK275 .D86 2025 | DDC 324.2732/7—dc23/eng/20241126
LC record available at https://lccn.loc.gov/2024031101

ISBNs: 9781541700215 (hardcover), 9781541700246 (ebook)

LSC-C

Printing 1, 2024

For Emilia, Helen, and, of course, Kathryn

"We have these honorary pigs like [San Francisco] Mayor Alioto . . . plugged into one gigantic system, one octopus spanning the continent from one end to the other, reaching its tentacles all around the world, in everybody's pocket and around everybody's neck. We have just one octopus. A beast with his head wherever LBJ might be tonight."
—CIVIL RIGHTS LEADER ELDRIDGE CLEAVER,
OCTOBER 1, 1968

"We are at a moment of history. You could have Robert Moses come back from the dead and he wouldn't be able to do shit."
—CLEAN ENERGY EXECUTIVE MICHAEL SKELLY,
APRIL 6, 2017

CONTENTS

INTRODUCTION

THE EXPRESSWAY AND THE TRAIN STATION

The most haunting story in *The Power Broker*, Robert Caro's Pulitzer Prize–winning history of New York, traces a singularly powerful man's determination to jackhammer an expressway across the South Bronx. Caro's subject, Robert Moses, was at the peak of his imperious glory when he decided during the mid-1950s to dig what amounted to a cavernous trench through some of the Big Apple's most vibrant working-class neighborhoods. Nearly everyone objected—even the mayor had taken sides with the parade of citizens, community groups, and elected officials begging the great man to modify the route. But those pleas fell on Moses's deaf ears. And by the point of *The Power Broker*'s celebrated release two decades later, the Cross Bronx Expressway had effectively turned a once lively and multicultural section of the globe's financial capital into an urban wasteland.[1]

Caro's telling of the horrors—Moses blithely imposing his will on enfeebled citizens—was not only damning but indicative of why, by the time of the book's publication in 1974, the public had turned against public authority. In nearly every realm, those wielding power in government appeared impervious to objection, high-handedly dismissing anyone with the moxie to raise a stink. Whether it was Richard Nixon's corrupt efforts to keep his hold on the White House, or the Pentagon lying about Vietnam, or Moses razing whole parts of New York without any mind to his victims, what had come to be called "the Establishment" seemed, by the 1970s, to have run completely amok. *The Power Broker* was simply the most erudite treatment of how public authority had gone awry. By that point, no one really doubted that it had.

In 2013, I reread *The Power Broker* during my weekly train commute to New York. At the end of each journey, following the conductor's announcement that we'd arrived in Manhattan, I would close the book, gather my belongings, and climb up into the daylight through the dingy, fetid basement corridors that serve as the city's front door. At the time, more people traveled through New York's Penn Station each weekday than traversed the region's three airports combined.[2] And yet, while the station had originally been described by the *New York Times* as "the largest and handsomest . . . in the world," its turn-of-the-century grandeur had been razed in 1963 to make room for the eyesore known as Madison Square Garden.[3] A once magnificent station was left to occupy the warren of dimly lit corridors below. And each time I traipsed through, I asked myself: Why hasn't anyone fixed this? Why was New York allowing its most important gateway to fester as a rat's nest?

Penn Station was not the only example of New York's torpor. Decades earlier, Moses had built all sorts of things, and often in short order. Not only neighborhood-destroying highways, but parks, and bridges, and tunnels, and apartment buildings, and major cultural attractions—Lincoln Center, the United Nations Headquarters, the World's Fair grounds in Queens, and, perhaps most celebrated, Jones Beach on Long Island. Venerated by many, he was, even then, considered a villain by others. But following the Verrazzano-Narrows Bridge's opening in the late 1960s—the same time, as it happened, that Moses was stripped of his last remaining influence—the city had essentially stopped building new infrastructure.[4] And that left me curious. What had changed? Why hadn't the globe's second most heavily trafficked transit hub been reimagined or redeveloped? Why had it been so easy for Moses to pursue bad projects when it was now so hard to complete good ones?

The problem, I quickly concluded, wasn't a lack of vision. In the wake of Penn Station's demolition and Moses's subsequent dethroning, a range of powerful figures had championed various plans for restoration. As early as the 1980s, New York senator Daniel Patrick Moynihan had begun speaking about Penn Station as his top priority—a massive public endeavor not only to restore some of Manhattan's lost splendor, but to spur development of Midtown's woebegone Far West Side. One iteration of the plan included a massive, 150-foot glass-and-steel canopy designed by the renowned architect David Childs—a flourish that promised to make Manhattan's new gateway a destination in and of itself.[5]

Moynihan's proposed redevelopment would, of course, be expensive—but set against all the projects Moses had pursued during his long reign, the dream of making Penn Station a front door worthy of the globe's financial capital was hardly out of the ordinary. Madison Square Garden might need to be moved, again. But few objected substantively to the senator's vision. Nevertheless, like so many other grand visions in New York—extending subway lines, erecting new housing, making it quick and easy to get from Manhattan to the city's airports—progress foundered for years, and then decades. Each time I arrived in the world's financial capital, I confronted a Penn Station whose replacement had been a sore subject for more than thirty years.

Hoping to gain some perspective on the dynamics holding back progress, I began reading up on the project's history, building a spreadsheet that tracked all the erstwhile attempts to answer Moynihan's call to action. I began reaching out to people who had been involved in various schemes, many of which had been abandoned years, if not decades, earlier. I spent hours listening to frustrations narrated by disillusioned representatives of City Hall, of the state's economic development agency, of both the national railroad that owned the station (Amtrak) and the state-owned railroads that delivered commuter trains from New Jersey and Long Island, of Madison Square Garden executives, and of the megadevelopers hoping to erect skyscrapers in the surrounding neighborhood. I soon came to accept that everyone had a legitimate interest in the project—and most had good intentions. But they simply couldn't divine a way forward because not everyone's interests were aligned.

I was surprised by my own conclusion. I'd suspected at the outset that some single roadblock was *really* culpable for the whole fiasco—that, for example, the Dolan family, which controls Madison Square Garden, was the fly in the ointment. But the truth turned out to be different: Nearly every player involved in the negotiation had something significant to lose if the redevelopment took any certain turn. And while nearly everyone was willing to show some flexibility in pursuit of the greater good, no one was willing to abandon their own interests too severely. The result was an impenetrable Rashomon, with everyone laying blame at the feet of some purportedly intractable partner. *If only* federal bureaucrats had approved more funding. *If only* Amtrak had been more flexible in scheduling track construction. *If only* the preservationists had approved demolishing a hidden wall. *If only* a peevish governor had exerted his leverage over the Dolans. *If only* the Dolans had relented. *If only, if only, if only.*

What I came to find so remarkable was that this whole Rashomon phenomenon had rarely flummoxed Robert Moses. Decades earlier, he'd managed to build the Cross Bronx despite a whole cacophony of objections—and yet the project had steadily moved forward. That contrast hadn't been lost on the figures involved in the negotiations over Penn Station. On more than a few occasions, midway through an interview at a Midtown coffee shop, one of my subjects would scan for eavesdroppers, lean forward, and whisper to me, not for attribution: "This is why we need another Robert Moses." Then, leaning back and reconsidering what they'd just said, they'd make all the requisite disclaimers. Not the racist parts of Moses. Or his taste for ever more expressways. Or his penchant for condemning the homes of working-class families. They simply believed it was time to install someone with sufficient authority to drive projects to their completion—someone who could cut through all the "if onlys."

The first half dozen times I'd been told Penn Station's morass had suffered for not having a Moses-like figure, I'd nodded along. In Caro's telling, Moses had been a kind of political savant, roguishly maneuvering to be appointed to a cluster of city and state bureaucracies—park commissions, state councils, transportation authorities—such that he could throw his weight around, impervious to the naysayers. Moreover, "the best bill writer in Albany" regularly managed to weave seemingly innocuous language into bills granting him ever more authority. The result was that Moses had managed to *centralize* power—to cull together leverage that would have otherwise been spread to a range of others.

A half century later, Penn Station was caught in the flip circumstance: Power had been so diffused that any minor objection would upend the whole thing. This wasn't a shift in personality—it was a transformation in the architecture of power itself. But, at that point, I still didn't understand what had prompted the change. Robert Caro's masterpiece had pulled the veil off Moses—*The Power Broker* revealed how, in ways both terrible and mundane, the Establishment had wielded power to catastrophic effect. I now wanted to understand what had happened in the decades since. This book traces what I uncovered.

This is an intellectual story in some sense—a battle of ideas. But it's also a window into one crucial reason government has lost the public's confidence over the last several decades. America is caught in a housing crisis today—we simply can't seem to build enough homes. We're trying to thwart a climate crisis, but we can't bring enough clean energy online to render fossil fuels obsolete. We're decades behind Europe and China in building high-speed rail lines. And despite massive investments from the Biden administration—resources unseen in generations—progress is too often halting.[6] In America today, government too often plays the buffoon. And while that's a problem in and of itself, it's a particular scourge for progressives who view government as a crucial tool for setting things right.

The chapters that follow argue that, for all the complaints, these frustrations aren't born for lack of what some term "political will." America still boasts its fair share of Robert Moses wannabes. Nor is it that conservatives have thwarted government by "starving the beast"—though that certainly hasn't helped.[7] Rather, this book argues that progressivism itself has changed. Once committed to galvanizing experts to tackle big problems, the movement has more recently turned in the other direction. Having come to see how men like Moses were wielding public authority, progressives haven't just taken more frequently to "speaking truth to power." Rather, we've remade our governing agenda in its entirety. We've broadly abandoned efforts to draw power into the hands of power brokers and worked instead to diffuse authority—to push it down and out.

Before going any further, I want to be clear that several things can be true here at the same time. First, conservatives can (and should) be assigned some bulk of the blame for convincing portions of the public that government is invariably bad—not only that public authority is wasteful, corrupt, and ineffective, but that it is an agent of moral decay.[8] That's long been their bread and butter, and they should own it. But progressives can't hide from the reality that we too have burnished the same narrative: the movement's determination to protect against latter-day Robert Moses types now serves not only to thwart abuse, but also to undermine government's ability to do big things. As we'll see, by helping to render government incompetent, we have pried open the door for MAGA-style populism. We share culpability for the public's frustration.

Fortunately, things need not remain this way. To paraphrase a Democratic luminary, there's nothing *wrong* with progressivism that can't be fixed by what's *right* with progressivism.[9] But to right the ship, the movement will need a new perspective on how its values inform its agenda, and how its agenda shapes its politics. Rather than remain dependent on vilifying (frequently villainous) opponents and focusing the public on the depths of their villainy, progressivism needs to seek to heal itself—to expand the movement's appeal so that it isn't so vulnerable to criticisms from the outside. But that will mean addressing the root causes of public failure. And to do that, progressives will need first to understand the conflicting impulses that have led so many Americans to feel as though nothing works.

PROGRESSIVISM'S GREAT SCHISM

This book makes three arguments. The first is that progressives have conned themselves into believing that they're focused on one thing when, in reality, the movement is broadly about something else. In fairness, that confusion has been born in large part from the fuzzy definition of the word "progressive."[10] Today, the label is sometimes taken to mean that someone leans far to the left. In other contexts, it suggests that someone subscribes to some smorgasbord of political positions—on abortion, climate change, gun safety, or simply on Donald Trump.[11] A further complication: if you asked a self-described progressive what it means to be progressive, many would simply define it as the antithesis of conservatism. And in a global context, "progressive" parties are generally thought to be the "party of government," set in opposition to the more conservative "party of business."[12]

The journalist Matthew Yglesias supposed in early 2022 that if you interviewed many among the young college graduates who typically staff Democratic congressional offices, they would argue "that transforming the United States into a European-style welfare state would be desirable, and the big question about the Democratic Party is whether it's too full of lame sellouts."[13] But I suspect that those same "progressives," if asked to list the issues that mean the most to them, would turn out to be less interested in expanding government authority than in boxing it in—that few pine for big government so much as they fear government coercion. They worry about the prying tentacles of abusive police officers, corrupt election officials, and conservative jurists much more than they dream of expanding access to health care—or so you would come to presume if you scrolled their doom-filled social media feeds.

In 2019, a group of political scientists at Vanderbilt and UCLA conducted an experiment seeking to understand which issues were most salient to various types of voters. Interviewing roughly half a million Americans in search of the "revealed importance" of various topics, their surveys packaged issues together in creative ways—combining, for example, the liberal positions on gun control and the minimum wage with the conservative position on immigration. They then asked survey-takers whether they preferred *that* slate or the mirror image—namely the conservative position on gun control and the minimum wage, but the liberal position on immigration. The results allowed them to better discern what was pulling at voters' guts, if not their minds.

What the researchers uncovered about the voters they termed "liberals" was noteworthy. Policies separating immigrant children from their parents, banning abortion, and preventing Muslims from entering the United States turned out to be *more* salient than policies increasing the minimum wage, providing Medicare for all, or capping carbon emissions. The issues that resonated most powerfully painted government as a *menace*—as an institution poised to rip families apart, rob women of their bodily autonomy, and discriminate on the basis of religion. Issues that framed government as a *salve*—proposals to raise family incomes, expand access to health care, and save the earth from a climate catastrophe—were less heartrending.[14] In essence, a movement that's purported to be bent on *growing* government appears, upon closer inspection, more driven to *paring* it back.

That's not to argue that progressives aren't, in many instances, eager to expand public authority. Obamacare broadened Washington's mandate, and three of the Biden administration's biggest early achievements—the bipartisan infrastructure bill, the Inflation Reduction Act, and the CHIPS and Science Act—had the effect of expanding government's reach. But if those triumphs were each a big deal, they elicited less attention among progressives than questions of endemic racism, access to abortion, and immigrant rights. In short, the research suggested that the progressive head and the progressive heart are in different places. And that, I will argue, is for a hidden reason: progressivism can't be boiled down to one governing impulse—it's actually a strange and awkward amalgam of two.

Before delineating the distinction, it's worth reconsidering how, exactly, we presume individuals come to their politics. If each individual's view of government were some immutable genetic trait—an engrained characteristic like someone's height or eye color—that would be one thing. If our thinking were an entirely academic exercise—if individuals typically investigated an issue before coming to a logical conclusion—it would be another. But, in reality, that's not how things work. Rather, our individual politics are brewed up from some combination of emotion and rationality, nature and nurture, logic and values, such that we come to issues of policy through *narrative*.[15] We develop stories to help us make sense of reality—the famed journalist Walter Lippmann termed these the "pictures in our head"—and we then use those frames to make sense of politics.[16] My argument here is that progressives operate with two separate pictures in their heads—two narratives that they hold simultaneously, often without even recognizing the distinction.

The first of the two is framed by the misery born of chaos—a narrative steeped in our images of tenement-dwelling immigrants, of the "Okies" making their way west in John Steinbeck's *The Grapes of Wrath*, of New Orleanians stranded after Katrina, of children starving in refugee camps, of polar bears trapped on melting icebergs. In the face of these privations, progressives rue *the absence of authority*—they long for a heroic figure equipped to save the day. Set amid various tragedies of the common, progressivism's first narrative dreams of pulling power up and into a node of authority equipped to make things better *from above*.[17] A relief agency, a benevolent bureaucracy, a Herbert Hoover in Belgium, a Mother Teresa in Calcutta, an Admiral Thad Allen in Louisiana.[18]

The second narrative is born not from chaos but from tyranny. Centralized authority, in this frame, is less a salve than a menace. King George. The slave driver. The bureaucrat requiring a rape victim to bring her pregnancy to term. The cop with his knee on George Floyd's neck. Robert Moses. In these circumstances, the progressive impulse isn't to push authority up—it's "to speak truth to power," to cashier the tyrant and shield the victim.[19] As one liberal once explained on Facebook during a period of intense debate over the war between Israel and Hamas that began in October 2023: "I will ALWAYS stand beside those with less power. Less wealth, less access and resources and choices."[20] The dream isn't to imbue some savior with the authority to fix things—it's to manacle a pernicious octopus. Power, within this narrative frame, isn't a balm—it's a scourge.

These two narratives aren't exclusive to progressivism—they represent, by some measure, a tension straight out of the Enlightenment.[21] Dueling impulses to pull power up and to push it down span the political spectrum. Nor were they born with progressivism's emergence at the turn of the twentieth century. Indeed, one hundred years earlier, during the late eighteenth century, they represented the core friction between two founding luminaries. Alexander Hamilton, leader of the Federalists, worried primarily about chaos. He wanted to place more authority in the hands of centralized officials and financiers capable of developing America into an industrial dynamo—a "Hercules" on the global stage.[22] His worry was that America would remain too disorganized, too divided, too chaotic to make the most of its opportunity.[23] Pulling power into a leadership class would deliver more for the public.

Thomas Jefferson's narrative, by contrast, was born of an entirely different frame. Horrified by the English Crown's treatment of the colonies, he was determined to *thwart* overbearing authority—to protect individuals (or, at least, white, male, landowning individuals) from the abuses of public authority.[24] Jefferson saw shadows of the Crown's cruelty in centralized national bureaucracy, and his attendant skepticism, paired with his belief that individual yeoman farmers were the heart of democratic practice, prevailed through the bulk of the nineteenth century.[25] As Henry Adams would write: "European travellers who passed through America [in the early 1800s] noticed that everywhere, in the White House at Washington and in log-cabins beyond the Alleghanies, except for a few Federalists, every American, from Jefferson and Gallatin down to the poorest squatter, seemed to nourish an idea that he was doing what he could to overthrow the tyranny which the past had fastened on the human mind."[26]

This book's first argument is that *both* of these narratives—one Hamiltonian, the other Jeffersonian—frame elements of the progressive worldview. They were *both* part of the movement's origin story in the late nineteenth century, and they have *both* framed progressive thinking ever since, despite being largely at odds. When progressives perceive a challenge through the Hamiltonian lens, the movement tends to embrace solutions that would pull power up and in. When, by contrast, a problem appears born of some nefarious centralized authority, the movement argues for pushing power down and out. But rarely does anyone notice that these two narratives, and their ensuing prescriptions, cut directly against one another.

That's not always a problem—the two impulses can, and do, coexist. Few, for example, would so much as raise an eyebrow if a young progressive today professed that her two top voting issues were reproductive rights and climate change. What *is* remarkable is that they are each respectively born of the two antithetical narratives. The fight for reproductive freedom is an explicitly *Jeffersonian* endeavor—it's designed to protect women from outsiders intent on controlling their bodies. The fight against climate change, by contrast, is explicitly *Hamiltonian*—activists want to imbue some institution with the power to stop people and businesses from spewing carbon and destroying the planet.

Support for centralized efforts to curtail pollution need not require you to believe that rape victims should be forced to bring their pregnancies to term. Those who advocate for choice need not ignore concerns that the earth may turn into a ball of fire. But if these two notions can comfortably coexist under progressivism's broad banner, those who subscribe to the movement's core tenets should not deny that they flow from wildly different and contradictory narratives about *power*. And that's the essential point. In *both* cases, progressivism means well. But, at root, the frames are different. In many ways, they are discordant. And often, as we'll see, they conflict.

THE CULTURAL AVERSION TO POWER

This discord might be more obvious if we could lean on a clearer definition of "progressivism." Unfortunately, instead of confronting this oft-overlooked ideological wrinkle, progressives today tend to be sidetracked by discussions of who is *more* or *less* progressive.[27] No one can doubt that members of today's Congressional Progressive Caucus, a group committed to making "Wall Street, big corporations, and the wealthiest pay their fair share," would be revulsed by Teddy Roosevelt's century-old Progressive Party agenda, if only because it was so explicitly pro-corporate.[28] But the ideological division between progressivism's Jeffersonian and Hamiltonian impulses doesn't track that distinction for a simple reason: *Every* progressive, from *every* stripe, is invariably drawn in, to various degrees, by *both* narratives. The battle for progressivism's heart is waged, in short, in the heart of every progressive.

The second argument of this book, then, is that the two progressive narratives are suspended in a kind of yin and yang, an everlasting symbiosis that has ebbed and flowed through the decades. To be clear, at no time has progressivism been exclusively in the throes of either impulse; Jeffersonianism and Hamiltonianism have always existed side by side. Nor do progressives typically view themselves as ideologically bifurcated along these lines, as evidenced by the fact that almost no one has registered how the campaign to combat climate change is directionally distinct from the movement to preserve reproductive freedom. But the tension has always been there, and for progressivism to thrive, I will argue, the two impulses need to be in the right balance. And that's our fundamental problem today: the movement has listed too far in one direction.

The basic arc of this story is fairly simple. In the beginning, namely at the turn of the twentieth century, Hamiltonian progressivism reigned supreme. The Jeffersonian strain held its own in the early years—as we'll see, Woodrow Wilson, running against Theodore Roosevelt and William Howard Taft in 1912, articulated a deep skepticism of centralized authority. But from the late 1800s through the early 1970s, with certain exceptions, and with important caveats, progressives tended to favor pushing power up into institutions controlled by what we would come to call the Establishment. The movement's prevailing view was that centralized institutions were the key to checking industrial excesses, and building public works, and expanding broad-based prosperity. Progressives were culturally *inclined* to power.

That proclivity was made evident in all sorts of ways: In the creation of regulatory bodies akin to 1887's Interstate Commerce Commission, a now forgotten bureaucracy designed to keep watch over the railroad industry. In the creation of "public authorities" to manage public functions, including the port of New York. In the creation of school boards to expand the promise of public education. It was evident in the founding of big bureaucracies like the Social Security Administration and the National Labor Relations Board, and in the standing up of a whole series of public and private bureaucracies that would come to be called the military-industrial complex. Progressivism's Hamiltonian bent fueled the creation of America's expressways, its space program, and the Peace Corps, as well as many of the programs that comprised Lyndon Johnson's Great Society. The movement generally conceived the core problem facing America as a lack of centralized control.

But in the 1950s, Jeffersonianism began to seek its level. During the postwar era, reformers became increasingly dogged by a gnawing notion that the Establishment wasn't always working for the good—that it wasn't uniformly wise, or effective, or even well-intentioned. Through the 1960s and 1970s evidence began to mount that the country's powerful bureaucracies were prejudiced, corrupt, and sometimes even delusional. But when reformers tried to rein them in, they frequently discovered that the System was too insulated to be brought under control.[29] As Greatest Generation sensibilities gave way to boomer skepticism, Hamiltonianism began losing its purchase. If progressivism had once been focused on building up centralized institutions, the new goal was to tear them down.

The seeds of Jeffersonianism's renaissance were planted by abuses rendered overseas—the atrocities of Nazism, Stalinism, and Maoism, among others. Totalitarianism unmasked centralized power's potential evil. So it wasn't much of a leap to apply the same lens to domestic institutions. The Establishment, reformers began to understand, was suffused with all sorts of villainy. It had spawned Jim Crow. It had pointed the country into the quagmire of Vietnam. It was responsible for "slum clearance," the country's disastrous reliance on foreign oil, the glut of pollution, and the rampant corruption made evident in Watergate. By 1974, when Caro published *The Power Broker*, there appeared little question that the most serious threats to America came not from below, but from above. And progressivism reacted by leaning into Jeffersonianism—by embracing a cultural *aversion* to power.[30]

At this point in most accounts of American history, Ronald Reagan's conservative revolution typically takes center stage. But a studied look at progressivism during what might be called the movement's wilderness era makes clear that the skepticism of centralized power never abated. Even after Bill Clinton's election victory in 1992 ended the Democratic Party's quarter century in purgatory, the pendulum never swung back. Progressivism's central narrative—its belief in the conservative philosopher

Lord Acton's famous aphorism that "power tends to corrupt and absolute power corrupts absolutely"—held firm.[31] And even today, progressivism remains profoundly suspect of the Establishment—a reality whose effects continue to reverberate in crucial but unexpected ways.

Most important, progressivism's cultural aversion to power has turned the Democratic Party—purportedly the "party of government"—into an institution drawn almost instinctively to cut government down. Progressives are so fearful of Establishment abuse that reformers tend to prefer tightening the grip on public authority to loosening the reins. The movement discounts whatever *good* government might do in service of ensuring it won't do *bad*. And as we'll see in the chapters that follow, that's driven well-intentioned reformers to insert so many checks into the System that government has been rendered incompetent. Public officials can't effectively fight climate change, or address the nation's housing crisis, or enhance the country's infrastructure because of strictures progressives themselves have installed to protect the public from abuse.

Conservatism, of course, hasn't been helpful on any of these fronts. But for progressives, that reality can quickly become a distraction. We can't control the MAGA agenda—but we *can* offer a more palatable alternative. If the progressive agenda is going to prevail—if government is going to be given the leash required to combat inequality, to solve poverty, and to fight prejudice—we will first need to convince voters that government is capable of delivering on its promises. At present, we're too inclined to cut public authority off at the knees. And that's why progressives so often feel like they can't win for losing. Our cultural aversion to power renders government incompetent, and incompetent government undermines progressivism's political appeal.

DARKNESS DESCENDS

Ed Koch was angry—and perhaps a bit embarrassed. It was the spring of 1986, and the wheels were beginning to come off for New York's irascible mayor, a Democrat now serving in the first year of his third term. Elected nearly a decade earlier on a promise to pull a crime-ridden Big Apple back from the brink of bankruptcy, Koch had cultivated a reputation for being both tough and savvy. But there was no getting around the reality that his Parks Department had wasted millions of taxpayer dollars trying unsuccessfully to rehabilitate Central Park's Wollman Rink. At the height of the crack epidemic, the skating facility's closure hardly represented the worst of New York's problems. But the Parks Department's ineptitude burnished a notion that New York was fundamentally ungovernable. A mayor famous for cheekily asking New Yorkers, "How am I doing?" appeared not to be doing very well at all.

The trouble had begun six years earlier when the happy little attraction near Midtown's Plaza Hotel was abruptly closed for repairs. Having constructed the rink during the go-go years following the Second World War, the city then let Wollman decay. To cut costs, the Parks Department had begun to explore the possibility of replacing its clunky brine-based refrigeration system with a more efficient new technology known as Freon, which was purported to cost $20,000 less per year to operate. So, in 1980, City Hall ordered the rink shuttered, the pipes beneath torn up, and the whole system uprooted to make way for a $4.9 million replacement that would take fewer than three years to complete.[32] The project quickly went sideways.

Having ripped up the old system, a contractor installed what amounted to twenty-two miles of new piping for the Freon. But when that initial phase was complete, the Department had yet to secure a contractor to pave over the new plumbing. For more than a year, the piping was exposed to the elements, flooded by an underground stream, and subject (according to subsequent investigations) to stray electric current. When, in 1982, pavers were finally hired to cover the new pipes, engineers underestimated how much concrete would be required to complete the job. Rather than call for more, they diluted their insufficient supply. Then, to protect the delicate piping below, the pavers chose not to deploy vibration machines typically used to collapse any air pockets.[33] The result was predictable. When the job was done, the ice on the surface melted. The rink simply didn't work.

As was typical in this sort of fiasco, everyone pointed fingers. The Parks Department excoriated the contractors. The contractors blamed one another. The public blamed City Hall. And the mayor was left to shake his head in disgust. In a kind of chef's kiss moment, consultants the city hired for $200,000 to audit the catastrophe punted as well: speaking to Joyce Purnick, an iconic columnist for the *New York Times*, one Parks Department employee later complained that the report read "very much like 'Murder on the Orient Express,'" where "the detective on the case finds out that . . . everybody was the murderer." Koch was incensed, not only because the project had been bungled, but because an opportunity to demonstrate that New York was turning a corner had instead burnished the city's reputation for incompetence.

At this point, the mayor had little choice but to order the Parks Department to begin anew. To rip up the piping. To abandon the new technology. To revert to the traditional refrigeration system. That, of course, would not only require the department to shutter Wollman for another two years, but to add another $3 million to the taxpayers' tab. The whole thing appeared like an unmitigated public relations disaster until, almost by the grace of God, Koch received an unexpected reprieve: a local developer offered to step in and make things right. In an unusual arrangement, Koch cut a deal to pay the developer to take control of the rink project, complete it for a fee, and hand it back to the city. "If it costs less, we'll pay less," the mayor explained when some questioned the wisdom of trusting someone outside of government to do something that would typically have been handled by a public authority. "If it costs more, he'll pay."[34]

Lost in the focus on the city's incompetence was a more nuanced reality. The Parks Department had been trying to rebuild the rink with a proverbial arm tied behind its back. More than sixty years earlier, the New York state legislature had passed a law designed to prevent mayors (and the machine bosses who controlled them) from throwing municipal construction gigs to politically connected contractors.

At the time, progressives in both parties rightly presumed that graft was rife throughout the state—that various construction companies were bribing city officials to secure city contracts at inflated prices. Wicks Law had aimed to solve the problem by requiring cities to hire, *separately*, the lowest-bidding general construction, plumbing, electrical, heating, and ventilation contractors on any municipal project slated to cost more than $50,000.[35] Mayors were prohibited from hiring general contractors. As a result, more than a half century later, Ed Koch's Parks Department was still legally prohibited from hiring a single firm to deliver a project on time and on budget.[36]

Asked why a private developer would be better equipped to move more speedily, a Parks Department official charged with managing capital improvements explained: "Parks is a city agency. We are bound by the city's rules and regulations and checks and balances. If [the developer] wants a certain contractor, he just picks up the phone and says, 'Look, if you ever want to do work for me again. . . .' He's got that type of clout."[37] Another former city official explained that private developers could consider skill, competency, cost, and trustworthiness. Moreover, they could move expeditiously ahead when selecting people to work on a project. But, he pointed out, "there is nobody in government who can do that. There are 15 or 20 people who have to agree."[38]

Fortunately for Koch, his collaboration with the outside developer turned out to be a huge success. The project *did* cost less than the original estimate—$750,000 less—and the rink opened ahead of the holiday season.[39] But from a public relations perspective, the developer's success just seemed to highlight City Hall's incompetence. The Parks Department, columnists and reporters liked to remind the public, had wasted six years and $13 million on a project the private sector managed to complete in six months and at roughly a sixth of the cost. Asked about the lesson learned from the whole episode, the developer responded: "I guess it says a lot about the City."[40] And with that wry remark, everyone understood how this episode fit into a broader narrative. City government was fundamentally incompetent. The municipal bureaucracy was a nightmare. Even liberal New Yorkers, many of whom reviled then president Ronald Reagan, would have been tempted to nod along to his famous quip that "the nine most terrifying words in the English language are: I'm from the Government, and I'm here to help."[41]

Not long thereafter, a reporter traipsed down to Central Park to interview members of the public. A local man enjoying a skate was asked his impressions of the rigmarole: "Anybody who can get anything done right and done on time in New York is a bona fide hero," the skater replied. Then, after a pause, he alluded to the sort of honor the city reserves for America's greatest luminaries. In recognition of a triumph of this magnitude, he declared, the developer "should get a ticker-tape parade."[42] Fixing a municipal skating rink was, in this New Yorker's view, an accomplishment to be venerated akin to General Dwight Eisenhower winning the Second World War or Neil Armstrong walking on the moon. And it's probably safe to say the developer would have agreed. Certainly he would have enjoyed the attention. His name, as it happened, was Donald J. Trump.

TOWARD FULL-CIRCLE PROGRESSIVISM

That then marks the third argument of this book. The first, to recount, is that progressivism is defined not by *one*, but rather by *two* divergent impulses. The second is that the two impulses have waxed and waned through time such that the movement's underlying zeitgeist has shifted, a bit like the tide. And the third, made so plainly evident by the catastrophe at Wollman Rink, is that the balance that's emerged since the late 1960s—the excessive tilt toward the Jeffersonian—is a seminal *political* liability for the progressive movement. Beyond conservatism, populism, MAGAism, and whatever other forces are pushing in contrary directions, progressivism is undermining itself. The cultural aversion to power hasn't just tied government in knots—it has diminished the movement's broader appeal. It is at the root of contemporary progressive exasperation.

Some will argue that's preposterous—pointing to Trump and his supporters, they'll dismiss out of hand any notion that progressivism should be held culpable for its own frustrations. They'll argue that the movement's real shortfall is its inability to overcome its antagonists—Rupert Murdoch, Tucker Carlson, Ben Shapiro, and a whole slew of others. But my contention that progressivism is largely responsible for its own foibles should be more a source of hope than of anger. After all, the best antidote to conservatism's enduring appeal may in fact be, quite simply, a progressivism that simply *works*.[43] And on this count, the movement need not wait on voters to wake up to how bad MAGA-style populism really is—we can forge a more balanced progressivism on our own.

The saga at Wollman Rink encapsulates the underlying dynamic. Wicks Law had been passed with good intentions—to thwart municipal corruption. Mayor Koch had wanted to restore Wollman Rink for good reason—to serve the public. Combined, however, progressivism's two impulses had served to undermine each other, and the resulting gridlock cleaved an opening for Trump. As we'll see in the chapters that follow, that same cadence has become so endemic that progressives no longer register or notice. But the evidence is everywhere.

America can't build housing. We can't deploy high-speed rail. We're struggling to harness the promise of clean energy. And because government has failed in *all* these realms—because confidence in public authority has waned through the years—progressives have found it increasingly difficult to make a case for themselves.[44] After San Francisco spent several years and $1.7 million trying to get a toilet installed in the Noe Valley neighborhood, one *New York Times* reporter asked: "If an army of more than 30,000 city employees with a $14 billion annual budget cannot build a simple bathroom in a reasonable way, what hope is there that San Francisco can solve its housing shortage and fentanyl crisis?"[45]

Or, put more universally: Who would want to give *more* power to an institution that, as Ronald Reagan sometimes quipped, would mess up a two-car parade?

There is a certain irony to progressivism's contemporary predicament. After all, as we'll see in the first chapter, the movement was born amid many of the same dynamics. The core problem at the turn of the twentieth century wasn't that powerful government bureaucrats were doing bad things—it was that feckless public authority couldn't get things done. The famed journalist H. L. Mencken rued that during the late 1800s in Baltimore "there was a great epidemic of typhoid fever every Summer, and a wave of malaria every Autumn, and more than a scattering of smallpox, especially among the colored folk in the alleys, every Winter."[46] But machine-controlled government remained incapable of crafting solutions. Across the country, machine-controlled city halls struggled to build sanitation systems, or public parks, or good schools. Robber barons corrupted public bureaucracies. Government was a mess, fenced in by judicially enforced doctrines of laissez-faire.[47] Progressivism emerged to steer the country in a different direction—and it prevailed.

Today, the *sources* of progressive frustration are different—but the underlying dynamic is largely the same. Things feel *stuck*. Nothing seems to work. And for all the efforts Democrats make to invest in the future—the Bipartisan Infrastructure Law, the Inflation Reduction Act—progress too often remains a vision of Charlie Brown's football. Reformers tout an achievement, but then a housing plan is abandoned after local opposition, a high-speed rail line is shelved for exorbitant costs, or an offshore wind farm is blocked by local fishermen. Often enough, *both* sides in any given debate—those who want to change things, and those who fear that change will be destructive—are well-intentioned. But the movement's inability to resolve its conflicting impulses has turned progressive policymaking into what drag racers call "warming the tires." A driver steps on the brake and accelerator at the same time. The wheels spin. The track screeches. But the car remains in place.

The *political* effect of the ensuing paralysis has been profound. In the early 1960s, nearly four in five Americans professed trust in Washington to "do what's right." By 2022, that figure had fallen to one in five.[48] And you need not discount conservative harping to acknowledge that progressives have *also* been arguing for decades that power can't be trusted—that public authority is captured by moneyed interests, that it lines the pockets of the powerful few, that it is a tool of white supremacists, xenophobes, sexists, and worse. No one can deny that centralized power can be used for ill. But even given that reality, attacking government turns out to be, for progressives, a ham-handed way of convincing ordinary people that government should be empowered to do *more* to pursue the public interest.

This book comprises eight chapters, the first four of which detail how progressivism evolved from a beacon of centralized authority into a movement culturally averse to power. The latter four chapters detail how this shift has played out in various realms—in the movement's effort to regulate greedy corporations, to keep housing affordable, to build public works, and to build a clean energy future capable of thwarting climate change. Every chapter begins with a story designed to illustrate how the progressive schism has framed a certain moment, or shaped the movement's approach to a certain challenge. Following that prologue, each chapter tracks back to trace the chronological narrative. And while the topics vary dramatically, the basic arc remains the same throughout: public authority's potential is eventually undermined by the impulse to "speak truth to power."

Which points to the book's final nudge. Having identified the core of progressivism's frustration, the solution presents itself: the movement needs to come full circle—to rebalance its Jeffersonian and Hamiltonian impulses. The unresolved question—one to which I've yet to divine an entirely satisfying answer—is how to avoid too drastic a pivot. How, in the end, can progressives pull the System back from the vetocracy we've created over the last fifty years without licensing a new generation of imperious, unaccountable power brokers? How can we clear a path for progress without beckoning another Robert Moses? In 1976, Daniel Bell argued that "if the society can respond, through a new public philosophy that commands respect and through institutions that work, then there may be time for the other, slower process of cultural reconstruction to take hold."[49] That should be the goal. In the face of today's imbalance, progressivism needs to reset.

The good news is twofold. First, the movement doesn't lack for gumption. Wonks, activists, and experts across the country are awash in plans and proposals delineating how America can build sufficient housing, address climate change, give people better access to transit, improve public education and health care, fight inequality, advance social justice, and more. Good ideas abound. Second, and perhaps more important, reformers need not wait on conservatism to come to its senses before changing course—progressivism can heal itself. With a proper balance, the movement can make a convincing case for how and why public authority is, in fact, a boon to the public interest—that it produces a good return on public investment. If we can convincingly make that true, ordinary people will be less inclined to fall for the other side's foibles and canards.[50]

To get there, however, progressives will need to step away from the impulse simply to attack whatever red meat Fox News throws on their screens. Rather than tear our hair out over *their* plans, we need to train more of our attention on our own ideas, our own impulses, our own narrative. That's not to invite a war within progressivism, if only because, as I argued above, nearly every progressive of every stripe harbors *both* progressive impulses to one degree or another. If there's any great reckoning to be had, it will be within each progressive heart—individuals will need to recognize that their underlying political impulses cut against each other and must be put into balance. To say it again, there's nothing *wrong* with progressivism that can't be fixed by what's *right* with progressivism. But to restore the movement's promise, we will need to grapple with our own demons, and place our good intentions in a balanced, productive tension.

1

Servant or Master of the Public?

PROLOGUE: STEALING THE PLANK

The fight over what would come to be known as the "stolen plank" of 1912's Progressive Party platform perfectly encapsulates the core tension that has bedeviled progressivism since the movement's founding. In that moment, set little more than thirty-five years since the end of Reconstruction, many believed America was on the brink of being swallowed by industrialization. The concerns weren't new—the economy had been changing for decades. And yet, to that point, neither of the two major political parties had emerged with a compelling vision of how to set things right. The ragtag Democrats were viewed as little more than an ineffectual collection of rural populists and immigrants eager to scapegoat the nation's behemoth trusts and corporations. The Republicans, by contrast, appeared too enthralled with laissez-faire economics to whip an out-of-control corporate world into shape.[1] Frustrated, a collection of reformers determined to form a third party—the Progressives—in the hopes of returning ex-president Theodore Roosevelt to the White House. Gathering in Chicago to write the nascent new party's convention platform, they were convinced both that the country demanded change and that "The Colonel" was the man to deliver it. What exactly he would do during his second stint as president—well, that was still to be determined.

It was exactly that topic that became the focus of debate late one night among members of the party's Resolutions Committee. The issue, more specifically, was whether to endorse what some had come to call the "business plank." On one side were the self-styled radicals who believed that government should combat the trusts by taking a much more aggressive hand in breaking them up. By 1912, the Sherman Anti-Trust Act, then nearly a quarter century old, appeared, with a handful of notable exceptions, like a failure; it was derisively known as the Swiss Cheese Act for being so full of loopholes. This first group wanted Washington to get tough. As one prominent radical explained in a letter to Roosevelt: "In the old days it was the Crown . . . against the people. Today it is the industrial oligarchy, the trusts against the people."[2] They had drafted the business plank to signal their intention to beef up the effort to break business down.[3]

But others within Roosevelt's orbit weren't convinced that trust-busting was the answer. Hovering behind the scenes in Chicago that summer was a deep-pocketed figure who was underwriting some great bulk of the Progressive Party's expenses. His name, now largely forgotten to history, was George Walbridge Perkins. Years earlier, Perkins had emerged as a business wunderkind when, as a middling executive at New York Life, he'd taken on the job of combatting the scourge of insurance "rebating"—namely the corrupt practice among agents of returning a portion of a customer's premium in order to win their business. Because more lucrative clients could demand heftier rebates, the practice effectively forced middle-class customers to subsidize the rich. Perkins had convened a conference of insurance executives to establish an enforceable convention against rebates, complete with an independent arbiter to settle disputes. And this novel regime proved a success.

That achievement not only propelled Perkins into the orbit of the famed banker J. P. Morgan—it came to frame his lifelong view of industrial capitalism: excessive competition was "cruel, wasteful, destructive, [and] outmoded." Cooperation, by contrast, was "humane, efficient, inevitable, and 'modern.'"[4] Now joined in Chicago by, among others, Indiana senator Albert Beveridge, he proposed a competing plank that argued that "the concentration of modern business [is] . . . both inevitable and necessary for national and international efficiency."[5] Better, in their view, to establish a centralized authority capable of keeping business in line—expert bureaucrats modeled on the rebate arbiter, each ready to snap the whip when the excesses of private-sector competition cut against the greater good.

The radicals' business plank and Perkins's alternative need not have been viewed as an either-or proposition—members of the Resolutions Committee debating adoption could have embraced an approach that promised to regulate businesses in some circumstances, and to bust trusts in others. But within the context of this particular moment—and in ways that would vex progressivism in the decades that followed—the two impulses cut directly against one another. The radicals viewed Perkins as a shill for the corporate world, with one framing his plank as "merely a means of perpetuating trust extortion."[6] Perkins and his peers viewed the radicals as impractical dreamers who had no real understanding of how business actually worked. As it happened, Governor Woodrow Wilson's Democratic Party agenda that year included language reflecting the radicals' vision for fomenting more intense commercial competition. The Democrats had dubbed their approach, "The New Freedom." But Perkins, seeing additional competition as a scourge that would only worsen economic conditions, argued Wilson's agenda "had better be called the Old Bondage."[7]

But there was something more going on. This singular dispute served as a proxy for a schism that extended well beyond progressivism's approach to economic consolidation. The underlying question of how to solve big, public vexations—or, really, how to target the sources of those challenges— tracked back to what Walter Lippmann would eventually term "the pictures in people's heads."[8] The radicals were convinced America's problems were tied up with corruption running rampant *atop* society—among robber barons, political bosses, corporate boards, and snooty lawyers. Absent their chicanery, radical reformers presumed the country would restore the better elements of what had come before. So they wed themselves to Jeffersonian solutions: salvation, in their view, would emerge from bludgeoning those at the top and pushing their power down to ordinary people.[9]

Perkins and those of his ideological ilk were skeptical of that diagnosis. They believed that any dream of returning the economy to the less efficient, smaller firms that had defined America's nineteenth-century economy was bound to fail. Perkins shared the radicals' concerns about the power wielded by the titans of industry—that's why he was a progressive. But he was less entranced with taking them down, and more inclined to building government up.[10] To his mind, *everyone* would benefit if power was simply better coordinated in a scientific way—if, rather than a mess of competition, those with authority in both the private and public spheres acted in cooperative consultation. But even as he made that point repeatedly that evening in Chicago, the radicals on the Resolutions Committee dismissed his alternative. The next morning, the finalized version of the party platform, complete with the radicals' business plank, was delivered to several newspapers for printing. The text was subsequently read aloud on the convention floor. It appeared they had won.

What then happened behind the scenes remains something of a mystery even now. It's possible that Perkins, having failed to prevail the previous evening, had gone directly to Roosevelt to complain. It also seems possible that, after the platform was read the next morning to the convention— Perkins was seen stomping out of the hall afterward in distress—Roosevelt or his aides had a change of heart. What's indisputable is that several hours after the platform's formal unveiling, Oscar King Davis, serving effectively as the party's communications director, walked into the Chicago office of the Associated Press to inform editors that the business plank had been included erroneously in the document delivered to them earlier that day.[11] As a result, subsequent editions of the same newspapers omitted it—in some cases with a note explaining the change. Perhaps more remarkable, printed copies of the platform produced by the Progressive Party in the weeks after the convention *also* omitted the language. In the months that followed, many of the party's radicals were left to wonder angrily what had happened. Who had "stolen" the plank?

This wasn't just a clerical question—it appeared to many progressive reformers to have real political import. As the general election campaign wore on that autumn, political discourse came to turn increasingly on the question of which insurgent candidate—Roosevelt or Wilson—was better poised to be a more potent reformer. And as it was, many radicals believed that the plank's omission had opened the door for Democrats to argue that their nominee was the truer beacon of progressive change.[12] Wilson ended up taking advantage, using a thinly veiled attack on Perkins, still generally viewed to be J. P. Morgan's right-hand man, to cast doubt on Roosevelt's promise to bring order from economic chaos. Speaking to a crowd on a campaign swing through the Midwest, Wilson argued: "These gentlemen say that these big combinations are necessary for economy and efficiency. The only answer I can think of that meets the suggestion is: Rats!"[13]

But if the historical details around the business plank's excision remain murky, the deeper truth of what happened isn't hard to surmise. Roosevelt, we can presume, was trying to have it both ways—to give both the radicals and Perkins's allies the impression that he was with them. The Colonel needed to maintain the radicals' support lest they follow their north star, future Supreme Court justice Louis Brandeis, into Wilson's Democratic camp. But Perkins and his cohort were the lynchpin to the Progressive Party's whole apparatus—they were funding the campaign.

Presumably, the ex-president knew that the radicals would balk if he embraced Perkins's position, and that Perkins would close his wallet if the convention was seized entirely by the radicals. And so the ex-president remained coy, receiving the Resolutions Committee's final language when it emerged from their deliberations, and then subsequently allowing an emissary to have the plank removed.

The root of the issue in the summer of 1912 wasn't whether Roosevelt would have been wise to be more transparently for one camp or the other. Nor was it that either camp represented the one true progressivism. Rather, as we'll see, the fight over the stolen plank spotlighted an underappreciated ideological divide within the progressive tradition—one that remains with us today. Progressives have, from the very beginning, been torn perennially between their desires to build public authority up and to tear centralized power down. In some circumstances, we're drawn to the Hamiltonian impulse to invest new authority in scientifically minded experts—in others, we're attracted to the radicals' Jeffersonian desire to curtail the discretion of haughty, imperious bureaucrats. That underlying tension was set in particularly stark relief in that moment—but it is an everlasting feature. And the manner in which the movement has worked to resolve that conflict at various moments has borne heavily on progressivism's capacity to win.

PUNCTUATED EQUILIBRIUM

The battle between the radicals and George Perkins in 1912 hardly marked the first time these two indelibly American impulses had faced off against one another. Right from the beginning of the republic, the nation's political life turned on questions of who, exactly, should be assigned authority to make decisions on behalf of the broad public. George Washington, Alexander Hamilton, and their Federalist allies tried to convince Thomas Jefferson's Democratic-Republicans to invest additional power in the national government. But through the 1800s, with rare and important exceptions, decentralization generally won the day.[14] Theodore Roosevelt's efforts to wrest back the presidency in 1912 brought to a head a decades-long struggle to break through Jeffersonianism's long domination. But, by some measure, Roosevelt's charge was simply the catharsis of a shift that had begun during the last third of the nineteenth century.

The country's long aversion to centralized power had, in no small part, been the product of searing experience. During the 1830s, a federal bank chartered to finance canal and turnpike improvements had sparked such widespread anger—many viewed it as a power grab from the eastern elite—that Andrew Jackson won the presidency explicitly in protest.[15] Three decades later, the federal government's incompetent prosecution of the Civil War—the Lincoln administration cycled through a whole litany of ineffective generals before prevailing over the outmatched Confederacy—deepened the notion that centralized bureaucracy was inherently inept. Reconstruction, the decade-plus-long federal effort to remake the South through 1877, was also viewed as a morass of organizational failure.[16] All of these episodes deepened an underlying cynicism about power imposed from afar.[17] Prevailing wisdom at the time suggested that, save for some limited circumstances, individual communities should be spared the mettlesome interference of people removed from the familiarity of everyday life.[18]

Today, during an era when inconsequential squabbles on Capitol Hill frequently elicit much more attention than debates over road maintenance at City Hall, that may seem odd. Presidential politics and cultural hot buttons dominate today's public discourse.[19] In the nineteenth century, by contrast, a citizen's worldview was largely concentrated on what they could see out the window and walk to with their own two feet. The next village over was, in many cases, a day's trip away, if only because the journey required resting and watering a horse.[20] Most Americans struggled to buy anything that wasn't sold by a local merchant. And while news traveled to some extent, people were much more consumed by what was happening nearby. America was, before the so-called Progressive

Era, a nation of "island communities."[21] For any individual family, the local mayor was likely to throw a longer shadow than the president of the United States.[22]

Not that these islands were out-and-out fiefdoms. They were, themselves, complex political organisms. Today, many will recall that checks and balances were written into the American Constitution in order to provide a certain political stability by distributing power between the various branches. This same ethos had long prevailed at the local level through the tension set primarily between courts, on the one hand, and parties, on the other.[23] By enforcing property rights, the judiciary served to protect each community's elite—to insulate the old-money aristocracy and nouveau riche capitalists from what the journalist H. L. Mencken would later term the "vulgar."[24] In what W. E. B. Du Bois would label the "counter-revolution of property," post–Reconstruction era jurisprudence gave judges explicit license to strike down legislative initiatives designed to placate the down-and-out.[25]

But the have-nots had their defenders as well—they were served, in theory at least, by political machines. Bosses gleaned the power by championing the interests of the voters who would otherwise have been hosed.[26] Even if, as was often the case, machine politics served the working class a bill of goods—even if the bosses were too corrupt or self-interested to deliver real protections—the tension between the judges and the parties provided a localized ballast, giving people at different stations of society the imprimatur of influence. Judges prevented the masses from overrunning the elite, and machines ensured that the upper crust couldn't entirely ignore the pleas of ordinary citizens.[27] The system wasn't foolproof—but it was workable. Within any given island community, it represented liberal democracy in action.

Moreover, within any given circumscribed place, the two institutions were often capable of finding mutual accommodation.[28] If the creek needed damming, if the fire brigade needed new buckets, if a mill was polluting the town's drinking water, courts and parties could frequently resolve the problem through local bargaining—that is, without assistance from above. Judges could bend when the greater good was in too much peril; machines could help metabolize frustration when a court seemed to stand athwart public opinion. Flawed as this system may have been—women couldn't vote, minorities were subject to rampant bigotry, life was hardly ideal—this was America's Jeffersonian tradition at its apex.[29] It set individual freedoms and majority demands in a productive tension. And the System generally provided a modicum of tranquility—or it did, at least, until trains changed everything.

Today, many will find it difficult to appreciate the degree to which the railroad industry emerged during the late nineteenth century to become for America what the Catholic Church had been to medieval Europe—an institution so suffused with power and so central to everyday life that its decisions rippled across the whole fabric of American society.[30] The telephone, the automobile, the television, the internet—disruptive as each technological breakthrough would prove to be, none was as disorienting as the train. From almost nothing, by the 1870s, the country boasted a full 70,000 miles of "road" (read: track), so much that you could load a train car nearly anywhere and have it arrive nearly anywhere else without a hitch.[31]

But it wasn't just that the railroads became thoroughfares connecting the whole of the nation's economy. The financiers and corporate executives who controlled the "iron horses" effectively became the nation's overlords in the course of a generation. No one—not the local bosses, not the local judges, not the federal government—was powerful enough to protect ordinary people from being bulldozed on a robber baron's whim. Nothing in American history approximates, to the same degree, cartoonish depictions of flying saucers darkening the sky. The railroad industry's power was effectively unchecked. This was, to borrow a phrase from the world of evolutionary biology, a moment of "punctuated equilibrium."[32]

At first, the railroads' impacts were primarily economic. Farmers in Indiana and manufacturers in Pennsylvania had previously been free to

engage in commerce more exclusively on their own terms—to sell locally, to ship their wares via barge, to charge their customers whatever
the market would allow. Now, suddenly, decisions ratified in corporate
boardrooms—where to extend a rail line, how frequently routes might be
traversed, what freight or fare might apply—had material impacts on their
lives. Yet customers had virtually no leverage to influence a railroad executive's decision. A farmer informed that the one nearby railroad would no
longer serve his region might have no recourse. As Louis Brandeis complained: "Politics as well as economic and social science noted these revolutionary changes. But legal science—the unwritten or judge-made laws
as distinguished from legislation—was largely deaf and blind to them."[33]

Today, most observers are familiar with the reaction many in America's
heartland have had to the pervasive sense that the financial elite are prone
to sell them out—Donald Trump's popularity highlighted the point. The
emergence of the railroads more than a century earlier elicited a similar
response, with one crucial caveat: in the nineteenth century, there appeared no institution capable of coming to their aid. Courts and parties
were powerless to push back.[34] The federal government was a shadow of
what it would later become, boasting a mere fifteen thousand civilian
employees as late as the early 1870s.[35] Within the context of Jeffersonian
democracy, the victims had nowhere to turn.[36]

The sheer inequity of the situation came into clearer focus when the industry's overgrowth morphed into an economic affliction. What had been
70,000 miles of road in the 1870s grew to become 200,000 by 1900.[37]
And all those new tracks had been financed by speculative investors now
demanding returns. So the robber barons and executives leading the various
roads schemed for ways to burnish their revenues—to ensure, for example,
that two corporations running trains between Ohio and Pennsylvania did
not undermine each other's profitability. In some cases, they merged—
between 1875 and 1900, the number of railroads running in Massachusetts
alone fell from more than sixty to a mere two.[38] In other instances, competitive railroads sometimes fixed rates at inflated prices. In still others, they

cut deals to rebate larger customers like John D. Rockefeller's Standard Oil, putting smaller independent oil suppliers at a vast disadvantage.

The upshot was to spread consolidation throughout the rest of the economy. United States Steel, Consolidated Tobacco, and Amalgamated Copper were all born in large part to protect smaller companies being squeezed by the railroads. And the great whoosh of consolidation often appeared frightening to the ordinary person on the street—a consumer, or a small entrepreneur who could not possibly fight back against the behemoths suddenly in their midst. Between 1900 and 1912, monopolies accounted for almost a third of the nation's industrial GDP growth. And few could mistake the upshot: giant combinations were protecting Wall Street interests, while those on Main Street were left to suffer.[39]

The ensuing economic turmoil eventually connected to something deeper—something cultural. The late 1800s were awash in tensions centering on questions of immigration, urbanization, and racism, among other topics. As industrialization threw wrenches into the norm of nineteenth-century life, social critics rued the newfound worship of money and castigated a depravity engulfing the nation's soul. But the frustration wasn't directed exclusively at the underlying shifts—it was born from a widespread notion that the country wasn't equipped to metabolize such monstrous change.[40]

In a world now where courts and parties were now incapable of protecting ordinary people against turmoil, the "invisible hand" of free enterprise wasn't a beacon of opportunity—it was an economic catastrophe. The virtues of hard work and thrift—what some would celebrate as the Protestant ethic—no longer appeared capable of lifting ordinary families from industrialization's undertow.[41] When a bomb went off in Chicago's Haymarket Square in 1886, fears of violent class warfare spread across the nation.[42] And while that explosion proved singular, it reflected the sense that America was a tinderbox—not entirely unlike today.[43]

A clear way out of the crisis appeared elusive. If localized power brokers were impotent in the face of corporate power, the nation's two political parties were similarly at a loss. The GOP, which dominated Congress, was tied at the hip to the industrial interests that prevailed throughout the Northeast, the mid-Atlantic, and much of the Midwest—as such, they had no intention of abandoning the doctrine of laissez-faire.[44] The Democratic Party, on the other hand, was steeped in the populist doctrines taking hold across the South and the nation's agricultural heartland—it had no substantive answer save for vilifying corporations. The ups and downs of the new economy were so uneven and unpredictable—the future so hard to fathom—that many Americans began searching for new ways to settle things down. The nation was going through something akin to what the journalist George Packer would later term an "unwinding."[45] And so, along those lines, a whole range of ideas, new and old, began to make their way through the body politic—socialism, anarchism, racism, antisemitism, temperance, religious fundamentalism, among others.[46]

Herbert Croly, who would go on to become a close advisor to Theodore Roosevelt and to found the *New Republic*, wrote in 1890 that Western civilization had been subject to three major transformations—the Protestant Reformation in the 1500s, the birth of democracy in the 1700s, and now the industrial revolution.[47] And it was from that sense of both fear and possibility—a combination of both nostalgia for the nineteenth century's simpler rhythms and an almost utopian sense of hope for what might emerge in the twentieth—that a new brand of politics began to emerge.[48] But if the movement that would come to be known as progressivism was ready to strike out in a new direction, it wasn't entirely clear where its ideology would point. And in the years that led up to the 1912 Progressive Party convention, reformers struggled to divine the best way forward.

ROOTS OF THE JEFFERSONIAN IMPULSE

Given that America's core institutions appeared outmatched by industrialization, many reformers were bent primarily on pushing back—to restore order, they put designs on countering the forces turning everything upside down. But how? Many argued that America would have to find some mechanism to thwart the rapacious characters steering society away from the broad public interest. The robber barons and the judges who seemed to do their bidding. The corrupt machine bosses. To set the country right, the thinking went, power would have to be returned to the people. As Louis Brandeis wrote to his sister in the 1880s, "I have spent much time of late before juries, and am becoming quite enamored of the Common Sense of the people." To save America, he and those who shared his perspective would argue, society would have to tap back into that precious resource. Power returned to the people.

Here were the stirrings of what would be woven into the progressive tradition as a Jeffersonian impulse. Of course, the desire to push power down—to shield decent citizens from the pernicious forces hovering above them—wasn't entirely new in the late nineteenth century. Thomas Jefferson's celebration of local democracy had flowered through the era of Andrew Jackson into an almost religious conviction. In this particular narrative, the Mayflower crowd—the white Anglo-Saxon Protestant men who had dominated the old colonial capitals—had typically been cast as the enemies of the commoner. And in many cases, they had served as a perfect political foil: through the 1800s, the Democratic Party mobilized voters by promising to protect the farmers, pioneers, and eventually the immigrants who might otherwise have been trampled by old money.[49] For decades, the Democratic Party carried the ordinary citizen's banner against judges who served to burnish patrician interests.[50]

But industrialization was now jumbling the stakes of that familiar nineteenth-century order. Suddenly the villains weren't the local blue bloods—they were powerful figures who smoked expensive cigars in oak-paneled boardrooms hundreds if not thousands of miles away.[51] It would no longer suffice for the working class to mobilize against the scrooges living up the hill—and yet all they could realistically do now was shake their fists in vain at the mysterious "trusts," organized on Wall Street, where financiers doffing top hats schemed behind closed doors.

And so, to survive, the old Jeffersonian impulse would have to take a new form; the impulse to pull power down would need to animate a different policy agenda. From this frustration, many reformers endeavored to take scalpels to big power. Ordinary people would be able once again to harness the promise of American life only if the country could neutralize the corrupting influence of those at the top.[52] This narrative came to frame the emerging movement's approach to at least three major challenges.

First, and perhaps the most important, Jeffersonianism animated the push to break up the nation's vast monopolies.[53] The Sherman Anti-Trust Act in the 1890s was born largely from widespread frustration that the mightiest of all robber barons, John D. Rockefeller, had managed to monopolize the oil market. Unfortunately for reformers, the law had been so rife with loopholes that it operated originally more like a fig leaf than like a battering ram; in fact, the new law posed so little threat to Standard Oil's interests that Rockefeller himself subsequently made a generous donation to the very senator who had drafted it.[54] But what would eventually become the touchstone for American antitrust enforcement nevertheless pointed to the progressive principle that government should do more to combat what Brandeis would label "bigness."[55] It represented a down payment on the movement's determination to break apart concentrations of private power.

As in other realms, the more purely economic focus on combatting trusts was part of a broader cultural zeitgeist. Brandeis, who would come to be known as "the People's Attorney" before joining the Supreme Court, wasn't merely focused on thwarting the power of monopolies.[56] He was more generally concerned that centralized institutions were a threat to the republic. And through that lens, powerful government bureaucracies were *also* liable to cut against the public interest.[57] Fueling their antipathy for big business, Brandeis and his intellectual allies wanted to restore the cacophony of small interests that had defined American society before the railroads had disrupted the equilibrium.[58] Getting Sherman's "Swiss Cheese Act" through Congress had represented an important first step for reformers in 1890. But the real barrier to any campaign to neutralize the trusts wasn't political—it was judicial.

In the late nineteenth century, the Supreme Court loomed almost without question as the most powerful branch of the federal government. And much as local judges had long been utilized as a check against majority rule, the nine justices then sitting in their Capitol chambers viewed themselves as guardrails against excesses of "democracy"—as protectors of the wisdom wielded by the enlightened few against an invidious public. Even if a progressively minded Justice Department led by a progressive attorney general appointed by a progressive president took a stand against monopoly power—passing a law, imposing a regulation, prosecuting anticompetitive behavior—the judicial branch was, at the time, poised to give the private sector a pass. And so the court loomed large for progressives at the turn of the century, much as the Warren Court would frustrate conservatives a century later.

The conservative majority made something of a game of nitpicking progressive efforts to bring corporate America to heel. The same year the Sherman Act was signed into law, the court issued a ruling curtailing states' ability to cap railroad rates.[59] Five years later, when Grover Cleveland's administration moved to break up the sugar trust controlled by the Havemeyer family, the court struck again. In *United States v. E. C. Knight Co.*, the justices ruled 8–1 that because the Havemeyers controlled a single enormous business rather than a collection of smaller firms, their company had not "restrained commerce," as the Sherman Act disallowed.[60] The ruling seemed absurd on its face. But the justices were sending a message about legislative efforts to interfere in private markets. Only twenty-four lawsuits were brought under the Sherman Act during the first fifteen years of its existence.[61]

In the wake of those rulings, federal antitrust law appeared like a limp arrow. But progressive reformers kept the pressure on, and as monopoly abuses worsened and public sentiment changed, the justices were eventually convinced to relent in certain circumstances. In 1905's *Swift*

& Co. v. United States, the court ruled that a single corporation could, in the end, be prosecuted by the federal government for antitrust violations, presuming it was engaged in interstate commerce. And then, in 1910 and 1911, the court reversed the precedent set in the sugar trust case, greenlighting government cases against Standard Oil and the American Tobacco Company. That then established a new standard, namely that restraints of trade could be lawfully prohibited, so long as they were "unreasonable."[62] This may not have been the anti-industrial counterrevolution some imagined, but it served, on the margins, to restore some semblance of the old balance.

The Jeffersonian impulse to slash at centralized power wasn't targeted exclusively at the big trusts—and for at least one obvious reason: the legions of laborers pouring into cities were being exploited by small firms as well. The owners of stand-alone textile mills, for example, were often engaged in cutthroat competition with other small mills. Each owner was incentivized to wring additional productivity out of their operation, if only to keep costs to a minimum. And so the foreman running a shift might demand that employees work endless hours at pain of losing their positions. The mill might pay unconscionably meager wages. Children might be sent to toil in abominable conditions. This sort of exploitation, pervasive as it was, was born less from grand concentrations of capital than from more mundane disparities of power *within* individual firms. If antitrust enforcement wasn't going to be an effective salve for this scourge, the Jeffersonian impulse to push power down flowed instead into a second desire to enshrine laborers with new "rights."

The desire to invest individuals with new protections was not new to American life in the late nineteenth century. The Civil War, still within living memory, had largely been fought over the "rights" of enslaved humans. But the limited success of efforts to protect newly free Black communities by enshrining various *civil* rights dimmed hopes that imbuing individuals with new power within the workplace could shield laborers from serious exploitation. Nevertheless, Jeffersonian reformers were determined to try. In the realm of economic abuse, they imagined articulating a set of protections that would limit the abuse employers could inflict on their employees—minimum wages, maximum hour limitations, and child labor prohibitions among them.[63] But here, as in the realm of antitrust, courts posed the most significant hurdle.[64] Beyond directly protecting the welfare of a worker, nineteenth-century jurisprudence largely prohibited outside interference in the workplace.[65] The same hurdle standing in the way of Jeffersonian design on antitrust policy now loomed over a separate campaign to protect workers at firms of all sizes.

The court, by then, had come to embrace a doctrine suggesting that, for the most part, employment arrangements, negotiated privately, should live beyond the reach of political interference. Most famously, 1905's *Lochner v. New York* limited the government's ability to impinge on what became known as the "liberty of contract" between employers and their employees. If a laborer agreed to accept a poverty wage, or to work inhumane hours, the court maintained that there was almost nothing elected officials could do to interfere.[66] While *Lochner* came to epitomize the court's intransigence, it was, in fact, just one example of the judiciary's opposition to progressivism's Jeffersonian agenda. As the country seethed amid riots, strikes, marches, and more, judges formed a kind of impenetrable black curtain. The ensuing frustration among reformers spurred a whole range of proposals to winnow judicial power. Theodore Roosevelt became so incensed that he openly flirted with proposals to let state court decisions be subject to popular referenda. The widely respected appeals judge Learned Hand proposed a broad reinterpretation of the due process standards.[67] Others suggested amending the Constitution to eliminate due process altogether.

None of these more audacious efforts to curtail judicial power ever came to pass. And as more conservative justices cycled off the court, and others loosened their grip, progressive reformers were able to glean various bits of satisfaction. Much as the *Lochner* ruling would stand until the 1930s, the court green-lit legislation capping working hours in 1908. In

1917, the justices let stand a law imposing a minimum wage for women and children—though it would invalidate another in 1923.[68] And yet even as the court's economic doctrines evolved, Jeffersonian progressives set their attention on shaving down a third bastion of centralized power: machine bosses. And that, then, became another leg of the Jeffersonian mantra: returning *political* power to the people.

Recall that during the bulk of the nineteenth century, political parties were a bulwark of democratic politics—they were the vehicle ordinary people employed to defend themselves against abuse from the well-off. Now, with the incumbent order in disarray, Jeffersonian progressives began to take a different view of the old political dynamics. Among those who shared Brandeis's aversion to bigness, machines looked almost unerringly like the corrupted tools of the country's economic overlords. As muckraking journalists frequently documented, many were on the take, serving more to exploit democratic impulses than to put muscle behind working-class demands. For reformers, that realization prompted an effort to reframe bosses as rapacious charlatans standing against the interests of ordinary citizens. Like those running the trust and the factory floors, they too needed to be taken down a peg.

This banner of political Jeffersonianism was particularly potent in the West, a region where fear of big businesses—mining and logging companies in many cases—prompted the (quite realistic) concern that big money would eventually buy off local legislators, turning them into rubber stamps for corporate interests. In that vein, California's governor Hiram Johnson proposed a mechanism to recall public officials, lest the state's honest citizens discover an elected official had been captured. A 1911 amendment to the state constitution similarly empowered citizens to place legislative initiatives on the ballot, bypassing what might someday become an intransigent legislature. These sorts of reforms, each providing ordinary people with opportunities to wield more authority *against* elected officials, took hold across the country.[69] Wisconsin senator Robert La Follette, who would run as the Progressive Party's 1924 presidential nominee, went so far as to make direct primaries, voter initiatives, and recalls pillars of his radical agenda.[70]

Combatting monopolies. Enshrining workers' rights. Lassoing political machines. These three priorities may appear to be largely distinct—reforms designed in each case to address a discrete challenge. But however different in target, they all reflected the same underlying conviction that the country's problems emanated from perversions born on high. The reformers who carried their banner subscribed to the same picture in their heads, believing that the key to the nation's progress was in returning authority to subjugated figures down below. But that, of course, wasn't the only ideological frame available to progressive activists at the time. Some reformers—and, in many cases, the very same people—began to embrace a notion that salvation would come less from tearing these institutions down, and more from building others up. They began to imagine new, public bureaucracies capable of holding the trusts, and foremen, and machine bosses more directly to account—or at least in check. And as we'll see, that more Hamiltonian notion spurred reformers to embrace a wholly distinct agenda—one that cut in a very different direction.

ROOTS OF THE HAMILTONIAN IMPULSE

It is difficult, today, to appreciate the menace the old robber barons posed more than a century ago. Twenty-first-century tech executives may control flows of information; they may manipulate the items we put in our virtual shopping carts. But the robber barons looming over the late nineteenth- and early twentieth-century trusts wielded much more power over the public's access to the basic necessities of life—oil, sugar, tobacco, steel, and much more. The figures running the trusts were more than celebrities boasting incredible wealth; they were beacons controlling the nation's subsistence. And so the notion that you might winnow the power wielded by John D. Rockefeller, Andrew Carnegie, or James Buchanan Duke by restoring some mid-nineteenth-century alternative replete with lots of little competitors seemed fanciful to many critics. These progressives came to believe that Brandeis's vilification of "bigness" was fundamentally off base. In their view, the salve wouldn't be in eroding concentrations of power, but in establishing new nodes of *public* power to hold vast concentrations in check.

Here is where progressivism's Hamiltonian impulse found its footing. Behemoth corporations, Hamiltonian reformers argued, were the natural outgrowth of progress. They were more efficient than smaller firms—better poised to exploit economies of scale. Boston, for example, competed with New York and Philadelphia for the business of midwestern farmers shipping their grain overseas. Few Bostonians believed that their port would be better served if grain had to traverse a whole bevy of little railroads on its way from Illinois to Massachusetts—they understood that a single large railroad would keep shipping costs lower.[71] The same was true across a whole range of industries. Better to have one enormous plant produce a lot of sugar, or aluminum, or tobacco, than to insist on a panoply of smaller facilities. And so many progressive reformers, skeptical that additional competition was a realistic salve, began looking for an alternative approach to keeping those enormous economic behemoths in line.

Like the impulse to push power down, progressivism's designs on enhancing public authority weren't entirely new at the turn of the century. In 1869, after two Massachusetts railroads merged, President John Quincy Adams's well-heeled grandson, Charles Francis Adams, argued that it would be "far easier and far cheaper to regulate than to destroy [the new monopoly]."[72] Reformers who shared Adams's sensibility imagined a centralized regulatory infrastructure capable of meeting the menace of bigness less by forcing competition than by exerting some control over how the private sector operated.[73] That is, limiting what corporations could charge, how much they could pay in dividends, and how they treated employees.

Those more inclined to this Hamiltonian approach saw a host of other advantages to building up public authority. A powerful regulator could ensure that every meat processor cut their beef in a sanitary way, that every steel mill constructed its beams such that buildings wouldn't collapse, that every railroad ran at speeds slow enough to ensure that trains did not jump the track. Unfortunately, as with the Jeffersonian dream of carving up huge corporations, the Hamiltonian vision of erecting a powerful new regulatory apparatus faced several steep obstacles.[74] Jeffersonian efforts to discipline the trusts faced the gauntlet of a suspicious judiciary; Hamiltonian designs ran up against the friction of a skeptical public. In the late nineteenth century, the American public generally held bureaucrats in very low esteem.[75] Perhaps worse, their skepticism was well-founded.

The most glaring contemporary example of bureaucratic incompetence centered on the federal government's enormous pension system.[76] Washington had established the program primarily to care for the families of Civil War casualties. But nearer the turn of the century, the program's intended beneficiaries were reaching old age. Oddly enough, however, the pension system's roster actually grew between 1880 and 1900: 60,000 pensioners had turned into 428,000. Payouts, which consumed a third of the federal budget, were higher in 1910 than they had been in 1890. And the growth hadn't been organic—it had been explicitly political. As much as half the Senate's legislative output during any given term was composed at the time of "private bills" granting new benefits.[77] And the new recipients were being sponsored, almost everyone presumed, on the basis of patronage. The subtext was unmistakable: government power was bound to come to abuse.[78] This, then, became the tide against which Hamiltonian progressivism had to swim. Those advocating for centralized public power were unavoidably vulnerable to the perception that they were the champions of incompetent public bureaucracy.[79]

If Hamiltonian progressives were going to establish a new vanguard of competent centralized authority, they would first have to devise ways to replace the incompetent hacks who had long been the common face of government. And because the movement was largely a creature of the nation's burgeoning middle class, reformers presumed that this meant replacing the working-class men who had traditionally claimed patronage appointments with experts exuding middle-class sensibilities.[80] Note that this was the explicit antithesis of Brandeis's faith in the "Common Man."[81] Jeffersonianism preached returning power to ordinary people; Hamiltonianism was grounded in a determination to erect a modern, scientific, professional bureaucracy full of disinterested professionals. Men like George Perkins and Charles Francis Adams viewed themselves as archetypes for the new managerial class. The new bureaucracies they dreamed of creating would have to be staffed with men who shared their sensibilities.[82]

That, then, pointed to a second-order question: How could reformers ensure that the new bureaucracies they envisioned would be insulated from the machines hungry to turn them into political boondoggles?[83] How could they preclude a local boss's inept nephew from being handed responsibility for overseeing a region's turnpike and canal projects? Moreover, reformers wanted to ensure that the new breed of professionalized bureaucrats was not beholden to those same bosses—that they would be empowered to act in the public interest without fear of being pushed out for doing the right thing. Put succinctly, it wasn't just that reformers wanted to exchange the government's incompetent hacks with educated experts—it's that they wanted those experts to wield authority unencumbered by the political patrons who had undermined faith in public bureaucracy. They wanted to replace a system defined by working-class graft with one characterized by middle-class professionalism.

Here, reformers faced elements of the same skepticism that thwarted fanciful desires to break up the trusts. Patronage was a staple of the nation's political system. During Democrat Grover Cleveland's first term as president, he forced forty thousand Republican postmasters out of their positions, replacing them with Democrats. When Republican Benjamin

Harrison subsequently defeated Cleveland, he replaced fifty thousand Democratic postmasters with Republicans. This churn was based not on ability or talent, but on political connections—those seeking appointments were required to contribute financially to their local parties.[84] For Hamiltonian reformers, the policy salve for this corruption was just as apparent: They would have to replace the "spoils system" of executive appointments with a civil service system based on merit—a project begun when Congress passed the Pendleton Act of 1883.[85] To insulate a new breed of publicly minded public servants, they would pull power up and away from the vulgar political class.

Unfortunately, the roster of *federal* bureaucrats was just a single, thin layer.[86] The real challenge during the Gilded Age and Progressive Era centered on state and local government.[87] As the eminent reformer John Dewey would write: "[City] agencies are the 'machines' of political parties, with their hierarchical gradation of bosses from national to ward rulers, bosses who are in close touch with the great business interests at one extreme, and with those who pander to the vices of the community (gambling, drink and prostitution) at the other."[88] In this realm, the rot extended beyond the incompetent clerks to the leadership itself. One activist in Iowa sounded the typical anthem: "The professional politician must be ousted and in his place capable business men chosen to conduct the affairs of the city."[89] That notion then spurred local reformers to amend city charters such that key decision-making authority was shifted from smarmy mayors to appointed "city managers" who would be unencumbered by petty politics, serving instead at the behest of the decidedly middle-class leadership of local chambers of commerce. By the 1910s, appointed managers were effectively running roughly six hundred cities around the country.[90]

That, then, pointed to Hamiltonian progressivism's third challenge. If they succeeded in building up a coterie of expert public professionals, and subsequently insulated those professionals from the corruption of politics, how could they ensure that important government decisions were made by this new breed of official? This was a primary concern for figures like Adams, who had understood early on that tension would emerge between elected legislators and expert regulators. Having concluded in the case of Massachusetts's railroads that there was more to be gleaned from establishing regulations than from smashing apart any new monopoly, he worried also that any legislative effort to keep watch over behemoth corporations would fail. "Knowledge," Adams argued, "cannot possibly creep into the legislature long enough to learn, [but] commissions—advisory bureaus—might scientifically study and disclose to an astonished community the shallows, the eddies, and the currents of business."

As others took stock of Adams's thinking, his prescribed model—a centralized body of experts empowered to keep the railroads in check—began to be applied elsewhere. To electric utilities, to water and sewer systems, and the like.[91] Here, taken together, was a Hamiltonian approach to solving the problem Jeffersonianism had tried to crack with an entirely different formula. Rather than chip away at the centralized institutions that were wreaking havoc on American life, the Hamiltonians would create new, publicly minded bureaucracies capable of keeping any rapacity in check. The problems of industrialization wouldn't be solved with renewed competition, but rather with new, competent organization. The nation's scientifically oriented middle class would swoop in to save the day.

To be sure, most progressives at the time, like most progressives today, were drawn to elements of *both* impulses. Many would have wanted both to establish workers' rights *and* to empower expert commissions. It would have been entirely normal, in fact, for a reformer to advocate both for busting trusts *and* ending the spoils system.[92] And, in that way, the movement's Jeffersonian and Hamiltonian impulses were not *always* in conflict. But if they could coexist, they were nevertheless rooted in fundamentally different stories about how the country could rise above the frustrations of the age. To borrow Walter Lippmann's phrase, progressives suffered from simultaneously having two pictures in their heads—one that preached that the elite were too awash in power, and another that they weren't powerful enough.

This distinction still frames a potent divide that resides deep within the progressive heart. Jeffersonianism was, and is, grounded in lionizing the wisdom held by the smallholder farmer, the working stiff, the person on the street. At the same time, many Hamiltonians were equating the word "democracy" with mob rule, some arguing that the "vulgar," as H. L Mencken would call them, were too drunk, stupid, corrupt, and immoral to be trusted with public authority.[93] Lippmann himself, almost explicitly repudiating Louis Brandeis's faith in the common man, put the Hamiltonian view plainly in 1922: "It is no longer possible . . . to believe in the original dogma of democracy."[94] Instead, he and those like him wanted the nation's well-heeled elite to impose their will to everyone's benefit. As the longtime progressive leader Henry Stimson explained of the early Progressive Era:

> Men began to think that irresponsibility was a direct result of scattered authority and divided power; fear of too much government had led to untrustworthy government. The true remedy for American misgovernment would lie, then, in exactly the opposite direction from that indicated by the advocates of direct democracy.[95]

Here, then, was progressivism's core divide in its purest form. And while, by some measure, their proposals seemed to hang together—it was easy, at first glance, to see why reformers would want to empower ordinary citizens to pass laws through referenda *and* to authorize expert commissions to issue regulations from insulated star chambers—a closer look makes clear that these two different approaches attacked the problems of industrialization from entirely different angles, girded by wholly contradictory narratives. Put another way, from the very beginning, progressivism represented the awkward marriage of two very different impulses. And that underlying contradiction sowed the seeds of the movement's subsequent frustration.

HAMILTONIAN MEANS TO JEFFERSONIAN ENDS

More than a century on, the Gilded Age and the Progressive Era have come to be remembered primarily as the setting of a grand political battle between trusts and reformers—a tug-of-war that pitted abusive industrialists against grizzled idealists eager to hold them accountable.[96] By contrast, the tension that prevailed during those years *within* progressivism is treated almost as a historical afterthought—an ideological spat without real consequence. Those looking to understand those decades can be forgiven for the oversight if only because, as we'll see, the gargantuan political fight between Theodore Roosevelt and Woodrow Wilson in 1912 was quickly resolved in the years that followed, with the Jeffersonian Wilson adopting most of Roosevelt's Hamiltonian approach. Caught midswirl of the ideas and movements defining the age—populism, socialism, Marxism, anarchism, feminism, racism, and more—the distinctions may appear marginal. But, on some level, that's the point: those seeking to understand the movement then and now can easily overlook the subtle dynamic that holds the two divergent impulses together.[97]

The late nineteenth-century populist insurgency that is often viewed as progressivism's immediate precursor leaned heavily toward the Jeffersonian bent. Widely extolled throughout America's agricultural heartland, the nation's farmers, in particular, were repulsed by the newly nationalized economy—they felt as though they were being crushed by eastern financial concerns.[98] William Jennings Bryan's still famous "Cross of Gold" speech, delivered at the 1896 Democratic National Convention, excoriated the faraway financiers who made no bones about the role currency had in driving debtors into bankruptcy.[99] And that dynamic drew on a widespread and latent desire to return America to a whitewashed nineteenth-century pastoral bliss, tilling the intellectual ferment for what would become progressivism's impulse to push power down and out.

But if the desire to spread power prevailed in some quarters, other reformers were increasingly drawn to a different critique. Awash in muckraked evidence that robber barons were fleecing consumers and abusing factory hands, many within the now burgeoning middle class were eager to hold bad actors to account. Even before the end of Reconstruction, several midwestern states awash in populism passed so-called Granger Laws to regulate intrastate freight prices, thereby capping what any given road could charge farmers shipping grain from one place to another. Here, right from the start, is an example of a Jeffersonian desire to push power down being pursued by a Hamiltonian directive, namely a collection of laws granting centralized state bureaucrats the power to set shipping rates. And, of course, the trusts didn't like any of it: determined not to let government interfere in their business practices, the railroads filed suit against the new intrusion.[100]

The Supreme Court's somewhat unexpected ruling permitting states (if not the federal government) to regulate the railroads set off a decades-long game of cat and mouse between various corporate interests, on one hand, and reformers grasping for ways to glean any sort of leverage over various industrial behemoths on the other. The railroads responded to the Granger Laws by consolidating their operations, creating interstate networks whose power states could not abridge. And then they engaged in a kind of conspiracy against reform. In 1883, they agreed to a uniform timetable. In 1886, they agreed on a common gauge allowing trains running on one road to traverse another's tracks.[101] And that same year, the Supreme Court gave them the gift of a regulatory reprieve. In *Wabash, St. Louis & Pacific Railway Company v. Illinois* the justices ruled that states were prohibited from capping rates on routes that crossed state lines.[102] Congress took a Hamiltonian turn in response, establishing in 1887 what became the first true federal regulatory agency—the Interstate Commerce Commission.[103]

For reformers, the Hamiltonian fantasy that the ICC would reestablish a balanced marketplace was short-lived. While the new agency explicitly forbade some of the railroads' most noxious practices, the robber barons running the corporations managed to find loopholes and gimmicks to preserve their leverage.[104] And eventually the Supreme Court issued a ruling that effectively handcuffed the ICC, leaving it to do little but collect and publish rate information. Thus, in the years immediately after its creation, the Hamiltonian ICC, like the Jeffersonian Sherman Anti-Trust Act enacted three years later, failed to deliver on its promise.[105] It wasn't really until 1901, when Vice President Theodore Roosevelt unexpectedly assumed the presidency, that reformers really had a champion on the national stage. At that point, a more profound battle for the heart of progressivism came into clearer view.[106]

For all his moxie, President Roosevelt didn't initially appear inclined to go to war with the nation's monopolies. He believed, like many of his upper-class contemporaries, that bigness was born from "natural causes in the business world," and that economies of scale generally "benefited the whole country."[107] But neither was he disposed to let corporate America have its way as a matter of course. Rather, while remaining open to enforcing antitrust law in certain egregious circumstances, Roosevelt became a beacon for the Hamiltonian desire to build a new federal regulatory apparatus.[108] This, remarkably enough, put him on something of a political island. Democrats, populists, and reformers in the ideological mold of Louis Brandeis wanted Washington to mount an all-out battle to break up the trusts. Many of Roosevelt's fellow Republicans, by contrast, remained committed to laissez-faire.[109] Few, it seemed, were particularly eager to give the national government's executive branch more unilateral authority. And yet that's exactly what he proposed.

Here things get complicated—but the underlying tension between the movement's Jeffersonian and Hamiltonian impulses remains constant. The conservatives wanted to keep government small, lest bureaucracy interfere with the private sector. Brandeis's acolytes and populists alike wanted to keep both business *and* government small so as to restore the norms of nineteenth-century life. Roosevelt and his allies, by contrast, envisioned a robust "administrative state," as it would come to be known. So when the Colonel proposed in 1903 to create a new Department of Commerce and Labor complete with a Bureau of Corporations empowered to investigate business, he was met with bipartisan opposition.[110] The best he could do was to prevail upon Congress to pass the Mann-Elkins Act, a law that put the onus on railroads to prove that rate increases were reasonable—hardly the bureaucratic Hercules Roosevelt envisioned.[111] He was forced to put his larger Hamiltonian project aside.

That said, Roosevelt wasn't above employing Jeffersonian tools when he thought them appropriate. In 1904, at a point when the Sherman Act was viewed as a law so pockmarked by loopholes that it could not be used to any real effect, his administration's Justice Department brought suit against J. P. Morgan's Northern Securities Company, which had managed to "organize" several of the railroads serving the nation's Northwest—and the government prevailed.[112] Yet even amid that Jeffersonian success, Roosevelt remained determined to build up the government's regulatory capacity.[113] Frustrated by a Supreme Court ruling that had prohibited the Interstate Commerce Commission from capping railroad freight charges, he championed the Hepburn Act, which explicitly granted the commission that authority. With its passage, the federal government reclaimed across the whole of the country the leverage that Granger Laws had once given states.[114] Roosevelt, in a phrase, braided progressivism's two impulses together in his pursuit of the public interest. And that then set the pattern.

Over the next several years, progressivism's two impulses continued to notch parallel, if incremental, political victories. After Upton Sinclair's *The Jungle* exposed the abuses running rampant in the largely unregulated meatpacking industry, Roosevelt signed into law both the Pure Food and Drug Act and the Meat Inspection Act. Senator Albert Beveridge, a prime sponsor, declared that the efforts marked "the most pronounced extension of federal power in every direction ever enacted."[115] Then, Roosevelt's successor, William Howard Taft, steered back toward a Jeffersonian bent, successfully forcing the breakup of both John D. Rockefeller's Standard Oil empire and James Buchanan Duke's American Tobacco Company.[116] This, then, was the setup for the 1912 campaign—the election during which George Perkins would battle with the progressive radicals over the business plank of the Progressive Party platform.

By the point of Roosevelt and Taft's epic showdown with Woodrow Wilson, it had been nearly a quarter century since the Interstate Commerce Act and Sherman Anti-Trust Act had been enacted as the respective lodestones for the movement's Hamiltonian and Jeffersonian impulses. Both approaches had been subjected to sniping from conservative legislators and skeptical judges. Both had enjoyed limited but notable success.[117] But the broader landscape had evolved as well. The appeal of nineteenth-century laissez-faire conservatism was at a low ebb. Federal bureaucracy had begun to look less incompetent. And so the core underlying question to be debated over the course of the 1912 presidential campaign was which version of progressivism—what mix of its Jeffersonian and Hamiltonian impulses—would define the movement going forward.

All three candidates tried to lay claim to the progressive banner—even the conservative Taft, who had worked hard to burnish a reputation as the nation's foremost trustbuster.[118] Roosevelt, trying to return to the White House four years after moving out, instead made robust government intervention the centerpiece of his appeal, even while endorsing direct primaries, supporting women's suffrage, and proposing to give voters opportunities to recall unpopular judges and decisions—each an explicitly Jeffersonian endeavor.[119] Ironically, the Democrat who would go on to win the general election was perhaps the most removed from the "big government" vision so often associated with the progressive label.[120] Wilson was, after all, the preferred candidate of Louis Brandeis.[121] In the New Freedom, Wilson's answer to Roosevelt's New Nationalism, Democrats explicitly vowed to strengthen the Sherman Act.[122] Perhaps more notable, despite having published an 1887 article calling for centralized, public administration, Wilson now claimed to be decidedly less keen on erecting a stronger regulatory regime.[123]

Note that here, again, the movement's two threads, spread across three candidates, were being braided together in ways that obscured their distinction. And the bifurcation was further confused by the reality that, after Wilson prevailed that November, he turned to embrace much of

Roosevelt's proposed agenda. In a phrase that would echo through time, *New Republic* founder Herbert Croly had, in 1909, defined the progressive creed as employing "Hamiltonian means" to achieve "Jeffersonian ends."[124] And that, increasingly, became the movement's approach. Brandeis remained a leading light in 1912—Wilson would appoint him to the Supreme Court. But the celebration of smallness that had been the hallmark of the justice's pre-court activism waned during the course of Wilson's presidency. As the eminent academic Christopher Lasch later described the contemporary thinking: "The trusts had brought order out of commercial chaos; public regulation of industry was the next step."[125] And so progressivism increasingly aimed to pull power up and in.[126]

To be fair, Wilson didn't abandon his campaign's Jeffersonian dogma altogether. He signed the Clayton Act in 1914 to strengthen the Sherman Act's protections against "unfair trade practices, such as interlocking directorates."[127] Beyond Brandeis's Supreme Court appointment, he made William Jennings Bryan, the celebrated populist, his first secretary of state. And the courts opened the door to new worker rights as well: by 1914, several states had enacted court-approved statutes outlawing child labor and limiting work hours.[128] But it was Wilson's embrace of Hamiltonianism that defined his two terms.[129] Most important, he championed the bill establishing the Federal Reserve—a publicly chartered central bank that functionally replaced J. P. Morgan and the so-called money trust that effectively set the nation's monetary policy. Perhaps just as important, after a decades-long fight over the federal government's authority to impose income taxes, Wilson signed into law the Revenue Act of 1913 following ratification of the Sixteenth Amendment. Those tax dollars would prove to be the lifeblood of the bureaucratic expansion to follow.

The drumbeat of Hamiltonian triumphs didn't end there. Wilson endorsed the ICC's once tenuous power to regulate railroad rates. He established a system to underwrite rural farm credits, and created a workers' compensation program for federal employees.[130] He signed into law the bill creating the Federal Trade Commission, a new body assigned the task of keeping tabs on the nation's commercial enterprises.[131] And that signaled a broader trend—a wholesale embrace of Charles Francis Adams's vision for a new legion of expert-led commissions. By the end of Wilson's tenure, the federal government boasted roughly four dozen commissions modeled on the ICC.[132] Given this string of victories, when the men who founded the *New Republic* endorsed Wilson for reelection in 1916, the magazine's editors, many of whom had supported Roosevelt four years earlier, felt confident declaring that the progressive agenda was ascendant.[133]

America's entry into the First World War served overwhelmingly to further the movement's Hamiltonian bent.[134] Facing an unprecedented international crisis, some had worried initially that mobilization would be undermined by the same incompetence that had hampered Union efforts during the Civil War a half century earlier. But Wilson appointee Bernard Baruch led a celebrated effort by the War Industries Board to reorganize the nation's industrial base in support of America's military.[135] Future president Herbert Hoover became an international hero by dint of his successful efforts to administer food aid through destitute parts of the continent.[136] And when the railroad industry, which Wilson had nationalized during the conflict, was returned to private ownership in 1920, few questioned the wisdom of empowering the ICC to take an even more powerful role balancing the interests of railroads, shippers, laborers, and ordinary passengers.[137] Administrative power, it seemed, was having a moment.

Again, Jeffersonianism was hardly vanquished. Many of the figures who had so enthusiastically championed centralized bureaucracy before 1912 came away from the First World War disillusioned. For as much as the War Industries Board appeared a beacon of professionalized management, insiders knew that it had often been twisted in knots, paralyzed by infighting.[138] Many of the same figures took umbrage at the way Wilson's administration had used public authority in a seemingly coercive way.[139] Wilson's decision to join the hostilities sparked a wave of domestic unrest, prompting the federal government to what some viewed as political suppression.[140] More than two thousand people were arrested during the war for speaking out against American involvement, some sentenced to as many as twenty years in prison.[141] And when, in 1920, a bomb exploded outside Attorney General A. Mitchell Palmer's home in Washington, a young Wilson administration appointee named J. Edgar Hoover ordered the arrests of a range of purported anarchists and communists, some of whom were summarily deported.[142] As horror stories of government oppression trickled out of the newly established Soviet Union, even many one-time Hamiltonians began to reconsider whether the stampede toward centralized power had gone too far.

Through the decade that followed, the movement's intellectual schism largely faded from view. Amid the "return to normalcy" Republican senator Warren Harding promised during his successful 1920 campaign for the White House, the Progressive Party disintegrated, and the "progressive" label, tarnished in the wake of Roosevelt's defeat and subsequent jingoism, was rebranded "liberal." As laissez-faire reemerged as an animating force in conservative circles—during the 1920s, the "Four Horsemen" of conservative jurisprudence on the Supreme Court struck down some 140 state laws designed to protect the public—the debate among liberals over whether power was better shifted up or down was swept from center stage.[143] But the underlying disagreement—the same divide that had separated the Sherman Act from the ICC, and the radicals from George Perkins—bubbled beneath the surface. It would rise to noticeable preeminence again only in 1932, when a charismatic young relative of Theodore Roosevelt's emerged as the Democratic nominee for president amid the turmoil of the Great Depression.

2

The Price of Progress

The Tennessee River runs a full 650 miles, meandering through seven separate southern states before merging with the Ohio near Paducah, Kentucky. Because the river basin's 40,000 square miles do not boast the flat terrain conducive to cash crops like cotton, the Upper South, as the surrounding region is better known, was never overrun by the plantation-centered lifestyle that prevailed across the Black Belt. That's not to suggest that slavery wasn't endemic in the Tennessee Valley before the Civil War. But the region, slightly smaller than England and defined more by forests than by fields, was typified less by Simon Legree than by Daniel Boone.[1] Whites may have wielded the power, but far from enjoying sweet tea on the veranda of the Big House, most survived through subsistence farming, with poor families of all races tending to maintain an isolated, hardscrabble existence. The Tennessee Valley was, by some measure, fly-over country before anyone coined the term.

In the decades that followed the Civil War, the Upper South's forests were abused by the timber industry, and over time the depleted landscape was left for dead. Robbed of its root systems and subjected to intermittent flooding, much of the area's fertile topsoil eroded. With the potential for agricultural prosperity deemed more remote, even those families boasting title to substantial plots of land often struggled to make a living. By the 1930s, the region's two million people subsisted on an average income merely half the national mean.[2] Tuberculosis and pellagra, a disease born from malnutrition, were common throughout. And while more prosperous parts of the country were being wired for electricity, only 2 percent of the region's farms had been connected to a grid.[3]

The region was not entirely forlorn. During the First World War, the federal government had initiated construction of a dam near Muscle Shoals, Alabama. The gigantic facility was designed to harness the river's flow to power the machinery required to produce nitrates for use in both bombs and fertilizer. At the end of the war, War Industries Board chairman Bernard Baruch proposed selling the facility off to Henry Ford, who promised to use the dam to power a "Detroit of the South." But Senator George Norris, a progressive Republican from Nebraska, balked, arguing that what had been a federally constructed facility should be used for the public's benefit.[4] And that disagreement led to a long stalemate. Both Presidents Calvin Coolidge and Herbert Hoover, avatars of private industry, vetoed bills that would have used the dam to provide "public power."[5] Through the 1920s, laissez-faire prevailed, leaving those farms and families in the region that were *not* served by private electricity producers largely to go without.

The battle over the dam's ownership coincided with a broader battle over electricity. Previously, during the Progressive Era, when electrical wires had first been strung across the country, municipalities had often taken the lead, establishing locally owned electrical systems under the direct control of City Hall. But if that appeared like progress to some, conservatives worried about the creeping tentacles of (often machine-controlled) local government. From that tension, a compromise was born. Rather than choosing between public and private ownership, government would charter "public utilities," entities that would be run independently and for profit, but with the imprimatur of public oversight.[6] In exchange for controlling the exclusive franchise to serve an area, a utility was contractually required to extend service to anyone who wanted a connection.[7] In theory, the public would get the benefit of municipal ownership with the efficiency born of private industry. Or that was, at least, the hope.

Already by the mid-1920s, however, many were questioning the wisdom of that arrangement. Legal agreements and secretive financial arrangements had opened the door for shadowy financial interests to claim effective control of the nation's utilities. Local citizens might have maintained the *impression* that the small power plant serving their single neighborhood was owned locally—but in many cases it was actually controlled by a corporation headquartered thousands of miles away. That left many Americans—most of them dependent on their little, local electrical utility—powerless to lobby for lower rates, better service, or new connections. Perhaps worse, profit-oriented ventures, however they might be governed, had no real incentive to string wires to faraway places that were unlikely to draw much electricity. And that market-based reality had left the vast countryside in regions like the Tennessee Valley bereft of service.[8]

Elected during the depths of the Great Depression, Franklin Roosevelt was determined to change the whole paradigm—not only to vanquish the now repudiated promises of laissez-faire, but to lay the foundation for a more rational economic system for electricity and beyond. As the historian Arthur Schlesinger would explain, as president-elect, Roosevelt determined that "the new economic order would have to enforce national standards, bringing great industries, such as mining, milling, manufacturing, and agriculture, under central control." And in his plan the Tennessee Valley would stand at the vanguard—a model for what vast public power could accomplish using rivers ranging from the Ohio, to the Missouri, and to the Columbia in the Pacific Northwest. Noting that, amid the catastrophe of the moment, America's economy seemed to be slipping backward, Roosevelt intended to reverse course: "The normal trend now is a back-to-the-farm movement. . . . I believe it is now time to tie up all these various developments into one great comprehensive plan within a given area."[9]

To the new president's mind, that meant something more than making the Muscle Shoals dam the generation plant for a federally run power grid. He wanted to use the facility to showcase how centralized, publicly administered electricity could draw undeveloped parts of the country into the modern economy. Rather than pour the system's profits into shareholder dividends, Roosevelt imagined investing that revenue back into the surrounding region.[10] The new federal authority would endeavor to control flooding, reforest the countryside, conserve the soil, burnish the region's agricultural economy, and build the foundation for a new industrial base.[11] Norris, realizing Roosevelt's vision was a supersized version of his old dream, was thrilled. And soon after the new president's inauguration, they worked together to usher through Congress a law creating the Tennessee Valley Authority.

Roosevelt had selected the Upper South as a demonstration project because it offered such a pristine example of the free market's failure to serve the greater good. The region was already dotted with power plants owned by various subsidiaries of Commonwealth and Southern, a holding company that controlled the Georgia Power Company, the Alabama Power Company, and the Tennessee Electric Power Company.[12] But Commonwealth and Southern's management, beholden to its shareholders, had chosen not to expand its service footprint for the simple reason that they did not believe the venture would be profitable—the cost of erecting wires across long stretches of the Tennessee River Valley would not justify the new demand for "load." That *appeared* like a purely economic decision— but it was grounded in cultural prejudice. The sophisticates who invested in and controlled the nation's utilities simply didn't believe the families dotting the countryside—the reporter H. L. Mencken would describe rural Tennessee in 1925 as "a sort of Holy Land for imbeciles"—would put public provision to good use.[13] Utility executives had little financial interest in helping people they viewed as hicks raise themselves out of the nineteenth century—and so they didn't.[14]

That's a crucial nuance. The TVA was conceived not just to deliver power to the countryside, but also to civilize what elites considered the country's heathens; electricity would simply be used as a civilizing cudgel. Roosevelt's venture proposed to deliver Muscle Shoals–generated electricity to unserved portions of the Valley. The new government-subsidized, publicly owned entity would erect wires to scattered farms and homesteads and then sell power at a rate 40 percent below what Commonwealth and Southern typically charged. Predictably enough, the private sector reacted to the scheme with fury, corporate executives viewing Roosevelt's plan as the camel's nose for out-and-out Bolshevism. If government was going to winnow down profits, how could businesses hope to compete? Wendell Willkie, Commonwealth and Southern's CEO, declared in a speech to the US Chamber of Commerce: "Subsidized government competition established in one industry, threatens all industry."[15] And that anti-government invective, which Willkie delivered with stinging effectiveness, fueled what would eventually propel him to the GOP presidential nomination in 1940.

But for all that Roosevelt's detractors viewed with suspicion the "brain trust" of White House advisors who saw great merit in the Soviet system, Roosevelt was less a communist than a progressive. The aristocratic new president's determination to help raise up the Tennessee Valley's impoverished families may have made him out to appear a "traitor to his class," but he nevertheless maintained a healthy disdain for the ordinary American citizen. He was less a man of the people than a country squire—a man of the upper crust determined to raise up the unwashed masses. "Power," the president explained when referring to the TVA, "is really a secondary matter. What we are doing there is taking a watershed with about three and a half million people in it, almost all of them rural, and we are trying to make a different type of citizen out of them." His was an explicitly paternalistic vision—one in which the riffraff were to be civilized by a paternalistic state.[16]

If Roosevelt was Hamiltonian in this respect, the progressive movement remained of two minds about the whole endeavor. To that end, the figure the president selected to chair the three-person board running the TVA, Arthur E. Morgan, brought a distinctly Jeffersonian sensibility to the mission. Morgan was a dam-building expert then serving as the president of Antioch College, and his desire was less to civilize the Upper South than it was to restore the rhythms of traditional Southern society. "If you give people the means for creating wealth and comfort, they will work out the situation without further help," he argued. "Yet today that most fertile land in America is the locus of the sharecropper tenantry, where poverty and bitterness are general, and violence appears."[17] Grand public works may have been straight out of the Hamiltonian playbook, but Morgan seemed convinced that, by providing power, the TVA could push economic power down to the yeoman farmers Jefferson had championed a century and a half earlier.

At the same time, another appointee to the three-member board was more explicitly Hamiltonian. A much younger man, David Lilienthal had spent the early part of his career regulating public utilities in Wisconsin, and he embraced a dogma very different from Morgan's—a sensibility that looked with much less favor on the private companies that had left so much of the Tennessee Valley in the dark. One 1932 study had revealed that the vast majority of farms across Tennessee, Alabama, Georgia, and Mississippi were not yet connected to the grid.[18] If the market was disinclined to provide ordinary people with a decent standard of living, Lilienthal believed the government should intervene.[19] He had almost no sympathy for Wendell Willkie's hysterical concern that electrifying these impoverished farms would spell the end of free-market capitalism. But he didn't think much of Arthur Morgan's hope that sprinkling new electricity on the region would reinvigorate nineteenth-century southern gentility.[20] As Lilienthal saw it: "We cannot return to a simpler standard of living, for that is to begin a retreat."[21] The Tennessee Valley was trapped in a tragedy of the commons, and he intended to use the TVA to lift the region out of that broader morass.

The tension, like so many disputes between and among progressives before and after, was a microcosm of the movement's efforts to balance its Jeffersonian and Hamiltonian instincts. Lilienthal, whom many viewed as an acolyte of Louis Brandeis, paid a certain lip service to decentralization, arguing, for example, that "the citizens' participation in the exercise of centralized authority must be increased." But he wasn't actually keen on ordinary people taking the wheel. Beyond stringing wires to the countryside, he wanted the Tennessee Valley's residents to *use* that power.[22] His paternalism wasn't so blatant as to suggest punishing farmers who refused to adopt modern agricultural practices. But he had no bones about pushing locals to purchase the washing machines, electric stoves, and refrigerators that prevailed around the country.[23] With a fully Hamiltonian zeal, he was going to pull the Upper South into the twentieth century whether the locals liked it or not.

Looking back, twenty-first-century progressives may wince, detecting a colonial bent to Lilienthal's thinking. The young Midwesterner viewed those living in the Upper South much as the European explorers had viewed the Native populations they encountered after crossing the Atlantic. And like a conquistador bringing news of the savior to the New World's pagans, he was determined to proselytize the miracle of rational administration to the victims of free enterprise.[24] Centralized public power would correct for a system that didn't work. And while, in other realms of the New Deal, Jeffersonianism would carry a brighter torch, in this corner of Roosevelt's agenda, Hamiltonianism won the day. Lilienthal, allied with a third member of the TVA's board, managed to sideline Arthur Morgan. And much as it is often overlooked among the alphabet soup of New Deal programs that served the nation as a whole—the Civilian Conservation Corps, the

Civil Works Administration, the Works Progress Administration, the Public Works Administration, the Social Security Administration—the TVA became arguably Roosevelt's most radically transformative reform. Perhaps never in American history has a single civilian bureaucracy had such a deep and transformative impact on any part of the country. And the impact has lasted.

The TVA, still in operation as late as 2025, would come to construct sixteen dams—a feat of engineering, many have argued, equal to a century's worth of the nation's railroad construction *combined*. And that publicly constructed system not only electrified vast swaths of the countryside—millions of dusty acres were turned into arable land, two hundred million trees were planted, erosion was curtailed, and farms and businesses both began to thrive. Despite displacing as many as fifty thousand people, the TVA was so successful that even conservatives lauded it.[25] Representative John Rankin, an unrepentant racist from Mississippi who would become Senator Joseph McCarthy's red-baiting ally, argued years on that "TVA is the most profitable investment the American people have made since the Louisiana Purchase."[26] This was a triumph of centralized, top-down, public administration.

The program was far from perfect. Like so many programs during this period, it was laced with racism—not only because Arthur Morgan was an unrepentant white supremacist, but because Roosevelt felt he had little choice but to heed the demands of southern Democrats determined to preserve Jim Crow.[27] But if the racial hierarchy remained, the TVA was nothing short of revolutionary. Without providing any real recourse for those forced to endure the costs of progress—people whose property was to be flooded behind new dams, and those whose homes would be inundated with smokestack pollution, and those forced to accommodate new power lines strung across their lots—the TVA plowed ahead. By dint of his perch atop this vast, unchecked federal authority, Lilienthal could not only brush past some of the most powerful corporations in the country; he could impose his will on a population without heeding much of any local opposition.

Roosevelt, for one, was thrilled by the TVA's progress. When celebrating the Tupelo, Mississippi, decision to abandon private power for electricity produced by the TVA's power, he declared: "What you are doing here is going to be copied in every state in the union before we get through."[28] And while that did not entirely come to pass—with the exception of a handful of smaller federal power authorities out west, the energy industry largely remained the province of private utilities through the New Deal—the TVA played a powerful role shifting the public perception of what government *could* do.[29] And it became a model.[30] The Marshall Plan—the Truman administration's scheme to rebuild Europe in the wake of the Second World War, was marketed to the American people as a "European TVA."[31] The Johnson administration's plan to rebuild the Mekong Delta was sometimes described as a "TVA for Vietnam."[32] During the 1960s, many including Martin Luther King Jr. and Robert Kennedy imagined creating a Marshall Plan for the nation's Blacks.[33]

The eminent historian Henry Steele Commager would come to celebrate the TVA as "the greatest peacetime achievement of twentieth-century America," an enterprise that "showed that public intelligence can operate most effectively through government and that government can be more efficient than business."[34] But he went further, crystallizing a notion that the TVA represented the triumph of progressivism's first story—a vision of heroic, centralized power at its best:

[The TVA] was the proving ground, as it were, of a dynamic democracy. Here were tested the broad construction of the Constitution, large-scale planning, the recasting of federalism along regional lines, new techniques of administration and new standards of civil service, the alliance of science and politics, and the revitalization of democracy through a calculated program of economic and social reconstruction. There was nothing new about any of these—broad construction dates back to the First Bank of the United States, science and politics were wedded in the world of the Smithsonian Institution and the Geological Survey, political regionalism was acknowledged in the Federal Reserve Bank System—but the TVA was the first institution to combine all of them in one tremendous experiment.[35]

IN SEARCH OF EXPERTISE

A decade before the TVA was born as one of the New Deal's early triumphs, few would have predicted that progressivism would take such a distinctly Hamiltonian turn. The push to centralize power had stalled in the wake of the First World War—reformers had been warded off by a newfound fear of abuse. David Lilienthal's mentor—the figure who convinced Roosevelt to install him at the TVA—was Felix Frankfurter, a young reformer whose unabashed prewar enthusiasm for administrative bureaucracy had flipped to turn him into a champion of Jeffersonian checks during the 1920s.[36] The American Civil Liberties Union was founded in 1920 expressly to defend against the government's coercive power.[37] And reformers by then had a range of good reasons to question the trustworthiness of public authority. In the wake of the Palmer Raids, and amid burgeoning fears of communist infiltration, the 1920s were not far removed from the nadir of American race relations.[38] Abuse was widespread, and the government was complicit—its authority used in a whole range of different circumstances unquestionably for bad.

But if progressivism's Jeffersonian impulse was on the march through the 1920s, something else was happening as well. The old populism that had predated the progressive tradition—the ideology typified by William Jennings Bryan, fueled as it was by southern and western notions that eastern elites were a threat to farmers and working people—began losing its purchase. Nineteenth-century Jacksonians had wanted to protect ordinary citizens from deep-pocketed financiers and self-styled experts. As Jackson himself had put it in 1829: "The duties of all public officers are, or at least admit of being made, so plain and simple that men of intelligence may readily qualify themselves for their performance."[39] But as the industrial economy had grown bigger and more complex, America's celebration of Johnny Appleseed had faded.[40] And that, perhaps more than any single feature, distinguished populism from progressivism.[41] Beneath their good intentions, many progressives came to believe that, to put it indelicately, the general public was too stupid to be trusted with any real influence. And that wasn't simply born of prejudice—it reflected the country's newfound draw toward new sources of expert wisdom.

Progressivism, in short, was being shaped by a *cultural* turn toward science. And the progress, driven by rationality, appeared to be everywhere. Researchers were unveiling new approaches to treat and protect against horrors ranging from cholera to scarlet fever, diphtheria, tuberculosis, smallpox, and typhoid. Engineers and doctors were spreading the miracles of improved sanitation, vaccinations, and medicine. And to the degree that the promise of scientific and engineering expertise spurred many progressives to call for replacing backwater public health officials with trained professionals, the same worldview began to frame the movement's approach to public policy more generally.[42] Matters of state, in the progressive worldview, should not be left in the hands of charismatic country bumpkins; they should instead be placed in the responsible hands of professionals, of experts, of the well-heeled and well educated.[43]

The turn to expertise wasn't exclusive to progressive reformers. America, as a whole, was becoming increasingly professional. In most little nineteenth-century businesses, bosses had prized employees who understood every part of an operation—they wanted generalists. But in the huge manufacturing facilities coming to prevail through the early twentieth century, specialization became coin of the realm. In 1895, Frederick Winslow Taylor had published a paper on what he called "scientific management." He called for planning departments to replace foremen in control of factory operations—and for those planning experts to dictate to cogs on the factory floor how to do their jobs. The *thinking* part of any industrial process, in Taylor's view, should be done by people who had divined the *right* way.[44] And that meant ceding the bulk of decision-making to people at the top—to professionals who knew better.[45]

Taylorism was controversial, viewed by some as a scheme to undermine the dignity of labor. But it nevertheless became a cultural touchstone.[46] Taylorism girded Henry Ford's embrace of the assembly line.[47] And while scientific management became a central nostrum in the world of big industry, its underlying thrust was applied much more widely.[48] Ordinary Americans began to put a greater premium on having their problems addressed by people who had acquired certified expertise.[49] Trained doctors supplanted the "quacks and nostrums" who dispensed medical advice. The slapdash legal profession was professionalized by bar associations. Universities reorganized themselves into academic disciplines that claimed dominion over various subjects. Chambers of commerce, unions, and farming associations all began establishing canons designed to burnish the public's faith in their members.[50] Even personal decisions became the province of outside experts. *Middletown*, Helen and Robert Lynd's iconic study of Muncie, Indiana, detailed how American families were turning to patronize banks and insurance companies explicitly because they preferred to place their financial well-being in the hands of financial professionals.[51]

The same zeitgeist framed progressivism's view of government. To the new progressive mindset, the hack country lawyers and freewheeling political bosses who had prevailed in the nineteenth century appeared amateurish, small-minded, and obsolete.[52] Better for the nation that public business be handled by those who understood the unique challenges of public authority.[53] At the root of the movement was a notion that government executives, ham-handed by special interest–dominated legislatures, were "not strong or responsive enough to deal with modern conditions."[54] The surgeon was to the hospital what the lawyer was to the courtroom and what, in theory, the bureaucrat should be to the government agency.[55] And so progressives began crafting reforms designed to insulate publicly minded experts from public interference.[56]

During the 1910s, for example, the nation's largest port, split between the states of New York and New Jersey, was a political mess, caught in the crosshairs of various machines bickering over systemetic improvements in ways that eroded efficiency and undermined long-term planning. The Port Authority was established in 1921 to pull the port free and impose a routinized, standard, rational system. While that rankled local bosses in both states, it typified the progressive longing for professionalized centralized authority.[57] And if that impulse to pull power up and away from purportedly corrupt bosses prevailed in progressive circles, reformers applied the same mentality to private corporations.[58] When Franklin Roosevelt became New York's governor in 1928, he dismissed proposals to let General Electric, DuPont, and Alcoa harness the hydroelectric power born of damming the Saint Lawrence River, choosing instead to invest that responsibility in a centralized public bureaucracy, the Power Authority of New York State.[59] In ways that privatization and public-private partnerships would mark the vanguard of subsequent reform movements, centralized public authority was the order of the day.

Because it's so often overlooked, there should be no mistaking here just what a break this explicitly Hamiltonian instinct was from the Jeffersonian tendencies that had animated Louis Brandeis and his accolytes just a few years earlier. Brandeis, of course, was preternaturally suspicious of "bigness." Reformers in his mold had striven to pull power *away* from machines and corporations alike, hoping to reestablish the nineteenth-century pastoral norms that prized small businesses and shopkeepers. Efforts to create the Port Authority and the Power Authority of New York State were in direct contravention of the impulse that had spurred radicals at the 1912 Progressive National Convention to demand stronger antitrust enforcement. And that shift wasn't born exclusively of a newfound faith in bureaucracy. Rather, rebranded "liberals" still maintained very little faith in the nation's judiciary, which still appeared during the Lochner era like a tool of the financial elite.[60] Better, as George Perkins and others had argued, to empower expert-led agencies to bring the private sector to heel. It was through this mentality that "planning" became popular among progressives.[61] Better than hackish, machine-controlled legislators or effete, imperious judges, many reformers wanted to empower expert-led bureaucracies.

Not that the newfound turn to Hamiltonianism eclipsed progressive Jeffersonian tendencies altogether. As has always been the case, many reformers were engaged in both traditions at the same, if in different realms of public policy. At the same time Felix Frankfurter was working to protect citizens like Nicola Sacco and Bartolomeo Vanzetti *from* prosecutorial abuse—an explicitly Jeffersonian endeavor—he was arguing that government regulators and publicly spirited bureaucrats should be given wider latitude to use their "temper of mind" with greater discretion.[62] "Democracy," he explained to a reporter from the *New York Times Magazine*, "is dependent upon clean and disinterested government. But these days the simple virtues of honesty and public devotion are not enough. . . . Forced to grapple with a world more and more dominated by technological forces, government must have at its disposal the resources of training and capacity equipped to understand and deal with the complicated issues that arise."[63] The public sector, Frankfurter's endeavors made clear, should have less discretion in certain realms, like criminal justice, and more in others.

Prosecutors should, in some realms, have their wings clipped—regulators should be empowered to soar. Newly empowered public bureaucracies, reformers realized, spelled a whole host of vulnerabilities. Government authorities might, as revealed during the First World War and the years that followed, become incompetent and abusive in their own right. Bureaucrats might be captured by big private interests. They might even wind up hemmed in by the same factors that rendered machine-led government departments so frequently ineffective. So the challenge wasn't just to empower these new bureaucracies; it was to ensure that they would be run by the right people. Smart people. Publicly spirited people. People who would rise above the muck, weigh the costs and benefits, and come to a rational, scientific, perhaps even *correct* decision.[64]

If Hamiltonian progressivism's paternalism was sometimes shrouded in the patina of expertise, its disdain for the working class was frequently out in the open. Frankfurter frequently took to quoting free speech's original champion, John Stuart Mill: "Mediocrity ought not to be engaged in the affairs of state."[65] His mentor Louis Brandeis, dubbed "the People's Attorney," was similarly caught dismissing the lowly opinions of ordinary people—often to the horror of his detractors.[66] And H. L. Mencken, the wildly influential Baltimore-based newspaper columnist who founded and edited the *Smart Set* and the *American Mercury*, forerunners to the *New Yorker*, complained that "politics under democracy consists almost wholly of the discovery, chase and scotching of bugaboos. The statesman becomes, in the last analysis, a mere witch-hunter, a glorified smeller and snooper, eternally chanting 'Fe, Fi, Fo, Fum.'"[67] Power, in his view, should be reserved more exclusively for the experts.

Not every reformer was quite so paternalistic. Leading progressives including Herbert Croly and John Dewey viewed robust public education as a salve for the public's ignorance and small-mindedness.[68] But, in the end, progressivism increasingly came to embrace Mencken's underlying desire to rid the public square of the backwardness.[69] Frankfurter's simultaneous embrace of civil liberties and expert-led bureaucracy can certainly be understood as a split reaction against his fear of the mob. Either way, progressivism increasingly came to view oppressive democracy as a far graver danger than overbearing bureaucracy.[70] As a result, by the eve of the Great Depression, the movement appeared ready to go big on big government.

A FOOL'S PARADISE

The better part of one hundred years later, progressives are often prone to look back on the New Deal with an air of wistfulness. Here was a moment, we tell ourselves, when big government dramatically and unapologetically stepped in to save the republic. Roosevelt's first reelection campaign in 1936 was such a rout—the president won all but two states,

and Democrats expanded their majorities in both houses of Congress—
that the results now loom as the high-water mark of progressive fantasy:
a catharsis when the movement could impose its will on the country
without having to account for conservative foot-dragging or Republican filibusters.[71] Government, for once, appeared to be operating on all
cylinders. And so, decades later, at times when Democrats sensed that
they might be on the precipice of similar dominance, various left-leaning
think tanks would sketch out similarly bold agendas—grab bags of ambitious ideas. For the better part of a century, progressives have dreamed
of having a second New Deal–like bite at the apple.[72] Oh, the places
we'd go.

Historians of the twentieth century know, of course, that the New
Deal was not the well-oiled machine sometimes conjured in the movement's contemporary imagination. Like any large, powerful bureaucracy
facing a crisis, the Roosevelt administration was riven with tensions and
disagreements, triumphs and grievances. And those arguments were born
from a whole range of factors—personality clashes, disparate priorities,
petty politics. But too often overlooked today is the role played by a core
ideological divide. Just like in 1912, when the Jeffersonian "radicals" and
Hamiltonian reformers battled over the business plank of the Progressive
Party platform, progressives warred among themselves over how to balance their competing impulses to drive power up and pull it down. And
through Roosevelt's dozen years in office, the calculation was perpetually
in flux.

It wasn't clear, at the moment of Roosevelt's first victory in 1932, how
exactly his administration would govern. As in previous and subsequent
eras, the Democratic Party was then an unwieldy coalition knitting together various schools of thought, each of which was inclined to balance
the movement's Jeffersonian and Hamiltonian instincts in its own way.
To begin with, a certain phalanx of Democrats, perhaps most potently
embodied by the new vice president, former House Speaker John Nance
Garner, was conservative in the most Jeffersonian way. They worried

primarily about government overreach and were often preoccupied by the specter of nationalization—namely the possibility that Washington might claim ownership of various businesses or even entire industries.[73] While Roosevelt was himself less enamored of what might be termed "tight" fiscal policy, the 1932 Democratic Party platform had called explicitly for the federal government to trim its sails.[74] And the president remained committed, in theory, to balancing the government's books.

But if Jeffersonian conservatives still had a place under the Democratic tent, the Great Depression muted the impulse to *de*centralize power. Amid a deep popular hunger for government to do *something*, almost anything, to end the misery, second and third schools of thought shunted fears of government overreach aside, urging Roosevelt to embrace not Marxism but Keynesianism, a newly emerging economic theory that prescribed public deficit spending in the face of plummeting consumer demand.[75] But beyond that, those urging more robust government intervention disagreed on where the government should invest those extra dollars, and how it should exact political power over the private sector. In the most simplified terms possible, various New Dealers harbored two separate visions of the role a centralized, powerful state could play in American life. And Roosevelt, a wily shape-shifter, vacillated between the two.

The men often described as FDR's original brain trust, Raymond Moley, Rexford Tugwell, and Adolf Berle among them, were broadly of the same mindset Arthur Morgan would take at the TVA, imagining that government could be used to reorganize the American economy to ensure that adversarial interests *cooperated* in pursuit of the greater good. Morgan hadn't wanted the TVA to compete with the private companies that had refused to wire up the Tennessee Valley—he had wanted the TVA to balance interests almost as a factory manager might scientifically tweak the workings of an assembly line to maximize efficiency. The brain trust held much the same view of how Washington should handle the economy as a whole. Government, in their vision, would serve as a grand convener, a conductor of the orchestra, a referee of the game.[76]

Of course, the analogy isn't perfect. If Morgan had been more sympathetic to Commonwealth and Southern than his peers atop the TVA, the brain trust was, by nature, more antagonistic to the scions of private industry—Tugwell, in fact, was so hostile to corporate power that he would eventually come to be known as "Red Rex." But as advocates for what came to be known as "associationalism," these advisors worked to convince the president during the early days of his administration that the government needed first and foremost to restore confidence in the System—to snuff out the "fear" that the new president had so famously highlighted in his first inaugural address.[77] So, averse as they were to the greed and corruption, those shaping what would become known as the First New Deal saw government as less the private sector's adversary than a partner in reviving the nation's vast economic machine.[78]

It was this "associational" approach that framed the most consequential legislation of the Roosevelt administration's first years—in particular the National Industrial Recovery Act, which authorized creation of the behemoth National Recovery Administration (NRA), and the Agricultural Adjustment Act (AAA).[79] Both initiatives were born from the intellectual tradition that had framed the First World War's War Industries Board, which had coerced cooperation among labor and industry in service of the military's European campaign. Excess competition, as Moley put it, "created as many abuses as it prevented."[80] And so the NRA, which was focused on bringing order to the nation's industrial economy, and the AAA, which was designed to settle the chaos that was befalling the nation's farmers, were assigned the challenge of saving the nation by wielding the same tools. The associationalists wanted to put disinterested experts in charge of managing the ballet of competing interests, thus ensuring that the nation's economic machine could run apace.[81]

Note that the brain trust, while not calling for explicit nationalization, had less use for the Jeffersonian strand of the progressive agenda—they were not frightened of "bigness" in either the public *or* private sector. The National Recovery Administration explicitly suspended the Sherman

Anti-Trust Act, thus giving industry and labor opportunities, through publicly sanctioned councils, to work cooperatively in establishing hours, wages, and prices. The AAA proposed something similar for farmers. The progressive brain trusters, in short, were encouraging the very behavior the progressive trustbusters had wanted to eviscerate just a few decades earlier.[82] Inherent in both programs was Theodore Roosevelt's notion that bigness was inevitable—and that cooperative planning was the only reasonable way forward.[83]

Well-intentioned as it may have been, the NRA proved to be a spectacular failure. The councils Washington convened to set norms and standards were dominated by well-established corporate behemoths and labor giants, leaving smaller players—small businesses, smaller unions, and, in many cases, consumers—without any real influence. Roosevelt's western allies in Congress, many of whom had joined the progressive movement with a mind toward pursuing Jeffersonian *political* reforms like the referendum, the recall, and the direct election, were aghast, believing that the administration was serving to shield powerful interests from upstart competition. And when the famous liberal lawyer Clarence Darrow eventually released a scathing report highlighting the NRA's incompetence, Walter Lippmann, a progressive journalist and thinker now well on the road to New Deal skepticism, wrote: "The excessive centralization and the dictatorial spirit are producing a revulsion of feeling against bureaucratic control of American economic life."[84] George Perkins's Hamiltonian vision of a managed ballet of economic interests, laid out decades earlier, now appeared a dead end. The First New Deal was in shambles.

Eventually, both the NRA and the AAA were put out of their misery by the Supreme Court.[85] In rulings that would thoroughly anger the president—speaking to the press, Roosevelt would argue that the justices were limiting government to the role that it had played in the "horse-and-buggy" era—the court established clearer limits on the role the federal government could play in regulating the economy.[86] But, perhaps as salient for progressivism, the rulings appeared like acts of revenge for those who held a torch for the movement's Jeffersonian tradition. Now Justice Louis Brandeis, who had been so dismissive of Theodore Roosevelt's New Nationalism a quarter century earlier, summoned one of the president's aides to the robing room moments after the court issued its rulings. "This is the end of this business of centralization," he seethed. "You must see that [Brandeis acolyte, Roosevelt confidant, and future Supreme Court justice Felix Frankfurter] understands the situation and explains it to the President. You must explain it to the men Felix brought into the Government. They must understand that these . . . decisions change everything. The President has been living in a fool's paradise. . . . We're not going to let this government centralize everything."[87]

And that then forced the administration to reconsider its approach—to reevaluate how to balance its Hamiltonian and Jeffersonian impulses. By then, most White House advisors, and even Brandeis himself, realized that the government could not return to championing the old aversion to bigness—there was no realistic way to pull the country out of the catastrophe of the Great Depression by championing what one of Franklin Roosevelt's advisors referred to derisively as "small proprietors . . . corner grocers and smithies under spreading chestnut trees."[88] And so Roosevelt's second approach would have to combine, in some new way, the adversarial nature of antitrust with the bureaucracy that had typified Theodore Roosevelt's designs on big public authority. This new breed of progressivism keyed in on this newfound embrace of expertise and professionalism. It prized a tool that the associationalists had been less keen to employ: regulation.

BOYS WITH THEIR HAIR ABLAZE

To be sure, the approach that would animate the Second New Deal wasn't entirely new to the progressive tradition. A generation earlier, in the years that predated the First World War, many progressives had wanted to let public authority loose by piercing the constraints courts and parties placed on robust government action—they had harbored designs on letting democracy rip. But despite their progress through the Wilson years, significant barriers remained. Political machines had been cut down on the margins by various reforms—the direct election of senators and women's suffrage each winnowed the control bosses could wield over elected officials. But often enough, bosses could still control which public works projects were given priority as New Deal funding poured into states and localities. Many reformers wanted to change that.

Of more concern for those now wanting to impose regulation, the judiciary remained a substantive headache. *Bailey v. Drexel Furniture Co.* (1922) had precluded government from outlawing child labor. *Adkins v. Children's Hospital* (1923) had thwarted progressive designs on imposing a minimum wage. The justices had green-lit yellow-dog contracts, which permitted employers to preclude unionization.[89] Justices Oliver Wendell Holmes and Louis Brandeis frequently wrote scathing dissents—but through the 1930s, the judiciary, even more than party machines, remained progressivism's most potent adversary.

Reformers might have been tempted, in the wake of the First New Deal's unraveling, to revert to their old Jeffersonian ideology. And almost on cue, populists emerged to demonize big business with an eye toward tearing it down. Louisiana senator Huey Long's famous call for a program to "Share Our Wealth" spoke more directly to old Jeffersonian fears about roguish elements like the old money trust.[90] But by the mid-1930s, many erstwhile champions of progressivism's aversion to bigness began to see the limitations of that approach. Particularly in cases where "natural" monopolies prevailed—utilities, for example, served markets where the costs of production or distribution were too much to split between firms—trust-busting seemed far-fetched. That said, if the associationalist approach of the First New Deal was a dead end, Hamiltonian progressives would now need to divine a different approach to shape the second.

It was at this point that a Yale Law School professor, Thurman Arnold, pointed to an alternative way forward: rather than managing the economy from above—treating economic actors as marionettes as the First New Deal had attempted to do—progressivism could seek to deploy government in a more adversarial role.[91] Instead of assigning executive branch agencies the role of serving as economic maestros, this Second New Deal would deploy executive agencies as players themselves. This approach preserved the role the judiciary had traditionally played as the ultimate referee: when private industry wanted to do one thing, and a government regulator demanded that they do another, a judge in Arnold's framework would decide whose prerogative would prevail. As in the First New Deal, executive branch agencies would be more powerful. But rather than shaping the game, they would actually play it. Arnold's scheme was as Hamiltonian as the brain trust's had been, if a bit different.

We can't know, of course, whether the justices of the Supreme Court would have been as averse to the underlying ideology of the Second New Deal if Roosevelt had embraced it from the outset—if he had bypassed the associational approach and immediately alighted on a more explicitly regulatory regime. But by the time Roosevelt switched streams, the court's jurisprudence had begun to change. In 1934, well before the court-packing fight that would hobble Roosevelt's second term, the court ruled narrowly in *Nebbia v. New York* that state government could, in fact, regulate the price of milk.[92] And that shift had served as a kind of signal to reformers. The justices seemed to suggest that executive branch officials *could* be granted more power as regulators, just so long as courts remained on their perch to decide when the "experts" hired by the government had gone too far.[93]

But if this second theory of government intervention seemed better poised to pass constitutional muster, another open question remained: Would it actually work? To that point, only two independent regulatory agencies of any real consequence had ever been established at the federal level—the Interstate Commerce Commission, born in 1887 to deal with specific problems created by the nation's railroads, and the Federal Trade Commission, created during the Wilson years but seen, by the 1930s, as something of a flop.[94] Roosevelt, nevertheless, chose to plow ahead. As the president declared in his second inaugural: "As intricacies of human relationships increase, so power to govern them must also increase. . . . We are fashioning an instrument of unimagined power for the establishment of a morally better world."[95] In that spirit, a younger generation of hard-charging advisors—what one observer labeled "the boys with their hair ablaze"—began erecting new executive bureaucracies equipped to tangle with avaricious business interests in a way that served the broader public interest.

The Roosevelt aides most integrally involved in the birth and implementation of this modern administrative state—Harry Hopkins, Harold Ickes, Frances Perkins, and Robert Jackson, among others—are now the most celebrated figures of the era.[96] Inside the White House, they were assisted by Benjamin Cohen and Tommy Corcoran, two young idealists bent on using government to hold both corporations and machine bosses to account.[97] And the tent poles of modern progressivism included many of the Second New Deal's greatest achievements.[98] The Wagner Act created the National Labor Relations Board, a federal bureaucracy tasked with insulating labor organizers from employer coercion. The Social Security Act created a bureaucracy to provide limited public pensions.[99] The Securities and Exchange Commission was charged with regulating large Wall Street investment houses. The Federal Communications Commission was assigned the task of regulating the telephone, telegraph, and radio industries.[100] The Civil Aeronautics Authority was charged with regulating the airlines.[101]

Each of these accomplishments demanded expertise within the ranks of bureaucracy.[102] James Landis, an early luminary of administrative law, would argue that those carrying torches for the public would need the wisdom that "springs only from that continuity of interest, that ability to desire to devote fifty-two weeks a year, year after year, to a particular problem."[103] And that was their Hamiltonian dream, if not their expectation. But even as this second phalanx of New Dealers began the work of pushing their ideas through a relatively pliant Democratic-controlled Congress, the Supreme Court loomed in the distance. Having witnessed the justices upend so much of the First New Deal, no one could be sure the court would bless this new progressive approach.

Here, history took a fateful turn when, amid the drama that surrounded Roosevelt's controversial second-term plan to pack the Supreme Court, the high court became remarkably pliant. In what is sometimes remembered as the "switch in time that saved nine," Justice Owen Roberts doubled back on a previous ruling barring the imposition of minimum wages—suddenly, in *West Coast Hotel Co. v. Parrish* the court ruled 5–4 that government *could* interfere to limit the discretion businesses had to pay at miserly rates. And Roberts's switch symbolically ended the court's opposition to Roosevelt's agenda. Within weeks, rulings blessed the Social Security Act and the National Labor Relations Act. And from that point in 1937, the court never again thwarted a New Deal program.[104]

This new template—one in which the big, centralized bureaucracies were given the authority to do big, consequential things—became progressivism's new standard and approach. And this explicitly Hamiltonian project flowed down from Washington into the states. The White House drafted model legislation for state and local governments to use in growing centralized bureaucracies that would work in the public interest. Washington deployed the Reconstruction Finance Corporation to help cash-strapped public authorities grow, and established the Public Works Administration to purchase their debt. With the New Deal's blessing, a new legion of experts and professionals began to seize an entirely new modicum of power across the country.[105] And with that, top-down progressivism appeared more permanently ascendant.

THE DREAM OF FULL EMPLOYMENT

The New Deal was hardly perfect—Roosevelt was undoubtedly slow to pursue progress on racial equality, for one. But the 1930s marked a kind of halcyon moment for the movement for a reason. Would that the president hadn't made the disastrous political misstep of trying to pack the Supreme Court—a grab for power that reawakened the nation's skepticism of administrative overreach—the march toward an even more powerful, disruptive, and efficacious government might have reached even greater heights.[106] But progressivism wasn't simply victimized by its own missteps, or by the resurgent appeal of the electorate's more conservative instincts. The movement's adherents, having tilted so drastically to its Hamiltonian impulse during Roosevelt's first two terms, began through the late 1930s and early 1940s to pull back, rediscovering in their critiques of the New Deal some of their more Jeffersonian instincts.[107]

Some of the shift was personality-driven. Western progressives who had been enthusiastic about Roosevelt and his agenda at the administration's outset—progressives like Montana Democrat senator Burton Wheeler, the Progressive Party's vice-presidential nominee in 1924—were later put off by the Hamiltonian pull of the NRA. They maintained their old aversion to "bigness" and believed that coordination between various interests was aiding the nation's big monopolies at the expense of smaller enterprises. Representative Wright Patman, a Democrat representing a district in East Texas, would come to champion a widely publicized bill to tax chain stores in ways that advantaged mom-and-pop competitors—a bill that Roosevelt's aides opposed in the name of efficiency.[108] Senator Hugo Black, the Alabama Democrat whom Roosevelt would eventually nominate to the Supreme Court, was of the same mindset—more inclined to push power down and out than up.[109] And that Jeffersonian strain reestablished itself slowly but assertively, eventually steering the movement to a place very different from what the boys with their hair ablaze might have preferred.

Hamiltonianism's lost momentum was evident in a variety of set-backs. The administration's plan to impose the TVA model on other parts of the country—seven "mini-TVAs"—petered out after facing heavy opposition from the nation's utilities. The Civilian Conservation Corps, the Works Progress Administration, and the Home Owners' Loan Corporation were all eventually discontinued.[110] But if the United States seemed poised to repeat the pattern that followed the country's triumph in the First World War—if the electoral setback Democrats suffered during the 1938 midterms suggested that the country was ready, once again, to "return to normalcy"—two crucial circumstances intervened. First, in a move that would end the Lochner era, the 1937 Supreme Court ruling permitting minimum wage legislation opened the door to much more robust government interference in other realms—a clear win for Hamiltonianism.[111] Second, and better understood, the specter of a burgeoning conflict in Europe began to dominate the national consciousness.

In an echo of Bernard Baruch's success leading the War Industries Board two decades earlier, America's preparation for the Second World War reinvigorated the nation's embrace of powerful bureaucracies.[112] The military, perhaps more than any other American institution, was a quintessentially top-down affair. And so, however fledgling America's embrace of the New Deal may have been by the late 1930s, the nation's faith in the wisdom of experts—diplomats, generals, and bureaucrats alike—was poised to grow. On the home front, Roosevelt established a new bureaucracy to manage inflation. With so many resources now being directed to the nation's war machine—factories retrofitted to build military equipment, agricultural products now being sent overseas—civilians were forced to adjust to an economy starved for both needs and wants. The Office of Price Administration (OPA) was established to create and enforce various standards. Here, as in earlier periods of the New Deal, Roosevelt's administration turned to centralized administration. And here, again, there would be a Jeffersonian backlash.

Donald Nelson, the now mostly forgotten figure appointed to fill the role Baruch had played in the previous war, was broadly criticized for incompetence. Absent strong civilian efforts, the military was left to provision for itself. Perhaps more pointedly, Leon Henderson, tasked with leading the OPA, became a public lightning rod, reviled, perhaps understandably, for limiting what people were paid and what they could earn. And so, rather than responding to global catastrophe yet again by championing a further consolidation of centralized power, many among the public turned to adopt an emergent new conservatism. In 1944, Friedrich Hayek's *The Road to Serfdom*, which argued that the growing administrative power represented a slippery slope to fascism, became a bestseller. By Roosevelt's third term, even some big-government liberals had begun to tire of bureaucracy, with Reinhold Niebuhr, a theologian who would emerge as the conscience of American liberalism, voicing concern about creeping centralized power. Facing yet another turn in the political landscape, Roosevelt and his successor, Harry Truman, adjusted once again.

Having abandoned the First New Deal's associationalism for the Second New Deal's centralized regulation, progressives now steered more directly into the increasingly influential doctrine of Keynesianism. Rather than manipulating companies and unions like marionettes, or bringing them to heel through administrative fiat, Washington began trying to affect the economy more exclusively through the public purse. Public works projects, guaranteed incomes for farmers, urban "renewal," public housing, the GI Bill—this broad portfolio of new federal investments was designed to promote, at the national level, what became the postwar promise of progressive politics, namely, "full employment." Southern Democrats in particular had begun to look with increasing skepticism at the burgeoning desire among northern liberals to interfere with the Jim Crow system of white supremacy—they wanted their region to be left alone. And so, rather than pursuing more aggressive reform, Democratic Party leaders intent on keeping their diverse coalition together became broadly content to enhance and maintain the "rising tide" that, as John F. Kennedy would later celebrate, "lifts all boats." The impulse to grow government dissipated some, even as many of the centralizing institutions remained in place.

Through the 1950s, progressivism settled into a new footing. The big reforms that had defined the New Deal might no longer have been feasible, but the large bureaucracies that had been created theretofore, now licensed by the Supreme Court's repudiation of *Lochner*, wielded enormous authority. Largely abandoned were the Jeffersonian dreams of restoring the norms of small-town life, or breaking up the big, bad trusts—those sorts of concerns had been rendered something of an afterthought. Now the challenge was simply to steer existing bureaucracies to invest. Democrats proposed federal programs to subsidize home mortgages and student loans. They proposed to use federal funding to clear slums and to expand access to health care. When a Democratic Congress dusted off a Roosevelt-era proposal to fund a national interstate system, Republican president Dwight Eisenhower not only acceded to it, but claimed its passage as his own accomplishment. The era of big federal funding had arrived.[113] And with that change came a new challenge—determining who, exactly, would control the money now flowing to a broad range of bureaucracies working on the nation's front lines.

THE ESTABLISHMENT TAKES HOLD

In 1955, Sloan Wilson, a military veteran who had returned from service overseas to become a journalist and university professor, published what would become an era-defining novel. *The Man in the Gray Flannel Suit* highlighted the burgeoning resentment within the ranks of the nation's middle-class businessmen that they were prisoners to a corporate culture stifling their creativity and demanding their deference. Two decades earlier, in the depths of the Great Depression, America had been hemmed in by the ravages of economic catastrophe. Now, however, even as the economy hummed, Wilson captured an emerging impression that life was colorless, monotonous, and oppressive.[114] America might now be more prosperous, but those climbing the corporate ladder had been reduced to peons, tools of some overarching "establishment."

That term—the Establishment—wasn't originally coined to describe the nation's corporate elite. It first came into broad use to describe the stuffy club of purportedly wise men who, in the postwar years, controlled the levers of the nation's foreign policy. President Harry Truman's national security apparatus comprised a whole coterie of prep school–bred, Ivy League–trained denizens of Wall Street who viewed themselves as members of a privileged clique uniquely qualified to manage grand strategy on the global stage: Averell Harriman, Robert Lovett, Dean Acheson, John Foster Dulles, and his brother Allen Dulles. Sometimes this group was called the Georgetown Set; sometimes, the Wise Men. Their personal wealth allowed them to jump in and out of public service without financial concern. And to that end, they believed they were, themselves, unencumbered by self-interest, and therefore summoned by noblesse oblige to steer the government toward shrewd policy.

Even at the time, the Georgetown Set appeared like a vestige of a different era—imperious torchbearers for the nineteenth century's old guard. But much as they may have been avatars for the country's stuffy conservatives, many were cut from a classically "progressive" mold. They were nothing if not beacons of centralized, expert-driven power. They were, almost to a one, contemptuous of the small-minded politicians who might deign to get in their way. They thought very little of the ordinary public, convinced that only the great few who tailored their suits, met at Union Leagues, and drank Manhattans were qualified to steer the ship of state. The Establishment might have been buttoned-down—but they embodied an ethos very different from the laissez-faire conservatives of decades earlier. They had grand pursuits in mind. Defeating communism. Growing America's sphere of influence. They wanted to spread freedom across the world.[115] And in keeping the Hamiltonian tradition, they were prone to believe that pursuing the public interest could be done best by ignoring the mettlesome concerns of the public.

If popular conceptions of the Establishment originated in the sphere of foreign policy, the prevailing archetype came to be applied more broadly.[116] Yes, Americans wanted true professionals to take charge where a false move might spur a nuclear holocaust. But given the events of the previous quarter century, many reformers came to believe that true experts should be put in charge of public pursuits no matter what the venue, foreign or domestic. Washington, after all, had spirited the country past the twin horrors of the Depression and the war. With prominent exceptions, the elites had earned their stripes. And so it made sense to let savvy minions of that same elite shape the future in other realms.[117] To implement the recommendation of blue-ribbon commissions. To shape public planning processes.[118] To impose their scientific expertise on the rhythms of everyday American life. It was right and good for wise men in Washington and London to shape the North Atlantic Treaty Organization—but so was it right for the wise men of Boston to shape New England.

Columbia professor Lionel Trilling's famous quip, published in 1950, that "in the United States at this time liberalism is not only the dominant but even the sole intellectual tradition," hinted at a supposition that, in nearly every realm of American life, Americans were now inclined to defer to the fedora-adorned Establishment.[119] When Harry McPherson, the longtime aide to Lyndon Johnson, was briefly appointed to a position inside the Pentagon, he remarked on the unspoken power wielded by the expert bureaucrats: "It seemed unlikely that former corporals and lieutenants would overrule generals in matters of 'Army policy.' . . . [but] civilian specialists were another breed altogether. Even national heroes were no match for economists and statisticians when it came to planning for a modern military force."[120]

The newfound deference to authority was primarily cultural. As Wilson's novel had illustrated, it was pervasive in the workplace. As future feminist scholarship would reveal, it often went without saying at home.[121] But it influenced the academy as well. Early twentieth-century "progressive" historians in the mold of Charles A. Beard had framed America's story as a battle of class interests, with the Constitution serving as a tool the elite utilized to undermine proletarian interests. Now, by contrast, historians began framing the American story with a different narrative. The country, they acknowledged, *was* exceptional. America had managed to avoid communism, socialism, fascism, and Nazism explicitly because *something* inherent to American society had tempered the nasty passions that might have prompted more violence. But what was it?

Was the nation's unique trajectory due to American individualism? To what some termed "pluralism"—namely a propensity to balance various groups' demands against one another? To growing confidence in capitalism? Scholars would argue about *why* America was exceptional—but few disputed the underlying premise. And the upshot, in many cases, was that the country had new reason to place faith in the nation's great men. As one historian put it, "The Constitution and the Founding Fathers became fashionable again."[122] And the Establishment came more generally to be bathed in the same reverence.

It was during this period, an era when Keynesian economic doctrine emerged as accepted wisdom in Washington, that Hamiltonian progressivism reached its zenith.[123] Government would fund great endeavors, and those endeavors would be run centrally by great men. It was emblematic of the thinking that spurred support for the Truman administration's Marshall Plan designed to help Europe rebuild after the war.[124] It was reflected in the Supreme Court's decision to leave important regulatory decisions—how, for example, utilities should value their assets and thereby charge consumers—to the wisdom of regulatory agencies.[125] It was reflected in the notion that the world of science was a "republic" of its own, with the general public blessed simply to be able to witness technological progress from the sidelines.[126] NASA, as one example, was a government bureaucracy erected to be run by the greatest scientific minds; it was conceived as a distinctly Hamiltonian institution to explore space.[127]

But the Hamiltonian impulses extended beyond the realm of Washington, even if the federal government's largesse was footing the Keynesian bill. In the same way David Lilienthal had remade the Tennessee Valley from his office in the Upper South, local planning commissions around the country were tasked with remaking towns and cities—of taming the element that had allowed tenements to flourish and slums to persist. And power wasn't exclusively to be vacuumed up into the government. Unions accrued greater power right through 1960 when, in a series of Supreme Court cases known as the *Steelworkers Trilogy*, the power of collective bargaining reached its apogee.[128] The context differed, but in nearly every venue, the underlying narrative was the same: power was placed in the hands of Establishment figures who would balance competing interests in a way to benefit the public at large.

This was, in many ways, a generational shift. The progressives of the 1930s had accepted the primacy of Hamiltonianism only begrudgingly. Senators ranging from Montana's Burton Wheeler to Idaho's William Borah to Nebraska's George Norris to Wisconsin's Robert La Follette had been deeply suspicious of concentrated power in any form. But the breed of progressives who replaced them in the 1950s—most specifically in the deluge of Democrats who won seats in 1958 midterms—were willing and eager technocrats.[129] As Senator John F. Kennedy would argue during remarks at Harvard's 1956 commencement, politicians needed "both the technical judgment and the disinterested viewpoint of the scholar, to prevent us from becoming imprisoned by our own slogans."[130] The notion that his administration would, five years later, comprise the nation's "best and brightest" was born of an explicitly progressive worldview.[131]

More than a half century later, during an era when progressives are much more skeptical of powerful institutions, many might presume that Establishment figures seized this authority against the public's free will. But on the whole, Hamiltonianism's rise was spurred less by any conspiracy than by widespread deference to those with expertise and professional wisdom. As Sam Beer, a White House speechwriter in the 1930s and subsequently a longtime professor at Harvard, would later explain: "Roosevelt taught us that in both spheres, domestic and foreign, 'government is the solution.'"[132] It was this same approach to doing the public's business that fueled the explosive growth of so-called public authorities, which grew four times over between the late 1940s and 1950s, becoming the go-to mechanism for building schools, water systems, hospitals, sewers, roads, and parks throughout the postwar boom.[133]

As Robert Moses, a paragon of this same Establishment, would explain, centralized power was born of necessity: "The individual has to yield in matters of this kind to the entire country, to the advantages and needs of the majority of people." If vast improvement championed by public authorities were held hostage to the demands of self-interested critics, "We wouldn't build anything! Nothing would be built. There'd be no highways. There'd be no housing. There'd be no public improvements. . . . There's just no other way out."[134]

Decades on, it would be hard for many progressives to imagine how the American public could have accepted this sort of coercion—why ordinary people would have let men like Moses impose their ideas from above. But at the time, many viewed these trade-offs as the price of progress. In 1960, the last year of Dwight Eisenhower's presidency, a TVA employee flying across western Kentucky noticed that the construction of the Barkley Dam, one of the TVA's installations on the Cumberland River, had created a little peninsula of unused land. Imagining how best to make something useful of what was geographic refuse, he suggested to his higher-ups that, for a fairly reasonable sum, the TVA could convert the sliver into a park. With a minimum of delay, the authority's brass agreed and construction began soon thereafter. Unencumbered by demands for transparency, or environmental reviews, or public hearings, this single federal bureaucracy expeditiously simply green-lit what seemed, to insiders, to be a good idea. And with that, the TVA created what became the Land Between the Lakes, a slice of greenery that would eventually come to serve more than a million visitors per year.[135]

The Land Between the Lakes represents, by at least one standard, the quintessential upside of Hamiltonian progressivism. Those with control over public authority were able to deliver something great without encumbrance. Edified figures were able to have a big impact with a minimum of delay. And while the centralized system progressivism helped to erect provided only negligible opportunity for anyone to raise meaningful objections, that was, as many progressives argued at the time, beside the point. As the old idiom suggested, you can't make an omelet without breaking some eggs. The greater good simply had to prevail. And the gruff old men who dominated progressivism during the postwar period—Establishment figures set in the mold of Robert Moses—rarely doubted that they knew best what was required to best serve the greater public interest.

3

Bodies on the Machine

PROLOGUE: MAXIMUM FEASIBLE PARTICIPATION

As any student of twentieth-century American history will tell you, the campaign of 1960 marked a generational shift in American politics, as Old Man Eisenhower was replaced in the White House with the young golden boy, John F. Kennedy. But the election also signaled a major demographic milestone: for the first time in the nation's history, half the country's Black population now lived north of the Mason-Dixon Line. A half century earlier, during the Progressive Era, nearly nine of every ten Black Americans had resided in the Jim Crow South. The morbid darkness of that era had helped to fuel what would later be termed the Great Migration. Over several decades, millions of Black southerners had trekked north in search of a better life. By the point of Kennedy's inauguration, the ripple effects were finally coming into clearer view.[1]

The Black families arriving in the industrialized North faced challenges different from those who had arrived early through Castle Garden and Ellis Island. Neither experience had been pleasant. Nativist concerns about immigrant riffraff had fomented the xenophobia that ran rampant in the country at the turn of the twentieth century—sociologists had worried then about the specter of "anomie" inciting unmoored newcomers to vice and violence.[2] But the norms and institutions that had helped to integrate European families into the fabric of urban life weren't available to many newly arrived Black southerners. Subject to rampant prejudice, precluded from settling in nicer neighborhoods, and facing steep prejudice in the job market, new arrivals often found themselves trapped in what many would come to call the "ghetto."[3] Cities that had once served as ladders to opportunity now isolated some of society's most desperate citizens.

Brown v. Board of Education of Topeka, the 1954 Supreme Court decision overruling the prejudicial doctrine of "separate but equal," was nearly seven years old when Kennedy assumed the presidency. Fresher in the nation's mind was the unrest that had followed the integration of Little Rock's public schools. When, in 1957, nine Black students had enrolled at Central High School, President Eisenhower was compelled to send in paratroopers to quell white violence. Now, with Black communities becoming more visible up north, what some labeled "the problem of the ghetto" had taken a turn. In polite conversation, the issue was often framed as a question of "youth crime." But the subtext was unmistakable: many of the same northerners who had professed to be scandalized by Jim Crow were now worried about the destabilizing effect of down-and-out Blacks living a few neighborhoods over.

Kennedy had purposefully downplayed race during the 1960 campaign. At the time, the Democratic Party's big tent still shaded many of the South's most virulent racists, and campaign strategists had worried that any significant focus on civil rights might wedge crucial elements of the electorate toward Kennedy's opponent, Vice President Richard Nixon. But once in office, Kennedy and his well-heeled staff—the journalist

David Halberstam would derisively label them the "best and brightest"—took the challenge seriously.[4] To their minds, if Washington could face down the Great Depression and the Nazis, government could certainly ameliorate the race problem. And so the Kennedy White House, steeped in the New Deal's Hamiltonian tradition, went in search of a top-down, centralized solution.[5] To that end, Congress appropriated $10 million to "demonstrate and evaluate" potential solutions through what would be called "The President's Committee on Juvenile Delinquency and Youth Crime."

The problem, of course, was that the challenge of "youth crime," to use the euphemism of the moment, wasn't solvable in the same manner. There were no rivers to dam or arsenals to build. And so Kennedy's staff was compelled to hunt for new ideas. The administration chose David Hackett to lead the initiative. Handsome, young, and vibrant, Hackett had not only been Robert Kennedy's prep school buddy, he had served as the inspiration for the character Phineas in *A Separate Peace*.[6] But as he toured the country in search of models to tackle "the problem of the ghetto," his charm and charisma were often met with scowls. Local officials engaged in the often ugly business of confronting "youth crime" took umbrage at this youthful Milton Academy alumnus lecturing them about problems he was just then coming to understand. Hackett quickly came to realize how difficult it was to discuss racial strife between classes, even among whites. Not everyone shared the best and brightest's can-do attitude, or even its sensibilities.

Upon his return to Washington, Hackett's anecdotal reporting sparked what became an intense debate among administration staff. The old liberals inside the White House remained bullish on the power of government to steer young ne'er-do-wells onto the straight and narrow. If given the wherewithal to calibrate public policy to specification, they were confident social engineers could pull residents of the nation's ghettos up the socioeconomic ladder *from above*.[7] But others, including Hackett, had concluded that centralization was not only a spent force but the root of the problem.[8] The northerners he'd failed to charm had no more interest in integrating Blacks than the protesters ringing Little Rock's Central High School. With that in mind, Hackett and his administration allies were more inclined to push power down so residents of the nation's ghettos could fight for themselves.

Hackett's point of view reflected an emerging literature. In 1960, a writer and theorist named Paul Goodman had published *Growing Up Absurd,* which indicted American democracy for serving as a foil for an oppressive political class.[9] From Goodman's perspective, the school officials, police departments, welfare agencies, and charitable organizations that claimed to be doing God's work helping the urban poor actually held them back.[10] Hackett and his cohort inside the White House agreed. In their view, if the Kennedy administration intended to do something for the nation's "ghetto youth," New Deal–style programming was bound to fail. They proposed instead to help victims of the Establishment get out from under its thumb. The watchword for their strategy was "institutional reform."[11]

Hackett hadn't conjured this explicitly Jeffersonian impulse on his own. Through the Eisenhower years, the Ford Foundation's Public Affairs Program, led by Paul Ylvisaker, had invested heavily in studying the northern Black experience. And while some in Ylvisaker's orbit still held a torch for big bureaucracy, many had become increasingly cynical about the efficacy of top-down reform.[12] They embraced a different model altogether: the Henry Street Settlement, an organization born decades earlier to help immigrants settling on New York's Lower East Side, had more recently established Mobilization for Youth, a program designed to train local Puerto Rican and Black kids to demand city government provide more and better social services. In essence, rather than empower the Establishment to fix a problem, Mobilization for Youth was designed to empower the Establishment's critics to demand better.

On the surface, the debate within the Kennedy White House centered on which of these two approaches held greater promise. But beneath the disagreement was the more endemic ideological battle. As Daniel Patrick Moynihan, a prominent Kennedy administration official, would later write, for the Jeffersonians who wanted to scale up the Mobilization for Youth, "The name of the game was *community action*, the vehicle that of an independent community agency."[13] Meanwhile, those invested in Hamiltonian solutions argued for prioritizing education and training. As Lyndon Johnson would later put it, Washington should focus on lifting up young people "whose background, health and education [left them] . . . least fit for useful work."[14] At the moment President Kennedy boarded Air Force One en route to Dallas in November 1963, he had yet to choose from between the two starkly different alternatives.

Reeling from the president's assassination, the vice president's ascension to the Oval Office likely appeared a setback for those hoping to scale Mobilization for Youth. Whatever else he was, Lyndon Johnson was a Hamiltonian through and through—a man who not only lionized Franklin Roosevelt but who cut his teeth working for the New Deal's National Youth Administration. The new president believed wholeheartedly in big, powerful, centralized government. Moreover, he was contemptuous of Hackett and his ilk, viewing Kennedy's prep school–trained advisors as eggheads and amateurs.[15] Johnson may have shared their desire to lift up the "ghetto youth"—his experience teaching poor Hispanic children on the Mexican border had imbued him with a moralizing sense of purpose— but he was fundamentally aligned with the Establishment institutions Hackett had come to disdain.[16]

Debates inside the new Johnson White House about how to shape what would become 1964's Economic Opportunity Act pivoted on this same ideological divide. "Liberals," holding a torch for the New Deal's more Hamiltonian thrust, wanted the president to champion old-school jobs and education programs. "Radicals," by contrast, were eager to steer the administration toward institutional reform. And the president, more inclined to one, but not wanting to alienate the other—Johnson worried about making moves that might appear like repudiations of his predecessor's legacy—decided to split the difference. The legislation he eventually sent to Congress included proposals for both job training *and* institutional reform.[17] Here was Johnson employing a strategy that he'd perfected as master of the Senate—giving both sides of a disagreement something they could count as a win.

This time, however, the tactic backfired—and for reasons that might have seemed counterintuitive. As members of Congress began to consider the bill, many of the same mayors and local leaders who had scoffed at David Hackett's *radical* ideas appeared to be even more miffed by the *liberals'* agenda. Organized labor, for example, didn't want the government hiring legions of unemployed youths to build projects that might otherwise be constructed by unionized workers. School officials didn't want federal bureaucrats layering new mandates onto federal money they now spent at their own discretion.[18] For decades, progressivism had worked to build up an Establishment—and now the various beacons of that same Establishment, scattered as they were across the country, were intent on maintaining their fiefdoms, whatever the public interest.

The Economic Opportunity Act that eventually passed Congress may not have comprised the whole of Johnson's war on poverty. His expansive agenda featured a whole range of quintessentially Hamiltonian efforts—expanding Social Security, creating Medicare and Medicaid, establishing food stamps, federal aid for public schools, and more. But here, in this negotiation, he was quick to fold. The ironic upshot was that a centerpiece of Lyndon Johnson's bill to fight poverty was fundamentally inimical to his Hamiltonian sensibilities. His effort to stamp out poverty would not be anchored in programs akin to the National Youth Administration, but rather around a Jeffersonian thrust to "empower" local residents in the spirit of Mobilization for Youth.[19] From the department of politics making strange bedfellows, this one was a doozy: President Lyndon Johnson had become a shill for David Hackett's "radical" agenda.

Here is how it would work. As conceived in the final draft of the Economic Opportunity Act, community action programs (CAPs) would help communities advocate for themselves *against* bureaucracies that, as Hackett's old friend Senator Robert Kennedy complained, "plan programs for the poor, not with them." The whole scheme would be run out of the newly created Office of Economic Opportunity (OEO), led, as it happened, by Kennedy's brother-in-law, Sargent Shriver. Through the OEO, CAPs would fund local community action agencies (CAAs), which would "provide stimulation and incentive for urban and rural communities to mobilize their resources . . . to combat poverty."[20] The legislation specified that each initiative should be "developed, conducted, and administered with the maximum feasible participation of residents of the areas and members of the groups serviced."[21] And that last phrase—"maximum feasible participation"—became the crux of the whole enterprise.[22] This wasn't a top-down affair—it would work from the bottom up.

The program's fate was likely sealed right from the beginning. Shriver's young and idealistic staff fanned out across the country. Ten months after LBJ signed the bill, they had designated more than four hundred CAAs for funding—a year later, there were more than a thousand.[23] The sudden availability of funding created a kind of feeding frenzy among local reformers and activists. Groups of all sorts wanted to know how to qualify and how to maximize their award. Amid all ensuing excitement and confusion, many in Washington lost sight of a more fundamental dynamic: the Johnson administration was now in the business of funding the very people who most irritated the nation's mayors and power brokers. The community organizers now applying for federal funds were explicitly promising to agitate against housing authorities, welfare agencies, and, perhaps most of all, elected politicians who were, in many cases, the president's most ardent supporters.

Once the spigots turned on, the inherent conflict was impossible to avoid. The White House began receiving irate phone calls from local leaders now being targeted by federally subsidized protestors. And if the substance of their complaints hadn't been so egregious, many would have been comical. A group in Syracuse had applied for a grant to train community organizers intent on disrupting local government meetings. After winning an award, they used the money to hire master agitator Saul Alinsky to plan new provocations. Similar, if less pointed, dustups riled mayors in Chicago, Los Angeles, San Francisco, Philadelphia, and elsewhere.[24] And the mess didn't end there. When the OEO chose *not* to approve applications from various civil rights groups, those denied funding accused the White House of fomenting racism. And when the OEO permitted programs in Chicago and New York to be co-opted, respectively, by Mayor Richard Daley and Harlem congressman Adam Clayton Powell Jr., others wondered aloud whether the White House was using the program as a slush fund. The program appeared a hot mess.

When Johnson realized there was no way to win, he beat a hasty retreat.[25] In 1967, Congress passed, and the president happily signed, legislation redirecting the program's funding to local governments; rather than fuel those agitating *against* the Establishment, CAPs would fund . . . the Establishment. Shriver, who had once been viewed as a rising progressive star, saw his reputation permanently blemished—to save face, Johnson appointed him ambassador to France. And with that, a program designed to be a cornerstone of Johnson's war on poverty was shunted to the margins, a well-intentioned initiative that appeared, from both liberal and radical perspectives alike, to have gone haywire.

Not all was lost. Mobilization for Youth would go on to serve as an impetus for New York's Civilian Complaint Review Board—a programmatic check on police brutality. And a subsequent study found that CAAs had served as training grounds for a new generation of Black leaders.[26] But if the Great Society would come to encompass a broad range of policy innovations and successes—the creation of Medicare and Medicaid, significant funding for primary and secondary education, the Fair Housing Act—the community action programs would endure as a symbol of government incompetence. Moreover, the chasm within the Johnson administration separating the liberals from the radicals rekindled the decades-old tension between progressivism's Hamiltonian and Jeffersonian impulses.[27] And that internal debate, paired with the dysfunction it bred within government, would go on to have profound political consequences.

THE GOSPEL OF BALANCE

The progressive journey from David Lilienthal's Tennessee Valley Authority to David Hackett's community action programs was hardly inevitable. New Deal reformers informed of what was going to happen thirty years hence likely wouldn't have believed it—and that's because the strange evolution was predicated on a crucial shift in the reform movement's underlying zeitgeist. By the end of Lyndon Johnson's presidency, the cultural *inclination* to authority that had fueled progressivism's enthusiasm for big bureaucracy had given way to the cultural *aversion* to power that had spurred staffers inside the Office of Economic Opportunity to claw at the Establishment. The change wasn't born of any grand strategy. Rather, the movement's journey from a predominantly Hamiltonian to a thoroughly Jeffersonian worldview reflected a deep-seated cultural shift. And, as we'll see in subsequent chapters, that narrative change would reframe how reformers pursued their agenda.

The evolution was fueled by fear—or, more specifically, by a shift in what progressives were most prone to dread. In the wake of the Second World War, the movement had been consumed by a fear of *chaos*. The hedonism of the roaring 1920s, many believed, had left the globe vulnerable to the turmoil that followed.[28] Many subscribed to the notion that societies pushed off-kilter were susceptible to what Hannah Arendt would later term the "banality of evil"—that upheaval opened the door to elements of human nature that could impel ordinary people to act on despicable impulses. In the wake of nearly two decades of bedlam, reformers were determined through the 1940s and 1950s to preclude any future descent into depravity. And so the underlying culture, as much as anything else, steered postwar progressivism to invest power in centralized nodes of authority capable of keeping the lid on. The movement's watchword, if not America's, was *stability*.

Easy as it may be to caricature the 1950s as the *Father Knows Best* decade—a period defined by a milquetoast president, processed food, and oppressive cultural uniformity—the nation's recent history hung like a dark cloud throughout. McCarthyism was born in no small part from a fear that communism represented the scourge to follow Nazism, and Americans were determined not to replicate British prime minister Neville Chamberlain's infamous attempt to appease Hitler in 1938. While progressives largely abhorred McCarthy's fearmongering, the movement's priorities were shaped by the same underlying concern. The Establishment had grown through the 1930s and 1940s to save the globe from chaos—now, progressivism would lean on centralized control to deliver continuing stability.

On the economic front, that meant embracing the doctrine of full employment. President Harry Truman and his Democratic successors would beat the drum for Franklin Roosevelt's iconic promise to build an economy that provided "freedom from want" well into the 1960s. And so Keynesianism—an economic theory centered on the notion that government could use budget surpluses and deficits to maintain steady economic growth—eclipsed elements of the movement's old economic agenda. Trust-busting was out of vogue. The Brandeisian celebration of smallness went by the wayside. In their place emerged a proactive embrace of gargantuan companies. None other than David Lilienthal himself wrote a book defending large corporations in the early 1950s titled *Big Business: A New Era*.[29]

In service of that stability, many progressive economists embraced the notion of what the prominent Harvard academic John Kenneth Galbraith termed "countervailing power."[30] At its root, yet again, was a *cultural* inclination to balance—an underlying belief that properly checked self-interest was the lodestone of prosperity. If government couldn't stage-manage the economy, as the associationalist brain trusters had wanted to do during the First New Deal, progressives could still harness the conflicting demands of industry, labor, and the regulatory state to pursue the greater good. Powerful bureaucracies would, under this doctrine, champion the public interest by giving all the various stakeholders seats at the table, taking their various concerns into account.[31] The nation's broader prosperity would presumably shake out in the wash.[32] *E pluribus unum.*

The gospel of balance wasn't limited to the realm of economics. "Containment," namely the foreign policy doctrine suggesting that the West could seek to keep the Soviets in perpetual check, drew directly from the same notion. Diplomats and strategists would need to divine ways to hold America's most potent adversary at bay without resorting to open hostilities. And progressives embraced a theory of domestic governance that reflected the same sensibility. In previous decades, reformers had striven to gut political machines and make democracy more direct.[33] During the 1950s, by contrast, the movement alighted on a promise of what some labeled "pluralism." As the celebrated political scientist Robert Dahl concluded in a study of New Haven, successful mayors would play a city's divergent enclaves against one another in pursuit of common prosperity.[34]

All of these doctrines—Keynesianism, containment, pluralism—were predicated, in the end, on a key factor: wise, measured, dispassionate leadership. If America was going to enjoy prosperity, peace, and stability, expert economists, strategists, diplomats, and mayors would have to take the tiller. Postulate to this notion was a supposition that if America *did* find those wise and measured leaders—if challenges *could* be managed with professional wisdom—then "any problem could be solved."[35] From this combination of fear and confidence, worry and gumption, progressives, like Americans more generally, developed a "picture in their heads" about what wise, measured, and dispassionate leadership might look like in the flesh. A charcoal suit. Perhaps a fedora. A wry grin or, if not, a stubborn frown. Arms crossed. A resolute, middle-aged figure, relaxed and in his element while wielding power. This was the Establishment incarnate.

These were the men—and they were almost invariably white men—who would protect Americans from the barbarians at the gate. And amid a culture of fear, there was no telling where danger might emerge. Fredric Wertham's *Seduction of the Innocent*, published in 1954, highlighted the widespread concern that comic books, wildly popular through the postwar period, were warping children's minds. Glamourized depictions of violence and brutality might, many worried, disrupt the maturation of impressionable adolescents. Liberal intellectuals, increasingly taken in by Freudian notions of conflict and trauma, worried that frightening ideas might stunt the boomers' development.[36] Theodor Adorno's *The Authoritarian Personality* reflected a progressive concern that working-class culture was poised to unleash a new wave of American brownshirts. From the progressive perspective, members of the ultraconservative John Birch Society appeared like the quiescent Nazis to come.[37] To combat all of these various threats, the movement invested its faith in the Establishment's dispassionate wisdom.

To be fair, progressivism didn't entirely abandon its Jeffersonian predilections. McCarthyism spurred a whole literature about the threat centralized authority could pose to individual freedom. Ray Bradbury's *Fahrenheit 451*. George Orwell's *1984*. William Golding's *Lord of the Flies*. But while that canon would be celebrated in later years, the zeitgeist of the moment prioritized keeping order from chaos, and keeping things regular meant making government *work*.[38] As Columbia scholar Todd Gitlin would later write: "Liberals traced their common lineage to the Enlightenment. They believed that society could be understood and, once understood, rationally steered through responsible action. Reason was the name of their faith, and the government its instrument."[39] David

Truman, perhaps then the nation's leading political scientist, argued at the time: "The great political task now as in the past is to perpetuate a *viable* system."[40]

In the end, responsibility for crafting that system and maintaining its viability was laid unquestionably at the feet of the men of the Establishment. Elites who had long viewed themselves as uniquely wise took advantage. And so, in almost every venue, and on every front, they steered authority to centralized institutions they were poised to control. The TVA remained the benchmark, modeling how progress and prosperity could be rendered by experts. But the same ethos applied everywhere. More power and authority to planners designated to oversee urban development. To generals equipped to counter the Soviet threat. To social workers to police private morality.[41] To censors to regulate comic books.[42] Moored in a culture of fear, progressivism leaned into the wisdom of experts. Or it would, at least, until the culture changed. The movement's Hamiltonian bent would not predominate forever.

THE SEEDS OF DISILLUSION

However much Americans prized stability through the 1950s, progressivism's fear of chaos was eventually eclipsed by something else—cynicism. Municipal scandals, seemingly rampant through the Eisenhower years, nibbled away at the public's faith in city fathers. New Dealers who had presumed that dispassionate experts would sit atop the growing administrative state were horrified when Republicans installed political hacks in positions of vast responsibility—a reality pointedly illustrated when President Eisenhower's chief of staff, Sherman Adams, was exposed for having accepted an expensive fur coat from a businessman being investigated by the FTC.[43] Even the Georgetown Set came under scrutiny when, during the late 1950s, hawks in both parties fanned concerns, however spurious, that a "missile gap" had opened between the United States and the Soviet Union.

But if the Establishment's competence was coming into question, progressives reacted initially not by attacking it, but by proposing to improve it.[44] Washington, after all, wouldn't solve the missile gap by deconstructing the Pentagon—it would need to augment the military-industrial complex's vast power. Cities wouldn't solve their problems by denuding the mayoral authority, but by strengthening pluralism's ability to overcome hackish opposition. The year after Eisenhower signed the bill funding the interstate system, the prominent critic Lewis Mumford excoriated the nation's highway planners for not having "the slightest notion of what they were doing. Within the next fifteen years they will doubtless find out; but by that time it will be too late to correct all the damage to our cities and our countryside."[45] But for all his fury, Mumford didn't propose to end the highway program—he prescribed *more* and *better* planning, consolidating municipal authority into regional governments that would cut through the stew of parochial interests.[46]

To that end, Hamiltonianism still predominated when John F. Kennedy was elected president in November 1960.[47] A dozen years after President Truman created a "slum clearance" program, Kennedy proposed to do more of the same—but better. He proposed expanding the federal government's role in school funding and wanted to erect a hospital insurance program for old people.[48] Indeed, much as Kennedy's election is remembered as a passing of the generational baton, his agenda was rooted in its embrace of the big institutions of old.[49] And yet, as he took the oath of office in 1961, the winds were beginning to change.[50] A burgeoning skepticism, embraced most readily by young baby boomers, levered a new spirit of questioning. Perhaps, some began to suggest, America had shown the Establishment too much deference. Maybe it was time to reconsider the movement's priors.[51]

The most serious scrutiny began inside the academy. During the 1950s, the Columbia sociologist C. Wright Mills had begun denouncing the influence of what he termed the "power elite."[52] At much the same time, a burgeoning phalanx of self-described "critical theorists," many associated with an academic community loosely termed the Frankfurt School, began to shape a strikingly different (and, in some cases, avowedly Marxist) narrative about American culture. None viewed Washington as the benevolent global savior Americans had fancied in the wake of the war—to them, the United States often played the menace.[53] In the world of political theory, a range of eminent liberals began debating whether nineteenth-century liberalism was culpable for the despots that had emerged to shape the twentieth.[54] Cynicism began to wind its way through a whole range of disciplines, and the collective critique paved the way for a deeper and more encompassing skepticism of the Hamiltonian project as a whole.[55] In this competing narrative, the Establishment was cast as a villain.

There was a generational element to this story. The boomers, coming of age during the early 1950s, had not directly witnessed the traumas of the 1930s and 1940s. Their early years had been defined more by abundance than chaos. Their parents' desire to steady the boat, to keep the lid on, to maintain a proper balance, did not, for them, hold the same appeal. To much the same end, boomers were less inclined to pay (what many increasingly viewed as) mindless fealty to the system such that it was. Plodding progress, from their perspective, appeared like no progress at all. Black kids in the 1960s *still* couldn't order a hamburger at Woolworth's department store years after *Brown v. Board of Education*. Joe McCarthy was gone, but the House Un-American Activities Committee was *still* hunting for subversives.[56] Much to many an older activist's consternation, this new ethos was growing stronger within the movement.[57] And slowly, these various currents of skepticism were braided together into a phalanx that referred to itself as the New Left.

In 1962, several of this nascent stream's young leaders gathered at a union-owned retreat north of Detroit to write the manifesto that would define their new ideology under the aegis of a new organization, Students for a Democratic Society (SDS). Written as a broad indictment of American society, the Port Huron Statement took issue not only with specific

elements of progressive policy, but also progressivism's generalized embrace of centralized authority. SDS was intent on replacing "power rooted
in possession, privilege, or circumstance [with] power and uniqueness rooted
in love, reflectiveness, reason, and creativity." In this critique, America's
problems were rooted less in chaos than in the big bureaucracies, corporate leaders, city fathers, the Establishment figures donning charcoal suits
and fedoras. The New Left was less interested in attacking the right than
it was in pulling the progressive tradition away from its embrace of centralized power.[58] That was its call to action.

Those leading the New Left, like those who would hold torches for
the variety of left-leaning movements that would emerge through the
1960s and after—second-wave feminists, various civil rights leaders,
many anti-war activists—were not born directly from the Jeffersonian
progressivism of old. They were their own thing. But their skepticism
of centralized authority echoed the concerns Louis Brandeis and other
avatars of Woodrow Wilson's New Freedom had articulated decades earlier. This particular wave of Jeffersonianism was different, however, in
the way it looped private and public authority together. Anyone wielding power of any kind quickly became suspect of being in cahoots. To
members of SDS, the elites running the big corporations were indistin-
guishable from the elites running the government—they were all appa-
ratchiks of "corporate liberalism."[59] And that vitriol quickly turned into
a call to arms. As Mario Savio, a leader of UC Berkeley's Free Speech
Movement would argue in December 1964:

There's a time when the operation of the machine becomes so odious,
makes you so sick at heart that you can't take part! You can't even pas-
sively take part! And you've got to put your bodies upon the gears and
upon the wheels, upon the levers, upon all the apparatus—and you've
got to make it stop! And you've got to indicate to the people who run
it, to the people who own it—that unless you're free the machine will
be prevented from working at all!![60]

Today, progressives often imagine Lyndon Johnson as the epitome of the backward-looking Establishment. But even more than Johnson, Kennedy personified the corporate liberalism the New Left despised.[61] As the debonair beneficiary of a Wall Street fortune, the King Arthur of a White House gauzily deemed "Camelot," the young president was, for the New Left, the embodiment of the elitism they intended to dismantle. It wasn't just Kennedy's suave persona they abhorred. The New Left wanted to extinguish the torch that had been passed from Theodore Roosevelt to Franklin Roosevelt to Harry Truman and now across the generational divide. They objected to the very notion that problems could be solved by siccing expert bureaucrats on the nation's problems. They weren't frightened of chaos. In the New Left's analysis, *order* was at the root of America's problems.

This wasn't a dispute over policy—it was way upstream of that. In 1937, frustrated by Supreme Court decisions that had upended the New Deal's efforts to aid the nation's farmers, protect defenseless children, and strengthen the labor movement, Franklin Roosevelt had rued that the three branches of government were pulling in different directions. But, he insisted, "If three well-matched horses are put to the task of plowing up a field where the going is heavy, and the team of three pull as one, the *field . . . will . . . be . . . plowed.*"[62] By the New Left's analysis, however, Roosevelt's dream was a nightmare. As SDS veteran Todd Gitlin would later write, the new wave of progressivism "valued informality, tolerated chaos, [and] scorned order."[63] Their goal wasn't to get the machine to work in rhythm, but to expose its conniving. They wanted to poke the bear so that when it lashed out everyone would see it for what it was. And once they did, those looking to upend the Establishment were convinced that others would be inspired to join the cause.[64]

A RELIGIOUS AWAKENING

The New Left served as something akin to a Jeffersonian pebble thrown into a Hamiltonian pond. Even given C. Wright Mills's indictment of the power elite, the critical theorists' worries about emergent authoritarianism, Hannah Arendt's concerns about the "banality of evil," and a range of other authority-skeptic influences, radicals in the early 1960s couldn't have predicted how, or even whether, their disgust with the Establishment would ripple across the movement's broader landscape.[65] But the battle for progressive hearts would have to be won before the boomers could claim progressive minds. The movement's great triumphs to that point had emerged out of big institutions like the TVA, the Social Security Administration, and the Marshall Plan. Given all that, getting the progressive rank-and-file to spurn the dream of building power up in favor of tearing it down appeared a tall order.

The shift, to be sure, would be gradual, and the tension was never entirely resolved—both the Hamiltonian and Jeffersonian instincts are inextricable from the progressive tradition, even as the balance is fluid. But in 1965, the Johnson administration, brimming with executive branch appointees, congressional allies, and White House aides eager to build on the New Deal's legacy of bureaucratic centralization, brought Hamiltonianism to its cathartic peak. Democrats passed legislation creating Medicare, Medicaid, and food stamps, among other new federal programs. President Johnson signed a bill establishing massive new investments in the nation's public schools. These triumphs epitomized the big, top-down approach to problem-solving that the president would lionize in his famous commencement address at Howard University—a *centralized* plan to create jobs and enhance prosperity.[66]

These were, to be sure, *policy* accomplishments—but they were all born of the same *cultural* predilection. They reflected the apotheosis of Johnson's belief that when the free market failed, progressives should be prepared "to vote for whatever legislation is necessary to let the Federal Government do it. If that be enlarging the power of the Federal Government, and if that be centralizing more power in Washington, [we should] make the most of it." Here the Democratic Party was embracing what Johnson loved most about the New Deal—why "LBJ" venerated

"FDR." Now, in 1965, Johnson was building on his political hero's legacy. Great Society–style big government was Hamiltonianism at its high-water mark.[67]

But even as Johnson was reveling in all his Hamiltonian glory, the movement's Jeffersonian impulse was on the march. Kennedy might have sidestepped discussions of race in the 1960 campaign, but his successor could not, by 1964, duck the burgeoning demands of the civil rights movement. That said, if Johnson felt compelled to take aim at the nation's racial caste system, expert-led bureaucracy hardly appeared the right tool to force privately owned hotels to lodge Black families, or to ensure that Black citizens could exercise the franchise. Bureaucracy might eventually play an important role—centralized institutions might serve to bridge vast economic disparities born from slavery and Jim Crow. But equality first required pushing power *down* to citizens, not up to bureaucrats. Individuals were rightly demanding to be treated as equal citizens under the law. To that end, the Civil Rights Act of 1964 and the Voting Rights Act of 1965, two of the Johnson era's most iconic achievements, were distinct in that they flowed directly from progressivism's Jeffersonian tradition.[68]

To be sure, both laws were a mix of the two impulses. The Civil Rights Act not only precluded businesses providing public accommodations (hotels, theaters, restaurants) from discriminating against individuals on the basis of race, color, sex, and a variety of other personal characteristics—thereby endowing those individuals with protections crafted in the spirit of the Jeffersonian *workers'* rights progressivism sought a generation earlier; the bill *also* created the Equal Employment Opportunity Commission, a centralized bureaucracy tasked with enforcing the law's provisions.[69] The Voting Rights Act not only guaranteed equal access to the ballot but also invested in the federal Justice Department responsibility for preclearing any changes in election procedures. And that's the important nuance—*both* progressive impulses were deeply woven into the culture and philosophy of Johnson's broader agenda.[70]

To linger here for a minute, it's worth noting that the feature distinguishing the various elements of Lyndon Johnson's agenda was not the degree to which any individual thrust was *more* or *less* progressive. The Voting Rights Act was not *more* progressive than the creation of Medicaid, or vice versa. Nor would creating a Marshall Plan for Black communities have been *more* progressive than passing the Civil Rights Act. But these various ideas were distinct from one another in that they were steeped in different conceptions of *power*. Those who believed centralized power was a force for good were more likely to want to empower bureaucracy. Those who thought it inherently bad were more likely to want to burnish individual rights. *Both* impulses were fundamentally progressive, but the factors determining whether someone is more prone to embrace either approach at any given moment were often less *ideological* than they were *cultural*. That's the key to understand. The stories—the pictures in progressives' heads—are upstream of any policy. And during the 1960s, the predominant story was changing.

If Jeffersonianism and Hamiltonianism were able to exist for a brief moment in a productive balance during the Johnson years, the balance didn't hold. In June 1966, a presidential conference established to point the nation's path toward great racial equality suggested that "the Federal government should assume responsibility for the quality of education in all parts of the United States." The impulse was quintessentially Hamiltonian—a response to the reality that schools in white and Black communities were of wildly different qualities—and federalizing the endeavor seemed, at the time, like the only way to guarantee that opportunity would be spread equally to children born everywhere. But, as Johnson White House counsel Harry McPherson later recounted, "A year or two later, many of the people who had attended the conference would be calling for community control of the schools."[71] They'd reversed course. Their Hamiltonian impulses had, by then, been subsumed by Jeffersonian fervor. And the same shift was evident everywhere.

Perhaps the most pointed illustration of the movement's cultural shift followed the publication of a Johnson administration study titled *The*

Negro Family: The Case for National Action written by then Assistant Secretary of Labor Daniel Patrick Moynihan.[72] The Moynihan Report, as it came to be known, had been drafted to argue that the civil rights bills would not suffice in the quest for true racial equality—that more would have to be done.[73] But whatever its intention, Moynihan's analysis argued that the Black community's miseries were born less from prejudice than from a "tangle of pathology" that prevailed within the community itself—that Blacks, critics of the report asserted, were responsible for their own predicament.[74] Black women, Moynihan noted, were disproportionately having children out of wedlock. Black children were disproportionately being raised in households without a father. In Moynihan's view, that disparity was poised to have a disastrous impact on Black America's ability to climb the economic ladder. The government, he argued, needed to intervene from the top down.[75]

Whatever others within President Johnson's orbit thought of Moynihan's broader theory, the report, when leaked, proved to be a public relations disaster—a flashpoint for the same discord that had riven the liberals and radicals debating the merits of community action programs. Among those who were deeply suspicious of the System, it appeared like little more than a clumsy justification for imposing new Establishment-born diktats.[76] Moynihan's decision to lionize white middle-class norms dripped of the same patriarchal impulses that, as the *Nation* argued, spurred many to treat Blacks as savages.[77] Perhaps, during an era when progressivism's cultural proclivities had been more inclined to TVA-style centralization, Moynihan's perspective would have been welcome. But in a moment when Jeffersonianism was ascendant, his analysis was met with intense denunciation.

Moynihan's report was completed in March 1965. The Voting Rights Act passed in August. The following November, SDS's Carl Oglesby delivered a speech to a march on Washington that typified the movement's new orientation: "We must simply observe, and quite plainly say, that this coalition, this blitzkrieg, and this demand for acquiescence are creatures, all of them, of a government that since 1932 has considered itself to be fundamentally liberal."[78] Oglesby wasn't delivering a policy critique—he was calling for a religious awakening. C. Wright Mills's indictment of the "power elite" and the Frankfurt School's suspicion of power were once cloistered inside the academy; their calls to action were now the anthem of a movement determined to free people from the System.[79] As Oglesby put it: "We are dealing with a colossus that does not want to be changed. It will not change itself. It will not cooperate with those who want to change it."[80] To the newly converted, power was suspect in any and all its emanations. And with that fundamental notion firmly established, reformers could turn to their next challenge—proselytizing to those who had not yet seen the light.

JUST ONE OCTOPUS

In the early 1960s, before the New Left had any real purchase on the mainstream—at a moment when critical theorists were still struggling to raise alarms about American oppression—members of the Establishment had rarely been compelled to pay Jeffersonian concerns much attention. That air of dismissiveness continued through the middle of the decade. Serious people, most liberals presumed, would inevitably continue to place faith in experts. Moreover, it seemed inevitable that the issues facing the nation would draw most lefty critics back into the fold. The Bull Connor types siccing dogs on civil rights demonstrators horrified the Establishment and the New Left alike. Sure, the Beats and the radicals reading C. Wright Mills might be miffed that Kennedy's "best and brightest" weren't pursuing various social reforms more expeditiously. But what were they going to do—throw in with the Barry Goldwater crowd? A serious breach within the New Deal coalition seemed inconceivable—or so it seemed before Vietnam.

Today, during an age when reporters are preternaturally skeptical of nearly everything politicians say or do, it may be hard to appreciate the degree to which early post–Second World War media made a practice of taking public officials at their word. When Truman administration secretary of state, and later secretary of defense, George C. Marshall spoke, journalists gave him the presumption of their deference; having led the army during the Second World War, he was revered. But boomers entering the news business in the 1960s weren't inclined to accept government claims so uncritically, and for good reason: officials were increasingly caught lying.[81] As David Halberstam, a *New York Times* correspondent in Saigon, would later reveal, journalists on the ground often referred to the military's afternoon media briefings as the "five o'clock follies." Members of the brass regularly bragged about accomplishments reporters in theater knew to be false or misleading. And that seeded a broader skepticism.[82] C. Wright Mills's indictment of the power elite was the better part of a decade old, but his cynicism began to appear prescient.

Authority figures were not only weaving tall tales but they were occasionally caught hiding true horrors. A generation earlier, the federal government's efforts to tame the Tennessee River had typically been framed as an entirely beneficent crusade to free helpless citizens from the grips of poverty. When, by contrast, news of the My Lai massacre emerged in late 1969, few journalists were inclined to give public authority the benefit of any doubt. American soldiers, it was revealed, had raped, mutilated, and murdered little girls—and the military brass had covered it up.[83] When the Pentagon Papers came to light several years later, no one could reasonably deny that the government had long known that the whole war effort was a catastrophe. And that raised a more basic question: How could ordinary people continue to believe that the Establishment responsible for pulling the Upper South out of misery was still a force for good?

The so-called credibility gap that separated military propaganda from reality became, for many boomers, a frame for understanding not just the Johnson administration but also institutions of power more generally.[84] Nearly everything the government proclaimed would eventually become suspect.[85] Establishment figures *claimed* to be accounting for the nation's long history of racism and prejudice—but were they actually in bed with the bigots? They *claimed* to be protecting the environment—but, as Rachel

Carson exposed in *Silent Spring* (1962), big agriculture was poisoning the nation's crops and farmland.[86] The gospel of balance had promised that big industry would deliver great prosperity at falling prices—but Ralph Nader's *Unsafe at Any Speed* (1965) revealed that regulators were allowing the automobile industry to sell death traps on wheels.[87] The pattern was endemic. It wasn't just that the Establishment no longer deserved the benefit of the doubt; big government began to appear entirely unworthy of the public's trust.

The specifics differed from realm to realm, but the core complaint remained the same. In 1965, the same year the Moynihan Report argued that the government needed to do something to "save" the Black family, Nader was arguing that the American people needed protection from their own government. "The bureaucratic apparatus of all state governments share similar traits which do violence to equal protection for citizens," he argued.[88] And you could hear echoes of that same concern in other realms as well. Suspicious not just of the military, or of the federal government, many began to see the outlines of a broader patriarchy, suffused by white supremacy, coordinating its various schemes across various institutions. In perhaps the most vivid indictment of the age, the Black Panthers' Eldridge Cleaver charged:

> There aren't any more state governments. We have these honorary pigs like [San Francisco] Mayor Alioto . . . presiding over the distribution of a lot of federal funds. He's plugged into one gigantic system, one octopus spanning the continent from one end to the other, reaching its tentacles all around the world, in everybody's pocket and around everybody's neck. We have just one octopus. A beast with his head wherever LBJ might be tonight.[89]

Without being explicit, Cleaver's imagery aligned with the same indictment Nader, Carson, and skeptical reporters in Vietnam had embraced: the Establishment and its minions were bad.[90]

As progressivism's cultural aversion to power grew more predominant within the movement, the public's growing mistrust of the Establishment began to seep into the culture at large.[91] You could make it out in the music scene, in the art world, even in growing suspicions about the safety of processed food. The counterculture, later to be remembered for its embrace of tie-dye, free love, and LSD, was suffused with a generalized notion that the march to sophistication was perverse—that humanity would do better for itself, and all living creatures, if it just returned to Mother Earth.[92] Radical Harvard psychologist Timothy Leary's call for young people to "turn on, tune in, drop out" went hand in hand with a desire to escape the oppression of the mainstream. Less of the Establishment's restrictive sexual mores, career trajectories, and sanitized music. America needed to break free—or, at least, so claimed the anti-Establishment wing of the progressive movement.[93]

It was in this context that 1968's Democratic National Convention appears, in retrospect, almost like a preordained prize fight. Inside the convention hall were Hamiltonians still enamored of the Establishment order. Outside were the Jeffersonians who rejected the very premise of "liberal" politics.[94] The two groups weren't at odds over questions of policy so much as they were fundamentally offended by the other's worldview. When Mayor Richard Daley, a Hamiltonian beacon as indelible as Robert Moses, licensed Chicago's cops to use what Democratic senator Abraham Ribicoff termed "Gestapo tactics" on the protestors outside, the tension came to a head.[95] As Jerry Rubin, the countercultural icon helping to organize the demonstrations, explained: "We wanted exactly what happened. . . . We wanted to create a situation in which the Chicago police and the Daley administration and the federal government and the United States would self-destruct. . . . The message of the week was of an America ruled by force. This was a big victory."[96]

From a purely practical point of view, Rubin's bravado was risible—the 1968 Convention was a disaster for progressives of Hamiltonian and Jeffersonian stripes alike. Richard Nixon won the general election that

November and Republicans would go on to win every presidential election, save one, during the following quarter century. But by another measure, Rubin was accurate in bragging that he and his fellow demonstrators had accomplished their ideological goal. If the tide had turned in 1965, then the Jeffersonian wave crested in 1968. At long last, the yin turned to yang, the ebb turned to flow, and the teeter-totter crossed its fulcrum. Those who continued to venerate TVA-style bureaucracies would remain in the Democratic fold, holding a torch for the old liberalism, and scoring intermittent victories in the years and decades to come. But in the wake of Chicago, progressivism's zeitgeist was different. In the cultural battle for the heart of the movement, the aversion to power had prevailed.

SPEAKING TRUTH TO POWER

In the prevailing historical narrative, this is the moment when the hopeful aspirations of the 1960s—the utopian visions of love, peace, and harmony—collapse inward. With Nixon's victory in November 1968, a silent majority of normie moderates rises up against the chaos put on display in Chicago. The northern white liberals who enthusiastically supported an end to Jim Crow turn against the school busing schemes that threaten to upend their own children's education.[97] Black leaders set aside Martin Luther King's anthem of nonviolence in favor of Stokely Carmichael's Black nationalism. SDS splinters, with more radical members forming terror cells that marginalize the New Left altogether. The Vietnam War ends in ignominy, with the nation's military chastised and deflated. The yippies turn to yuppies, and the utopian dreams of the 1960s are replaced by the cultural narcissism of the 1970s.[98]

The problem with this arc isn't that it isn't true—much of it is. The issue is that the underlying narrative treats the tumult of the 1960s as a kind of historical anomaly in the progressive journey—a temporary aberration from the norm: progressivism was one thing *before* all the craziness—then, when the country tired of upheaval, the movement retreated back into a wounded dog version of its previous self. With this framing, progressivism limps along in the same direction it had taken before Port Huron, with leaders arguing primarily about how aggressively to pursue the movement's agenda. In the decades that followed, those looking to rekindle the fervor of the 1960s would deride the so-called moderates as sellouts and traitors, and those looking to beckon back the silent majority—soccer moms, for example—would castigate countercultural torchbearers as self-defeating radicals. Nearly every subsequent Democratic presidential primary has been interpreted through some version of this frame: McGovern v. Humphrey, Hart v. Mondale, Bradley v. Gore, Sanders v. Clinton.

Unfortunately, much as this narrative makes some sense of the movement's demographic fate—progressivism undoubtedly became caught in a tug-of-war between those championing divergent notions of how to build an enduring Democratic majority—it glosses over the reality that the 1960s were less of a temporary aberration than a permanent progressive metamorphosis. Not that there weren't ideological threads tying the before with the after—there were. But the cultural aversion to power reframed progressivism's understanding of what ailed American society. Political battles between liberals and moderates—each an echo of the fight between those inside and outside the 1968 DNC—overshadowed the fact that the movement's previous inclination to build power up had been replaced by an almost insatiable desire to tear things down.

This more fundamental shift was overlooked at the time for a whole variety of reasons. One was circumstance: With Richard Nixon's victory in 1968, reformers of all stripes were compelled to unite against a common enemy. Almost no one wanted to see the Democratic Party self-destruct like that again. But there was another reason we've largely failed to register the shift: the now predominant Jeffersonian impulse was baked so thoroughly into the progressive cake that it went unnoticed. The New Left's underlying ethos and call to arms—to fight the System "[because] it is only when that system is changed and brought under control that there can be any hope for stopping the forces that create . . . all the incalculable, innumerable . . . atrocities that are worked on people all over—all the time"—became the movement's north star.[99] Progressivism, once home to the American Establishment, had become, at its core, a movement of liberation.[100]

Not everyone bought in, of course—Hamiltonianism maintained a place in most every progressive heart, even if less prominent. But remarkably enough, as the 1960s turned to the 1970s, even progressive groups that had stood at the vanguard of efforts to build up the hulking institutions of the postwar era were eager to disavow their roots. When legendary *Village Voice* journalist Jack Newfield accused Americans for Democratic Action of being part of the "Liberal Establishment," the organization that would have once delighted in that recognition scrambled to highlight how it had pushed back against President Johnson's foreign policy.[101] Progressives weren't calling for Americans to "ask not what you can do for your country" anymore; they were promising to shield citizens from what the government might do to them.[102] Perhaps the New Left had shriveled, but the Port Huron Statement had won.

This shift delighted Nixon because, as he may have understood better than anyone, the New Deal coalition's survival hinged on the Democratic Party's ability to keep progressivism's impulses in balance. Now, if the movement's prevailing view suggested that, as Gitlin described things, "for every face of authority, there [needed to be] someone to slap it," conservatives could more easily claim working-class whites away from the Democratic coalition.[103] Realizing just how deeply so many Americans resented the radical likes of Abbie Hoffman, Ralph Nader, and Eldridge Cleaver—the silent majority didn't want every authority figure slapped— the White House purposely baited progressives into taking positions out of step with the president's mainstream appeal.[104]

In what was perhaps the most dastardly element of Nixon's tenure, his own misbehavior only served to steer progressives further into the swerve. Watergate, after all, was nothing if not the apotheosis of authority being abused—a presidential conspiracy to manipulate government to tighten the president's hold on power. When "Tricky Dick" was finally exposed, progressives might have expected voters to tack back to the ideology that had predated a decade of turmoil—perhaps they would plot a return to Camelot. If anything, however, Watergate just burnished progressive distrust of the Establishment. By the point of Nixon's resignation, few reformers could doubt that power corrupted, and that absolute power corrupted absolutely.[105] Better to keep it locked away at all costs.

What's more, Watergate emerged as a kind of cultural lodestone. Bob Woodward and Carl Bernstein, the *Washington Post* reporters who would forever be lionized within the media for their dogged reporting on Nixon, became icons explicitly because they employed a more skeptical journalistic lens. But Woodward and Bernstein weren't muckraking journalists in the mold of Ida Tarbell or Lincoln Steffens, both of whom had wanted to expose how trusts and corporations were corrupting government. Nor were they political columnists like Jack Anderson and Drew Pearson, who traded more in gossip. Rather, Woodstein, as the pair was known together, was driven to make news simply by exposing the machinations of power— it went without saying that something was awry.[106] If they weren't *of* the New Left—many presumed Woodward was a conservative—they were nevertheless imbued with the Port Huron Statement's underlying view of the power elite. Their impulse wasn't just to *explain* what the Establishment was doing; it was to hold the Establishment to account.[107]

A similar shift became evident inside the academy. By the 1970s, a range of scholarly disciplines were already decades into a project designed to unearth the roots of totalitarianism—the critical theorists, members of the Frankfurt School, and what some would come to call "Cold War liberals" among them.[108] During the 1950s, most had presumed that serious threats to democracy were ensconced more firmly on the right. But the 1960s had seen bulwarks of the New Deal coalition direct firehoses at civil rights protestors, threaten free speech on campus, and order the Vietnamese countryside to be sprayed with Agent Orange, among other atrocities. In reaction, a wider range of academics began thinking more deeply about where the octopus's tentacles might extend.[109] And eventually, the search for power and its attendant corruptions became, in some academic realms, nearly the whole project.

French theory, as some have termed that broader impulse to deconstruct the institutions of modern life, was not born exclusively from the struggles of the 1960s and 1970s. But scholars including Jacques Derrida and, perhaps most notably, Michel Foucault echoed the cultural aversion to power.[110] Their work prompted scholars to ask questions about all received knowledge, to challenge received assumptions, to query whether any given conclusion had been derived from some set of preconceived notions.[111] As Todd Gitlin summarized the thinking, "All assaults on authority could count on the presumption of innocence; all authority started out with the presumption of guilt."[112] The subtext was unmistakable: power was in and of itself nefarious. As in the world of journalism, academia increasingly became focused on holding authority in all realms to account.

The case for popular cynicism only seemed to grow stronger and more pervasive. It wasn't just Vietnam and Watergate. A prison rebellion at Attica, in upstate New York. A full recitation of the atrocities in My Lai. The Manson Family's cultish rampage through Southern California. The infamous Stanford prison experiment, where students pretending to be guards began to abuse students pretending to be inmates.[113] When *Rolling Stone* published Hunter S. Thompson's *Fear and Loathing in Las Vegas*, gonzo journalism's almost dystopian quality read to some as an indictment of the drug-riddled counterculture of the 1960s. But the piece more broadly alluded to a notion that everyone was phony.[114] Thompson wasn't explicitly political, but the subtext illustrated just how mainstream the cultural aversion to power had become.[115]

In the late 1970s, the eminent professor and critic Christopher Lasch contextualized the impulse to vilify authority as one element of a broader "culture of narcissism."[116] Hannah Arendt complained that older desires to construct a shared public happiness had been replaced with a voracious materialism and consumerism.[117] And their indictment connected America's burgeoning political cynicism with something deeper, namely a personal desire less to fit in, as had been so pervasive during the 1950s, and more to sit beyond the reach of judgment and do what felt right to the individual. To discard oppressive parenting techniques in favor of helping children develop at their own pace. To give spouses the license to leave unhappy marriages without assigning fault. To free atomized families from ticky-tacky suburban houses. To break the unfulfilled out of sterile religions in favor of communities that offered them authentic joy.[118] Whether the nation's culture shaped progressivism, or progressive thinking shaped the nation's culture, the prevailing zeitgeist was unmistakable.[119] Indulgence might beckon chaos—but that was better than oppression.

The message was everywhere. In 1974's *Chinatown*, the ghoulish figure wielding power over Southern California's water system is too influential to combat. *One Flew Over the Cuckoo's Nest* (1975) indicted the oppressive power of the nation's psychiatric institutions. The film's now iconic Nurse Ratched, a cold and unfeeling agent of the medical establishment, brutalizes mental patients committed to an asylum.[120] The famous line from 1976's *Network*, about the stilted influence of television news—"I'm mad as hell and I'm not going to take it anymore!"—encapsulated that same feeling. Power, wherever it resided, appeared to be inherently dangerous.[121]

When, during the Watergate summer of 1974, Robert Caro published his voluminous takedown of Robert Moses, the spellbinding narrative mirrored what was, by then, an entirely familiar worldview. Moses had been a progressive in the original Hamiltonian mold—a man who believed unerringly in the wisdom of experts. But as he had become more powerful, he'd been unable to resist the temptation to deploy his authority against a hapless and unsuspecting public. It wasn't just that he had imposed his will without considering the implication for those without power; it was that his imperviousness had left New York trapped within a tangle of clogged expressways, soulless neighborhoods, beleaguered ghettos, and bankrupt bureaucracies. Moses personified the Establishment—he was, in fact, a figure out of central casting. Caro's long exposé, released within weeks of Nixon's resignation, was yet more evidence of power gone awry.

A half century earlier, in 1919, the progressive theologian Reinhold Niebuhr had published a letter in the *New Republic* complaining that progressivism lacked "fervency . . . [the] spirit of enthusiasm, not to say fanaticism, which is so necessary to move the world out of its beaten tracks. . . . Liberalism is too intellectual and too little emotional to be an efficient force in history."[122] By the mid-1970s, that was no longer the movement's problem. With an almost religious zeal, progressivism could see and taste its enemy. Lyndon Johnson, Richard Nixon, Bull Connor, Nurse Ratched, Robert Moses—they were all fiendish representatives of the octopus, all beacons of oppression. The details differed, but the script remained the same. And so, in the main, progressivism shunted its Hamiltonian instincts aside, putting Jeffersonianism at center stage. And with that picture in its collective head, the movement began to craft a new agenda.

4

Manacling the Octopus

PROLOGUE: BRIGHT LIGHTS AND RUBBER HOSES

Vincent Ragosta Jr. hadn't been out of law school long when, late on a Friday night, the phone rang in the small apartment he shared with his wife in Providence. A colleague was calling with an urgent request from a longtime client: her husband had been arrested outside a bar downtown— disorderly conduct—and someone would have to bail him out. As a young associate at his family's law firm, and, during the 1970s, one of its younger employees, Ragosta was the next man up. He had, by that point in the evening, already begun to unwind. But, perhaps because he was so green, he felt a rush of excitement. The young lawyer had never been drafted to do anything like this. So he threw on a suit, grabbed his briefcase, and headed down to the Fountain Street police station.

Even if Fountain Street served as the department's city-wide headquarters, the station house felt sleepy, if not relaxed, when Ragosta arrived—it was, after all, a routine weekend evening, with not much doing. So he was caught off guard when, while sitting on a wooden bench, the room suddenly came alive. When the young lawyer looked up, he saw that Providence's chief of police, who would rarely have made an appearance during the evening shift, had swept into the building. Ragosta sensed that everyone was suddenly on edge. Officers behind the desk rapped to attention, each attempting to wear a studious expression while paging through piles of presently important papers. Everyone wanted to appear busy.

To this day, Ragosta isn't sure why the chief came downtown that night. In the mid-1970s, Providence was, admittedly, a rough town. As in other working-class cities in New England, the decline of manufacturing—most notably, in Rhode Island, the textile and costume jewelry industries—had left working-class communities restive and angry. Beyond that, Mayor Buddy Cianci's Providence was haunted by the barely hidden menace of organized crime. Against that backdrop, policing Rhode Island's rusting capital was a challenge. To do the job well, you needed to cut a fearsome profile—to elicit discipline in the ranks. And so it was no wonder that when the chief walked in, the cops on duty bristled in fear. You didn't trifle with department brass, and you certainly didn't want to be seen disrespecting the chief.

Unfortunately, at the moment the chief arrived, one poor slob of an officer wasn't able to get himself together—he was too far gone. Had this Friday evening been like most others—a lazy parade of inebriated bar patrons being booked for minor offenses—the young cop wouldn't have had any reason to stand on ceremony. Even by his mere posture, you could tell he was just biding time before the end of the shift. He was fat—"corporeal," as Ragosta described it, years later. He was slouching. He wasn't wearing his hat, as department policy required. Perhaps worse, his shirttails were out. He looked a mess, and when the chief walked past, the young cop was caught utterly out of sorts. It was like a scene out of a sitcom—but without the humor.

Describing what happened next more than forty years later, Ragosta still professes shock. The chief stopped, gave the officer a quick up-and-down, cocked his arm, and slapped him with an open hand. As the younger man recoiled, the chief began barking commands. "Tuck in your shirt. Where's your fucking hat? Get your act together!" The disheveled cop, humiliated, scurried into the back of the station to clean himself up. And Ragosta, embarrassed enough to look away, suddenly gleaned a much clearer understanding of what it was like to serve in the ranks of Providence's police department.[1] However fearsome the city's officers might have appeared while walking the beat, they were themselves vulnerable to violence from above. And as would soon become clear, the dynamic on display that evening in Providence was indicative of the norm across the country.[2]

At the time, that dynamic was only beginning to change. Amid the tumult of the 1960s and 1970s, America's perceptions of law enforcement had begun to evolve. Previously, during the period when authority figures had been more summarily venerated, cops had often enjoyed broad public esteem. If not every community was entirely satisfied with the ways officers comported themselves—Black communities were more regularly subject to disproportionately harsh treatment—the men and women charged with upholding law and order were typically shown a great deal of deference, even among progressives. But as the movement's cultural aversion to power had taken hold, cops had become subject to more intense scrutiny. Victims of misconduct and brutality had begun bringing suits against the blue. And in many cases, the Supreme Court responded by issuing rulings that required officers to raise their standard of conduct.

Mapp v. Ohio (1961) had directed courts to rule out evidence that police had collected from unconstitutional searches. *Escobedo v. Illinois* (1964) excluded statements made to investigators after suspects requested a lawyer. *Miranda v. Arizona* (1966) required officers to advise suspects of their rights.[3] By the late 1960s, the message had been made clear—officers had, in the past, too frequently abused their authority. Their wings now needed to be clipped. By the time news cameras caught cops whaling on protestors outside the 1968 Democratic National Convention, progressive attitudes had broadly shifted. Time to clamp down. Whatever fly-by-night practices had previously been permitted would need to be stamped out moving forward.

That change elicited a variety of responses. Some officers, of course, accepted the new procedural regime without protest. Some resented the new strictures, irritated that, in their view, a bunch of bleeding-heart lawyers were hog-tying the brave men holding a thin blue line. Still others began ignoring the rules, imagining themselves as Dirty Harry types—vigilantes in uniform. But what few outside the police community seemed to realize was that there was another reaction as well: insofar as lawless hippies, smelly vagrants, and out-and-out criminals were now being protected *from* abusive police behavior, officers themselves remained vulnerable. As would be made clear to Vin Ragosta during his visit to Providence's Fountain Street station, many of the men and women charged with keeping the streets safe were more vulnerable in the station house than some criminals were in the wild. And that disparity spurred varying degrees of resentment and bewilderment in the ranks. Who, at long last, was going to protect the officers from the chiefs?

The question fit into a broader context. By the 1970s, many Americans had come to embrace a certain idea about the abuse of power. It was all too easy, many had concluded, to compel ordinary people to do terribly depraved things. Mao had convinced millions to torture their neighbors during the Cultural Revolution. The Vietcong had convinced their adherents to inflict untold horrors on American captives in the jungles of Southeast Asia. And while few, if anyone, would make the comparisons explicit, it was easy to imagine something similar might have happened before Chicago's police had beaten protestors outside the DNC, or before members of the National Guard had murdered students at Kent State. Not that the perpetrators weren't themselves responsible on some level—but perhaps they'd been cowed into their demented behavior by the beacons of some cruel Establishment order. Perhaps, in fact, members of the rank-and-file felt as if they'd had no choice.[4]

It was in this context that, decades later, Vin Ragosta used the phrase "bright lights and rubber hoses" to describe the way chiefs had taken to interrogating rank-and-file officers during that period. Providence's police chief had made no bones about slapping a disheveled officer late on a Friday night. But that was just a peek behind the curtain. There was nothing to stop a chief from throwing a wayward officer into an interrogation room and torturing him until he confessed to running a racket, or placating a mobster, or, for that matter, *not* running a racket or *not* doing favors for the local mob. Many officers presumed that the only way for them to advance up the ranks, or avoid a hazing, or even keep their jobs, was to be entirely supplicant to the brass. Put simply: individual officers were powerless against the System.

At the time, few would have been confused about who exactly constituted that system—in the popular imagination, they were all of a type. Chicago mayor Richard Daley. Birmingham, Alabama, public safety commissioner Bull Connor. General George Patton. In Baltimore, the System was personified by Donald Pomerleau, a former marine who would serve as the city's police commissioner from 1966 to 1981. Pomerleau relished his role as Charm City's chief enforcer. And while he was credited near the outset of his tenure for bringing order to a flailing department, his detractors came to view him as a kind of municipal dictator.[5] When asked at one point if he'd directed his undercover officers to keep tabs on political figures, he'd brashly replied, "Just the blacks. Just the blacks. Just the blacks." He explicitly intimidated other public officials in the style of J. Edgar Hoover—compiling dossiers and hinting ominously at the leverage he wielded.[6] He was a man who many in Maryland feared. And as it turned out, some among those who feared him the most were members of his own department.

Early in his tenure, Pomerleau had been rumored to have assembled Baltimore's entire command staff into a single room and defied anyone to deny that he was the "sole boss."[7] He'd instituted a practice of subjecting

officers to lie detector tests—and firing them if they failed.[8] Some claimed
he had often taken to placing officers in a "sweatbox," questioning them
for hours until they finally admitted to a crime, real or contrived.[9] And
as the nation's judges had begun clamping down on police abuse of ordinary citizens, the chasm between *suspect* rights and *officer* rights had only
appeared to widen. Pomerleau was doing to his rank-and-file what the
rank-and-file were precluded from doing to suspected perps (even if, in
some cases, they did anyway). It didn't seem fair.

In Baltimore, leaders of the local police union were quick to highlight
the discrepancy. One complained that, while criminal suspects were sure
to be released in the absence of being read their rights, "a policeman is
never advised of his rights because he has no rights." Officers argued that
the city's beat cops operated perpetually under a "black cloud," fearful that
they might at any time be subject to suspensions or ruined careers without
even facing any incriminating evidence.[10] In the wake of news that 1,250
bags of heroin worth $100,000 had been taken from the department's
evidence control unit, the strong suspicion was that higher-ups—perhaps
some of the Commissioner's favorites—had been involved. But Pomerleau
was connected to the Nixon-appointed US attorney who purportedly
gave him a heads-up. And when a local prosecutor threatened an investigation, Pomerleau sent a message by withdrawing two officers from the
prosecutor's office.[11] You were either with the Commissioner or against
him—and if you were against him, Katy bar the door.

Progressives had cheered when the judiciary began requiring cops to
adhere to more rigorous standards of professionalism. And now, many
wanted to apply the same approach to another circumstance defined by
vast disparities of power. The problem here wasn't just Pomerleau's pension for abuse—it was Pomerleau's system. By the 1970s, inured in the
culture of the moment, reformers wanted to do something that many of
their peers would have considered anathema during the 1950s and early
1960s: rein in the authority of the purportedly wise men running powerful institutions. The Baltimore chief's shenanigans weren't stand-alone

failures; they were just the latest illustrations of an Establishment gone wild. And so, for progressive reformers, the solution wasn't simply to replace one abusive chief with another. It was to impose checks that would prevent power from corrupting men and women of goodwill. Here was an opportunity for the movement's Jeffersonian impulse to take flight.

In what would appear like a strange bedfellows moment just a few decades later, unions appeared to be on the side of reform.[12] Beyond banning corporal punishment, organized labor also wanted to institute procedural reforms to ensure that officers were given opportunities to correct bad behavior before being let go—no more summary firings. To many progressives looking on from the outside, that just seemed fair: if tenured professors at public universities enjoyed job security, officers putting their lives on the line should get something similarly robust.[13] And it just went from there. The details of the various state laws passed as Law Enforcement Officers' Bills of Rights varied by jurisdiction: in some places, chiefs were prohibited from interrogating officers except under certain supervised circumstances; in others, the brass needed to warn officers before subjecting them to discipline.[14] In some places, complaints had to be kept confidential, and in others disputes had to be settled by "neutral" arbiters. Across the board, however, the intent was largely the same: Pomerleau-like reigns of terror *inside* police departments would have to end.

Decades later, many progressives coming late to the scene would presume that these guardrails were the handiwork of archconservative villains—legislators eager to carry water for the police unions in exchange for campaign donations and endorsements. In the 2010s and 2020s, as demonstrators filled streets across America in protest of the police killings of Michael Brown, Tamir Rice, Breonna Taylor, and, most pointedly, George Floyd, progressives typically derided LEOBORs. Arduous due process protections made it impossible, in many cases, to get wayward officers fired from the force. Bad cops appeared free to wreak havoc without repercussion. Racist cops patrolled with impunity. Similarly frustrating, LEOBOR-connected confidentiality provisions prevented chiefs from commenting on accusations of misconduct, giving communities the impression that their complaints were falling on deaf ears—and, in some cases, they certainly were.

Lost amid the frustration, however, was a realization that, upon their inception, LEOBORs had frequently been viewed as progressive victories—the means to pare back the power of devious figures like Commissioner Pomerleau. Working off the assumption that the line cops would be kinder and gentler if they were liberated from the nefarious influence of the bad chiefs—that cops on the beat would uphold a standard of morality if they did not work in fear of the brass—LEOBORs had been framed as a great leap forward. With the same sorts of protections that guaranteed university professors the ability to say no if a dean demanded they adopt a racist curriculum, cops would now be able to reject a chief's demand that they beat up protestors, or plant evidence, or gratuitously pull over Black motorists. LEOBORs would protect Black cops from being harassed by white chiefs. Or so many reformers at the time had initially presumed.

Decades later that perception would change. If progressive reformers and police unions had been allied against the chiefs during the 1970s, by the late 2010s the chiefs and reformers were aligned against the rank-and-file. By then, *both* rued LEOBORs for protecting abusive officers, wrapping disciplinary measures in an absurdity of red tape, and precluding responsible supervisors from maintaining proper compliance. The effect had been an outrage: to exact a minimal level of discipline, chiefs often chose to punish more serious misbehavior with slaps on the wrist, lest they get wrapped up in the vortex of a LEOBOR review. But then, if the officer fell out of line again, the first offense could not be used as precedent for a firing.[15] When reformers became aware of this racket, they were rightly incensed. But chiefs, even while facing the public's wrath, believed their hands were tied—had they pursued more punitive justice in the first instance, they might not have been able to impose any penalty whatsoever.

In the years following his eye-opening experience on Fountain Street, Vin Ragosta built a practice as the lawyer many of Rhode Island's cities, towns, and police departments turned to when seeking to discipline errant officers. And his exposure to the System eventually convinced him that Rhode Island's LEOBOR had overcorrected for the abuses of the postwar era. A political independent, Ragosta hailed from a Democratic family. His heart had gone out to that "corporeal" officer slapped years earlier by Providence's imperious police chief. But *post*-LEOBOR, he'd seen too many unfit officers retained for the wrong reasons. And he'd come to conclude that nearly *everyone* was suffering as a result. Citizens were wary of the police. Officers faced skepticism from the people they had sworn to protect. And police departments found it increasingly difficult to recruit good new cops. A vicious cycle.

Nationally publicized instances of police brutality—most notably Derek Chauvin's videotaped 2020 murder of George Floyd—sparked demonstrations and spurred a renewed interest in LEOBOR reform. But more mundane episodes of impunity were born of the same dynamic. In 2021, the City of North Providence, Rhode Island, tried to fire Scott Feeley, a police sergeant charged with a whole rash of violations. He'd been insubordinate to his superiors. He'd lied in the course of an internal affairs investigation. He'd failed to call in traffic stops. In all, Chief Alfredo Ruggiero Jr. brought ninety-seven different charges against him, and the LEOBOR tribunal empaneled to evaluate those charges found him guilty of seventy-nine of them.[16] But the panelists decided, in the end, not to strip him of his badge, as the city demanded. Instead, he was simply demoted to patrolman after serving a forty-five-day suspension. North Providence's mayor, Charles Lombardi, responded in outrage: "What do we do with this guy? He was found guilty of failing to obey, truthfulness. . . . This is insulting."[17] And yet there was nothing the mayor could do to keep him off the beat.[18] Feeley returned to service.

The stories differed from place to place, but the underlying dynamics were rarely distinct. Chauvin, the officer eventually found guilty of murdering George Floyd, had previously been subject to twenty-two complaints and internal investigations as a Minneapolis police officer.[19] Whatever his reputation for brutality, he'd remained on the force, protected in no small part by reforms often championed by progressives decades before. Those protections now appeared like vestiges of Jim Crow—invitations to abuse. In fact, however, they had been born in large part from the reform movement's Jeffersonian impulse. Feeley's and Chauvin's impunity, like that for so many officers whose misconduct remained shrouded by process, had been husbanded by the cultural aversion to power. The ugliness of Hamiltonian power had spurred progressives to pursue reforms that invited a different form of abuse. The movement had undermined itself—and this wouldn't be the only time.

THE RIGHTS REVOLUTION

As we saw in the last chapter, the tumult of the 1960s marked a *narrative* turning point for the progressive movement—its zeitgeist was changed substantively by the upheaval. Downstream of that philosophical shift was the movement's policy agenda—the nuts-and-bolts approach progressives would propose to address various challenges. If, after the change, the movement was more driven to push power down than up—if, beyond losing faith in the Establishment, it was bent on prying off the octopus's tentacles—progressivism's practical approach would also have to evolve. As we'll see, the substantive thrusts of an explicitly Jeffersonian agenda would turn out to be very different than those born from the movement's now more muted Hamiltonian impulse. The shift wasn't merely narrative—it was practical as well.

Before tackling how, exactly, the cultural aversion to power rippled out across the progressive agenda, we need to recall the context. Decades earlier, during the movement's formative years, reformers had frequently been consumed by their frustration with the courts. Time and again, nineteenth-century judicial doctrine had frustrated the reform community's designs on improving working conditions, raising wages, and much more. What is now remembered as the Lochner era was defined by a jurisprudence determined to thwart government interference in the private economy, thereby enfeebling centralized government. Progressives ranging from Theodore Roosevelt to Robert La Follette to Franklin Roosevelt proposed at various times a range of reforms designed to diminish the guardrails judges erected around executive action, from judicial overrides to court packing. Time and again, they failed. If progressives were going to overcome the judicial barriers to centralization, the change would have to emerge from within the courts themselves.

And it did come—and with it a great sense of relief. *Lochner's* repudiation in the late 1930s made a relic of the old progressive desire to push past the nation's judiciary. Suddenly flush with Roosevelt appointees, the Supreme Court appeared less like a menace than an opportunity. Perhaps, beyond merely *deferring* to the New Deal's newly expanded administrative state, the courts could be jerry-rigged in a progressive force for good.[20] With liberals now in control, reformers began to consider a previously unheralded question: Where now could judges serve as the tip of the progressive spear?

The intellectual journey that followed began with what many legal scholars refer to simply as "the Footnote." Written by Justice Harlan Fiske Stone and appended to the Supreme Court's 1938 *Carolene Products* decision—a ruling that effectively curtailed the scope of the judiciary's review of most economic regulation—the Footnote suggested a series of issues where courts, in Stone's view, *should* take a more proactive role.[21] As sketched out in the justice's brief delineation, and then colored in through subsequent jurisprudence, the judiciary reoriented itself to take a more aggressive role in guaranteeing democratic fundamentals (like voting rights), protecting minorities who had been victimized by prejudice, and upholding other rights conferred explicitly by the Constitution.[22] Quietly, this represented a watershed: by shedding the court's traditional role as a

bulwark *against* the movement's Hamiltonian impulses, Stone was pointing the judiciary to become an agent *for* Jeffersonianism.

This seemingly subtle shift in American jurisprudence, begun in the
late 1930s, did not spark a wholesale change overnight—it was not the lightning rod *Brown v. Board of Education* would prove to be. But the Footnote
did plant a flag or, perhaps more accurately, lay the seedbed for changes
that would flower several decades later. In a decision designed broadly to
pare back judicial interference—*Carolene Products* is largely remembered
for the fact that it was one among many decisions green-lighting big, centralized, Hamiltonian regulation—Stone was specifying areas where the
court *could* take a more proactive role. But in the late 1930s and right
through the era when progressivism was more focused on stability, exercising the "rights" Stone delineated was not nearly so high on the movement's agenda. The New Left, maximum feasible participation, Eldridge
Cleaver's "one giant octopus," and the cultural aversion to power were still
a quarter century in the future; *Brown v. Board of Education* was a ways
off as well. Jeffersonianism had, at that point, only a fraction of the same
purchase on progressive minds and hearts. But come the late 1960s and
early 1970s, Stone's tools remained there for the picking. And it was only
a matter of time before those wanting to chip away at the Establishment
would find ways to use them.

To be clear, these two separate shifts—the evolving *culture* examined
in the last chapter and the changing *jurisprudence* mentioned here—
weren't entirely unrelated. But for the most part, they evolved in parallel. In the immediate aftermath of the New Deal, various elements of
the administrative state had license to operate almost entirely without
guardrails. The National Labor Relations Board and the Securities and
Exchange Commission, for example, were initially empowered to implement rules without any substantive review, and it wasn't clear when
or if someone who believed the rules were unfair could complain, let
alone challenge them in court. Hoping to establish a thoughtful mechanism for weighing competing concerns, a nascent movement among

legal scholars, the Legal Process School, emerged in favor of regulariz-ing judicial review—ensuring that those under the thumb of regulatory power had recourse if the regulators overstepped their bounds.[23] This was, by some measure, the gospel of balance applied to the worlds of bureaucracy and regulation.[24]

The scholars and jurists who composed the Legal Process School weren't alone in fearing Hamiltonian progressivism gone wild. Other progres-sives had simultaneously begun to worry about the "threat of capture"—namely the concern that regulators might become tools for the indus-tries they were supposed to oversee (as many would complain during the Eisenhower years). The ACLU, which had, to that point, largely viewed the courts as beacons of moneyed interests, began in the post-Footnote era to conceive of the judiciary more as an institution uniquely equipped to serve as a backstop against government abuse. While less iconic than the organization's work protecting free speech rights, progressive civil lib-ertarians were determined to rein in the administrative state for much the same reason they were interested in defending individualized expres-sion: having unleashed the power of big government—the same power, by some horrific notions, that Benito Mussolini had infamously used to keep the trains running on time—they worried the centralized bureaucracies progressives had lionized might eventually be used for ill.

The touchstone of this rearguard action became the Administrative Procedure Act (APA) of 1946.[25] Less celebrated than other iconic progres-sive achievements, the APA mandated a certain cadence of rulemaking within federal bureaucracies, requiring them, with certain exceptions, to publish proposed rules, to make accommodation for public comment, and then to consider the reaction.[26] The law precluded regulators from adopting rules that were "arbitrary and capricious" or "unsupported by substantial evidence."[27] And it stated explicitly that regulatory procedures were subject to judicial review—put another way, it specified that outsid-ers could sue if they believed action by an administrative agency wasn't just or fair.

These new protections were important—but many among those watching the amoeba of the administrative state grow in the aftermath of the Second World War began nevertheless to articulate a growing sense of alarm. And this is where cultural predilections and judicial doctrine began to intermingle. Five years after Truman signed the APA into law, a Roosevelt appointee to the court stated in clear and concise terms why checks on the bureaucracy were so important. In a scathing dissent to a court opinion blessing a determination made by the Interstate Commerce Commission, Justice William O. Douglas wrote: "*Expertise*, the strength of modern government, can become a monster which rules with no practical limits on its discretion. Absolute discretion, like corruption, marks the beginning of the end of liberty."[28] Here, more than a decade *before* the Port Huron Statement, Douglas was articulating some of the same underlying concerns, namely that the centralized institutions that previous waves of progressives had fought to empower were liable to go rogue.

Through the 1950s, even as these concerns grew, the new "rights" created by the APA were rarely invoked. Without a lot of friction, the government proceeded with big projects reminiscent of the still-thriving Tennessee Valley Authority—projects including the Hoover and Grand Coulee Dams and a raft of massive nuclear power plants. Even when a Democratic Congress passed (and President Eisenhower signed) the law providing a mechanism to fund the vast highway program Roosevelt had conceived years earlier, there was little discussion of whether ordinary people should be guaranteed some opportunity to question government decision-making.[29] Whatever checks the APA provided, deference to authority was the unwritten rule.

In the years that followed, Jeffersonian efforts to corral the administrative state weren't pursued in a vacuum. Progressives during these years were kicking the tires on new uses for the judiciary in a whole range of contexts, none more famous than *Brown v. Board of Education* (1954), which employed judicial authority to do what the elected branches of government had failed to get right—namely to desegregate the nation's public schools. Often considered separately as beacons of entirely different realms of the law, these initiatives were born nevertheless from the same underlying notion that deliverance would come not by amalgamating authority, but by pushing it down to individuals. The proposition that judges could be the essential ally of those victimized by centralized power had been laughable during the Lochner era—judges had then shielded private interests from the demand of what many elites viewed as the democratic mob. Now, with the judiciary having a much more liberal bent, the courts appeared poised to be a crucial bulwark for the beleaguered outsider.

The same year that Congress passed the Civil Rights Act, a professor at Yale Law School wrote a law review article that would take this notion a crucial step further. Charles Reich's "The New Property" framed the bureaucracies progressivism had once celebrated less as salves than as scourges. In Reich's view, the administrative state had become such an omnipresent force in everyday life that, by the 1960s, a bureaucrat's decision to deprive an individual of any certain service was tantamount to stealing that citizen's personal property. People *needed* to drive their cars to work, for example, so if a bureaucrat withdrew an individual's driver's license without cause, or for some reason that might be deemed "arbitrary and capricious," the government was essentially robbing that citizen of their income. Reich argued that administrative agencies should have no more discretion to deprive someone a routine privilege than they had authority to summarily lay claim to someone's home or business.

Reich went on to provide a litany of the various ways in which the "gigantic syphon" of government improperly stole personal property. New Jersey's director of the Division of Motor Vehicles had suspended a citizen's driver's license even after he had been acquitted of committing any underlying crime. New York State had rescinded a citizen's welfare benefits when he refused to stop sleeping in a dirty barn that wasn't up to code. After a man was deported, the Social Security Administration had denied his wife the benefits due to her for the years he had paid into the system. These were, in Reich's view, violations of individual rights, and so he proposed a salve designed to protect the individual against the Establishment: "The denial of any form of privilege or benefit on the basis of undisclosed reasons should no longer be tolerated. Nor should the same person sit as legislator, prosecutor, judge and jury, combining all the functions of government in such a way as to make fairness virtually impossible."[30] And as important as the substance, that principle was the subtext. Reich was translating the New Left's antipathy for power into a specific agenda.[31]

Without overstating the influence of any single law review article, the New Property's significance was born from the grist it added to the new progressive zeitgeist.[32] Reich wasn't just arguing on behalf of a guy sleeping in a barn, or an exonerated driver deprived of his ID. What became known to some as the "rights revolution" broadly encompassed Jeffersonian progressivism's strategy of pushing authority down by investing individuals with new rights. Not only were progressives now averse to power—they were conceiving of specific ways to chisel at the authority Robert Moses types had come to wield. Culture had shaped the boomers' politics, and now their sensibilities were prompting a new policy agenda. Jeffersonian means to Jeffersonian ends. In ways that would have been inconceivable just a few years earlier, individual rights, protected by liberal judges, would become the tools reformers used to beat the Establishment into submission.[33]

SALT IN THE WOUND OF POVERTY

Perhaps nowhere in the public policy lexicon has the clash of progressivism's Hamiltonian and Jeffersonian sensibilities come into clearer contrast than in the realm of public assistance—what some pejoratively call "the dole." More than a quarter century after the Clinton administration's overhaul of America's welfare system, two different, if familiar, narratives still frame the debate.[34] Progressives tend to view recipients as deserving victims of systemic inequality. Conservatives are more likely to frame the same population as "welfare queens." Lost in this dichotomy are the basics of a once-heated debate *within* progressivism. If, as most reformers have long believed, those in need of public assistance are fundamentally worthy, they have frequently been of two minds about *how* best to help them. And that internecine policy dispute is derived from the movement's divided heart.

This oft-overlooked disagreement centers on what, exactly, welfare is supposed to accomplish—or, perhaps more pointedly, what the public can reasonably expect of those receiving taxpayer-funded subsidies. In some instances, and in certain periods, the movement had explicitly wanted welfare to be paternalistic—or, perhaps put more accurately, maternalistic.[35] Progressives in the early decades of the twentieth century wanted social workers to do for young women receiving public assistance what a doting parent might do for a struggling adult child—help them up and on their way.[36] But since the 1960s, many progressives have come to see that maternalism as a patronizing burden on families already mired in poverty. As a result, like in other realms, reformers became more inclined to manacle the octopus.

The program most commonly understood as "welfare" was established during the New Deal and known originally as Aid to Dependent Children. To that point, the federal government had played only a more marginal role caring for the nation's poor, leaving primary responsibility to families, private charities, local businesses, and, in some cases, states.[37] But in a progressive leap spurred largely during the ravages of the Great Depression, Democrats conceived a system designed primarily to aid single mothers—and in their prevailing conception, widows. During an era when the pervasive expectation was that, in a *proper* family, a father would serve as the breadwinner and a mother would raise the kids, reformers were bent on keeping the traditional roles intact—that is, in keeping mothers from *having* to work outside the home.[38]

Decades later, as conservatives attacked welfare for incentivizing indolence, that original intent would be overlooked. But if the progressives who originally shaped the program had hoped to preclude single mothers from *having* to leave their children in order to earn an income, the government's largesse came explicitly with strings attached. Aid to Families with Dependent Children (AFDC), as the program would later be renamed, may have been funded overwhelmingly by the federal government, but it was administered through state agencies and local bureaucracies dominated by professional social workers. Informed by progressivism's embrace of scientific expertise, these social workers were credentialed professionals, many steeped in the legacy of the old progressive "settlement house" movement. Like the settlement house employees determined to mold the immigrant classes into responsible American adults, those dispensing welfare saw it as their charge to mold the poor into responsible, middle-class citizens.

True to form, the army of social workers tasked with serving as something akin to surrogate mothers were not content simply to dispense checks. They saw it as their charge to help single mothers stay on the straight and narrow, raise their children right, and avoid the temptations of single life: indolence, substance abuse, alcoholism, promiscuity.[39] Public assistance, for the social workers who controlled it, was a carrot that could quickly morph into a stick—a tool that middle-class marms could use to keep poor women "moral."[40] And that maternalistic notion defined the program's ethos from its inception in the mid-1930s through the early 1960s: armies of social workers were generally granted wide berths of authority to mentor, mother, and cajole single mothers as they individually saw fit.

Some among the nation's social workers were gentle and nurturing— they took care to cultivate a loving touch. Others, however, led with a heavier hand, treating their charges in ways that many viewed as cruel. Regardless, there was no mistaking who wielded power in any given relationship. No one in the early years could deny that, at root, the program was a scheme to compel working-class and poor women to adopt middle-class values even if, as increasingly became the case, many resented the imposition. The bulk of progressives, and certainly the social workers themselves, dismissed those sorts of objections: Being infantilized by an expert seemed to them a mild penance to pay for relying on the public dole. If, as many conservatives would later argue, these women had wanted a different life, they should have chosen a different path.

Decades on, it may be hard to appreciate how it might have felt to have the Establishment hover over you as these social workers loomed over their cases. But, in many cases, the dynamic was not just infantilizing—it was oppressive. Social workers often took it upon themselves to police the role men played in recipients' lives. On the one hand, they figured, government shouldn't be cutting checks to women who were otherwise being supported by male breadwinners. On the other, they didn't want taxpayers subsidizing promiscuity. And so, in some instances, welfare agencies adopted "man-in-the house" policies designed to smoke out mothers shacking up with their boyfriends. That left many recipients to live in fear of what some called "midnight raids"—unannounced visits seeking to unearth who was present inside a given home during the late-night hours.[41] If someone discovered a man hiding in the closet, the recipient's checks might be curtailed entirely.

This was, almost by any measure, Hamiltonian progressivism at its very worst. In reaction, reformers in the 1960s began mobilizing, as on so many other fronts, to pull the whole scaffolding down. While authority, in this realm, wasn't wielded by a singular bureaucracy, the social workers essentially acted as little Robert Moseses in the recipients' lives—personalized Nurse Ratcheds. The other social movements of the era—against the war, for civil rights, in search of a flower-powered counterculture—were not directly akin to what became a collective uprising against the infantilization of poor, single mothers. But they all drew from the same cultural desire to liberate the oppressed from a heavy hand of one sort or another.[42] The question was how to manacle these particular tentacles.[43] And so, as we will see, in other realms, it soon became clear that the most expeditious route was to draw on Charles Reich's conception of the New Property.

From AFDC's inception, benefits had been used as a cudgel—social workers threatened to curtail payments if recipients failed to fall into line. Reformers, in turn, viewing this dynamic as a scourge, began lobbying governors, state legislators, program administrators, and anyone else wielding influence to reconceptualize the benefits as a right. Their thinking was clear: if social service agencies were compelled to cut checks regardless of whether a single mother followed a social worker's strictures, recipients could be brought out from under the government's thumb.[44] Reframing welfare not as a benefit but as an entitlement was an explicit swipe at the Establishment. It took authority from state-empowered matriarchs and transferred it to women who, from the reformers' perspective, were doing their best to raise children in dire circumstances.

The exact mechanism of this Jeffersonian reform varied from place to place. But the judiciary struck one universal blow when, in 1970, the Supreme Court established in *Goldberg v. Kelly* that welfare recipients were entitled to a hearing before the government could terminate a benefit—thus winnowing the discretion of individual social workers.[45] But the crusade to push power down to recipients didn't end there. Under pressure, some states updated their policy manuals to make payments automatic. And the impact of that sort of mundane change could often be profound: instead of being subjected to a social worker's prying questions, an applicant now simply had to proffer a few facts to determine whether, if by formula, she qualified for benefits, and at what amount. If you were poor, if you had one kid, if you had additional kids, you needn't worry about the presence of a boyfriend, or if you broke up with your boyfriend, or if you were engaged in a more casual relationship. The system was less personalized, and more routine.[46]

To be sure, recipients weren't powerful in this system—but neither were they at the same mercy of the marms. Nevertheless, there were trade-offs. The ordinary kindnesses that had once been within the purview of a social worker's discretion were now off the table—there was no one to bequeath a struggling mother an extra few taxpayer dollars if her car needed an unexpected repair, for example. And that was for the same reason that it was now harder for racists to shave down an applicant's benefit: the tasks that had once been handled by *social* workers were now being done by clerical *case*workers. As the paradigm shifted and the bureaucrats running social welfare agencies bought into the new depersonalized approach, they began seeking out employees capable of resisting the urge to interfere. As one senior Massachusetts official explained: "We've been trying to get the people who think like social workers out and the people who think like bank tellers in."[47]

Depending on your perspective, progressivism's new Jeffersonian approach represented something of a great leap forward. As a result of the change in orientation, many more poor people both applied and qualified for assistance. From 1966 to 1971, the percentage of eligible families *not* receiving welfare benefits fell from a third to a tenth.[48] In New York City alone, welfare rolls grew from 240,000 people in 1959 to 1,165,000 in 1971, and the costs to the federal government nationally grew more than five times over.[49] But if the new regime was more generous, it was, by progressive design, colder. Reformers were intent on getting bureaucrats out of the practice of orchestrating a woman's climb up the socioeconomic ladder. Massachusetts abandoned its practice of sorting cases by geography explicitly to ensure that caseworkers would not develop a working knowledge of a neighborhood's social service agencies. Instead, the Bay State began assigning cases directly by alphabetical order.

The shift to depersonalization had profound impacts—and not entirely for the good. Recipients who once bristled at being patronized now lived in perpetual fear of a bureaucratic snafu. In the old model, the social workers dispensing aid were (theoretically) rooting for a recipient's success. Caseworkers, by contrast, were charged merely with adhering to the letter of the law—and they risked trouble of their own if they bent the rules.[50] Here it's easy enough to understand why so many bureaucrats embraced what some called an "attitude of impersonality." If anything, their incentive was to deny or limit benefits lest their supervisors accuse them of misconduct.[51]

And that was understandably infuriating for recipients: the last thing a young mother struggling to raise her children needs is the added burden of tracking down a letter to prove her family's eligibility for a little plus-up in their monthly check.[52] Salt in the wound of poverty.

What was perhaps most remarkable about the shift was the alacrity with which advocates went from ruing midnight raids to castigating the miserliness of the new impersonal regime. A broad range of organizations—the National Welfare Rights Organization, the Children's Defense Fund, the Legal Aid Society—fought vociferously to prevent impersonal bureaucracies from denying benefits to the recipients who were legally entitled. Some even embraced an audacious strategy to deluge the program with recipients such that the entire enterprise would go bankrupt, presuming that a lack of resources would force the government, eventually, to create a guaranteed income.[53] But the growing *feeling* was one of frustration.[54] The public was given the impression of a system in turmoil. And that impression was often accurate. With images of disinterested caseworkers swimming in seas of paperwork, few were given to imagining that the system was defined by competence and efficiency.

It's worth taking note of the narrative arc here because it tracks a pattern that will be made evident again and again in the chapters that follow. A policy conceived *before* the 1960s, imbued with an explicitly Hamiltonian ethos, becomes the object of Jeffersonian ire. Well-intentioned reformers then begin to conceive of ways to push that centralized power down and out—to disrupt the Establishment's hold on its victims. In order to manacle the octopus, reformers work to endow the victims of the old regime with new rights—leverage of the kind Charles Reich conjured in "The New Property." Last, amid generalized frustration with the end result, government is made to appear generally, and specifically, incompetent. *To wit, nearly every element of the story can be explained without incorporating the (generally nettlesome) influence of conservatism.* Progressives serve at the forefront of every successive change. And yet there was no doubting who benefited politically from the change: the right.

In this case, the figure who first took advantage of the corner progressives had painted themselves into was Richard Nixon. Machiavellian as he was, Nixon understood how more conservative elements of the New Deal coalition would react to the notion that their tax dollars were being promised to unappreciative recipients by an overwhelmed bureaucracy. With racial prejudice woven into the subtext, conservatives replaced the public's sympathy for widowed mothers with the notion that "welfare queens" were bleeding the system. A former *New York Times* editorial board member recalled a comment one mother on welfare made to New York City mayor John Lindsay at a legislative hearing: "It's my job to have kids, and your job, Mr. Mayor, to take care of them."[55] Seeing the opportunity to drive a wedge, Nixon proposed what amounted to a guaranteed income for those at the bottom of the income scale, making himself appear to be sympathetic to the poor while castigating the same system that progressives were also prone to flay. While the Family Assistance Plan died on the vine, Nixon won by letting progressives walk into a trap of their own creation.[56] The nation's welfare system, by the movement's own testimony, was now perceived to be a fatuous mess.

The ultimate irony was that progressivism's effort to preclude social workers from prying into people's personal lives created what felt like *more* government. Absent a system where individual social workers could exercise personalized discretion, policymakers were compelled to lay down increasingly specific ground rules, guardrails, limits, and operating instructions. How, exactly, would someone qualify for assistance? What would exclude them from eligibility? How might they be reinstated? What proof did they need to provide to maintain their benefits? As in other realms of policy, decisions once made by experts were now decided by rule. In the decade that followed Nixon's inauguration, the federal register of regulations grew a full four times in length, with decisions including how welfare was administered now subject not only to layers of bureaucracy, but a new reign of judicial oversight as well.[57]

In the decades that followed, the welfare discourse reverted to the old tropes, with conservatives arguing with Nixonian fervor that big government was incentivizing indolence, and progressives arguing that miserly government was failing to serve those most in need. Some would try, on occasion, to break out of that vice, as happened among progressive supporters of welfare reform in the mid-1990s. Lost amid that tension was any serious attempt to grapple with the reality that the system was a mess largely by progressive design. The old Hamiltonian conception of the dole had been plagued with problems—but the Jeffersonian alternative was deeply flawed as well. In the end, the movement's cultural aversion to power had left progressives with the worst of both worlds: a program that was cold on the one hand, and insufficient on the other.

And then there was the role welfare had come to play in the public discourse. Here, the political implications come into clearer view. A program established during the New Deal to help mothers in need had become, a half century on, a poster child for bureaucratic incompetence. It served as Exhibit A for those wanting to sap confidence in government more generally. In the decades to follow, whatever progressives subsequently suggested to do to help the nation's poor—however they proposed to strengthen the social safety net—they were now forced perpetually to swim against a tide of public cynicism. Progressives had teed it up, and conservatives hammered it home. Government, observers were induced to believe, was indelibly incompetent, and only a fool would presume that public bureaucracy could work effectively in the public interest. Even if that wasn't true—and, to be clear, it wasn't in many cases—few could have come away with the impression that progressivism was poised to deliver on its broader promise.[58]

A NEW AND DIFFERENT AGENDA

The cultural aversion to power served not just to reframe progressivism's approach to combating police brutality, or awarding driver's licenses, or provisioning welfare to the poor. The impulse to push power down, combined with the policy tools born from endowing individuals with new "rights," proved particularly potent in the realm of environmental protection. At the turn of the twentieth century, America had been riven by a fear that the country was running out of space, driving progressives, most notably Theodore Roosevelt, to charge centralized authorities with keeping the nation's great expanses wild.[59] By the 1960s, however, the nation's natural resources appeared to face a different threat. Beyond conservation, a burgeoning new environmental movement wanted to combat other forms of degradation. That new mission would require new public policy tools—and activists would discover them within the Jeffersonian tradition.

The problems, at that point, were both dire and obvious. The postwar economic machine had made no bones about plying the landscape with chemicals, toxins, and filth.[60] Rachel Carson's *Silent Spring* served as the touchstone of a new back-to-the-earth environmentalism that aimed not only at preserving nature but also at combating industrialization. Carson wasn't simply indicting human selfishness—her ire was targeted at centralized power more generally. As she argued in a speech delivered a year after the book's publication: "The fundamental wrong is the authoritarian control that has been vested in the agricultural agencies" that put farming interests ahead of the underlying ecology.[61] This, she contended, was part of a larger problem: wherever the preservation of the environment came up against the Establishment, the public interest appeared destined to lose. The only potential salve was to push power down and out, from the centralized nodes to the otherwise helpless victims.

The Establishment's scourge extended everywhere, and its tentacles reached far beyond the agricultural machines poisoning the nation's farmland. Highway planners and engineers, six years into constructing the interstate system at the time of *Silent Spring*'s publication, were selecting routes that often lay needless waste to the underlying flora and fauna. Highway engineers may not have been *purposefully* destroying the environment. But their mandate was to enhance mobility *at minimal cost*.[62] That perversely incentivized ecological destruction: Not only were pristine natural patches of land fair game when selecting routes, but they often marked the path of least resistance. Better, Establishment figures concluded, to disturb a forest

than a neighborhood. Better to displace a bird habitat than add a few min-
utes to a suburban commuter's drive downtown.[63]

Regardless of whether progressive leaders explicitly understood how
the movement's zeitgeist was changing, they were quick to pick up on the
public's growing antipathy. In 1964, the Bureau of Public Roads, later to
become the Federal Highway Administration, directed state engineers to
consider not only convenience and price, but also the social, economic,
and environmental costs of any given route. Ralph Nader, a young lawyer
then emerging on the scene, viewed highway engineers much as Carson
had viewed the bureaucrats at the Department of Agriculture—indifferent, at
best, to the public interest, and more likely in cahoots with the profiteers
(farming and construction companies) making fortunes off the march
to progress. The alternative, in his mind, was obvious and in line with
other reformers of his generation: empower the public to advocate for
itself *against* the System.[64]

It's worth pausing here, once again, to appreciate just how revolutionary this turn was within the world of progressive policymaking. The old
Hamiltonian zeitgeist—the one that favored centralization—had cast the
central tension in public life as the pull-and-push between public and
private interests. Roosevelt's "boys with their hair ablaze," presumed that
the government was out for the greater good, while businesses were out
for themselves. Their agenda was erected upon that narrative foundation.
Public officials of all stripes—the august figures of the Georgetown Set,
the city fathers managing local affairs, the experts fanned out across all
the various bureaucracies—were presumed to have good intentions.

But now, as articulated by the likes of Carson, Nader, and others, those
same big public bureaucracies weren't balanced against private interests—
they were co-conservators. The public interest had been captured, corrupted, and worse. Even Louis Jaffe, a New Dealer who became a luminary
of administrative law, was by 1965 writing about "the most monstrous
expression of administrative power."[65] And that meant, logically, that the
only real way to pursue the greater good was to reverse course—to push

power down and out, to give ordinary people the opportunity to advocate for themselves, to establish outside watchdogs designed to keep the system honest.[66] It wasn't enough simply to throw your body on the machine. Per the *new* zeitgeist, law and policy would give citizens the tools they needed to manacle the octopus.

The ideological whiplash was rife in nearly every realm.[67] Between 1965 and 1977, Congress passed a rash of environmental bills, some of which—the Clean Air Act of 1970 and the Clean Water Act of 1972 among them—compelled strong, centralized, executive agencies to take tougher lines against polluters.[68] Rather than accept an industry's explanation for why it couldn't wean itself from whatever harmful environmental practice it had embraced to date—smokestack emissions, toxic runoff—Congress set explicit standards and timetables. These were "command-and-control" regulatory regimes: the demands came from government, and industry was compelled to fall into line. Power was vacuumed into the hands of bureaucrats who would fix problems from above.[69]

But at the same time progressives were championing these command-and-control solutions, they were *also* pursuing an agenda that pointed power in the other direction. Late in 1969 Congress passed, and in early 1970 President Nixon signed, what some have called the "magna carta" of environmental legislation—the National Environmental Policy Act (NEPA).[70] In fairness, the bill's authors and champions in Congress weren't aware of how drastically the law would impact environmental law or, for that matter, government. But NEPA was remarkable in that its aim wasn't to pull power up and into a centralized bureaucracy— it was to force big, imperious government bureaucracies to pay attention, at long last, to the damage they were inflicting on the nation's landscape. The bill merely required that the bureaucracies sponsoring big projects review potential drawbacks. A mandate that the bureaucrats draft "environmental impact statements" was designed primarily to prompt more *internal* dialogue about potential degradation. Look before you leap.

At the time, few thought seriously to object to the proposed bill, largely because few predicted much would change upon its passage. When NEPA's House champion, the automobile industry–friendly Representative John Dingell (D-MI), was asked in a public hearing whether the new bureaucracy created by the legislation, the Council on Environmental Quality, would now be involved in reviewing every project, the answer was unequivocally no: "The conferees did not view NEPA as implying a project-by-project review and commentary on Federal programs. . . . Rather it is intended that the Council will periodically examine the general direction and impact on Federal Programs in relation to environmental trends and problems and recommend general changes in direction or supplementation of such programs when they appear to be appropriate."[71] Indeed, most everyone viewed the bill as fairly innocuous—a statement of "good principles" that would cost little more than $1 million in staff work a year.[72]

But if NEPA had been created largely in the Hamiltonian tradition—if it was conceived to induce those *within* the behemoth agencies to be more ecologically sensitive while reshaping the nation's natural landscape—it inadvertently gave outsiders new Jeffersonian leverage. Those determined to drive power away from centralized nodes realized that the process for drafting environmental impact statements was subject to the Administrative Procedure Act's requirement that decision-making not be "arbitrary and capricious." If judges could be convinced that a project's environmental impact would, in actuality, be different from what an agency projected, ordinary citizens now had a Reichian cudgel to bring the bureaucracy to heel. And while the legislative language within NEPA never explicitly contemplated that litigants would be empowered to challenge the quality or thoroughness of environmental impact statements, a new phalanx of lawyers saw an opening.[73]

The impact was almost immediate. Mere weeks after Nixon signed NEPA into law, a newly formed progressive nonprofit, the Center for Law and Social Policy (CLASP), filed suit on behalf of the Wilderness Society,

Friends of the Earth, and the Environmental Defense Fund against the secretary of the interior demanding a halt to construction of the trans-Alaska oil pipeline. Their contention was that the government had not properly accounted for the project's environmental impacts. A judge issued an injunction. And while, in this case, the pipeline was eventually built, the judiciary's willingness to consider the case established a precedent that expanded well beyond NEPA.[74] Now, when an executive agency was assigned responsibility for protecting the environment, outsiders contending that the agency was doing an insufficient, incomplete, or incompetent job weighing various concerns could draft the judiciary to hold those executive agencies to account.

Federal bureaucrats quickly began to appreciate how the old system's familiar rhythms were under assault. Two years on, a Federal Highway Administration official attending a conference in Wisconsin on environmental impacts complained that a federal judge had halted a highway project for lack of an environmental study. The plaintiffs, he explained, had been able to file suit without posting bond—they weren't being required to cover the small fortune their lawsuit would cost taxpayers if the government prevailed and the project was eventually green-lit. Worse, this was part of a trend. In 1971, twenty-four similar suits had been filed across the country.[75] The Federal Highway Administration then managed a $5 billion budget with a mere five thousand employees. The agency's bureaucrats and lawyers were already overwhelmed, and the Nixon White House was trying to *reduce* the size of the federal workforce. If the government had to do this sort of study on every project, something *would* have to give.[76] And something *would* give—but it wouldn't be the environmentalists.

Over the next several years, states and cities began using NEPA as a model for similar bills, some of which came to mandate protections not only for governmental action, but for private projects as well. And before long, what had appeared initially as an innocuous requirement that federal bureaucracies simply look before they leap had reshaped not only the process for building things in America, but the very contours of power.[77] No longer could a figure like David Lilienthal swoop in from above and remake an entire river valley, as the TVA had done during the 1930s. Now, an agency would make a decision, a public-interest group would file a lawsuit, there would be a tussle in the press, and ultimately in a courtroom.[78] The parties might come to a compromise "consent decree."[79] But the core dynamics were unmistakably different: centralized power was finally being held to individual account.

As in the realm of welfare policy, the political implications of progressivism's shift were also profound. Ahead of his 1972 reelection campaign, Nixon would growl to his chief of staff: "We've had enough social programs: forced integration, education, housing."[80] His grousing was typical for any anti-Establishment conservative. Nixon had long made a sport of skewering what Donald Trump would, a half century later, label the "deep state." What was odd was that Nixon's Democratic opponent that year, Senator George McGovern, embraced much the same attitude. He promised at one point to combat the "empty decaying void" of an "establishment center . . . that commands neither the confidence" of most Americans "or their love."[81] Conservatism's antipathy for government was narratively resonant with progressivism's aversion to power.[82] Nixon's promise to fight for America's "silent majority" against the institutional elite wasn't so different from cynicism typified by C. Wright Mills, Abbie Hoffman, Eldridge Cleaver, Rachel Carson, and Ralph Nader. Both ends against the middle—both against public power.

Today, many may scoff at the notion that progressivism was somehow in sync with Richard Nixon, or vice versa. And, indeed, during this period, progressives remained supportive, in theory, of a whole range of more Hamiltonian proposals embraced by the Democratic mainstream at the time. (To repeat, progressivism has always embraced elements of both its Hamiltonian and Jeffersonian impulses—even if the balance is often in flux.) The congruence between the likes of Richard Nixon and Ralph Nader wasn't that they shared some broader dream of the same social justice—it was that they both sought ways to hack at nodes of centralized authority. And by the 1970s, the evidence of the Establishment's rot was so pervasive that, in many cases, Hamiltonian approaches to problem-solving were beyond the pale.

The evidence of bureaucratic incompetence and malfeasance was, at the time, almost overwhelming. When Saigon fell, few doubted that the Pentagon had gotten in over its head. The oil crises under-mined faith in America's economic machine.[83] Cities that had been riot-ing in the late 1960s appeared to be decaying through the 1970s—with New York, in particular, edging toward bankruptcy. In the years that preceded what would be (mis)remembered as Jimmy Carter's "malaise" speech, the public shared a notion that the country, led by tired institu-tions, was in decline.[84] Even the great exponents of the Hamiltonian New Deal were demanding a change. Arthur Schlesinger, who had venerated Franklin Roosevelt in an epic trilogy before serving as special assistant to John F. Kennedy, now argued *against* the centralized power of executive agencies.[85] And a new generation of Democrats, many of them elected in 1974 as "Watergate babies," saw curbing power as their *cri de coeur*. That year, a young Democrat named Gary Hart won a Senate seat in Colorado by explicitly flaying the Establishment. "The time is now for *all* of us to rise up and take our country back from the power-hungry corrupters, the fat cats and . . . the comfortable, complacent, backward-looking old men."[86]

Through the 1970s, the Jeffersonian impulse came to define more and more of progressivism's legislative agenda. Congress passed the War Pow-ers Act, limiting the president's ability to take the country to war without explicit authorization. Legislators created the Church Committee in 1975 to thwart the abuses of the intelligence community. Legislators passed the Developmentally Disabled Assistance and Bill of Rights Act to protect people with extra challenges from abuse and neglect. Congress passed the Ethics in Government Act in 1978 to attack conflicts of interest.[87] The list of laws pushing power down and endowing new groups rights just seemed to grow. Hamiltonian ideas sometimes garnered lip service, but they were rarely center stage. And the effects of these various Jeffersonian triumphs, from NEPA on down, would become increasingly clear in the years and decades to come.

A PUPPET CONTROLLED BY WARRING HANDS

Throughout Hamiltonianism's long reign as progressivism's predominant impulse, municipal reformers tended to castigate ordinary city agencies as lumbering creatures of corrupt political machines. To bypass the bosses— to ensure true experts were in charge of building a new water system or managing a complex transit network—the reform community frequently favored transferring control to what were innocuously termed "public authorities." Governed by appointed boards of directors, public authorities were conceived to be free of corrupt entanglements—more prone to being "businesslike" and "nonpolitical" than the bureaucracies with line authority from City Hall. They represented a kind of Hamiltonian ideal—a centralized bureaucracy capable of combining private and public sensibilities to the common good.[88]

During the 1970s, however, public authorities lost their luster. If Eldridge Cleaver's octopus had ever come to life, its most fearsome tentacles would almost certainly have taken their form. Designed explicitly to be insulated from politics, their executives appeared like distilled emanations of the Establishment. Their boards were filled with business elites, their priorities aligned with upper-middle-class sensibilities, and their finances tied to Wall Street. To build that new sewer system, authorities would hire financiers to sell tax-exempt municipal bonds to institutional investors who would siphon interest from the water bills paid by ordinary taxpayers. To maintain the system, authority executives often appeared more interested in maintaining their bond ratings (lest they be denied subsequent opportunities to borrow) than in fulfilling their public mandates. For reformers, these were the archetypical examples of the

Establishment gone wrong. And the evidence of abuse was, in many cases, jaw-dropping.

The Chesapeake Bay Bridge and Tunnel Commission, for example, had issued bonds to enhance and maintain the various bridges and tunnels on the Eastern Seaboard. Wall Street banks earned sizable commissions selling the bonds to investors who then expected to earn steady returns. When, however, toll revenue wasn't sufficient to pay the bondholders, it wasn't entirely clear who would be forced to eat the loss. The authority, the banks, and the bondholders all viewed the underlying terms of the deal as nonnegotiable, thus requiring taxpayers to make up the shortfall. And there was no one, save a few outside critics, positioned to raise a stink. Here was the Establishment at its most devious—a public enterprise, designed to pursue the greater good, crafting a bait and switch that benefited the wealthy and powerful. This was the octopus at work.

The problem was bigger than the financing. Public authorities were often taken to pursuing projects ordinary citizens abhorred even while neglecting improvements that the public might have deemed more worthwhile.[89] This was part of the rapacity that Robert Caro exposed in *The Power Broker*—Robert Moses used his power atop the Triborough Bridge Authority, among other bureaucracies, to engage in projects that served his predilections rather than the public good.[90] And it wasn't just Moses. Austin Tobin, running the Port Authority at much the same time, resisted entreaties to subsidize the woebegone railroad ferrying residents between New Jersey and Manhattan for fear that the cost might preclude the Port from engaging in projects more to his liking. He would eventually lose that fight—the PATH system was born as a result. But here was yet more evidence to prove that the Establishment had its own agenda and that its priorities weren't necessarily aligned with the public interest.[91]

But what to do to rein public authorities in? By the point of *The Power Broker*'s release in 1974, the New Left had dissipated, and SDS was defunct. Many of the organizations that had sounded the alarm had, it seemed, vanished from the scene. But if the whirlwind of protest had ended, the cultural aversion to power remained in full force. Not only were many veterans of the New Left now elected to office, the Jeffersonian ethos had come to own a much bigger slice of progressive discourse. To boot, by the 1970s, those eager to push power down and out had at their fingertips a whole playbook of moves at their disposal—new oversight boards, new reporting requirements, a new spirit of litigiousness.[92] Finally, girding all of these various blows against centralized executive power was a judiciary that was willing and eager to join the fight.

This judicial element was, by some measure, the *coup de grâce* of the whole transition. It wasn't just that progressivism had changed culturally. It wasn't just that the movement had developed new tools to hack away at the Establishment. By the 1970s, a new generation of judges eager to cut Robert Moses types down to size had arrived on the scene. One particularly influential figure, Judge David L. Bazelon of the DC Circuit Court of Appeals, wrote approvingly of a new day when courts would "insist on strict judicial scrutiny of administrative action."[93] And so a branch of government progressives had once been so desperate to sideline began providing "injunctive" relief against government plans in some cases, and taking over executive departments in others.[94] Here was the thrust of Justice Harlan Fiske Stone's famous Footnote in full flower.

In 1967, a mere three lawsuits had been filed to enforce federal statutes for every one hundred thousand Americans. That figure would quadruple by 1976, and grow seven times over by 1986. And for all the attention paid post-Watergate to the threat of an imperial presidency, the judiciary had perhaps a more powerful effect hobbling the same administrative agencies the Establishment had once lionized. A full half of the major regulations issued by the Environmental Protection Agency during the 1980s were blocked at one point or another—as were a host of Forest Service management plans, port dredging proposals, and vehicle safety regulations. In 2000, at least thirty of the nation's welfare agencies were operating under court orders demanding improvements. Even in 2016, the child welfare systems in twenty states were operating under consent decrees, and the courts were processing ten thousand appeals each year for benefits from government agencies.[95]

To read those statistics today, many progressives may be tempted to cheer, if only because it's so easy to imagine a Jane Jacobs type taking a Robert Moses–like figure to court, or a Ralph Nader acolyte convincing a judge to prevent a Republican appointee from leasing publicly owned forests to a corporation controlled by a GOP donor. Moreover, if a city's child welfare bureaucracy *isn't* protecting vulnerable children, why *wouldn't* progressives sue to force caseworkers to do their jobs? If an environmental regulator appears inclined to green-light pollution, why *not* enjoin her to uphold the public interest? If a police chief is firing good cops to hire incompetent good ol' boys, why *not* give upstanding officers more protection? Why *not*, in the end, use every possible mechanism to ensure the *real* public interest comes first?

In some cases, there is no good riposte to those questions—progressives are right to hold the authority to account. But there's a balance to be struck if only because, by limiting the discretion public officials have to do bad, the Jeffersonian agenda also narrows the path for other public officials to do good. By curtailing opportunities for centralized power brokers to wreak havoc, reformers risk immobilizing the public sphere, rendering the big, hulking bureaucracies that were once the apple of progressivism's eye incompetent. Controlling for the vices of Hamiltonianism, progressivism loses virtues as well. The scholar Jonathan Rauch, describing the New Deal, illustrated how nimble the government had been during the era when progressivism celebrated centralized power:

On the seventeenth day of his administration, [President Franklin Roosevelt] proposed the Civilian Conservation Corps; three weeks later, it was law. On November 2, 1933, he was given a proposal for a Civil Works Administration employing people to repair streets and dig sewers; by November 23, the program employed 800,000 people; five weeks later, it employed 4.25 million people or 8 percent (!) of the

American workforce. Just as important, Roosevelt was able to get rid of programs. He ordered the Civil Works Administration shut down at winter's end; its total lifespan was only a few months. Similarly, the Civilian Conservation Corps went away in 1942, once the war made it superfluous.[96]

Few of the items on Roosevelt's agenda would have struck a public chord in the absence of a Great Depression. But by the late 1970s, neither would they have even been possible. Scholars and analysts have long debated why faith in government has declined since Watergate. Some of the impetus, no doubt, was born from Nixon's villainy. Some of the subsequent decline has undoubtedly been due to the fact that the purported "party of government" has never boasted the filibuster-proof majorities that made Roosevelt's flexibility possible in the mid-1930s. Some of the public's frustration has surely been born from the role entrenched interests play frustrating efforts at reform.[97]

But beneath and beside these explanations is another omnipresent reality: government today suffers from an endemic diffusion of authority. The ability of presidents, police chiefs, social workers, public authority executives, and others to exercise discretion has been severely curtailed. In many cases, too many disparate voices now wield a proverbial veto.

This new dynamic was not prompted by any single shift. It wasn't *just* progressivism's cultural aversion to power that sparked the transformation. It wasn't *just* Charles Reich's new conception of personal property, or the subsequent development of a jurisprudence investing new rights in those affected by decisions above. It wasn't *just* the judiciary's new willingness to interfere more directly in the machinations of executive branch decision-making. But braided together, these shifts swung a great balance of power *from* central nodes of government *to* individuals on the periphery. Power that previous generations had pulled up and in has subsequently been pushed down and out. Subjected to legislative demands, judicial injunctions, and executive orders, the administrative state has become, in many cases, a puppet controlled by warring hands. And the effect, in many cases, has been dysfunction.

From a progressive point of view, this new constellation of power at first appears advantageous. When nefarious characters like Richard Nixon or, say, Donald Trump head the octopus, their administrations are now bound to be more limited in the damage they can do—they can't so haphazardly dismantle the programs progressives care about most. If a municipal welfare agency is operating under a consent decree enforced by a judge, presidents, governors, mayors, and others have considerably less opportunity to curtail the benefits it affords the poor. If a law gives regulators flexibility setting smokestack pollution standards, bureaucrats captured by industry now have a tougher time giving them a pass, if only because outside groups can sue the executive agency in the public interest—and win. All this is seemingly for the good.

But the downsides have been profound. It's not just that LEOBOR-like statutes sometimes have the perverse effect of making it harder to do good things—like get rid of bad cops. As we'll see in subsequent chapters, the new regime has also made it more difficult to build affordable housing, and to construct new high-speed rail lines, and to site the transmission lines required to deliver renewable energy to places eager to overcome their addiction to oil and gas. But the most profound detriment of the system Jeffersonian progressivism has created is that it has made government, in many realms, authentically incompetent. That, as we'll see, has now become progressivism's great political burden. Who in their right mind would seek to give *more* power to this sort of dysfunctional, do-the-least-possible version of government?[98] Is it any wonder that many Americans who might typically have found a home in the old New Deal coalition have ventured so far outside—even to the point of lionizing a man who rants against the "deep state"?[99]

A generation ago, when Ronald Reagan famously quipped that government would inevitably screw up a two-car parade, progressives bristled. But the Gipper's critique wasn't really directed at the government incarnated by the New Deal, the centralized system where, in the eminent legal scholar James M. Landis's words, experts were given "grants of power which with to act decisively."[100] Rather, Reagan and his conservative allies were indicting this new, perverse, impenetrable, Kafkaesque alternative. And when progressives, not entirely registering the distinction, fought back by claiming that government *was* somehow good, or worthwhile, or productive, they came to look untethered to the reality they themselves had helped to create. And yet the distinction was real.

In the decades that followed the 1960s, progressivism became a movement defined by the parks department unable to rebuild ice skating rinks, and the railroad unable to build a train station—a movement of social justice activists unable to act against brutal cops, of climate activists incapable of delivering clean energy, and of housing activists incapable of erecting new homes. By tipping the scales too far from Hamiltonianism, and too far toward Jeffersonianism, progressivism became, in short, a movement of do-gooders unable to do enough good. The diffusion of power hasn't just undermined government—it has short-sheeted progressivism's *political* appeal. And that is perhaps the most important lesson of the last several decades. Absent a progressivism that works, what reformers get is a progressivism left vulnerable to demagoguery. When government appears incompetent, voters turn to figures like Donald Trump.

5

More Harm Than Good

PROLOGUE: BOTH ENDS AGAINST THE MIDDLE

President Franklin Roosevelt established the hulking regulatory bureaucracy that would govern the airline industry through the postwar era for a simple reason. The upstart companies trying to stabilize their businesses during the Great Depression were being run by cowboys more entranced with the novelty of flying than the challenge of building a sustainable new industry. The Roosevelt administration's burden wasn't to keep the airlines in line—it was to prevent them from spinning off into bankruptcy. As in the case of the TVA, progressives worried in the 1930s that, absent some significant government intervention, the public wouldn't benefit from what appeared like a promising new technology. And so a progressive president sicced centralized authority on an industry caught in an almost archetypical tragedy of the commons.

Flying was a relatively new phenomenon at the time—Orville Wright himself was still in his sixties. And it had been merely a quarter century since the president's distant cousin, Theodore, had painted a vision of a government capable of managing the nation's corporate interests from above. Now, George Perkins's early twentieth-century concern—namely that too *much* competition was undermining the public interest—was being put on display by the pioneering capitalists trying to make their fortunes in the sky. Every airline was perpetually vulnerable to an upstart competitor. No one company knew when or if another might propose to fly the same route. And so, in the spirit of Theodore's Hamiltonian worldview, the second President Roosevelt endeavored to create a bureaucracy that would do for the airline industry what the Interstate Commerce Commission had done for the railroads: control "entry, prices, and routes." Thus the New Deal bore the Civil Aeronautics Board, referred to more frequently as the CAB.[1]

From the outset, many of the airline industry's pioneers appeared grateful for Washington's intervention. Caught in precarious financial straits, outsiders had begun to worry that some of the industry's cowboy executives might be tempted to cut corners on safety and maintenance. Roosevelt's CAB was designed to incentivize the industry *not* to put the public in that sort of danger—its mandate was to help the industry grow safely and steadily by limiting competition to those companies who earned, from the CAB, a certificate of public convenience and necessity.[2] And the scheme succeeded. Over the following two decades, what would become the sixteen "trunkline" airlines would grow with the confidence that government bureaucrats would protect them against upstart competitors. Washington, by some turn, had saved a fledgling industry from competing itself into extinction.[3]

Here appeared an example of Hamiltonian progressivism in its finest form. Absent a referee, the traveling public might not have had an airline industry to patronize. Moreover, the industry's bounty extended downstream. By the 1950s, labor unions, financial lenders, and aircraft manufacturers were all benefiting from being part of what amounted to a regulated cabal. And the regulators could justify their continued existence by touting the benefits they had extracted from the industry. No need now to worry that airlines would engage in a race to the bottom on service and maintenance. Maybe more important, the government began requiring the airlines to frequent small airfields that might otherwise have been left unserved. If an airline wanted to run more flights from New York to Los Angeles, Washington could compel it to serve Sioux City and Mobile as well. A chef's kiss for the Establishment.

It was for exactly this reason that most progressives bristled when, in the 1960s, critics began suggesting that the public was getting a raw deal. Casting aspersions on the government experts making purportedly scientific decisions about routes and fares, the doubters wondered whether the CAB was actually doing more for the airlines than for the nation's consumers. Would prices drop, they asked, if the regulators got out of the way? Progressives looked askance at these sorts of questions. Many worried about the downstream implications of opening the industry up to a free-for-all. Without the CAB, the trunklines might decide to fly exclusively to the big markets. Unionized employees might be replaced by cheap labor. The market for planes, for airports, and for air travel itself might spin into chaos.[4] And so the CAB maintained widespread support and esteem. It thrived as an enduring emblem of the New Deal.

But that deference began to erode during the 1970s. For one, consumers themselves began to chafe at the CAB's lumbering, onerous style. Would-be competitors proposing additional flights were almost always thwarted by CAB bureaucrats expressing confidence that the existing service was sufficient. The trunklines, of course, applauded the CAB's intransigence—the government was protecting them from market competition. And it would have been one thing if CAB officials weighed these conflicting concerns in an open and expeditious manner. But it often took the CAB years to make final determinations. At no time between 1969 and 1973 did the Board approve a new route.[5] Meanwhile, mergers reduced the number of trunkline airlines from sixteen to ten, meaning the public had fewer options. Ticket prices went unchecked. Critics began to grouse more openly.

Amid growing cynicism, two airlines that *weren't* subject to the bureaucracy's edicts touted evidence that the CAB was a market hindrance. Southwest Airlines was, by then, serving several markets in Texas. Pacific Southwest was flying a variety of routes in California. And because these two airlines were flying *intrastate* routes, the CAB was prohibited from micromanaging their fares, which, as it happened, were significantly lower than the regulated competition. Executives at the trunklines were, of course, incensed by the comparison, complaining that their rates were higher because they were obligated to subsidize flights to more remote parts of the country. But these natural experiments out of California and Texas undermined some of the CAB's self-justification; you couldn't now reasonably argue that additional competition would imperil safety or undercut the customer experience.

In the early 1970s, a theory emerged within progressive circles to explain the problem: the CAB had been "captured" by those it was supposed to regulate—the bureaucracy was working for the airlines rather than the public. Then a young aide on Capitol Hill, future Supreme Court justice Stephen Breyer saw a passing mention in the *Washington Post* about a meeting between airline executives and CAB staff about the role "chartered" transatlantic flights were playing in undercutting Pan Am's ability to attract customers. The government had responded by vowing to impose price floors on charter flights. Breyer was aghast: "It was a cartel, a simple cartel organized by the government," he explained to his boss, Senator Edward Kennedy (D-MA). This archetypical triumph of the New Deal had turned . . . bad.

In the decades since, the story of airline "deregulation" has often been told as a kind of fable of free enterprise. As it goes, conservatives, drawing on research conducted by beacons of the neoclassical Chicago School of economics, were at the time trumpeting a whole variety of plans to claw back government regulation wherever possible. Consumers would be better served, they argued, if the market was liberated to operate with less bureaucratic interference. The CAB, in this conservative view, was a vestige of an old progressive regulatory apparatus that had outlived its usefulness. And as lore has it, it was only when conservative politics gained a popular foothold ahead of Ronald Reagan's 1980 election that the administrative state finally began to succumb.

While there's some truth in that narrative, the focus on conservatism's ascendency largely obscures what was happening within the progressive movement at the same time. If Republicans led with their chins excoriating big government, progressives were seeing their cultural aversion to power bloom at mostly the same time. The antipathy the New Left had expressed for centralized bureaucracy—a seed that had flowered through the protests and demonstrations of the 1960s and 1970s—had by Jimmy Carter's presidency taken deep root in the progressive mentality. And so, as Democrats began to look at the industry with fresh eyes, progressivism's once blind fealty to big institutional, expert-driven bureaucracy was almost entirely set aside. It was the Democrats, more than the Republicans, who wanted to take a hatchet to the CAB. And it was, ironically, the industry itself that wanted to maintain its shroud of regulatory insulation.

Carter was, in a more measured way, an avatar for Jeffersonian progressivism's renaissance. Early in his tenure, he selected Alfred Kahn, a Cornell economist serving then as chairman of New York state's Public Service Commission, to chair the CAB. By the moment of Kahn's arrival in Washington, no one was under any illusion about his intentions. Here was a progressive figure who struck fear in a regulated industry not because he intended to clip its wings, but because he was determined to open it to market competition.[6] And that seemed to reflect a part of Carter's underlying governing sensibility: the president had appeared in 1976 to be a voice of moderation—a pious southerner promising to break from the divisiveness of the recent past. But his desire to hack at Franklin Roosevelt's behemoth bureaucracy wasn't fueled by a hope he could placate conservatives as much as it was his desire to do the bidding of progressive activists. And by then, the activist community, convinced that the regulators were captured, was out for blood.

To be fair, Carter might well have embraced deregulation regardless of the politics—stripping down big, lumbering bureaucracies was, by the late 1970s, at the forefront of the progressive zeitgeist. But it was the man who would challenge him for the Democratic nomination in 1980 who would force the president to lean in. If John F. Kennedy had been a beacon of the Establishment the New Left had abhorred, the slain president's younger brother Ted appeared less a beacon for the "best and brightest" than a critic of the proverbial octopus—or so he would seek to frame himself in the coming primary. His brother John had lionized expert bureaucracies; Ted was going to make a reputation for himself by tearing one down.

Using his perch on the Senate Judiciary Committee, Kennedy convened a series of hearings to study the issue. In one, a now nationally exalted Ralph Nader made the case for deregulation from the left: "Throughout the land, people are repulsed by arrogant and unresponsive bureaucracies serving no useful public purpose, and they are looking to this Congress to get on with the national housecleaning job that is needed. Can you think of a better place to start than the Civil Aeronautics Board?" And Kennedy echoed that sentiment from the dais: "Regulators all too often encourage or approve unreasonably high prices, inadequate service, and anticompetitive behavior. The cost of this regulation is always passed on to the consumer. And that cost is astronomical."[7] Kennedy and Nader, it seemed, were out to attack the New Deal. And the new president, also a Democrat, not only wanted to join them but he wanted to wrangle credit for the whole deregulatory initiative.

Looking back, the most remarkable oddity of deregulation's role in late 1970s progressive politics—namely, that the two leading contenders for the 1980 Democratic presidential nomination were competing to dismantle one of Franklin Roosevelt's prized creations—was the coalitions erected for and against maintaining the CAB's broad mandate. On one side were the old-timers—the industry executives who wheeled out the same tropes about the destructive chaos of unrestrained competition, the routes that would be shelved, the unionized workers who would be furloughed, the way service and safety would suffer. On the other were what *Fortune* labeled "an odd coalition of academic economists, Naderite consumerists, liberal Democrats, and conservative Republicans."[8] They argued that the free market would solve these problems—that the bureaucracy was more a hindrance than a help.

A decade earlier, the status quo might have won out—and progressives almost surely would have sided with the industry's old guard. But by the late 1970s, the melded interests of industry executives, union officials, and captured members of the CAB were deemed *bad*, even among the politicos and others who had once venerated experts and professionals. Conservatives who were, at the time, becoming more and more intellectually tied to the fanciful promise of supply-side economics, were happy to join in the fight. And so the broader infrastructure of airline regulation was, in successive waves, demolished. Kahn used his authority as chairman to approve routes that previous CAB chairmen had rejected. And Kennedy helped to usher in the Airline Deregulation Act of 1978, which Carter signed triumphantly. With that, Washington edged its way (mostly) out of the marketplace.[9]

In the decades that followed, progressives would quietly debate among themselves whether airline deregulation worked—whether, in fact, the public would have been better served by reforming rather than eviscerating the CAB. Over time, as upstart competitors began to serve the routes the legacy carriers had once dominated and unionized employee benefits were pared down to be much less generous, some began to wax poetic for the old regime. A quarter century after the fact, several carriers that had once provided their employees with "defined benefit" pension plans— guaranteed payments over the course of a retiree's life—abandoned them in the course of bankruptcy proceedings, costing both beneficiaries and taxpayers, who were compelled to cover a portion of the difference.[10] The irony that Ted Kennedy, a figure who would long enjoy a reputation as one of organized labor's greatest champions in Washington, had prompted the underlying shift would largely be overlooked.

But if some of the benefits wrought by the old regime had been stripped away, even critics would have to acknowledge that the traveling public had come out ahead—at least for a time. Over the next quarter century, real prices for airline tickets would fall by roughly 40 percent. Low-cost carriers would extend their reach to roughly 85 percent of the flying public. The bulk of those cost savings would redound to the benefit of consumers traveling along more heavily trafficked routes. So, whatever had been lost in the spirit of deregulation—the employee benefits, the cross-market subsidies, even, in some cases, the quality of service—the flying public enjoyed more options at lower cost.[11] And to many on both ends of the political spectrum, Naderites and the neoclassical economists alike, that equated to a win.

What's perhaps most remarkable is that even now, more than forty years later, airline deregulation is often overlooked as a progressive accomplishment explicitly because it does not fit neatly into the prevailing narrative of left versus right. If Republicans are purported to be the party of business, and Democrats the party of government, how could it be that the nation's leading progressive voices led the fight to denude a New Deal–era bureaucracy designed to keep the private sector under heel? But within the framework of progressivism's two prevailing narratives— one in which Hamiltonianism pushed for more centralized control, and Jeffersonianism pulled explicitly in the other direction—the enthusiasm among progressives for airline deregulation makes more sense. Here was an early triumph for those who had embraced the cultural aversion to power.

In this case, reformers had targeted the power held by a cabal of airline executives, union officials, and federal regulators. Conservative economists and liberal activists were strange bedfellows only in the sense that they embraced different political proclivities—on the question of government power, their narratives were almost entirely aligned. That said, this wasn't some blip or aberration in progressive thinking. It was, quite in contrast, a signal of the cultural realignment that had begun in the early 1960s and crested in the wake of the 1968 campaign.

Not every reform effort would end with the same resolution—but that's not because Hamiltonianism was poised for a roaring comeback. Rather, as progressivism's impulse to check centralized power became almost reflexive, the movement's efforts quietly took a different turn. Beyond peeling back regulations that no longer worked in the public interest, progressives began inserting regulatory vetoes into public processes right and left. In a perverse but unacknowledged synchronicity, the impulse to free the airlines from the CAB would tie up other public bureaucracies in processes rendering public authority absurd. Progressives had come to loathe the administrative state so much that they were poised to undermine government. And while that would appear a victory in some circumstances, the resulting regulatory "vetocracy" would become the bane of the next generation's reformers.

THE SCOURGE OF BIG JOHN

With the overwhelming majorities Franklin Roosevelt ushered into Congress, progressives had largely been able to bulldoze conservative objections through the 1920s. The New Deal was shaped to the movement's will on passage. But the judiciary, stacked still with conservative appointees, remained both beyond the movement's grasp and cynical about the administration's hard-charging agenda. "It is common sense," Roosevelt had argued early on, "to take a method and try it: If it fails, admit it frankly and try another. But above all, try something."[12] This was terrific political rhetoric. But right through the most important setback of Roosevelt's presidency—his failed second-term effort to pack the Supreme Court—judges would be the most significant check on his decision to build a new, experiment-driven administrative state. And that power struggle would largely set the outline of his presidency.

Roosevelt's intention wasn't to divine new power for the federal government, exactly. Rather, he wanted to vacuum up authority where it had previously existed and deposit it in new expert-controlled bureaucracies. The authority to purchase or seize plots of land for highways, railroads, and electrical lines, to weigh public health concerns against economic expediency, and to answer big economic questions had always existed in America, but it had typically been wielded by individuals, businesses, party bosses, bankers, and state and local governments. Now, with the old configuration having proven itself unequal to the task of combating the nation's economic catastrophe, Roosevelt proposed a more centralized architecture of power.

As the White House would quickly discover, conservative jurisprudential objections rested on decades of precedent. The courts had been designed explicitly to preserve minority rights—to protect the well-off and well-heeled citizens perpetually worried about majoritarian demands. And to that point, judges had taken a skeptical eye toward proposals that "delegated" legislative power to the executive branch. Bureaucrats, per a certain strain of American jurisprudence, were not supposed to do things that were the province of elected legislators. Now, amid the crises born from the Great Depression, when it seemed the country needed a jurisprudence that would allow experts to wield a stronger hand, conservative judges were loath to embrace anything like it.

What emerged over the course of the next several decades—what Richard Stewart, one of the towering figures in the study of twentieth-century American administrative law, would term the "New Deal constitutional revolution"—was a complex new framework designed to allow for an ordered transition to more centralized control.[13] Per the strictures of the Administrative Procedure Act that would become law in 1946 and the jurisprudence that followed, newly empowered agencies would be required to follow strict procedures when making decisions—they were prohibited from behaving as star chambers. They would have to be evenhanded and consistent, applying the same rules and decrees across the board. And Congress was required, to varying degrees, to set the parameters within which government bureaucracies were permitted to tread.[14] But the APA, while setting limits, also served as a kind of permission slip for the administrative state—a road map for the permissible use of executive authority.

There could be no guarantee, within this new constellation of power, that the experts appointed to wield this awesome power would actually be effective. And in fact, that concern quickly came to the fore. Presidents Harry Truman and Dwight Eisenhower both appointed commissions led by former president Herbert Hoover to examine the workings of the federal government. Hoover's reports were frequently scathing about the quality of the nation's bureaucracy. Academics, including Harvard's Samuel Huntington and Louis Jaffe, worried about regulatory independence.[15] And the underlying dyspepsia often came from the same place: it seemed, in many cases, as though the regulators were too enthralled by the institutions they were charged with keeping in check. During the New Deal, Hamiltonian progressives had imagined regulators and industry advocates pulling in opposite directions, with the public benefiting from that balanced tension. Now, many feared, the two were pulling in coordination against the greater good.

In the early 1960s, for example, the Southern Railway found itself in dire financial straits. The railroad was losing its grain-hauling business to barge and truck companies. Southern's executives were under no illusions about why. When farmers shipped over its rail network, their foodstuffs were deposited in old wooden boxcars that were frustratingly inefficient. Grain invariably seeped out through the slats. Worse, the old boxcars loaded from the side, meaning that product spilled out when the doors were opened. To shore up their business, Southern designed and introduced an alternative railcar that was twice as big, loaded from the top, and constructed from aluminum. Big John, as the new container car was nicknamed, was so efficient that Southern's executives promised to slash its grain-hauling prices by more than half—a boon for both the nation's farmers and consumers.

But there was a hiccup. To make the switch, Southern needed approval from the old Interstate Commerce Commission. And when the ICC began the process of considering Southern's proposal, waterway operators registered an objection that was as compelling as it was self-serving: if Big John was put to work on the railways, and Southern began marketing the same basic service at a 60 percent discount, many operators of the nation's barge fleet would be put out of business. There was simply no way for companies that had invested huge sums in new vessels, docks, and distribution networks to remain profitable when competing against Southern's new discounted rates. And under that rationale, the ICC ruled to preclude Southern from updating its fleet, prompting a whole deluge of legal wrangling that ended with two hearings before the Supreme Court. While Southern would eventually prevail, the whole process took four years.[16] And this wasn't an outlier in regulatory jurisprudence; it was just one example of a prevailing pattern.

Some progressives had seen wisdom in the ICC's position—better to block innovation than to endure the downsides of creative destruction. And some detractors argued that the long delays were merely bureaucratic: if better *experts* were appointed by the regulatory state, agencies could surely come to better *decisions* more expeditiously. But during the late 1950s, another view began to take hold—namely that the problem was structural. Regulators were making decisions that cut against economic efficiency. The Eisenhower administration, for example, had chosen to limit oil imports less to insulate domestic producers than to enhance national security— Ike didn't want foreign companies to have too much leverage over the American economy.[17] But consumers had then been forced to swallow the higher prices demanded for domestically drilled oil to account for an illusory national security dividend, which prompted the question: Was the juice worth the squeeze?

The regulatory state, as it evolved, wasn't merely preventing an excess of competition from upending the economy, as Theodore Roosevelt and George Perkins had imagined a half century earlier. It was being used to weigh economic growth against other noneconomic interests. And it wasn't always clear that the experts making those determinations knew what they were doing. Borrowing from the broader theory of pluralism, many regulators appeared more driven to balance the interests of various constituencies than they were to champion the greater good. Here was the gospel of balance—the fear of chaos—woven into a political agenda. Regulatory complication was a weapon taken up explicitly to keep things *stable*, and regulators used it with abandon. The *Federal Register* compiling government decisions grew from 2,400 pages in 1936 to 20,000 in 1970, to a remarkable 60,000 pages in 1976. From 1970 to 1975 alone, the *Code of Federal Regulations* grew by a third.[18]

Worse, as the rhythms of the postwar regulatory state became more familiar, warring economic interests began to develop more nuanced understandings of how they could use regulation to their own advantage. Agency processes became political footballs, and the terms of each fight appeared to center less on economic wisdom than political power—who had more sway over the regulators. America's oil producers were averse to oil imports, but refiners welcomed them.[19] If the market was permitted to resolve these concerns expeditiously, some companies were bound to fail. The bureaucracy became a tool to protect entrenched interests to insulate firms that could not compete. The regulatory state, conceived as an institution committed to the greater good, had become, in too many instances, a haven for free enterprise's losers.

For scholars associated with the neoclassical Chicago School, this was an object lesson in why regulation was bad. If Eisenhower had wanted simply to protect domestic production, Washington might simply have slapped a tariff on oil imports. But oil industry executives, by that point well-versed in navigating the nexus of business and politics, had preferred a quota system that could be manipulated to their advantage. So an administrative state that had been designed for the express purpose of enhancing national security became a tool firms could use to beat their more efficient competition. And when the nation faced the oil crises of the 1970s, the culprit seemed fairly obvious to the public: this was the government's fault.[20]

When, in 1975, California governor Ronald Reagan went on Johnny Carson's *Tonight Show* and succinctly answered a question about what ailed America with the quip "Well, Johnny, I think one of the things is that people keep looking to the government for the answer—but government is the problem," he was clearly on to something.[21] But what Reagan's emergence as a Republican gladiator tends to obscure is the degree to which progressives were enthralled by much the same concern. From their perspective, the problem was less that government was interfering in the private sector—after all, industries like the barge operators and domestic oil producers had benefited from that interference. Rather, in their narrative indictment, Establishment figures in the private and public sectors were working in cahoots against the public interest. The octopus's tentacles had aligned the powerful against the people.[22]

Perhaps because Reagan would go on to win the 1980 presidential election, history tends to focus on deregulation as one of his brand of conservatism's early triumphs. But deacons of the neoclassical Chicago School, many of whom would become fervent Reaganites, were singing from Ralph Nader's hymnal. In what can only be described as the deepest of ironies, political movements that had been at odds when the economy was good—with progressives pushing for *more* government while conservatives demanded *less*—began tugging in the same direction during the 1970s.[23] Progressivism's turn against regulation wasn't explicitly derived from the New Left's Port Huron Statement, or from the civil rights movement, or the anti-war movement, or the counterculture. Few would even have thought to make the connection. But they were all linked—each born from the same cultural aversion to power.

More than a half century earlier, Teddy Roosevelt, channeling George Perkins, had embraced the notion that competition was a scourge on free enterprise—that individual companies were often compelled by dint of greed to do things they purportedly did not *want* to do: to underpay their employees, to pollute the environment, to ply the public with unsafe or unsanitary products. Responding to that challenge, progressives had worked to shape an architecture of power that countervailed the vices of excessive capitalism. But by the 1970s, that entire approach appeared to a new generation of reformers to be a complete failure.[24] The movement's new crusade was to tear down the very institutions it had previously worked so assiduously to build up. The only real question was how.

A QUESTION OF STANDING

As we've seen, the impulse to raze powerful institutions wasn't entirely new to progressive thinking during the 1970s. Decades earlier, the reformers who most loathed George Perkins had beaten the drum for busting private-sector trusts. Now, it appeared as though the clique of robber barons and financiers who had controlled the country from Wall Street in the early twentieth century had morphed into the combination of public and private interests that constituted Eldridge Cleaver's octopus. And whether the monster slept where J. P. Morgan or Lyndon Johnson laid his head on any given evening, reformers reacted with the same impulse— namely to shear the tentacles wherever they appeared severable.[25] By the 1960s, that meant focusing on the cabal of scheming corporate executives, captured regulators, and two-faced politicians who had perversely turned the administrative state against the public interest.

This new campaign would be distinct from the old antitrust efforts because there was little reason to believe that the mere *size* of any given corporation corresponded to its penchant for rapaciousness. It wasn't the *size* of agricultural companies that spurred farmers to spray dangerous chemicals on crops. Slicing up monopolies and disallowing anticompetitive behavior might once have been a worthwhile enterprise, but for many progressives it was hard to see how attacking bigness would achieve the movement's ends. What emerged instead drew from the same spirit that had animated progressivism's old crusade against monopoly power. This time, however, the old Jeffersonian ethos now applied to a different area of jurisprudence. It aimed to harness the new "rights" bubbling up in other realms of the law as cudgels against the octopus.

It had been one thing to establish the "right" to integrated schools, and the "right" to have a lawyer present during a criminal interrogation. From there it hadn't been too dramatic a jump to imagine how reformers might establish a "right" to beat back a highway department's "arbitrary and capricious" plan to seize a home, or to protect a single mother's "right" not to lose her welfare benefits.[26] But what "right" could be invoked to stop a polluter from capturing an environmental regulator? What "right" could stop an automobile manufacturer from wielding power over the bureaucracy charged with making cars safe?

Put another way: if progressives were intent on using *de*centralized Jeffersonian tools to glean what big Hamiltonian regulatory bureaucracies had failed to secure, reformers would need to develop approaches that allowed public interests to put a heel on the neck of private avarice. If reformers were going to protect public lands, to preserve vulnerable neighborhoods, to speak public truth to private power, they would need a new venue. That venue wasn't going to be provided by the executive agencies already captured by private interests. Instead, however ironically, the nation's judiciary emerged as progressivism's last, best hope. A decade after *Brown v. Board of Education* had illustrated how the Supreme Court could deliver on progressive desires, progressives began to think more expansively about how the third branch of government could serve their interests moving forward.

The fight that followed hinged on whether courts should defer to executive branch experts or take a more skeptical "hard look" at agency decisions.[27] But that broader question was fought in the context of much more mundane and seemingly technical questions, like who exactly had standing to bring complaints against government agencies. In the wake of the New

Deal, Hamiltonian progressives had managed to narrow the universe of interests who could claim that their legal rights had been breached by an agency decision—better to protect the likes of the TVA against the private corporations who might otherwise file suit. Wendell Willkie's Southern Company had no standing to sue the Roosevelt administration over rate decisions, a dynamic that gave David Lilienthal more latitude to act as he pleased.[28]

But that limitation was re-scrutinized as reverence for the Establishment waned in the 1960s and 1970s. Even before figures like Ralph Nader began beating the drum for more radical notions, progressive agitators in the form of public-interest lawyers argued that individuals with tenuous connections to an agency decision should have additional opportunities to have their grievances heard in court.[29] As early as 1942, Justice Felix Frankfurter ruled in *Scripps-Howard Radio, Inc. v. FCC* that a competitor could challenge the FCC's granting of a radio license, expanding standing beyond parties who could explicitly claim their "rights" had been violated.[30] Now, two decades later, a further expansion of standing appeared prerequisite to ensuring that concerned citizens could disrupt plans that threatened to pollute the air, or raze a minority neighborhood, or do something else that cut against the greater good.

One of the crucial initial steps on the journey that expanded standing came at the unlikely behest of the judge that Richard Nixon would eventually appoint as the nation's chief justice. In 1969, while serving on the DC Circuit Court of Appeals, Warren Burger wrote an opinion on a case that turned on whether the Federal Communications Commission had erred in renewing the broadcasting license of Mississippi's WLBT.[31] The Fairness Doctrine, established by the FCC, required public broadcasters to provide the public with an understanding of *both* sides on any major topic of public discourse. WLBT had consistently painted the civil rights movement in the worst possible light, often failing to inform viewers of the protestors' grievances.

Burger, whose preternatural conservatism would eventually catch Nixon's eye, was not known as a beacon for civil rights. But in this case, he inadvertently handed progressives a significant victory: If the FCC had failed to account for the interests of the listening public when deciding to renew the license, then, Burger concluded, the public was entitled to standing in any court case that bore on the FCC's decision-making.[32] That was, in the view of one progressive advocate, a signal that the "courthouse door was open" to those who wanted to raise flags for the public interest.[33] As it would turn out, the future chief justice's decision represented more than just a tweak to the nation's existing jurisprudence. It cleaved open an entirely new and different role for this third branch of government.

Recall that, decades earlier, the courts had operated primarily as *barriers* to public participation—they were the bulwark for minority rights against majoritarian demands. Sure, courts had been the venue by which government lawyers might bring antitrust suits—but in the late nineteenth and early twentieth centuries, judges loomed more often as the trusts' great protectors. As such, progressives had schemed then to move power from the courts to the government's elected branches. Now, the movement took pains to reverse course. With agencies captured by the Establishment, judges appeared more like a cudgel against corruptible institutions. Previous generations of progressives had wanted to empower bureaucrats over imperious judges; now they wanted judges to help them push past imperious bureaucrats. As David Zwick, one of Ralph Nader's young associates, explained, he wanted to "government-proof" the government.[34]

More important, a judiciary now brimming with liberals appointed by Roosevelt, Truman, Kennedy, and Johnson appeared eager to accommodate. From the mid-1960s to the mid-1970s, reformers imposed new standards far in excess of what those who had written the Administrative Procedure Act of 1946 had likely envisioned. Judges and legislators began demanding that agencies conduct oral hearings in the course of drafting rules. That regulators respond to comments and give "reasoned responses" to critiques. That agencies allow interests affected by a proposed rule to cross-examine those giving the regulators information. That they create a rulemaking record. In sum, regulation, which had been enshrined as a means by which disinterested experts could quickly impose their will on the chaos of free enterprise with some degree of discretion, became much more laborious.[35] Now, the regulators needed to carefully trace their path through an administrative labyrinth, or else face a judge who would take them to task. Just as important, members of the ordinary public, unhappy with how a regulator had wielded their expertise, could challenge that wisdom in court.

The shift prompted not only a stampede to the courthouse door but also the creation of a new cottage industry of "public interest" organizations.[36] The Environmental Defense Fund was early to the call. The group filed suit in 1967 to bar the use of DDT, an insect repellent farmers sprayed on crops that, when consumed by pregnant women, caused horrific birth defects. Then a slew of other similarly oriented nonprofits emerged in much the same mold. The Center for Law and Social Policy (CLASP) in 1968. The Natural Resources Defense Council in 1970. Public Citizen in 1971. Washington had long been crowded with interest groups. But this new coterie of reformers wasn't simply going to lobby legislators to do the right thing, or offer their opinions to regulators as part of the rulemaking process laid out by the Administrative Procedure Act. They would harness the courts to be the muscle behind the movement.

The Sierra Club and the National Audubon Society had been party to only a single environmental law decision in the 1960s. That number grew to 149 in the 1970s, 337 in the 1980s, and nearly 500 in the 1990s.[37] Meanwhile, the number of annual applications from organizations for nonprofit status—many designed to pursue this very sort of "public interest"-oriented work—tripled from the late 1960s to the late 1970s.[38] And as this new front in the battle for progressive reform took hold, the old approach, the one that the "boys with their hair ablaze" had forged inside Franklin Roosevelt's White House, fell by the wayside. It wasn't that regulation was dead—but as the movement's zeitgeist had changed, so had its approach to the nuts and bolts of policymaking. The locus of opportunity had moved from the elected branches to the appointed one.

IDEOLOGICAL PURGATORY

Five decades later, Jimmy Carter's single term in the White House—a four-year blip set amid a quarter century of Republican presidential dominance—can appear inscrutable. But if the Georgia Democrat's victory in 1976 was born primarily as a reaction to Watergate, it also marked what may be the crux of progressivism's big pivot. While serving as the Peach State's governor in the early 1970s, the "man from Plains" had witnessed the way members of Congress earmarked funding such that the Army Corps of Engineers was compelled to build dams in their districts. These dams did less to improve the natural landscape than they did to ensure that their sponsors' names were permanently affixed to a great public work.[39] This was the vice of centralized power, and the future president was scandalized.

Holding a torch for Naderite complaints about the country's big regulatory bureaucracies—the "deep state" Donald Trump would later warn about—Carter entered national life intending to root the bad out of the System. As he explained in a Georgia Law Day address delivered seven months before his national victory: "The regulatory agencies in Washington are made up, not of . . . people to regulate industries, but of representatives of the industries that are regulated. Is that fair and right and equitable? I don't think so."[40] He would put an end to the mischief.

But still, in the late 1970s, not all progressives had gotten the memo. Many of Carter's Democratic allies on Capitol Hill remained steeped in the Hamiltonian ethos. Beyond having designs on seeing *their* names affixed to new projects, they carried torches for centralized bureaucracy. The Nixon and Ford years had seen the Environmental Protection Agency established in 1970 and the Consumer Product Safety Commission created in 1972. The Department of Labor had been empowered to regulate workplaces, and the Federal Trade Commission to take a more active role keeping watch on warranties.[41] These various Hamiltonian institutions were birthed and buttressed even as reformers were simultaneously defanging purportedly captured bureaucracies in the courts. That progressives were of two minds was perhaps best illustrated by a confrontation that began even before Carter's inauguration over trucking regulations.

As with the airline industry, many reformers viewed the Interstate Commerce Commission's (ICC) onerous restrictions on "common carriers" as concessions designed to appease a small roster of unionized trucking companies. They argued that the ICC had been captured by a cabal of fleet owners and Teamster officials representing the truck drivers.[42] The economic effect had been to force shippers to pay for inefficiency. One licensed carrier, for example, had been compelled by regulation to stop regularly in Salt Lake City when traveling between Denver and Albuquerque, turning what would have been a 440-mile journey into a 730-mile trek.[43] And the extra miles appeared to outsiders like a federally endorsed extortion plot against those sending wares between Colorado and New Mexico.[44] To Naderite reformers, the path forward was obvious—greenlight more competition.

But not all progressives shared the deregulatory impulse. In 1975, before being appointed as Carter's transportation secretary, Representative Brock Adams (D-WA) argued for *more* trucking regulation. Writing in *Reader's Digest*, Adams contended that defenestrating the ICC would simply open the door to all the abuses that had prompted its creation in the first place. Transportation companies would be able to pick and choose their clients. They might charge different rates to different customers, disadvantaging upstart competitors. And as with airlines, some less profitable destinations might be unmapped—shippers might decline to serve those locations altogether. Instead of curtailing the ICC, he proposed to create an even more powerful centralized bureaucracy with access to additional taxpayer dollars to subsidize better routes.[45] Nader's approach was fundamentally Jeffersonian, Adams's explicitly Hamiltonian.

In this case, the Jeffersonians would win. Under Carter's watch, the ICC eased up on its restrictions, enlarging the zones within which new carriers could operate without having to seek federal approval, and opening the market up to new competition. In the last year of Carter's presidency,

Congress passed the Motor Carrier Act of 1980, sanding down what remained of the trucking industry's antitrust exemption, and thereby preventing trucking companies from coordinating their rates.[46] But here, as in so many other realms, the progressive movement remained on a knife's edge, even if the ideological combatants were mostly unaware that each similar battle was part of a broader struggle. That tension between the Hamiltonian and Jeffersonian approaches was perhaps most potently apparent in what may well have been the most defining issue of Carter's presidency: oil.

The oil crisis had been born from OPEC's decision to raise oil prices by constricting supply. The ensuing debate in Washington centered on whether government was, in fact, responsible for creating the crisis, and how it might divine a way out. Those embracing a most Hamiltonian ilk, led by Secretary of Energy James Schlesinger, wanted to use centralized regulation to drive down consumption. To impose a national building code requiring more heat efficiency. To prohibit banks from writing mortgages for homes that lacked proper insulation. To provide tax incentives for fuel-efficient cars, even if that advantaged Japanese imports. But many on Carter's White House staff argued not for centralizing to reduce demand for oil, but for granting more authority to oil companies to drill.[47] They were steeped in the notion that the government's scheme to insulate the domestic energy sector, now nearly two decades old, had backfired.[48]

Carter's decision ultimately to take Schlesinger's side in a variety of intra-administration fights burnished a sense that the president was not, deep down, the reformer many wanted him to be—he was less the master of progressivism's two competing impulses than a fickle mistress. He *wanted* to deregulate, and he embraced efforts to let cable companies, railroads, and even banks get out from under what he deemed as the heavy hand of government meddling, claiming just a few weeks before being trounced by Ronald Reagan in the 1980 election that "we have secured the most fundamental restructuring of the relationship between industry and government since the time of the New Deal."[49] But deep down he was just like the progressives of old. A *Saturday Night Live* sketch of him absurdly micromanaging the federal bureaucracy drew on his instinct to pull power up and in.[50]

Carter was not alone in his ideological purgatory, but his agenda ended up being more a jumble than a thoughtful balance. He installed inspectors general in every government department and charged them with snuffing out waste, fraud, and abuse. He signed what some called a hair-trigger special prosecutor law, ensuring that any government malfeasance would be investigated by figures sufficiently independent to speak truth to power.[51] And even while promising to thwart the "imperial presidency" by pushing decision-making power back down to the agencies, he created a new unit within the White House, the Regulatory Analysis Review Group, which was tasked with analyzing any new regulation that would impose costs of $100 million or more.[52] In some cases, power flowed up; in others, down. But in nearly all instances, the effect served to limit the bureaucracy's freedom of action. Checks upon checks to ensure public servants were compelled to serve the public.

The logic of Carter's agenda was born to some degree from the circumstances of his election—the first president elected in Nixon's wake. Few doubted that his intentions were good, or even that, in his mind, new checks on government were a prerequisite to augmenting public power. As his domestic policy advisor, Stuart Eizenstat explained in a speech at the National Press Club: "If we are to build on the record of the New Deal and the Great Society, and if we are to continue to have a constituency for social programs in this country, we are going to have to convince the American people that those social programs are going to be administered in a fair and efficient way, with a minimum of red tape and an absence of fraud and abuse."[53]

But that just illustrated the degree to which his approach was a bundle of contradictions. He wanted to pare back the regulatory burden even while demanding that the regulatory bureaucracy accomplish more. He wanted to empower the agencies' professionals but hem them in at the same time. He wanted to sic independent watchdogs on centralized institutions even while centralizing oversight over various independent nodes of authority.

No matter how those inheriting this mess of directives might have reacted, one thing was clear in the end: progressivism was undermining itself.

THE OSSIFICATION OF GOVERNMENT

It's at this moment in the broader American political narrative that Ronald Reagan takes center stage. Beginning in 1981, the Reagan administration set Carter's conflicted efforts to check public authority aside, vowing instead to chisel away at the power of government with near-reckless abandon. But if Reagan's no-holds-barred attitude appeared a hallmark of conservatism, his animus might well have been born from the spirit that had animated the New Left. Conservatism's veneer was distinct and, for progressives, utterly abhorrent. But in ways few seemed to register, Reagan's agenda reflected progressivism's desire to manacle the octopus. Conservatives wanted to slash government; Jeffersonian progressives had wanted to check it. And now, unhampered by the Hamiltonian tradition that had countervailed against Carter's deregulatory agenda, Reagan and his allies gleefully looked to take a scythe to the administrative state.

There were limits to the damage they could do single-handedly. Even before Franklin Roosevelt's tenure in the White House, presidents had frequently availed themselves of what was popularly known as "reorganization authority," namely the power to move bureaucracies around within the executive branch, much as a corporate CEO might have a free hand to merge or separate a company's communications and marketing departments.[54] Between 1932 and 1984, presidents had used this authority more than one hundred times, making everything from small revisions to massive changes. Reorganization authority was used to create the Department of Health, Education, and Welfare in 1953, the EPA in 1970, and the independent Federal Emergency Management Agency in 1979. The process was simple and expeditious: the president would propose a change, and absent a veto from either house of Congress, his proposal would take hold.

In the 1960s, Congress began clawing back that authority in bits and pieces. Rather than providing a blanket grant of power, Lyndon Johnson was prohibited from proposing new departments. Carter was precluded from proposing to *eliminate* cabinet-level departments. Reagan was robbed early on of the ability to eliminate even agencies or subcabinet departments. And finally, in 1984, Congress allowed reorganization authority to expire in its entirety. By some measure, stealing that power from Reagan's White House appeared like a victory for progressivism—a president with a seemingly insatiable desire to slash government down was now hampered, at least through this particular mechanism. But government was simultaneously made more brittle, implacable, unresponsive, and impermeable. And while subsequent presidents of both parties would ask for reorganization authority back, Congress refused to relent.[55]

Amid a deluge of concern in recent decades about the specter of an "imperial presidency," the legislative branch's decision to withhold authority from the Oval Office appears an exception to the rule. But in other realms—and, in particular, for those figures the president appoints to make regulatory decisions in various agencies of the executive branch— decision-making latitude has been put under continuous and sustained assault.[56] The guardrails did not all come from one place, but the blows to centralized authority, thrust from Reaganite conservative and Jeffersonian progressive corners alike, fundamentally changed the experience of public service. Through the 1970s and 1980s, whatever reverence the public had once had for the grizzled, patronizing, purportedly disinterested wisdom of the old Establishment was extinguished. And if Americans had already grown increasingly wary of centralized power, rigidifying government ensured that bureaucracy would maintain its bad name.

The shift was tied to a change in the sorts of regulations Washington was choosing to pursue. By the 1970s, the regime of *economic* regulations that had prevailed in previous decades—the notion that august federal bureaucrats at the CAB should get to choose which routes airlines maintained—was largely out of vogue. Instead, Washington had begun engaging more in what some called *social* regulation—environmental, consumer-focused, and workplace safety–oriented requirements that were designed less to regularize the rhythms of free enterprise and more to sand down capitalism's excesses. Economic regulation had been targeted and acute in most cases—with bureaucracies like the CAB focused exclusively on one industry. Social regulation, by contrast, touched a much wider swath of the population—every company with a warehouse, for example. In many cases, members of the public who had never dealt much with federal bureaucracy were now inundated.[57] And the reaction was often swift.

The result was a strange amalgam—the country was deluged with *new* regulations even as it was awaking to the oppression of the *old* regime. Now, however, a whole infrastructure was available to those who wanted to push back. The Administrative Procedure Act had guaranteed those affected by regulations an opportunity to participate in the rulemaking process. A whole cottage industry of lawyers, some representing individual clients and others representing the "public interest," had emerged to government-proof the bureaucracy. And the judiciary, now more sympathetic to those scrutinizing the bureaucracy, had not only imposed new procedural hurdles and substantive standards, but had expanded "standing" to give many more Americans a seat at the decision-making table.[58]

The effect was to put bureaucracy in a straitjacket. Where it had once been easy for the CAB to tell a new airline that it could *not* begin flying between New York and Los Angeles—bureaucrats could quickly dispatch the complaints of the upstart company looking to disrupt the system—the Occupational Safety and Health Administration's regulations were vulnerable to the objections raised by the legions of companies happy to finance waves of opposition. In 1978, the Supreme Court issued a ruling significantly curtailing many of the *procedural* hurdles lower courts had imposed on administrative agencies. But the case *Vermont Yankee Nuclear Power Corp. v. NRDC* established in clear terms that courts were well within their right to judge the merits of an agency's decisions—that judges could apply what some called a "hard look" to whatever it was the purported experts had decided.[59]

As Robert Caro had illustrated so convincingly in *The Power Broker*, Robert Moses's influence in New York was drawn from his nearly unimpeachable authority—under the old Hamiltonian regime, his discretion was often impervious to criticism. He could bulldoze the opposition, literally and figuratively. And while not exactly the same, that imperious form of government authority had reflected a certain model of decision-making in public life: officials who made decisions about welfare cases, or agricultural adjustments, or infrastructure improvements, were empowered to throw their weight around. But now, those officials were subject to such a wide array of checks and balances—so many people and institutions had some level of purchase over their authority—that they appeared more like functionaries than power brokers. The tables had turned.

No single change had prompted the shift, but waves of reform had turned the underlying dynamic upside down. Make a wrong step—make any step at all—and onetime decision-makers were sure to find themselves vulnerable to incoming fire. From public-interest lawyers believing the underlying decision benefited a private interest rather than the greater good. From small businesses fearful the mandates would shave down their margins. From members of Congress angry that they weren't consulted. Even from White House overseers determined to ensure that purportedly independent agencies were aligned with the president's agenda and interests. And it wasn't just that these various figures could rail against a decision-maker's plans in the press or in the comments submitted through a rulemaking process. If they didn't get what they wanted, there was no barring the courthouse door.[60]

Federal courts had received little more than seven hundred appeals from administrative agency decisions in 1960; by 1983, that figure had grown to more than three thousand. Circuit courts had received fewer than fifteen hundred appeals in 1969; by 1983, the figure had risen to nearly five thousand.[61] And while this monumental change didn't mark the end of planning per se, it shifted much of the power once held by executive branch officials into the hands of the judiciary. The eminent legal scholar Richard Stewart termed the new dynamic "central planning through litigation."[62] And while this change had the veneer of enhanced public accountability, it was actually more opaque, by some turns, than the norms during the Moses era. Certainly it could not have felt to the ordinary citizen as though government was more accessible, or understandable, or responsive. Who ultimately made the decisions? Who really wielded control? Now, there was no Moses-type figure to rail against. Power had been diffused. If anything, the process had become more Kafkaesque.[63]

The effects of this shift were often hidden from the public—or, at least, the impacts were too diffuse to discern the breadth of the pattern. But they were legion. The Civil Rights Act of 1964, for example, had created an Office of Civil Rights (OCR) within the Department of Health, Education, and Welfare to push for more integration throughout the nation's schools—a mission that the small office's young and mission-driven lawyers took up with vigor. So when, a few years later, the Nixon administration made a political point of coming out *against* elements of progressivism's civil rights agenda, essentially directing HEW's Office of Civil Rights to stand down—the NAACP sued and received a court order requiring the OCR to continue assisting local efforts in North Carolina to integrate public institutions, colleges, and universities. The court decision created an odd sort of schism within the executive branch: despite the White House's opposition to the underlying policy, this one little cohort of lawyers housed within a Nixon-led federal bureaucracy was suing some of the same (often southern) school officials whose prejudice had led them to support Nixon's election.

When, in 1977, President Carter appointed the liberal firebrand Joe Califano as HEW secretary, the new secretary discovered that 80 percent of the Office of Civil Rights's work fell under the mandate of that nearly decade-old court order. Califano wanted to change the unit's focus, and other beleaguered groups—women and Latinos, among others—began to complain that too much of the OCR's attention was being paid to this long-running dispute even while other civil rights abuses festered. But the federal judge overseeing the case refused to rescind the original court order. More than that, he felt it within his purview to micromanage the office's activities, asking HEW's lawyers, at one point, to "describe the vigor" with which Califano was asking the White House for more personnel slots.[64] It was a remarkable tug-of-war, with this little office inside a behemoth federal bureaucracy subject to conflicting demands from the White House, from their nominal boss in the secretary's office, and from a federal judge who, from most angles, appeared entirely outside the chain of command.

Set aside the underlying merits of the cause, and perhaps the Carter administration *should* have made the North Carolina dispute its top priority, despite Califano's desire to focus elsewhere. The subject at issue was one of managerial control. It had originally made *political* sense, from a progressive point of view, to keep Richard Nixon's devious little fingers off this precious bureaucratic creation of the movement's great achievement—the Civil Rights Act. But the precedent set during Nixon's tenure now applied in Carter's. Was it good for reformers to strip the secretary of Health, Education, and Welfare of the power to set his own bureaucracy's priorities—particularly when the secretary was as liberal as Joe Califano? The federal judge overseeing this single case had essentially become the agency's puppeteer.[65]

If this whole conflagration was befuddling to the public, it was demoralizing for those inside the bureaucracy itself. Less than two decades removed from President Kennedy's call for Americans to "ask not what your country can do for you—ask what you can do for your country," public service now appeared more like an invitation to endless frustration. Legions of young progressives had joined the ranks of government—taken civil service exams, accepted more modest salaries than those on offer in the private sector—to pursue the dream of making a lasting impact as federal bureaucrats. To help in building glorious new public works, or protecting the environment, or propelling poor families to climb the economic ladder. But what some came to term "the ossification of rulemaking"—a notion that no one had the power to push through unpopular decisions that would, in the end, deliver a public good—reflected a broader diffusion of power.[66] Government had become increasingly hamstrung. And the resulting morass turned idealism into futility.

When Harry Truman signed the Administrative Procedure Act into law in 1946, most would have laughed off any prediction that Moses-like figures would be reduced a few decades later to glorified clerks. Government authority was simply too ascendant. If anything, the APA had seemed like a modest effort to ensure that imperious bureaucrats applied their power in a consistent, fair, and, to some degree, transparent way. By the 1980s, however, the worm had turned. It wasn't just that bureaucratic discretion was more limited. It was that the APA's requirement and the subsequent jurisprudence requiring decision-makers to apply the correct standard to each decision had effectively turned once powerful civil servants into pencil pushers.[67]

Amid all the public frustration, the image of bureaucracy shifted even more bleakly to give the impression that a sinecured workforce enjoying guaranteed retirement benefits simply did not care to do their jobs well. This pattern was repeated across the government, but perhaps no place was it more pronounced than at the Environmental Protection Agency. Conceived during the Nixon years, the EPA had originally been given a wide berth to make rules, issue sanctions, and even police other government bureaucracies. But as was the legislature's wont, Congress imposed new mandates on the agency.[68] During that same period, the White House tightened its grip on agency decision-making, often through standards and regulations designed to ensure the agency's bureaucrats weren't captured by polluters.[69] And of course those same polluters, along with their Naderite adversaries, were rarely bashful about drawing on the courts to require the EPA to steer policy in one direction or, often enough, entirely in another.

The picture that emerges of the agency through the 1980s is one of a bureaucracy under constant siege, unable in most cases to meet demands coming at it from all sides.[70] Between two-thirds and three-quarters of

EPA-proposed rules were revised by the White House before being issued in 1985, 1986, and 1987, with the Office of Management and Budget typically overriding the administrative state's proposals when the two were in conflict. William Reilly, administrator of the EPA under President George H. W. Bush, testified that in the less than two decades of the EPA's existence before 1989, Congress and the courts had imposed eight hundred separate deadlines—and the EPA had only met 14 percent of them. And while that appeared at first an indictment of the EPA, it also reflected another reality: more than four in every five of the EPA's major rules were challenged in court.[71]

The whole tenor of public life changed within the bureaucracy. Small missteps, tiny deviations from the legislated standards, any slight against a prescribed process for weighing some combination of concerns was likely to lead to a delay or denial.[72] Buffeted by demands from their congressional overseers, from their White House bosses, from various judicial diktats, bureaucrats had little choice but to hunker down, anticipate incoming fire, and deflect blows as best they could. One study completed in the 1980s suggested that policymakers at the National Highway Traffic Safety Administration had essentially given up on rulemaking altogether, choosing through recalls to react against bad vehicles instead of demanding that carmakers affirmatively improve designs through regulation.[73]

Few Americans would have believed, immediately after robust public authority had pulled the nation out from the depths of the Great Depression, remade the Upper South, and built the highway system, that, as Reagan liked to joke, government would eventually be capable of messing up a two-car parade. But by the 1980s, that was conventional wisdom. Even if conservatives were purposefully throwing wrenches in the works—and they were—culpability fell in no small measure at the feet of well-intentioned reformers. Progressives had set traps for themselves, and were then enraged to find that government had fallen in. At best, bureaucrats were seen as indifferent to the public good—at worst, they personified the irritating nuisance portrayed by the EPA's Walter Peck in 1984's *Ghostbusters*. And that was the real shame of it. The original impetus for the reforms born in the spirit of the APA—to make the bureaucracy *more* responsive to the public interest—had been turned on its head. Steeped in its cultural aversion to power, progressivism was failing itself.[74]

THE UNFILLED POTENTIAL OF VOICE

By the mid-1980s, the specter of Robert Moses's bureaucratic imperialism buffeted the movement at one extreme, and the scourge of procedural morass was consuming the promise of reform at the other. Nevertheless, even as frustration metastasized, few progressives were prepared to consider how they might put the movement's two impulses in harmony. The cultural aversion to power was simply too consuming, the desire to whack at the Establishment too fundamental. Faced with the outrageous and absurd tropes of Reaganism, reformers endeavored to keep hacking, and Reagan provided no shortage of fodder.[75] Early in his administration, he proposed to slash funding for school lunches; then, to obviate the government's obligation to serve children nutritious lunches, the Food and Nutrition Service reclassified ketchup as a vegetable.[76] In the face of such clear incompetence, what progressive would ever even consider *re*-empowering federal agencies? Reagan was proving the New Left's now-two-decade-old point: American bureaucracy was bad.

Trapped unwittingly between conservatism's vilification of government and their own skepticism of the Establishment, progressives alighted on what felt like a safe riposte to Reagan's excesses: open the government to more outside scrutiny. Force disclosure of what was being discussed along the corridors of power.[77] *Voice* would be the magic bullet. With truth-to-power reforms, public authorities wouldn't build a highway through neighborhoods without giving residents an opportunity to weigh in. Pollutant-emitting power plants wouldn't be constructed without locals having a chance to object. Developers wouldn't be permitted to build new housing without giving the neighbors a venue to register their concerns.

Girding this new truth-laden progressive tentpole was an unspoken presumption that if everyone was simply able to voice their objection—and if those in positions of power were made to incorporate those concerns into their planning—only worthwhile initiatives would move forward.[78] We wouldn't have all these problems, reformers told themselves, if we just made democracy more authentically democratic. You wouldn't *need* a Robert Moses–type Establishment figure to champion the public interest if you let members of the public champion their interests on their own. That ethos had girded progressive thinking when a Democratic Congress passed, and President Nixon eventually signed, the National Environmental Policy Act.

At the time, legislators had wanted to force bureaucrats to consider all the potential impacts of any given decision. And in their conception, once all the potential concerns were on the table, the people in charge would presumably craft solutions that addressed community concerns. They would steer the highway around the town green, rather than through. They would require "scrubbers" atop polluting smokestacks, rather than let the toxic air permeate the surrounding area. They would restrict new housing construction so that it would not impact those already living in the neighborhood.[79] Progressives now wanted to apply that approach across the whole of the policymaking landscape. If government had gone wrong, progressives told themselves, it was because ordinary people hadn't been able to get a word in edgewise. Fix *that* element, and things could be steered right. For that reason, voice became a kind of sine qua non for many in the movement.

What progressives rarely acknowledged in this turn—what they still struggle to accept today—is that voice is not in and of itself a strategy for weighing the trade-offs born in public policy. It's not sufficient simply to engage a community worried about getting bulldozed by a highway project, or devalued by a proposed homeless shelter, or skunked up by the rank smells coming from a new factory nearby. Few of those directly affected will be inclined to be more accommodating simply because they've been consulted, or given more time to object, or provided a platform to voice their opinion earlier in the process.[80]

Which is not to say that those communities hadn't been shorted adequate notice during the Moses era. Wily figures had undoubtedly managed to shroud their intentions in order to avoid public scrutiny. But no one is ever going to divine a forum where, simply by dint of everyone articulating their concerns, a controversial proposal elicits universal support. The residents of the South Bronx would have been unlikely to support the Cross Bronx Expressway even if Moses had been willing to negotiate the route. And that was (and is) the problem: at its most benign, participation is ineffective; but if given real teeth, it holds the potential to render government incapable of making hard choices.

This is a crucial but nuanced point. Giving communities voice isn't bad per se—those affected by public policy *should* have an opportunity to participate, to voice their concerns, to have their interests taken seriously. But from complaining that the bureaucrats hadn't *listened* emerged a means of wishing away the quandaries Establishment figures had once resolved through their discretion. A new highway will inevitably be a benefit to some and a burden to others—but is the net result a win? A proposed new regulation might protect some consumers but undermine an industry and its workforce—do the benefits outweigh the costs? A new development will change the character of the neighborhood—but where else will the people who would have moved there be able to live?

It was, and is, easy to argue that the downsides of any given decision could have been avoided if everyone affected had been given sufficient *voice*. But the reality was, and is, that progress involves ratifying trade-offs that distribute burdens across communities, fair and unfair. And so a progressive agenda centered in almost every context on providing ordinary citizens with new tools to thwart that centralized authority—opportunities to use their voice to lobby an official, to file a lawsuit, to register a complaint—too frequently fails to answer a crucial question: Who, after everyone has spoken, should make the final choice?

Perhaps the most pointed and extreme example of this impulse is a once popular if obscure regulatory tool known as negotiated rulemaking, or NegReg for short. NegReg was conjured decades ago to short-circuit the intense and overly adversarial notice-and-rulemaking process laid out earlier in the Administrative Procedure Act. Rather than simply impose rules on industries sure to take umbrage, NegReg created a formal structure where regulators and those they regulated sat down together and collaborated in crafting mutually agreeable regulations. Then, once the two sides agreed, their negotiated rule could be put through the ordinary pace of notice and comment, but with the presumption that everyone would wave through what was a consensus-driven bargain.

Used only sporadically during the 1980s, NegReg was authorized for more general use in the early 1990s and, with very little public notice, woven into the jurisprudence created by the Administrative Procedure Act in 1996. Many insiders were thrilled, believing that the new process was well suited to reduce the adversarial tenor of environmental regulation in particular. If EPA bureaucrats were brought to appreciate an industry's concerns *earlier in the process*, and if factory executives could be made aware of how their facilities spoiled nature *before* being subject to onerous demands, perhaps the two would be able to come to some mutual accommodation.

In one instance, NegReg was deployed to rework the regulatory regime applied to the thousands of iron and steel facilities scattered throughout the nation's rust belt. Federal regulators and industry executives, among others, were asked to hammer out some mutually agreeable framework. But despite meeting more than a hundred times over four years, the negotiators were able to consummate only a handful of marginal improvements: a proposal to create a website listing best practices; a promise to organize a workshop on the disposal of the "pickle liquor" produced when cleaning steel; and a small tweak to furnace pressure standards. And that was typical of NegReg more generally: in case after case, venue after venue, the process left negotiators at loggerheads on major topics of disagreement.

The underlying reason was obvious: environmental advocates and industry representatives weren't at odds because they'd failed to see the wisdom of the other's perspective; they were stuck because they had fundamentally different interests. No matter how deeply they listened to the other side, neither party was interested in cutting a deal. Moreover, nothing prevented parties who *did* participate in a NegReg process from subsequently throwing up additional hurdles—commenting on proposals, lobbying Congress, litigating the outcome—to upend a consensus they'd previously agreed to support.[81]

NegReg wasn't born of malice, even if many progressive reformers eventually deemed it a failed experiment.[82] It was simply an extreme manifestation of the movement's Jeffersonian impulse gone awry. The dream—or, perhaps more accurately stated, the fantasy—was that giving everyone voice would ensure an optimal solution. But in too many cases, there is no way to serve the greater good without exacting some cost on at least someone. Mitigating ecological damage is expensive—and those costs will be passed on to some producers, and potentially to some consumers. Giving everyone a seat at the table doesn't by any stretch guarantee a mutually agreeable fix. But, as we've seen, giving anyone at the table a veto almost ensures that nothing will be accomplished. Yet that's what happened.

Voice has become a lightly shrouded proxy for gridlock. It has become the slight leverage opponents need to stop the Establishment, or anyone else, from doing anything they find objectionable.[83] That was, of course, a welcome development when government initiatives were clearly cutting against the public interest. In the wake of decades during which the Establishment could impose its will with impunity, and the powerless needed new weaponry, voice appeared a reasonable salve. But when voice turned to veto, and the choices were more muddled, the new regime made progress more complex, difficult, arduous, and tendentious to get things done.[84] And that was, in the end, for one reason: rarely was anyone empowered to render a final decision.

During the era of Robert Moses, Lyndon Johnson, Richard Nixon, Richard Daley, Bull Connor, and the other imperious men of mid-twentieth-century America, it had been too easy for government power to be wielded *against* the public interest. Captured bureaucrats and self-dealing experts had been able to mold policy to their liking, almost no matter the outcry. Now, by contrast, regulatory authority is so diffused that nearly anyone can upend even the most well-intentioned effort to do good. The protections, reforms, rights, and processes have combined, in too many cases, to make government incompetent. And progressives, once the Establishment's biggest boosters and now among its primary antagonists, have played a pivotal role in creating the mess that emerged in its stead.[85] The Jeffersonian impulse has prevailed.

For reformers, neither extreme in this is good, or even acceptable—neither the one where bureaucracies can impose their will with impunity, nor the alternative where public officials have been made feckless in the face of a vetocracy run amok. But the deeper shame is that progressivism has yet to grapple intellectually with the implications. Government, in the end, needs to be able to make decisions that impose costs—and, in many cases, it needs to be able to do so with some degree of alacrity. No one should be denied an opportunity to voice their opinion on a question that affects them in general or in specific. But neither should voice give any figure the ability to hijack the decision-making process altogether. Government needs the ability to render difficult judgments even when they impose costs or remain unpopular.[86] If, by contrast, public institutions appear like mazes of dysfunction, progressivism is bound to lose.

6

No Place to Call Home

PROLOGUE: MORE THAN JUST A STATUE

When aides called to share the bad news, New York's governor Nelson Rockefeller was en route home from Reverend Martin Luther King's funeral in Atlanta. It was 1968, and just weeks earlier the presidentially appointed Kerner Commission had released a damning report blaming systemic racism for the fury pouring out of the nation's Black neighborhoods.[1] Rockefeller was sympathetic to complaints that government had played a powerful role in undermining those living in what many then called "the ghetto"—that same year he would push Robert Moses, one of the figures most responsible for decimating many of the city's minority neighborhoods, off of his last powerful perch. In the early days, the governor had figured that King's assassination would spur lawmakers at long last to solve the state's housing crisis.[2] Now, over the phone, he was learning that his supposition had been wrong. And beyond being disappointed, he was angry.

Rockefeller's proposed salve centered on creating a centralized bureaucracy, a national Urban Development Corporation (UDC), to correct for the scars Moses had left during his long tenure as New York's most powerful man. Following the Second World War, Congress had appropriated vast sums for "urban renewal," a program designed to fund state and local efforts to demolish run-down neighborhoods and erect modern new buildings with a bounty of additional housing in their stead. But "slum clearance," as the policy was more popularly known, had been particularly devastating in New York. Having wrested control of the program, Moses used it in many cases not to target slumlord buildings, but rather to clear whole blocks for redevelopment. Unfortunately, the empty lots had been less enticing than Moses presumed—developers thought it better to invest their resources in building out the suburbs. As a result, New York City had been left for decades with festering blocks of rubble.

By healing those scars on the urban landscape, UDC would be, in Rockefeller's imagination, "a monument to King that's more than just a statue."[3] If the private sector wasn't going to address New York's housing crisis, the state of New York would. But lawmakers in Albany were skeptical. By the late 1960s, progressives had already begun questioning the wisdom of empowering imperial figures to condemn property and construct buildings with impunity—hadn't that been Moses's strategy? And many conservatives didn't like the precedent: if the UDC was authorized to usurp local control over new housing projects in the big cities—to override zoning and ignore local building codes—the new bureaucracy seemed likely to drive projects that would invite urban (read: Black) residents into prosperous, lily-white bedroom communities, not to mention towns and villages farther out.

Rockefeller had proposed the UDC before King's assassination, but the legislature had refused to bite. Now, amid the threat of rioting, he urged the Assembly and Senate to give the idea a second look—and he wasn't beyond bargaining. Realizing that the legislators who had objected earlier might need an extra inducement to green-light the new agency, he sweetened the pot for the Senate's Republican leader, Earl Brydges, by agreeing to support a proposal to build a new international airport in Buffalo. But in the state legislature's lower house, Rockefeller's charm offensive fell short. So, when the governor's aides reached him in Atlanta to relay news that the Assembly had balked, the governor directed them to employ a different tactic—coercion.[4] And what happened in the hours that followed marks what likely represents one of the most brazen exercises of political power in the state's history.

The threats were both personal and pointed. Bob Douglass, Rockefeller's legendary chief aide, purportedly told one dissenting Republican from Rockland County: "If you don't change your vote, you'll wake up one morning to find the runway of Stewart Air Force Base extended right through your goddam house."[5] Still no luck. Finally, the governor resorted to a tactic that amounted to a legal bribe: in return for them supporting the UDC, Rockefeller agreed to what some would later call the "rip-off legislative pension plan," namely a guarantee of 50 percent pay to legislators upon retirement after a mere twenty years of service.[6] With that new feather bed, members of the Assembly relented. Hours after rejecting the proposal, they voted 86–45 in its favor.[7] Rockefeller, a Hamiltonian through and through, now controlled a bureaucracy that boasted many of the powers the TVA still wielded in the Upper South. And New York's governor, imagining himself walking in Franklin Roosevelt's footsteps, believed that the UDC might eventually punch his ticket to the White House.

In the early days, few understood quite how much power the UDC would claim. Beyond the ability to override local zoning, Rockefeller also outfitted the new bureaucracy with a relatively novel way of financing project construction. Rather than back the UDC's debt with the state's "full faith and credit," a privilege limited by the state's constitution, he proposed that the new agency issue so-called moral obligation bonds, debt that *suggested* Albany would make good on any financial shortfall without providing any legally binding commitment.[8] To lead the agency, he selected Ed Logue, a planner who had, by reputation, worked wonders in New Haven and Boston.[9] Logue, Rockefeller imagined, would be a good guy's Robert Moses—a figure who, far from pursuing his own imperious ends, would use centralized power to build housing in the public interest.

Logue got right to work. Quickly tapping Moses's standard trick—namely breaking ground on projects such that they would be nearly impossible to cancel—he green-lit in short order eight projects in Manhattan, eleven in Brooklyn, ten in Rochester, and three in Buffalo. This zeal came at the cost of financial due diligence. Eager to deliver results, Logue largely looked past the issue that preoccupies most private-sector developers—namely concerns over whether the rent paid by future tenants (and any associated subsidies) would cover the debt. What appeared a quibble to Logue had, of course, scared off many a private developer. But with Rockefeller's backing, the UDC's financial viability was a mere detail, a distraction. Logue, and perhaps a future President Rockefeller, would cross those bridges—solve those problems—down the road.

Whatever anyone thought of Logue, he was a force of nature—a bulldog, not entirely unlike Moses. The UDC proposed, for example, to erect housing on the East River's Roosevelt Island, a sliver of land long used as a sort of colony for societal outcasts. Logue's intention was to erect buildings for low-income residents first, subsequently building middle-class housing that could subsidize their rent. Adam Walinsky, one of Robert Kennedy's former speechwriters and the Democratic nominee for state attorney general in 1970, objected to the sequencing, arguing that the deluge of poorer residents would scare off any prospective middle-class tenants. But Logue, betraying a tendency to treat his detractors much as Moses had when wielding much the same power, turned a deaf ear. "Fuck it," he told one aide. "I'm going to do that anyway."[10]

And the UDC's ambitions weren't limited to Rockefeller's desire to correct for urban renewal. In his pursuit of social justice, Logue began pushing the state's wealthier, whiter residents—many of whom had fled New York City during the postwar years for the leafy suburbs—to permit new suburban housing for outsiders. After warning the governor that "shit might hit the fan," he unveiled what he termed a Fair Share Housing plan to build nine hundred affordable units spread between nine of suburban Westchester County's most well-to-do communities.[11] Predictably, local residents were enraged—flabbergasted that a Republican governor they had supported was now proposing to pierce their suburban bubbles. Logue himself was subject to death threats. When thousands of people showed up to protest at a town hall meeting, he required a police escort. Only when it became clear that the opposition was imperiling Rockefeller's political base did the governor lean on Logue to stand down—which he did.

What happened next remains a Rashomon even decades later. Logue and his progressive supporters would claim that political opposition to his utopian vision emerged to check his ambition—that he'd awakened too fierce an opposition by threatening to build new housing in the state's white suburban communities. But others pointed to a different culprit, namely the way Logue had approached what some call "project financing." The projects he'd green-lit had been financed by private banks— Wall Street had lent the UDC the money to pay for construction. The loans had been predicated on the assumption that various federal subsidies would help the UDC cover the payments due to the banks. Unfortunately for Logue, the Nixon administration had begun slashing those subsidies. Cash-poor, the UDC began struggling to pay its bills.

The UDC was hardly alone in this predicament—but it was nevertheless at the vanguard. Logue, like many other Establishment figures running arms of the state government at the time, had set any short- and medium-term concerns aside, confident that Rockefeller would tide over any shortfalls with cash infusions from the state's general fund. After President Nixon's resignation, however, when Gerald Ford elevated Rockefeller to the vice presidency, Logue was left hanging.[12] And when the UDC's tenuous financial situation was suddenly exposed, many of Logue's lenders were quick to worry that the UDC was poised to default.

By the point in early 1975 when Democratic representative Hugh Carey was sworn in as New York's next elected governor, the UDC and New York were more universally in a world of financial hurt. By then, Robert Caro's *The Power Broker* had become a sensation, entirely upending whatever faith remained in the Moses, Rockefeller, and Logue approach to governing from on high. Speaking almost directly to the notion that centralized authority was equipped to save the UDC, let alone the state as a whole, the new governor announced in his inaugural address that "the days of wine and roses are over." Few understood exactly what he meant; but soon it became clear, at least as it pertained to Logue's empire: entering office, Carey discovered that the UDC was spending $1 million every day to cover the costs of ongoing construction, but had a mere $10 million in the bank.[13]

Moral obligation bonds, federal subsidies, and the Rockefeller administration's largess had long nurtured confidence among bankers that lending to Logue was a safe bet. Now, bank executives began hinting that they intended to demand immediate repayment of their loans, for fear that the UDC would go bankrupt. So long as Nelson Rockefeller had been governor, few thought Wall Street had any reason to worry, if only because Chase Manhattan Bank was run by his brother David, and Nelson would swoop in if necessary. But now that Nelson was in Washington, David's banking colleagues began to panic because what those suddenly furiously studying New York's fiscal situation quickly realized was that the financial rot wasn't limited to the UDC—it was seemingly everywhere.

In 1974, New York State maintained a phalanx of 230 separate public authorities, each operating on its own charter. Many of these bureaucracies, each a manifestation of the Establishment, had been created to build and maintain massive public works: a housing project, a dam, a highway, a train network. Many issued debt and then serviced that debt with various revenue streams: rents, tolls, fares. They had, for decades, been praised for the virtue of being "apolitical"—for pursuing the public interest without fear or favor.[14] But now, with the UDC under strain, lenders began to worry more generally that the state would not, in the end, keep private-sector lenders whole. Perhaps New York State was itself a financial house of cards. And that tipped off what became a cascading fiscal crisis.

The new governor's thirty-four-year-old budget director, Peter Goldmark, was not initially aware of how pervasive the problem really was. Sitting in his new office on the second floor of the state capitol, he began receiving, on a frighteningly regular basis, desperate calls from various cities, counties, agencies, and commissions living beyond their means, each having presumed that the Rockefeller administration would bail them out if push came to shove. And quickly Goldmark realized that the state itself might soon become insolvent. So he took to calling off whichever major investments the state could cancel. He mothballed tunneling for what would become, decades later, the Second Avenue Subway. He shut down plans to build a dental school on Long Island. Not knowing where the next hit might come from, he cut back on what often appeared to be worthwhile public investments.[15]

Eventually, Goldmark concluded that Carey would need to do more than trim the fat. Between 1962 and 1974, when the GOP had controlled state government, public authority debt had grown from $129 million to $12 billion. Albany's fiscal obligations so far outstripped revenue projections that the state would either have to raise more revenue (read: raise taxes) or the state's lenders would have to "take a haircut"—that is, banks would have to agree to accept less back on the loans they'd made to bureaucracies like the UDC. That presented a big problem: the state of New York was suddenly at odds with many of the big banks that were headquartered in Manhattan. And much as they had long profited from the "moral obligation" bonds they had financed for figures like Ed Logue, New York's banking elite, including Rockefeller's brother, worried about the "moral hazard" of letting even one bureaucracy off the hook. That now put them at odds with the new governor.

In February 1975, Richard Ravitch, a young real estate scion whom
Carey had installed to replace Logue at the UDC, paid a visit to National City Bank (later Citigroup) CEO Walter Wriston at the financial
behemoth's offices overlooking Park Avenue. Ravitch carefully laid out
the state's perspective on the crisis: put simply, the UDC didn't have the
cash to honor the payments due the banks in the coming weeks. Albany
would be willing to pay the banks what they were owed, but only if the
banks agreed beforehand to lend additional money to the UDC immediately thereafter. Wriston listened quietly, asked for a moment to confer
with one of his banking peers, and then turned back to the young state
bureaucrat. "Mr. Ravitch," Wriston said, "pay your debts, and then we'll
talk."[16] Put in starker terms, the imperious older man wasn't going to cut
the state or its taxpayers a break. If the state had gotten out over its skis,
then taxpayers would have to take it on the chin.

Following his meeting with Wriston, Ravitch flew back to Albany and
explained to Carey in dramatic fashion what had transpired: "The banks
of New York have closed their doors to the people of New York."[17] That
put the governor off. Wriston and his colleagues on Wall Street, Carey
figured, had been complicit in letting the UDC get into trouble—they
had happily taken on the risk of lending to fiscally irresponsible public authorities. That being the case, it was now Ravitch and the governor's view
that the banks had an obligation to be flexible. And that set the terms of
a standoff. The banks figured that Carey and Ravitch would fold, fearing
the reputational hit the governor would take presiding over the first major
public bankruptcy since the Great Depression.[18] But Carey knew that the
banks had a lot to lose as well—bankruptcy would leave them to fight
over the state's assets as the broader economy spiraled into recession and
the state struggled to pay teachers, cops, and nurses.[19]

The tension reached a climax almost like in a movie. On Carey's orders, Ravitch ordered the UDC's lawyers to prepare a bankruptcy petition. He then invited the bankers to a Sunday afternoon emergency
meeting in the governor's Midtown Manhattan office. When the bankers

arrived, they found copies of the petition sitting in front of them, ready for filing when the federal courthouse opened the next morning. If it was filed, they understood, they were *sure* not to be paid, and they would be left to divvy up the UDC's remaining assets as meager compensation. It was in that moment that they blinked, agreeing to extend the UDC a new $300 million credit line in exchange for new collateral. And with the immediate crisis averted, attention turned to the reality that the UDC's mess wasn't an anomaly—it was the rule. New York state government was a financial house of cards. In the wake of Watergate, the public was growing suspicious that the problems were born of corruption.[20] And so Governor Carey endeavored to appoint an investigative commission charged with figuring out how things had gone so awry.

To lead the new inquiry, Carey appointed Orville Schell Jr., a well-respected Wall Street attorney, who quickly began receiving applications from young attorneys eager to get on the ground floor of what appeared to be the next Watergate-like investigation.[21] Perhaps they too would have an opportunity to expose the crooks who, like Nixon's allies, had taken advantage of an unsuspecting public. But after months of digging, Schell and his young peers determined that the debacle in New York had *not* been born out of greed or graft. Logue had simply moved too far, too fast. And the appropriate salve, in Schell's view, wasn't to throw anyone in jail; rather, it was to impose a Jeffersonian balance on the state's Hamiltonian bureaucracies. To that end, he recommended that New York establish a new temporary Public Authorities Control Commission, appointed by the governor, and charged with ensuring that agencies like the UDC managed the public's finances responsibly.

The Schell Commission's recommendation was received in Albany with a nod. Given the state's dire financial situation, few could reasonably object to a new layer of oversight. But when the Commission's report was delivered to the legislature, Assembly and Senate leaders insisted on what seemed like a minor change: The new body, which they would rename the Public Authorities Control *Board* (PACB), would *not* be controlled exclusively by the governor. The Assembly speaker and the Senate majority leader would be given the power to veto individually any major new outlay of taxpayer dollars. And that added an odd little wrinkle to the new bureaucracy. Until the PACB expired, the governor and his appointees would no longer be able to pursue projects entirely of their own volition—they would first have to win approval from the state's legislative leadership.

In the early days, the new veto power proved to be a nonissue: Governor Carey had no grand designs on big projects, if only because New York was so hopelessly cash-strapped. Nor did many connect this seemingly innocuous new emblem of Jeffersonian caution, eventually made a permanent fixture, with others being erected throughout the rest of American life. But they were everywhere—and particularly in the realm of housing. In 1976, revisions to New York City's municipal charter awarded community boards new influence over land use decisions that had once more exclusively been the province of City Hall. In 1978, the Supreme Court affirmed the power of the Landmarks Commission to protect private property from an owner's wrecking ball.[22] The lessons born from *The Power Broker*, the abuse made evident by Watergate, the financial tolls imposed by Rockefeller and Logue's grand machinations had proven that the government needed more guardrails. Creating them became the order of the day.

Over the decades that followed, and as New York emerged from the detritus of the fiscal crisis, the PACB remained little more than an afterthought—a bit of red tape to clear near the end of consummating any state-financed project. Indeed, few thought much about it until, in 2004, New York City mayor Michael Bloomberg proposed to construct a new football stadium in Manhattan as part of a bid to host the 2012 Olympics. Fearing the new stadium would steal convention business, members of the Dolan family, who controlled nearby Madison Square Garden, objected, turning to a friend in Albany, Assembly Speaker Sheldon Silver, for help. The Speaker, who would later die while serving a long prison sentence for public corruption, didn't care that the stadium was the lynchpin of New York's Olympic bid. He was perfectly willing to use his PACB veto at the

Dolans' behest. And much to many an observer's surprise—many hadn't heard of the PACB beforehand, let alone been aware of its power—that's just what he did.

During the Moses/Rockefeller/Logue era, centralized power had been nearly unimpeachable—no one could stop a project the Establishment backed even if was a bad idea, or threated to bankrupt the state. But the PACB, erected as a Jeffersonian check on Hamiltonian power, had been turned into a plaything wielded by a corrupt public official. At the end of 2006, for reasons that still remain somewhat mysterious, Silver used the same bureaucratic mechanism to shut down a proposal to renovate Penn Station. Beyond that, the PACB emerged as a tool so powerful that, in some cases, worthwhile projects died before even being vetted. One developer, for example, floated in Albany a proposal to move a state-run community college in lower Manhattan into another state-owned building so as to open up the old campus to residential development. But when it became clear that Silver opposed the project, the developer simply gave up—no need to have it vetoed officially at the PACB.[23]

We may never know how many other projects were stifled for the same reason, or how many times developers abandoned projects for fear that they could never clear the PACB gauntlet. But more than a decade after Silver's veto of the stadium—after he'd been unceremoniously removed from office and tried for corruption—the Jeffersonian excesses of the PACB struck again. After a widely publicized search, Amazon announced in November 2018 its intention to build the company's second headquarters across the East River from Manhattan, promising to site 25,000 jobs with an average $150,000 salary at a new campus in Queens.[24] The company proposed to invest more than $3.6 billion in the new facility and pay more than $27 billion in taxes over the course of the following quarter century. In exchange, Amazon executives asked the state and city to provide $3 billion in incentives and expedite the approvals required to complete the move.[25] For New York, boosters claimed, the project promised a whopping 900 percent return on public investment.

But not everyone was thrilled. Nearby landlords might benefit if Amazon purchased their property at a premium, but what about the New Yorkers who rented apartments in those buildings? Other critics questioned whether Amazon would hire resident New Yorkers or simply import outsiders. A rash of social justice advocates, among others, were ideologically opposed to the public subsidies, whatever the return.[26] But if a small minority of seemingly gadfly complaints presented the veneer of a public debate, almost all of the region's powerbrokers remained enthusiastic. And conventional wisdom, given the overwhelming support for the project, was that whatever demands locals made, their kvetching would never upend the sort of massive investment Amazon promised to make in the city and region.

What cheerleaders did not take into account, however, were the concerns of a single state senator representing parts of northwestern Queens. And as it happened Senator Michael Gianaris was serving then as the state senate president's designee on the PACB. And that meant that he wielded the veto. If Gianaris was hardly a rubber stamp, he hinted that he was inclined to support Amazon's plans if the company made a few additional concessions. But when nearby Representative Alexandria Ocasio-Cortez, newly anointed as one of Congress's most charismatic members, announced her opposition, Gianaris found himself in a tough spot. Exercising the veto might be bad for New York, but failure to put his full weight behind Ocasio-Cortez's opposition would make him a pariah to her supporters.

Had he been less integral to the project's success—one vote among a whole state Senate that would almost surely have supported the deal—he could have railed against Amazon, opposing the project without scuttling the whole thing. As elected officials representing nearby neighborhoods, Gianaris and Ocasio-Cortez were certainly justified in speaking up for their angry constituents. But as a member of the PACB, this single state senator *did* have the power to stop it, and if he failed, he risked Ocasio-Cortez's ire and, with it, the prospect of being reelected. So in the end Gianaris didn't feel as though he had any real choice.[27] In public comments, this single figure representing a small corner of Queens indicated that he was *likely* to exercise the veto. Understanding what that meant, Amazon decided to abandon the project altogether, sending those billions of dollars to an alternative HQ2 site outside Washington, DC.

That completed a remarkable arc. The PACB had been created at a point when the Establishment had disqualified itself—when progressivism's Hamiltonian impulse to concentrate power in the hands of well-intentioned power brokers had clearly gone wrong. Progressivism's yin and yang had come unbalanced, and the movement's Jeffersonian impulse to put checks on the bureaucracy found a new outlet. But several decades later, the movement's burgeoning aversion to power had come to stand in the way of new projects. Whether or not Amazon's proposal was worthwhile, no single state senator should have the authority to scuttle a deal of this magnitude on his own. And yet the PACB's story was not an exception; it was a single manifestation of a broader pattern. In a nation desperate to build, progressivism's imbalance had left the government unable to deliver. And those who suffered most from the resulting paralysis were often the people progressives cared most to serve.

GROWTH AND RENEWAL

Housing has long been one of the progressive movement's preoccupations. If turn-of-the-twentieth-century reformers were steeped in a notion that American society would benefit from centralized, expert-driven control, few venues called out for planning more than the nation's physical landscape. The sudden spread of industrial power—the move from farm to factory—was jumbling the patterns that had long defined where families lived and worked, drawing many more people from scattered hamlets into burgeoning towns and cities. So, at issue for many reformers was whether the nation's neighborhoods and metropolitan regions could be molded to ensure that urban living was healthy, clean, and productive for the masses.

At root was a concern about order. As slums emerged across the country, many progressives grew convinced that organic growth would lead to chaos, disease, and worse.[28] A distinctly middle-class movement worried that people of lower status were liable to become victims of what some called "anomie," the depressing, detached, depraved routines that were thought to prevail in poorer quarters. Middle-class America worried that poor people would be unable to resist the temptation of alcohol, gambling, prostitution, and crime. And the proper salve seemed intuitive enough: those determined to bring order from chaos proposed to erect a system to empower expert professionals to plan the future in a rational way.

Urban planning, then, emerged as something more than a mere professional discipline, like architecture or engineering. It became a primary tool reformers intended to use in service of saving the despairing masses from themselves. Fearful, for example, that factories were likely to spring up in residential neighborhoods—that bucolic communities stood in danger of being disrupted by the noise, pollution, and worse that came with big industrial enterprises—progressives wanted to instill a separation between home and work. Railroads had induced a natural separation of residential and industrial districts, if only because factories were typically erected adjacent to tracks, and homes further away. But as trucking became a more mature enterprise, industrial plants could more easily be sited near residential enclaves—factory owners might prefer, in fact, to set up their smokestacks near the places laborers lived.[29] So, reformers became convinced that government should work to separate the two—to impose reason on the urban jungle.[30]

The courts, almost invariably a barrier to domineering *public* authority in the late nineteenth century, maintained a fairly broad aversion to restrictions on private property rights. If, in line with the nation's pioneering spirit, you bought a plot of land, it seemed only right that you maintain license to do with it what you wanted. But life at the turn of the twentieth century made that increasingly untenable. Adjacent properties owned by different interests inevitably impacted one another.[31] If one owner's property spewed soot, or caught fire, or was a haven for licentious behavior, it was liable to affect those in the property next door, or around the corner. So, many progressives began looking for ways to establish new standards to balance property rights with an expert-driven order. Within (or at least adjacent to) progressivism emerged a movement known as City Beautiful. Adherents believed that city planning and architecture could protect against the despair many presumed the lower classes endured in tenements and shacks.[32]

By the beginning of the twentieth century, Europe had already begun experimenting with what would become widely known as zoning. A handful of German communities had imposed restrictions in an explicit effort to *reduce* property values such that more Germans could afford to purchase homes. The thinking was that if a purchaser was precluded from constructing a factory on a plot of land, wealthy industrialists would look elsewhere, leaving homes on the residential market that might otherwise have been razed. But among zoning advocates in the United States, the logic was inverted: restrictions stood to *enhance* a property's value. If you needn't worry that a soot-belching factory was going to be sited in any of the blocks nearby, buyers might be willing to pay more for a home. A European tool deployed to American ends.

Soon, zoning ordinances delineating areas for housing, commercial, and industrial use were adopted in many of America's growing cities—Boston and Los Angeles in 1909, New York in 1916.[33] And with this tool, bigots saw an opening: here, it seemed, was a good way to keep white communities white. Nevertheless, even at the height of "separate but equal," the Supreme Court was unwilling to go that far, ruling eventually that racial zoning was unconstitutional.[34] The racists would variously try other strategies: deed restrictions, covenants, and redlining, for example. Before the regulation was struck down by the courts, Baltimore prohibited people of any given race from living on blocks where a majority were of another race—a restriction that, in theory, applied to all races equally.[35] But perhaps most insidious, Berkeley, California, zoned a residential area exclusively for single-family homes—a restriction that worked in effect to preclude Black families (and, to that end, poor or "ethnic" white families too) from moving in.[36] When a housing developer sued the Cleveland suburb of Euclid, Ohio, for adopting a similar ordinance, the Supreme Court ruled it constitutional.[37]

But if *exclusion* was an important impetus for zoning, there was more to it than that. This was an indelible progressive idea. *Planning* had been envisioned as a way to make life better—to prevent self-interested property owners from ruining a neighborhood with self-interested schemes. Avaricious landowners needed to be controlled so they wouldn't demolish a home on a tree-lined street to make room for a junkyard, or place an oil refinery by a school. And that meant, in essence, pulling power up and out of the hands of individuals, investing that authority instead in some incarnation of the city fathers.[38] These city fathers would presumably hire expert planners who would divine the way forward. They would decide where streets would be plotted; how sewer systems would work; where schools, and electrical wires, and trolley lines would go; and which sorts of buildings could be constructed on individual plots of land.

In 1926, the Department of Commerce published a model piece of legislation to help municipalities impose standardized zoning schemes: local boards would make land use decisions, the public would be invited to offer their input, and those disappointed by a board's decision would have a process for appeal.[39] It went on to suggest that, rather than making determinations on a piecemeal basis, the whole process be done as part of a general plan.[40] Eventually adopted in some form by every state, this *process* was the apotheosis of Hamiltonian progressivism, and systematizing the urban landscape appeared, by many estimates, to harness real benefits. Between 1900 and 1940, for example, the mortality rate due to infectious disease—spread widely by deficient water and sewer systems—declined by 75 percent.[41] That would have been seemingly impossible without the order imposed by planners from above.

Through the 1930s and 1940s, as the nation endured first the Great Depression and then the Second World War, real estate development fell off. But the underlying infrastructure of planning and zoning, paired with the nation's limited housing stock, largely remained the same. The tenements that had long predominated in certain low-income neighborhoods— perhaps, most famously, on Manhattan's Lower East Side—loomed large in the public imagination as poverty traps.[42] It was only after the United States prevailed over fascism that reformers began to imagine how they might use the Hamiltonian tools created by various localized zoning regimes to spring slum dwellers free.[43] And while their various machinations were tinged by racism and ignorance, many still imagined that they were doing for the beleaguered masses what the beleaguered masses could not do for themselves.

What emerged over the next two decades was a breathtaking endeavor to remake America's housing stock. From 1932 to 1937 alone, the federal government established more than a half dozen new agencies to build housing, some of which were used to direct massive subsidies at developers churning out freestanding homes on farmland outside the nation's cities.[44] Many of the new homes were outfitted with a set of modern conveniences— washing machines, dryers, electric stoves—previously limited to those better off. To weave the suburbs into metropolitan regions, Hamiltonian planners constructed new roads and highways into and through cities—a choice made, oftentimes, in lieu of building new transit lines. And within cities, this broad endeavor prescribed demolishing derelict neighborhoods purportedly so those trapped inside could enjoy something better.[45]

To be sure, these efforts weren't defined by any communist plot— the Establishment was, in many cases, responding to market demands. During the postwar era, many Americans *wanted* to escape the city and settle in the car-centric suburbs.[46] But the effects were unquestionably shaped by policy choices. In the prewar years, cities had been segregated largely *by neighborhood*. Now, by inducing wealthier, whiter residents to move outside the city limits, the federal government effectively segregated regions *by municipality*. Washington *chose* to subsidize the mortgages borrowed by families migrating to the suburbs, particularly for veterans who might otherwise have raised their young families in cities. The government subsidized roadbuilding, funded largely by a dedicated tax on gasoline (see Chapter 7). And within cities, Congress created, President Truman signed, and President Kennedy expanded a massive bill to clear "slums" and replace them with homes more suitable for mid-twentieth-century housing—a program that came to be known as urban renewal. The Establishment that had led the nation through depression and war would now lead a domestic rebirth.[47]

Often analyzed separately, it's worth remembering that these various endeavors were all tentacles of the same progressive project. And the same basic story of city fathers endeavoring to drive local progress played out along the same arc in communities across the country. When, in 1950, New Haven mayor Richard Lee toured his city's Oak Street slums, he was made queasy by the stench of sewage piled up in and around homes that had neither electricity nor gas. He was aghast that people in his own city lived this way. This was, in his view, an illustration of systemic failure—a tragedy of the commons. Developers did not, by themselves, have the ability to evict the tenants, raze their homes, and replace them with something better. New Haven, Lee concluded, needed a "unity of approach." And so, as an archetypical midcentury progressive, he went about building an Establishment capable of fixing the problem.

Functioning not only as mayor but more broadly as the city's chief executive, he maestroed together a grand alliance—business executives, Yale University administrators, union brass, and representatives of the city's Irish, Italian, and Black communities, among others—who would serve as what some termed New Haven's "growth machine."[48] City Hall would bring local powers of eminent domain to bear on derelict neighborhoods, keenly aware that Washington would pick up two-thirds of the cost through urban renewal. Developers could then buy those plots at a steep discount—thirty cents on the dollar—with the presumption that they could then construct modern new homes.[49] The cabal might, or might not, work to accommodate the impoverished families they were displacing. But that wasn't really their concern.[50] The Establishment, led by Mayor Lee, believed that it knew better how to serve New Haven's broader interest.[51] To make an omelet, you needed to break some eggs.

This was the postwar norm—this is how city fathers were *supposed* to behave. Laws created to control development were harnessed to lend authority to august figures who would enhance a community's housing stock, and its economic standing, and its transportation infrastructure, and whatever else. What academics came to label "pluralism" was, in reality, an approach designed to let city fathers impose their vision on purportedly pliant communities. And to be clear, that was as many progressives thought it *should* be. The octopus that now governed American society had been born of the smoldering frustration that dour old judges and small-minded machine bosses had schemed to keep America in the horse-and-buggy era. Progressivism's Hamiltonian impulse was now finally in full flower. And from the Establishment's perspective, that appeared all for the better.

GROUNDS FOR EXCLUSION

The "pluralism" that defined Mayor Richard Lee's long run leading New Haven had been predicated on a certain metropolitan diversity. Within any given city, people from different stations, races, and ethnicities—the well-to-do and more marginal alike—would frequent many of the same commercial strips, send their kids to schools governed by the same boards of education, and pay their municipal taxes into the same coffers. They may not have been friendly—they may, in fact, have hated, resented, or even harbored deep prejudice against one another. But they all remained in the same figurative boat.[52] Mayor Lee's growth machine, like its counterparts elsewhere, had been predicated on a notion that wealth *wanted* to remain in the city—that middle-class residents would be eager to reside in the buildings that replaced the slums. But that would turn out to be a bad bet.

As white flight spurred many middle-class residents beyond the city limits—often to suburbs where they no longer had to shoulder the burdens of urban life, including the taxes—Establishment growth machines began to sputter and fail.[53] But if derelict public housing projects came to be a symbol of the shift, urban renewal proved to be a more profound and pervasive catastrophe.[54] Around the country, figures like Robert Moses razed scores of communities—more than three hundred thousand families were displaced between 1950 and 1974 alone—not for concrete towers, but for private-sector development.[55] Absent demand, developers often balked at investing in them, leaving once vibrant neighborhoods—Pittsburgh's Golden Triangle, Detroit's Ragweed Acres, St. Louis's Hiroshima Flats—as barren wastelands, blocks of rubble supplanting what had once been bustling, if sometimes rough-hewn, neighborhoods.

There was a racial subtext to the whole exercise. City fathers who had never particularly warmed to the southern Blacks arriving through the Great Migration saw "slum clearance" as an easy way out.[56] As James Baldwin once put it, "urban renewal means Negro removal."[57] In 1964 alone, two-thirds of those "removed" by slum clearance were minorities.[58] But poorer whites were victimized as well, and that was often because, as Jane Jacobs would eventually point out in *The Death and Life of Great American Cities*, the Establishment discounted the importance of social connection.[59] The slums may have been ragged, but many were suffused with community ties. And the sputtering failures of an indelibly progressive strategy to *fix* cities eventually forced reformers, by the mid-1960s, to question their prior assumptions. Here was another incarnation of the debate that had riven Johnson aides shaping the war on poverty (see Chapter 3). Would it be better to double down on the growth machine model, or to divine an entirely different strategy?

New York governor Nelson Rockefeller's Urban Development Corporation epitomized the first approach. Robert Moses, who had been an urban renewal czar in New York, had razed poor neighborhoods and then left them to decay. Rockefeller's answer to Moses's failure was Ed Logue.

And among many progressives, this appeared like the natural order of things. To their way of thinking, when planning and centralized control failed, government could solve the problem with *more* planning and *more* centralized control. Senator Henry "Scoop" Jackson, a Democrat from Washington State, went so far during the 1970s as to propose three pieces of legislation designed to establish a more rigid *national* planning regime, such that land use decisions would put all of society's diversified interests in harmony.[60]

Meanwhile, something else was happening to the nation's housing market. During the early postwar era, renting and owning homes offered Americans much the same financial proposition: because home values typically grew only on a modest scale—stocks and bonds often offered much better returns—homeowners were less apt to view property as a nest egg. In the 1970s, by contrast, with inflation high and the stock market flat, many Americans began to see growing home values as a ticket up the socioeconomic ladder.[61] As a result, a project that might change the "character" of a neighborhood wasn't just a mere nuisance—it was a potential threat to a family's financial well-being. If a homeowner's middle-class community turned working-class, or their lily-white suburb became "mixed," they *personally* stood to lose—or so many presumed.

In the suburbs, that steered residents and their elected representatives to view with great skepticism anyone proposing to construct new housing. In cities it meant that residents began to take a much more derisive view of the wealthy insiders conspiring with Robert Moses types to develop new complexes. In both cases, those looking to thwart development often couched their dislike for African Americans, or poor people, or immigrants, in worries about how change might dilute the quality of the local public schools, or erode the quality of the neighborhood, or simply diminish the value of nearby homes. But whatever the motivation, the concluding impulse was the same: pull power down and away from any state-level master of the universe (like Ed Logue) in order to give more authority to local figures averse to change.

222 | WHY NOTHING WORKS

Here, then, was the (now familiar) wrinkle. To pursue their Jeffersonian ends, progressives employed tools created previously to open Hamiltonian possibilities. During the postwar era, when progressivism had
been more inclined to lean into centralized power, the Establishment had
clandestinely pirated the whole zoning process through a fairly mundane
system known as variances. The process of zoning, chartered in the US
largely during the early twentieth century, had demanded as a first step
establishing a comprehensive plan such that anyone desiring to do something out-of-bounds—erecting a new apartment building in a parcel designated for industrial use, or constructing a new plant near a residential
neighborhood—was compelled to ask the city fathers for an exception.
Variances had thus become the currency of the Establishment: get in good
with the mayor or else your variance was likely to be denied.

The results had been predictable. Studies of urban zoning codes maintained in the 1950s and 1960s revealed that variances were granted less on
the basis of *rationality* than on *power*.[62] Very little housing was constructed
as of right because the Establishment understood that they benefited more
if developers were forced to request variances to a more rigid code. If you
wanted to build something, you needed to be in good with the powers
that be. In Manhattan, 40 percent of the buildings would have been disallowed by zoned restrictions on height, density, and use. In Somerville,
Massachusetts, not far from Boston, only twenty-two buildings in total
would have been permitted given contemporary zoning restrictions. Developers were often asked to build a park, or add parking spaces, or pass
an envelope under a table to get a green light.[63] Regardless, this was how
the growth machine worked by design.

In the 1970s, reformers eager to protect their communities from developers scheming to build more housing realized they could use the very
same tools to the opposite end. Rather than make zoning so strict that
only the powerful few could get their variances through, they worked to
make the system even more rigid.[64] Beginning in the suburbs, but eventually in the cities as well, the notion that a well-connected developer

might get special permission to build a project was turned on its head. Now, zoning would be used to ensure that even when the elite *did* approve a project, locals could thwart any proposed variance.[65] And here, as in other realms, those objecting to development shrouded their concerns in altruistic intentions. Offense at insider deals. Worries about limited water resources. Strain on the existing electricity grids. Additional traffic. Local animal habitats.

Some of the objections were legitimate. But they quickly became vehicles to shroud the concerns wielded by existing residents looking to simply preserve their own home's value. And so, without much notice, *insider* zoning became *exclusionary* zoning. Just as Berkeley had led the way on zoning decades earlier, California was at the vanguard of the new movement. During the early 1970s, an insurgent slate of antidevelopment "residentialist" town councilors in Palo Alto imposed a fifty-foot, five-story limit on all new housing within the small city's borders.[66] The town of Petaluma put a quota on building permits. Other places charged thousands of dollars for hookups to municipal utilities, claiming that water or electricity might otherwise run out.[67] And there was something else: the new effort to give homeowners vetoes over proposed changes to the surrounding neighborhood not only protected home values, but it gave bigots new tools to keep the unwelcome out.

The shift here is nuanced but profound. Under the old regime, places like suburban Levittown, New York, had managed to exclude Blacks by imposing a top-down system where homeowners were effectively precluded from selling to Black buyers, either through covenants or through a system known as redlining. The new regime erected hurdles from the bottom up—exclusionary zoning was redlining by another name.[68] Many Black families struggled to purchase or rent homes in communities where housing costs were inflated by "environmental" concerns. And that was among the ultimate ironies. The same political zeitgeist that had been born to push power down from Jim Crow legislators so that ordinary Black people could enjoy the full fruits of American citizenship—the

Jeffersonian impulse that had birthed the civil rights and voting rights bills in the early 1960s—was now being used as a tool by white home- owners determined to keep their neighborhoods functionally segregated.

UPENDING THE GROWTH MACHINE

If rigid (and often exclusionary) zoning marked the most apparent ev- idence of progressivism's new approach to what some call "land use" reform, it hardly marked the movement's only rearguard action against growth machines. Men like Robert Moses, Richard Lee, and Ed Logue had wielded power because they'd managed, in various ways, to claim li- cense from the two political branches of government. Now, to push back, progressives sought, as in other circumstances, to enlist the authority of the courts, which had historically been more deferential to those who con- trolled various zoning regimes. Now, the movement's new skepticism of centralized power spurred them to seek out judges who might construct a new jurisprudence endowing individuals with new protective rights. And the nation's judiciary was, by that point, eager to oblige.[69]

Here, the issue wasn't just the *outcome* or the *merit* of any objection, but the *process* by which the government made decisions, and the *standing* various stakeholders had to have their concerns heard by a court. On those fronts, the tide turned in 1973 when a group of homeowners in Washington County, Oregon, sued the Board of County Commissioners, which had previously rezoned a thirty-two-acre residential parcel explicitly in order to permit a developer to build a park for mobile homes. Nearby residents charged that the Board had erred by changing the county's comprehensive plan absent a process that allowed for other affected residents to voice their concerns and have them weighed. A police chief might be permitted to move patrols from one neighborhood to another—that decision was clearly the province of that department. But in *Fasano v. Board of County Commis- sioners*, a court ruled that municipalities were more circumscribed than the police chief in making changes to the existing zoning regime.[70]

Fasano reflected a wave of reforms—some done through the courts, others through state legislature and local ordinances—that would eventually prevail across the country. Under the new system, the processes for determining what could and could not be built would have to be open and formal—decisions would have to be made on the record, with the affected parties given an opportunity to present and rebut evidence. Local government would be compelled to establish a good reason for making exceptions—they couldn't simply do a favor for a friendly developer—and the decisions would be subject to judicial review.[71] This was, in short, a cut against the postwar norm of making development decisions in the proverbial, and sometimes literal, smoke-filled back rooms. Here was another effort to bring self-serving, back-scratching, insider deals into the sunlight, where they could be disinfected.

Had the new processes served simply to ensure that land use decisions were transparent, orderly, and fair, the old growth machines might have learned to adapt. Mayor Lee would have provided his rationale for supporting a new development in New Haven, various neighbors would have voiced their objections, and an apolitical Board would have issued a decision informed by its view of the greater public interest. In some circumstances, the parties might have negotiated a modification *before* a proposal went before a planning board. A developer might have spoken with opponents and tamped down the height of a proposed new tower or the number of new homes to fill a cornfield. In theory, the quasi-judiciary element of land use planning could be used to balance various interests to everyone's satisfaction without the courts having to get involved.

But that's not generally how things played out. In practice, the new system simply opened up even mildly controversial development proposals to a nearly endless litany of objections. Even when a developer managed to accommodate one set of concerns, another would emerge. And if a zoning board approved a plan over local objections, the disappointed interests would sue, arguing that the zoning board's *process* had been deficient in some way—that it had been arbitrary, or capricious, or contrary to the law, or been approved via a process that somehow failed to measure up.[72] In short, the system designed in the years that followed *Fasano* was, unexpectedly, one where the threat of consecutive objections sometimes made it impossibly difficult for developers and communities to arrive at compromise solutions—to balance the demand for new housing with concerns about environmental (or whatever other) impact.

The chasm between what *Fasano*-era reformers envisioned and the land use vetocracy that emerged was gaping. But the connection is indelible. Because so many residents had standing to sue, the process almost guaranteed that any significant development—and often those that were less significant to boot—was almost endlessly vulnerable. If developers had been impervious to public objections during the previous regime, many now appeared powerless to push aside even a scurrilous concern. The new hurdles often added months, if not years, onto the gestation of worthwhile projects, meaning that housing proposed during a boom might still be under consideration when the economy hit turbulence and demand melted away.[73]

What's more, to exacerbate the hurdles community members could exploit to thwart change, reformers leaned into restrictions that imposed parking minimums, density limits, and other criteria.[74] But the most powerful tool reformers devised in the campaign to push power down to ordinary citizens centered on the environment. By 1975, twenty-five states had begun requiring developers to study how their proposal might impact the local water table, or harm nearby wildlife, or worsen traffic patterns, or create some other potential problem before moving forward. And beyond adding cost to each project, the studies themselves became an invitation to litigation. Disaffected neighbors could sue over whether the study had been comprehensive. And regardless of the outcome, the resulting uncertainty served to discourage would-be developers from proposing new projects.[75]

This growing anti-growth machine wasn't fed exclusively by local planning processes or by increasingly development-skeptical courts. The political branches got involved as well. Not long after President Nixon signed NEPA into law, Governor Ronald Reagan scrawled his signature on the Golden State's echo, the California Environmental Quality Act, or CEQA.[76] Beyond its NEPA-like requirement that developers delineate all the potential environmental impacts of a project, CEQA required that cities *mitigate* whatever environmental impacts might occur from local land use decisions.[77] And courts interpreted the statute broadly to include not just projects on public land, but any project that required public approval—which, of course, was mandated for most *private* projects. The upshot was that a developer on the receiving end of a cheap-to-file CEQA lawsuit was put at an almost insurmountable disadvantage. They would be forced to cover the costs of any delay, of any litigation, and of any mitigation measure.[78]

The CEQA bar almost immediately became a theater of the absurd. And while the low barrier to entry surely precluded some bad projects from moving forward, the new law and the ensuing jurisprudence proved in practice that there was no mechanism to weigh the environmental costs against the attendant benefits—like the additional housing.[79] In 1973, a two-hundred-unit condo project in San Francisco was held up for a year and a half because a Boy Scout filed a case. And word quickly got out among those eager to prevent their little corner of the Golden State from becoming any more population-dense. By 1976, the federal government was producing only a quarter of the number of environmental impact reports as California.[80] By the 1980s, CEQA's impacts were clear: Californians incensed by the cost of housing simply weren't willing to abide its construction anywhere nearby.[81] And while this phenomenon was not as abject in other parts of the country, the same basic drama played out across the board.

It was during this same moment that New York City developed the Uniform Land Use Review Procedure, or ULURP, a mechanism designed to give local residents a larger voice in determining the fate of proposed changes to their corner of the five boroughs. Now, the working-class residents of an apartment building would have a voice in whether a nearby residential parcel was rezoned to be a school bus depot. But, in time,

ULURP evolved to give each individual member of the City Council effective veto power over each proposed change. And members of the City Council turned out to be much more inclined to pursue the interests of their incumbent constituents than any prospective newcomers. Wielding the power to veto, detractors might negotiate for some benefit—perhaps a developer could win a green light by promising to construct a public playground nearby.[82] Absent that, they could just stand pat.

And it wasn't just big cities. Guilford, Connecticut, created a land trust in 1965 to acquire land that might otherwise be purchased by developers looking to erect new housing. The land trust was born for palatable reasons: to preserve the scenery, to prevent overdevelopment, to maintain home values. But over the years it became a giant amoeba, absorbing most opportunities for new housing, and the effective check on development was so powerful as to render new construction nearly impossible. Only 2 percent of Guilford's land had been set aside as open space in 1918—by 2015 it was a full third of the town.[83] An observer need not be an advocate of wall-to-wall condos to understand that the limits had essentially precluded significant population growth. After a period of remarkable growth that lasted through the 1970s, Guilford essentially froze in size.[84]

This turn toward Jeffersonianism wasn't entirely born from bad-faith arguments or what some now term NIMBYism (Not In My Back Yard). New housing developments *can* impact the environment. They *can* worsen traffic. They *can* imperil endangered species. They *can* force the demolition of historic buildings. With that said, the composite effect of all these objections has drastically curtailed the nation's supply of homes. And curtailing the supply has served powerfully to drive up prices. The old growth machine model had allowed the Establishment to impose its will on the powerless without paying any heed to the social costs. But the new system was so rife with veto points that society had no way to meet the demand for homes. Progressivism had swung from one extreme to the other—the first Hamiltonian, the second Jeffersonian.

And that shift has had profound effects on the housing market across the country.

VETO BY VOICE

In 1974, Samuel LeFrak, a legendary developer who worked primarily in New York's outer boroughs, wrote an op-ed in the *New York Times* excoriating housing reformers for working to ensure that "the entire world should look like Greenwich Village." He was particularly vexed by the growing celebrity of Jane Jacobs, the public intellectual who had emerged as Robert Moses's archnemesis while stymieing a plan to build an expressway across lower Manhattan. Now considered the godmother of preservation, Jacobs was the nation's foremost critic of centralized urban planning.[85] LeFrak bristled: "For many years I have built six-story apartment houses in Brooklyn and Queens. They were basic. The windows opened and closed. You opened them in the summer and closed them in the winter. Middle-class New Yorkers could afford to live in them and raise families. The planners [by which he meant Jacobs] didn't like them so I can't build them any more."[86]

The details differed in various settings around the country. But the underlying dynamic was almost always the same. LeFrak, like Moses, held a torch for the old, top-down Hamiltonian system where gruff old men imposed their will on a pliant public. Jacobs, like the Boy Scout suing to hold up residential developments in California, was a beacon of an emerging Jeffersonian philosophy bent on allowing communities to evolve from the bottom up. If the cost of LeFrak's mentality was blight and displacement, the downside of Jacobs's approach was a deficit of new housing. To the developer's point, efforts to preserve neighborhoods as they were—to preclude projects that had negative impacts on traffic, or the environment, or historic buildings—made it difficult for supply to meet growing demand. The new system wasn't working.

In the late 1970s, seeing political opportunity in the public's frustration, conservative activists in California pushed for Proposition 13, a ballot initiative designed to cap taxes at 1 percent of a property's value, and limit any subsequent rise to 2 percent a year. Prevailing by nearly a two-to-one margin in one of the nation's most progressive states, the initiative stood at the vanguard of a right-wing resurgence born almost entirely from progressivism's failure to balance its two impulses.[87] Ordinary people hadn't liked the excesses of the Moses-style growth machines—all the additional homes threatened those who were already settled. But nor were they now willing to abide the excesses of Jacobs-inspired limits, which curtailed in-migration but drove up property values and attendant tax burden.

Now, utilizing two mechanisms that had once been considered progressive triumphs—the referendum process passed by progressives in the early twentieth century and the environmental laws passed by progressives in the 1970s—Californians crafted a world where they could have their cake and eat it too: they could preclude new development in their neighborhoods without having to fork over larger chunks of their income in property taxes.[88] What some viewed as the most progressive state in the country had now boxed the government in, insofar as anyone might want to maintain a reasonable housing market. And the impact was essentially foreordained: housing inflation put many middle-class homes out of reach of anyone offering anything less than a fortune; taxes stayed low, at least relative to the value of the property; very little *new* housing came on the market.

Nowhere is this phenomenon better illustrated than in Silicon Valley. During the 1950s and 1960s, developers, working with the local growth machine, had managed fairly easily to meet housing demand by constructing new homes in the area. But once the worm turned, and those already ensconced had the power to limit nearby development without shouldering the burden of rising property tax bills, home values rose with abandon. A Palo Alto tract house that sold for $16,000 in 1952 was sold in

2019 for $2.5 million.[89] During the 2010s, the Bay Area added more than seven hundred thousand new jobs, but its housing supply grew by little more than one hundred thousand.[90] And while more pronounced in the Bay Area, the same basic story prevailed across California. Government was powerless to respond.

Through the decades, journalists in California would regularly report stories detailing how CEQA had been abused, with project opponents invoking environmental concerns as the thinnest veneer for naked self-interest. The law required those proposing new structures to address nearly one hundred issues—noise, endangered species, traffic, etc.—many of which had their own subcategories. And opponents simply needed to find a flaw in a developer's proposal to mitigate impacts on anyone to put the entire project on ice.

A plan to turn an old, polluted aircraft manufacturing facility in Los Angeles into a vibrant new development with housing, office space, and a park was subject to twenty CEQA suits over twenty years.[91] In 2015, an antiabortion group filed a CEQA lawsuit to stop construction of a new Planned Parenthood clinic in San Francisco. Their complaint: that the protest they, themselves, would subsequently organize outside the clinic would prove to be adverse to traffic and public safety.[92] In 2018, owners of a restaurant in Boyle Heights, a neighborhood in Los Angeles, filed suit against a proposal to build housing for mentally ill homeless veterans. They claimed that the city had not sufficiently investigated whether the proposed site was contaminated, but it was not hard to surmise that they worried more that strung-out veterans would end up idling on the sidewalks.[93]

The results, predictably, were dreadful. As the median home price across the state grew to $700,000, Governor Gavin Newsom promised in 2018 to build 3.5 million new units by 2025—well more than four hundred thousand a year on average. But as of early 2021, the state had yet even to crack one hundred thousand in any given year.[94] And that wasn't for lack of trying—it was simply too easy for opponents to block development. In 2018, a bill to clear away barriers to developers who wanted to build five-story buildings near bus and subway stops went down in defeat at the hands of Democrats in the state legislature. They astutely feared backlash from progressive voters who would complain that the increased density would damage the environment, or worsen traffic, or overtax the electricity grid, or undermine historic preservation.[95] Everyone *wanted* more housing, it seemed—but they wanted it built *somewhere else.*

In September 2021, California's legislature finally eked out a bill allowing homeowners to construct duplexes on single-family plots and empowering cities to rezone small parcels of land without having to endure CEQA review.[96] But if it took this long to address even this small element of the problem in a progressive state burdened by some of the most extravagant housing prices, many worried about how the fight might unfold elsewhere. In 2022, the Biden administration estimated that the United States was short a full 1.5 million housing units. Others estimated the deficit to be as high as nearly 4 million.[97] By then almost half of the nation's renters were paying more than the recommended 30 percent of their income for housing.[98] And while some of that could be attributed to greedy landlords, the problem was more basic: in markets where demand exceeds supply, prices are bound to rise. And decades' worth of Jeffersonian reforms had made it increasingly difficult to build.[99]

Progressives were not entirely blind to the problem as it emerged. But for decades, the movement was focused primarily on what some call the demand side of the housing market. In that vein, reformers sought to cap rents and subsidize mortgages so that those with more modest incomes could afford to buy or rent. By contrast, problems on the supply side have been shrouded by the movement's disgust with landlord greed. You needn't lionize slumlords to acknowledge that today's incentives have skewed. But progressives are fundamentally conflicted about the solution. Construction is, by its very nature, viewed as coercion for those who stand in opposition. Almost by definition, gentrification cuts against the residents of poor or minority neighborhoods. In the wake of urban renewal, which still looms in the collective memory, Jeffersonian rights represent nothing short of salvation.[100] Proposals to sand them down appear like an invitation for Robert Moses's return.

Reformers have tried at times to strike a better balance. During the early 1970s, for example, Massachusetts enacted an "antisnob" zoning provision, creating a committee empowered to overrule exclusionary zoning decisions where less than 10 percent of a community's housing stock was deemed affordable. Six other states have since embraced similar strategies. Even more stringent by some measures, the so-called *Mount Laurel* decisions sparked the creation of a Council on Affordable Housing in New Jersey that works to incentivize inclusionary zoning.[101] These and various similar efforts were thought to represent the beginnings of a "Quiet Revolution" where local zoning decisions would be moved up to regional and state bureaucracies that could make decisions that served the greater good.[102]

But the pull to decentralize control during this period was simply too strong, and a whole slate of new environmental laws—the Coastal Zone Management Act of 1972, the Housing and Community Development Act of 1974, and the Resource Conservation and Recovery Act of 1976, among others—worked largely to replace, by other means, the zoning restrictions the Quiet Revolution had sought to pierce.[103] As with Senator Scoop Jackson's spoiled dream of creating a national planning regime and Ed Logue's abandoned efforts to force suburban communities in New York's Westchester County to allow for additional development, progressivism was simply too allergic to imposing power from above.[104] And still is now.

In a strange political inversion, by the 1980s, some Republicans—many of whom had been suspicious of public developers like Ed Logue—were taking up the cause of housing construction. Jack Kemp, while serving as President George H. W. Bush's HUD secretary, spearheaded the publication of a 1991 report, "Not in My Back Yard: Removing Barriers to Affordable Housing."[105] But because the push for a supply-side response was coming from a Reagan acolyte, many progressives were suspicious: Was Kemp just cheering on avaricious developers and slumlords?[106] By the early

234 | WHY NOTHING WORKS

2000s, advocates without the same conservative baggage began making similar arguments, but progressives were still too seized by fears of going back to the bad old days. Much as many might agree that housing was too expensive, it appeared easier to vilify rapacious landlords or demand more housing in *other* places than to repeal the crazy quilt of Jeffersonian protections erected in the wake of urban renewal.[107]

Given these limitations, progressives generally embraced two approaches. The first, born from the same spirit that fueled the embrace of NegReg (see Chapter 5), was to create land use planning processes that took fuller account of every possible voice. The supposition was that by inviting every affected stakeholder to weigh in—the developers, the community, the advocates, the would-be tenants—planning would be able to fashion a path forward that boasted universal buy-in.[108] Perhaps the developer would agree to a slightly smaller build, or to construct a community amenity. But as with NegReg, consensus represented an impossible dream. No playground proposal was going to satisfy the concerns of a community worried about gentrification. No suburban community frightened by the prospect of "urban youth" was going to be placated by a new bike trail. To the degree that some were willing to engage, their strategy was most commonly to run out the clock, at which point they were likely to sue as though they'd never been engaged in the first place.

A second more recently developed tactic, put on display in California, has aimed to turn NIMBYism against itself—that is, to bring Jeffersonian rather than Hamiltonian tactics to bear on the fight for more housing. Before it sputtered, the Quiet Revolution had been an explicitly Hamiltonian affair, seeking to pull the power to decide where and if housing would be constructed up from the local to the state level. Today, by contrast, so-called YIMBYs are often prone to embrace what amounts to a Jeffersonian approach, freeing the individuals who own given plots to build what they want regardless of local opposition. Their fight is to allow property owners to build granny flats above their garages as of right—that is, even if the neighbors object. And this latter approach seems to be catching on.[109]

In December 2018, the Minneapolis City Council voted 12–1 to end single-family zoning in the half of the city zoned that way, marking a dramatic shift in a municipality where half of renters were spending more than a third of their income on rent.[110] Property owners were thereafter permitted to carve up their lots into apartments or even raze a structure and rebuild a small apartment building—local NIMBYs, in theory, having no recourse. Seattle soon followed with a similar initiative, though it applied to twenty-seven zones rather than the whole city. Austin followed suit, creating a similar right to develop additional housing on single-zone lots—assuming the developer promised to keep the units affordable. And in July 2019, Oregon passed a similar law for all cities in the state with ten thousand people or more.[111]

Not every progressive housing reform reflected the same underlying aversion to power. Some proposals, including a bill to withhold federal funding to states and localities that fail to meet certain affordability benchmarks, were undeniably top-down.[112] The relatively liberal Republican governor Charlie Baker of Massachusetts managed during his last year in office to push through his state's legislature a measure making it easier for developers to win zoning changes for affordable housing.[113] But if these various efforts nodded at the notion that the broader public interest demanded greater supply, the effort did little to empower a centralized executive authority to decide what, if anything, should be built. And given the problems wrought by previous Hamiltonian regimes, that seemed to many reformers to be much for the better.

That said, Jeffersonian efforts to address the nation's housing shortage have yet to prove a panacea. And that's for the same reason that previous efforts to bestow rights have, in certain ways, frustrated progressives. Pushing power down to a property owner *sounds* good. But when the "right" to build a multi-unit building on a parcel previously zoned for single-family homes runs up against the "right" to preserve a habitat for endangered species, or to ensure the sanctity of a local noise ordinance, or to do whatever else some creative NIMBY lawyer conjures, a judge is required to resolve the conflict. And that judge won't decide exclusively on the basis of sound public policy, but by interpreting the law as written by legislators.

There is, of course, an alternative. Progressives *could* seek to reestablish a planning mechanism that both allows for everyone to be heard (which Robert Moses never cared to do) and empowers some centralized authority to make expeditious final determination, after weighing various national, regional, community, and individual interests. Pursuing that sort of solution would likely involve two prerequisites: first, a guarantee that a community's input would be taken seriously—that concerns about environmental or quality-of-life issues would not be ignored, even if they did not prevail; and second, that, in exchange for guaranteeing voice, an authority's decision would be insulated from the Kafkaesque series of veto points that have left too many public policy choices to the wilds of the judiciary.

That sort of reform would take a leap of faith for many progressives. What if a developer were to capture the process? What if a revolving door gives charlatans control over the outcome? Even the most minor Hamiltonian correction would need to be pursued with great care because, as some will argue, nothing would be worth allowing the old growth machine to reconstitute itself—powerless communities can't be forced to face, again, the threat of imperious and coercive elites reasserting their power. Even a half century after *The Power Broker* won the Pulitzer Prize, progressives have no desire for the pendulum swinging so far the other way. But this again is where the political dimension becomes clear. The housing shortage can't be subsidized away, and our collective failure to expand supply simply provides more evidence that the government *still* can't be trusted.

It is one thing to argue that the specter of Robert Moses's resurrection is too much to bear—that progressives should bar the door to the imperious Establishment figures who would happily raze whole blocks in poor and minority neighborhoods. But if the result is a housing market so tight that the nation's supply cannot meet demand—that people are forced to pay much too much for their homes—then government can't reasonably be called competent. And when government is viewed as entirely incompetent, people look for alternatives like Donald Trump.

Put more simply, if housing remains forever a symbol to ordinary citizens of why progressives can't be trusted with power, the movement undermines its own viability. To make a serious claim on shaping the nation's future—to offer a more compelling argument than the conservatives, populists, and demagogues—progressives need to make the public-sector work. And while acknowledging that perfect balance of Jeffersonian and Hamiltonian impulses will always prove elusive—that any public policy decision comes with trade-offs—progressivism's best foot forward is to create a system that can be trusted to look at public concerns, weigh the choices, and come to a reasonable decision.

7

The Bridge to Nowhere

The glut of new suburban housing erected after the Second World War created a cascade of new challenges. Among them, many Establishment figures worried about how to keep the blood flowing to the nation's downtowns. With the (largely white) middle classes pouring out into various suburbs full of single-family homes—many of them purchased with generous federal subsidies—urban business districts became increasingly dependent on commuters. Planners, who had come to imagine downtowns as something akin to a living organism's beating heart, began to worry that surface street traffic would become so clogged that businesses would move out as well. In response, city fathers around the country alighted on the idea of building something akin to cardiac stents—namely, new expressways that would whoosh people from the outskirts directly into the center city. To save the city, they argued, you needed to build *through* it.

Decades later, this whole notion would seem preposterous. The urban expressways that cut through previously tight-knit if sometimes ragged neighborhoods would be recast as gashes sliced through fragile living organisms. As we'll see, reformers early to that realization responded by building up a series of defenses making it almost impossible to build new infrastructure, good or bad. But at the time, many held to the prevailing view that downtowns would die *without* expressways. Planners extolling the demand for new urban circulatory systems made the case for urgency, worried that each traffic-clogged city might otherwise fall behind its competitors—that the metropolises that completed their urban highways most expeditiously would glean a competitive advantage. It was with this as a backdrop that city fathers in two midsize American cities, San Antonio, Texas, and Memphis, Tennessee, began thinking about how to ensure they wouldn't be left behind.

San Antonio's wealth had by then begun pushing north from downtown, with middle- and upper-class families putting down roots in neighborhoods on both sides of McCullough Avenue, a thoroughfare streaming up toward the city's newly constructed airport. And while the region was already blessed with circumferential roads and expressways going east and west, planners soon began noting the difficulty for locals commuting north and south—particularly for downtown businessmen rushing to catch a flight. In June 1959, city leaders asked the Texas Highway Department for a new north-south highway capable of delivering residents living north of the city straight into downtown. Better, the experts believed, to get speeding commuters off the slow-going surface streets.

Seven hundred miles to the northeast, residents of Memphis were having much the same debate, but their challenge was to connect the city's downtown to neighborhoods and suburbs farther east. As in San Antonio, those living farther from the Mississippi River were navigating increasingly clogged surface roads when commuting downtown. As in San Antonio, the local Establishment (the Chamber of Commerce in San Antonio, the Downtown Association in Memphis, among others) determined that the logical fix was to extend an expressway straight into the city center. But here, local leaders had an extra leg up: the federal government had already begun planning an interstate, I-40, from Greensboro, North Carolina, to Los Angeles. It seemed possible that this *federal* project could be the solution to fix Memphis's *local* challenge.[1]

If the broad outlines seemed clear in both cities, the specific routes remained undefined. Some of San Antonio's nicest neighborhoods, places like Olmos Park and Monte Vista, sat directly between downtown and the airport. Similarly, wealthy white residents of Memphis had splayed out in eastern communities ranging from Central Gardens to Bellaire Woods. Planners knew that however easy it might be to displace the residents of poor and minority neighborhoods, cutting through well-to-do white neighborhoods was fraught.[2] Fortunately, both cities boasted big, beautiful parks between the endpoints. Build *through* that urban greenery, planners figured, and you wouldn't have to condemn nearly so many nice homes.

But the two parks were, in fact, crown jewels. San Antonio's Brackenridge Park was a serpentine slash of green bound by resplendent houses and the idyllic campuses of Trinity University and the University of the Incarnate Word. Memphis's Overton Park boasted a zoo, a 170-acre forest of oak and hickory trees, a nine-hole golf course, and a band shell.[3] Nevertheless, the trade-offs seemed clear: in Memphis spoiling 26 of Overton Park's 342 acres would save at least six hundred homes and twenty businesses.[4] And there were financial considerations as well: the government is obligated to provide compensation when taking possession of a home or business. The parks were already public property—they could be claimed for a song.[5] And so planners and engineers worked up plans to drive these two new highways through Brackenridge and Overton Parks, confident that, as experts, they'd divined the most rational solution to a pressing public challenge.

Predictably enough, not everyone in either city was elated. Animated groups of local residents spoke up for keeping both parks pristine. But leading figures in both communities argued to mostly receptive audiences that to grow and thrive, postwar metropolises needed to enhance their *mobility*. They weren't entirely dismissive of the trade-offs—to compensate, San Antonio committed to replacing whatever green space was taken by the new highway, and Memphis would convert five thousand acres into new parkland.[6] And so, eventually, the vast majority of citizens in both cities fell into line without much complaint. The same month John F. Kennedy was elected president, voters in San Antonio supported a bond to purchase the right-of-way shooting north of downtown by two-to-one.[7] In the same vein, the Memphis City Council would pass a resolution supporting the highway through Overton Park.[8]

But if the proposals were broadly popular, the ragtag local opposition refused to acquiesce. Often viewed as gadflies—it's not hard now to envision the *very serious* men extolling the project rolling their eyes at *housewives* convinced that their picnics in the park were more important than regional progress—oddball collections of detractors began asking questions that reached beyond their immediate self-interest. Were expressways worth the enormous cost to taxpayers? Was government doing enough to mitigate the environmental impacts? Did urban planners *really* know what they were doing? Arrayed against their respective Establishments, each city's troublemakers looked small and powerless. In most measures, they were.

These dynamics prevailed in cities across the country. And, in time, the gadflies began to find each other—to join together in a national network of organizers fighting various highway schemes across the country—New York, New Orleans, Nashville, Washington, Baltimore, and Boston among them.[9] One New Yorker, Helen Leavitt, eventually highlighted the San Antonio fight in a widely read book, cementing a notion that little platoons of expressway detractors across the country were aligning into a grassroots movement.[10] But however many tree-hugging activists wrote letters to their local newspapers, they were rarely able to glean any real leverage over the Establishment. And, in many cases, the power differential was so stark that the opponents were dismissed without reply.

San Antonio, however, turned out to be different—there, the gadflies had a powerful ally. Texas senator Ralph Yarborough, remembered today as the last true liberal to represent the Lone Star State, shared some of the protestors' pique. He too had been put off by the ways San Antonio's elite had so nonchalantly chosen to sacrifice the city's crown jewel for a dirty, noisy highway. And as a senator, he was uniquely equipped to do something about it. In 1966, Yarborough was negotiating the specifics of the complex bill that would wrangle the scattered federal agencies overseeing roads, rails, air traffic, and more into a single, federal Department of Transportation. And during the course of that negotiation, he inserted language designed to nudge officials in Texas to find an alternative route—one that would more likely leave Brackenridge Park undisturbed.

The amendment that Yarborough crafted, and then succeeded in getting his colleagues to accept, became section 4(f) of the underlying bill. It said, quite simply, that funding issued by the new Department of Transportation could not be used in ways that disrupted public greenery "unless (1) there is no feasible or prudent alternative to the use of such land, and (2) such programs include all possible planning to minimize harm."[11] His fellow senators, who accepted the language, understood what Yarborough was trying to do. Many sympathized, but simultaneously wanted to be clear that 4(f) was not a directive *requiring* planners to route highways around parks and through neighborhoods. So, in an accompanying report, the Senate specified the following:

> [4(f) was not intended to issue] a mandatory prohibition against the use of the enumerated lands, but rather, a discretionary authority which must be used with both wisdom and reason. The Congress does not believe, for example, that substantial numbers of people should be required to move in order to preserve these lands, or that clearly enunciated local preferences should be overruled on the basis of this authority.[12]

244 | WHY NOTHING WORKS

At the time of its enactment, the nation's highway program was merely a decade old, and the Yarborough rule was just one of a broad range of provisions, written by various members of Congress, designed to rein in the upheaval that highway construction was creating in communities across the country. The same year 4(f) became law, for example, Congress passed the National Historic Preservation Act, a bill designed to nudge planners to take greater account of the buildings that might be sacrificed for highway projects.[13] And so it wasn't immediately clear, when President Lyndon Johnson signed the bill creating the Department of Transportation, whether the Yarborough rule would actually serve to disrupt Texas's plans to cut through Brackenridge Park. Regardless, Establishment figures in San Antonio didn't much care. If Ralph Yarborough and his friends were going to force them to consider alternative routes, they would consider them, and then dismiss them out of hand. Their counterparts in Memphis felt the same way. They knew what was best for their cities. Buoyed by the broad support of the general public, the engineers plowed ahead.

The question for opponents at this point was what if anything they could do in the face of the Establishment's intransigence. And they quickly realized they really had only one potential path forward: if the city planners and state highway engineers were going to turn deaf ears to their objections, the courts offered them their only leverage. The notion that a judge might rule in their favor seemed far-fetched at the time—America's courthouses were, with certain exceptions like *Brown v. Board of Education*, still viewed as bastions designed to protect the Establishment from the excesses of democracy. But if highway opponents were going to save Overton and Brackenridge Parks in the face of public sentiment favoring construction—if they were going to cut against majority rule—they had no other recourse. And the two localized fights played out almost in parallel.

In 1967, the same year that the Memphis City Council voted 4–1 in support of extending I-40 through Overton Park, a group in San Antonio led by the local Conservation Society filed suit in federal court.[14] Not long thereafter, Citizens to Preserve Overton Park, a group of activists organized by local Memphis firebrand Anona Stoner—a woman who might perhaps be best remembered as Memphis's answer to Jane Jacobs—filed a similar suit in Tennessee. Both groups faced the same dispiriting challenge. For decades, progressives had been preaching the virtues of judicial *restraint*.[15] August figures ranging from Oliver Wendell Holmes to Louis Brandeis to Felix Frankfurter had been determined to holster judicial interference so that executive branch officials could exercise *more* discretion when working in the public interest. Now, Stoner and her peers were asking courts to flip back—to substitute their judgment for those wielding public authority.

Given the prevailing jurisprudence, few were surprised when a federal judge in Memphis refused to require highway officials to select an alternative route. Or when the same argument failed on appeal before the Sixth Circuit Court in Cincinnati. For all that various courts might have questioned the underlying merits of these federally financed, state-administered, locally endorsed schemes, Stoner's counsel failed to convince judges that the decisions had been "arbitrary, capricious, an abuse of discretion, or otherwise not in accordance with law," as specified in the Administrative Procedure Act passed two decades earlier. The Yarborough rule had been written to require officials to consider alternatives to plans that would affect greenery, not to dictate that officials *couldn't* choose to drive roads through public parks. And so it came as something of a shock when the Supreme Court decided, despite what seemed like a clear standard, to take up the appeal. And in the majority opinion he subsequently authored in *Citizens to Preserve Overton Park v. Volpe*, Supreme Court Justice Thurgood Marshall issued a ruling that not only turned Anona Stoner into a sainted hero, but also proved a crucial pivot manifesting progressivism's cultural aversion to power.

At the outset, Stoner's crusade had appeared so unlikely to succeed that she struggled even to find lawyers willing to take up the case. But with the Supreme Court's surprise decision to hear the appeal, a whole range of national environmental interests—Friends of the Earth, the Wilderness Society, the National Audubon Society, and the Sierra Club among them—joined her cause.[16] Their legal team faced a formidable task: to convince a liberal court to cut against progressivism's embrace of judicial restraint, they would have to focus on *procedure*. It wasn't that the expert officials were prohibited from cutting through Overton Park, they would argue. It wasn't even that they'd erred in their judgment—it was, and remains, entirely within the government's discretion to build public works where they deem best. At root, the problem was that the figures who had planned this particular route had not, as the Yarborough rule required, explored in sufficient detail alternative routes that would have left Overton Park intact. They'd arrived at their decision the wrong way.

Justice Marshall's opinion, signed by six of his colleagues, represented nothing less than a Jeffersonian earthquake.[17] Repudiating the district and circuit court decisions, the court's liberal majority interpreted Senator Yarborough's rule in a manner entirely at odds with the Senate report accompanying the legislation. As Marshall argued: "It is obvious that in most cases considerations of cost, directness of route, and community disruption will indicate that parkland should be used for highway construction whenever possible." That is, in most cases, the cheapest, most expeditious, and least destructive path for a highway will almost always point officials to build across greenery. But, he went on to argue, "Congress clearly did not intend that cost and disruption of the community were to be ignored. . . . The statute indicates that protection of the parkland was to be given paramount importance."[18] In short, green space *could* be disrupted, but "only [in] the most unusual situations." Until the federal secretary of transportation determined, with sufficient study, that there were no "feasible and prudent alternatives," engineers could not proceed. And when they did, they would have to make every possible effort to mitigate the harm.[19]

Environmental activists and highway opponents reacted to Marshall's decision with unadorned glee. Already in the early 1970s, progressivism was well into its turn against centralized power. And now, here, in this revelatory judiciary opinion, Anona Stoner had proven herself to be David facing down the Establishment's Goliath. The president of the Sierra Club compared the fight over Overton Park to Gettysburg and Yorktown, claiming that it was "the first place where individual citizens used the law to stop the state and federal highway building and all the money and power behind them."[20] The *New York Times* editorialized the ruling was "good news for cities across the country that are still contending with the mania of those who would sacrifice the serene values of a green parkland to frenetic movement through a concrete wasteland."[21] By the summer of 1972, thirty-two similar lawsuits had been filed against various highway plans—in places as diverse as Boston and Seattle.[22] Marshall's decision was a new arrow in the quiver of anyone, no matter how marginalized, who wanted to thwart a project that impacted public greenery.

The Establishment, taken aback by the ruling, scrambled to adjust. To that point, the Tennessee Department of Transportation had intended to drive a $35 million trench through Overton Park, of which 90 percent, or all but $3.5 million, would be reimbursed by Washington. Now, to avoid impacting the park, the engineers would instead have to build a tunnel beneath the greenery, a feat of engineering that would cost a staggering $176 million ($1.3 billion in 2024 dollars), quintupling the state outlay.[23] Tennessee appeared happy enough to pursue the tunnel—provided that Washington was willing to cover the difference in cost. But the federal Department of Transportation flatly rejected that request, worrying about precedent. That left Tennessee in a pickle. Two thousand Memphis-area families had, by then, already seen their homes east and west of Overton Park taken in preparation for the new expressway. And if the engineers couldn't go through the park, their only alternative was to take homes and businesses elsewhere on the periphery—something the community would surely reject. And so the project just stood there in suspended animation for weeks, and then months, and then years.

Marshall's *Overton Park* decision had come down in March 1971. More than seven years later, with the project still on ice, Tennessee's Democratic governor, Ray Blanton, traveled from Nashville to Washington to testify before Congress in support of finally moving the expressway to completion. Resolution, he argued, was "important to all Tennesseans, because we have people being maimed and killed almost on a weekly basis because we do not have this important artery. And I believe now it is the only link of I-40 from coast to coast that doesn't afford our citizens a safe transportation route."[24] He and the mayor of Memphis, Wyeth Chandler, were both desperate to have Congress somehow point the way out of the impasse—to clarify 4(f), or to shave it down, or to replace it so that Justice Marshall's opinion no longer stood in their way. But by that point in the late 1970s, the highway system was no longer so popular. Four years after the release of *The Power Broker*, the public was less inclined to rubber-stamp the Establishment's decisions. Senators had no political incentive to give highway engineers more latitude to bulldoze public greenery.[25] And so absent any congressional action, Tennessee folded. In the last weeks of Jimmy Carter's presidency, the state requested that the federal money set aside for I-40's route through Memphis be directed elsewhere. Anona Stoner and her allies had won. David had slain Goliath.

San Antonio, whose threats to Brackenridge Park had inspired 4(f), took a different tack. There, as in Memphis, local conservationists had brought suit. And there, in the wake of the Supreme Court's *Overton Park* decision, the conservationists had found relief. Citing the precedent set in March 1971, Fifth Circuit Judge Homer Thornberry criticized Texas's highway planners for failing to establish that they could find no feasible alternative to disturbing Brackenridge Park: "Our task is simplified greatly to begin with because it is undisputed that the Secretary of Transportation complied with none of the . . . statutes. . . . No environmental study under N.E.P.A. has been made . . . and the Secretary has demonstrated no effort by anyone to examine the section 4(f) 'feasible and prudent' alternatives."[26] Once again, the local Establishment was stupefied. One of the North Expressway's fiercest supporters, former San Antonio mayor Walter McAllister, reacted by saying that he was "about ready for Texas to secede from the union." The elected branches, representing the will of the people, wanted the new expressway—but the courts were standing in their way.

In June 1971, Gruen Associates, an engineering firm based in Los Angeles, published a 120-page environmental impact statement of San Antonio's plan—a study of the sort mandated by the National Environmental Policy Act, signed by President Nixon a year and a half earlier. The report evaluated a series of routes the North Expressway *could* take, identifying one that would avoid any impact on the zoo and sunken gardens. The Green Plan, as it was called, would have taken less right-of-way and demanded less than a sixth as much "fill" than Texas's preferred route through Brackenridge Park. But it would also have required demolishing at least ten "substantial" houses in the tony neighborhood of Olmos Park.[27] And while unappealing, the mere possibility precluded highway officials from claiming that they had no "feasible and prudent" alternative. It seemed, then, as though Senator Yarborough was likely to win, much like Anona Stoner.

But San Antonio's Establishment refused to give in. In September 1971, a group called the Citizens' Committee for the Completion of the North Expressway collected 40,000 signatures on a petition demanding the road's completion; two months later, the roster had grown to 100,000.[28] And by that point, Yarborough had been unseated by former congressman Lloyd Bentsen, a Rio Grande Valley Democrat who had run in the 1970 primary employing the slogan: "It would be nice if Ralph Yarborough would vote for his state every once in a while." Bentsen went on to defeat George H. W. Bush in the general election, and in 1972 he mobilized with his Senate peer, Republican John Tower, to give San Antonio the expressway it wanted. The question for the bipartisan pair was how to get around Justice Marshall's ruling.

It was not a simple challenge. By dint of *Overton Park*, no federally funded project—not a new highway, a new train track, a new runway, a new port—could impinge on a public green space except in the most limited circumstances. And advocates were aware that those circumstances might not apply in the case of Brackenridge Park. How would courts define a "feasible" alternative? Was a plan that displaced twenty families preferable to one that took several acres of public green space? Ten? Two? It just wasn't clear that the Texas Department of Transportation would be able to clear the bar. So, the two Texans settled on a different legislative strategy: Rather than attack 4(f), they would pull the North Expressway from the federal system. If the state shouldered the financial burden on its own, the Yarborough rule wouldn't apply.

That, in the end, is what happened. Despite opposition from the minority of San Antonians who opposed the new road, the Federal-Aid Highway Act of 1973 included a provision deleting the proposed North Expressway from the interstate system altogether. Work recommenced twenty-four hours after President Nixon signed the bill into law.[29] Further legal efforts to thwart progress were rebuffed. And the new state highway opened to the public in 1978, named in honor of the former mayor, Walter McAllister.[30] I-40 would remain forever broken through western Tennessee, but San Antonians have their straight shot to the airport. And for the most part, that marked the end of the debate over the Yarborough rule.

Section 4(f) remains on the books today, modified only on the margins, and subject to the same interpretation. Anytime a federal transportation dollar is invested in any improvement—any new road, or high-speed rail line, or pedestrian bridge, or bike trail, or airport, or seaport—that has any significant bearing on a bit of public green space, it must undergo a 4(f) review. The impact has not been to make it entirely impossible to build new infrastructure in the United States.[31] Rather, the change has impacted *who* chooses to build *what*. Justice Marshall's ruling was apiece with a whole range of other procedural changes that spread decision-making power so wide and thin that nearly anyone with an objection could exert powerful leverage over what can or can't get done. And the question today, as we'll see, is whether that shift has all been for the good.

THE YELLOW BOOK

In contemporary progressive lore, the nation's urban interstates are framed almost as an unadorned evil. When Biden administration secretary of transportation Pete Buttigieg contended in late 2021 that "there is racism physically built into some of our highways," he was acknowledging what progressives know in their bones to be true: certain routes were chosen explicitly to divide communities along racial lines.[32] Perhaps as noxious, America's mid-twentieth-century inclination to favor roads over rail and transit pointed the country to a whole slew of policies that incentivized a slate of realities contemporary progressives revile: suburban sprawl, white flight, an utter dependence on (often imported) oil, and degradation of the nation's natural environment. Girding that antipathy is a notion that the car-dependent society we've inherited wasn't inevitable, and that America's leaders could still change things if they just summoned the requisite *political will* to do something different.

More than that, the seemingly retrograde infrastructure we've inherited isn't in good shape. Americans returning from continental Europe, or Japan, or China almost reflexively savage America's public works. More than a decade after then–vice president Joe Biden complained that New York's LaGuardia Airport was like "some third-world country," the nation's infrastructure was *still* a shambles when President Joe Biden signed a law investing massive new resources in a fix.[33] But why had things gotten so bad in the first place? It hadn't always been like this.

At the turn of the twentieth century, the country's private-sector rail networks put the rest of the world to shame. In 1916, the country boasted more track than every other nation combined.[34] But therein lay the problem. As with the electric wires that private industry refused to string to poor farmers in the Tennessee Valley (see Chapter 2), the railroads of that era had not been interested in serving isolated small towns and hamlets across the countryside—the costs outweighed the potential revenue. And so progressives at the time, much to the derision of conservatives, set about crafting a plan to connect the isolated and forlorn corners of the country—the places where the railroads didn't run. In that spirit, progressives endeavored to have government build roads.

If any single figure can be considered the father of America's road system, it's Thomas MacDonald, the largely forgotten civil engineer who served as something akin to the nation's highway czar from 1919 to 1953. MacDonald was a beacon of the original progressive creed, having been trained by Anson Marston, a turn-of-the-century engineering professor who taught that scientific rigor was the key to social progress. An almost humorless figure, MacDonald rose up through Iowa's public works bureaucracy before being hired by the federal Bureau of Public Roads, which he eventually came to run.[35] Like many progressive bureaucrats, throughout his career he imagined himself as a figure removed from politics, charged with solving problems of limited mobility in disinterested, rational ways. MacDonald endeavored to impose order on chaos—to centralize scattered sinecures of roadbuilding authority so that dour engineers could make responsible decisions in the public interest.

Crucially, centralizing power in MacDonald's vision didn't mean locating it in Washington. During the decades he lorded over the federal Bureau of Public Roads, the nation's road systems remained largely the province of the states, with state highway departments maintaining responsibility for tackling the formidable challenges of connecting far-flung locales. MacDonald's mandate was simply to incentivize often bare-bones and politically captured state highway departments to approach this challenge in systematic, rational ways. While some in Washington dreamed during the 1920s about building super-roads across the country— Eisenhower famously became obsessed with improving the nation's roads after accompanying a mud-slogged transcontinental military convoy in

1919—speeding up protracted journeys was only a secondary concern. Railroads already made it possible to get people and goods between cities. The network's weak links were the connections from various railroad hubs to isolated farms and factories.[36] Only roads could fill those gaps.

A century on, many progressives presume the federal government's massive investment in roads served primarily to subsidize a wildly profitable automobile industry, thereby stunting the development of what might otherwise have been a robust rail economy. But in the 1920s, it was the other way around: progressives wanted to subsidize roadbuilding as an alternative to wildly profitable private railroad corporations—the Pennsylvania and the New York Central among them. In 1921, reformers managed to enact a federal-aid highway system that required Washington to pay for the construction and maintenance of no more than 7 percent of a state's primary and secondary roads. If the money was a bounty for states, it came more directly as an inducement. To be eligible, state governments were forced to consolidate roadbuilding power in the hands of the expert officials who would begin using scientific methods to choose where the roads would be built.[37] This was Hamiltonian progressivism in its early glory—but there was more to come.

By the latter part of the 1930s, as Americans began to place even greater confidence in public authority, many began to dream more seriously about a system of national highways. In 1939, the same year General Motors sponsored a Futurama exhibit at the New York World's Fair sensationalizing expressways, the Bureau of Public Roads published a book, *Toll Roads and Free Roads*, exalting how modern roadways could work to fix the nation's teeming, impoverished, and often fetid cities. As with "slum clearance," many imagined that government could use new highways to spring those trapped in squalid neighborhoods by razing dilapidated homes and speeding access to cities from farther away.[38] The progressive mandate to connect isolated places was morphing into imagining ways of fixing purportedly broken ones as well. Centralized, disinterested expertise deployed, in yet another realm, for the greater good.

But even as progressives and bureaucrats schemed for a brighter future, two major hurdles stood in the way of real progress. The first centered on how the government would lay claim to the right-of-way required to build an interstate network. From the beginning of the federal-aid system, conservatives had prohibited federal dollars from being used to *acquire* land—those costs, they argued, should be borne exclusively by state and local governments. That changed only ahead of the bombing of Pearl Harbor, when Congress realized that the military was struggling as a result to erect new access roads to various military installations.[39] That, then, proved to be the camel's nose under the tent—once the military began purchasing land for roads, there was no going back. In 1944, mere months before Roosevelt's untimely death, he signed into law a bill that authorized a forty-thousand-mile "limited access" system to supplement the primary and secondary roads Washington was already subsidizing.[40] Three years later, Congress passed a bill designating the routes, with the presumption that Washington would pay for the bulk of the land, in addition to the construction.[41]

And that then pointed to the second hurdle: funding. Roosevelt, enamored of big public authorities like the TVA, had wanted Washington to finance the new system by seizing excess land for roadways, developing the adjacent lots, and using the revenues from those developments to subsidize construction. In much the same way the TVA had competed with Commonwealth and Southern in the market for electricity, he imagined a United States highway corporation competing with local real estate firms. But for the same reason many objected to the TVA—private developers weren't keen to compete with the federal government—the bill went nowhere.[42] Others proposed financing construction through tolls, but through the Truman years, old bulls on Capitol Hill, particularly Democratic chairman of the Senate Committee on Finance Harry Byrd, scoffed at the notion that toll revenue would be sufficient to pay off the astronomical expense of interstate construction. And so Roosevelt's

Hamiltonian dream of a new interstate system remained shelved for lack of money.

The postwar economic boom changed that. Robust growth prompted more families to buy cars. And those new car owners, many of whom settled in the new suburbs, began to fulminate over the traffic building on the nation's surface streets. So when, in 1955, the Bureau of Public Roads published what became known as the "Yellow Book" of maps sketching out where proposed new interstates were likely to be constructed, younger members of Congress began to agitate against the reluctant old bulls. What emerged was a classic legislative compromise. Per the desire for a new interstate system, Congress would authorize appropriations for their construction. But the new road system would not be funded by tolls or general revenues. Rather, the costs would be covered by sequestered gas tax receipts, and construction would commence only so fast as those coffers were filled.[43] Conservatives in both parties, wary of the grandiosity of progressive intentions, felt they had protected taxpayers against Washington writing a gargantuan blank check; progressives, eager to get building already, finally received a green light.

With that bipartisan agreement in place, the bureaucratic octopus that would come to be known as "the highway lobby" was born. Road builders, auto manufacturers, oil companies, and those developing the nation's suburbs were all, for the moment, aligned in common interest. And while viewed today by many reformers as the moment of original sin, President Dwight Eisenhower's signing of the National Interstate and Defense Highways Act in 1956 merely marked the apex of progressive efforts to connect isolated parts of the country. This was an archetypical Hamiltonian project— an effort to centralize power such that Americans would be able to "drive from Maine to California without hitting a traffic light."[44] It was a distilled example of government solving a tragedy of the commons by pulling power up from down below. And what emerged in the decades that followed was, to both its champions and detractors, nothing short of remarkable.

America would go to the moon during the same period, and the military-industrial complex would emerge to counter communism's global ambitions. But here, with the nation's expressways, was an illustration of how government could alter life in ways that citizens could see and touch. The whole program, which would eventually grow from forty thousand to forty-nine thousand miles, took almost forty years to complete.[45] By the late 1960s, interstates had come to occupy more than fifteen million acres of the nation's landscape—a combined landmass roughly the size of West Virginia. And what the *Wall Street Journal* would eventually label the "highway-auto-petroleum complex" would come to employ 20 percent of the nation's workforce.[46]

The interstate highways were, by any measure, a feat of ingenuity. But they were also a monument to the American Establishment. And not just to the powerful figures in Washington who championed the financing mechanism that made the system possible—the system vested the bulk of its authority in an octopus of state and local figures empowered to designate the routes, negotiate the purchase (or seizure) of private property, and manage the construction. And as with the alphabet soup of New Deal programs that had helped to lift the country out of the Great Depression, and the military that had defeated fascism, this was centralized power being used effectively for the greater good.

Here, as in other realms, power gave officials a remarkable degree of mostly unchecked discretion. Through the years, Establishment officials, spread across various bureaucracies in various states, were slated to take possession of more than three-quarters of a million parcels of land in the name of expressway construction.[47] And to do that, they would collectively have to prevail over an innumerable slate of objections—people who didn't want their homes, or their farms, or their parents' graves destroyed in service of a new road. And that would mean creating a bureaucratic apparatus that could push past obstacles—giving public figures the power to bulldoze the opposition, literally and figuratively. If, as the experts had concluded, it was in the *national* interest to have a highway system, *parochial* concerns would have to be kept at bay. And despite that, the whole project initially proved popular.

Some bristled, of course—protestors in New Orleans and in Cambridge, Massachusetts, mobilized early on to thwart new routes.[48] But more abject than any widespread fear that a new interstate would ruin a town or city was the concern that accompanied being bypassed.[49] As in San Antonio and Memphis, the pervasive worry was that *absent* expeditious ways to drive around and through parts of the country, designs on growth were more remote. People wanted quick access to the interstates for fear of being left behind. And that was the entire endeavor's core appeal: much as subsequent generations would see expressways as tools that had been used to divide America—to create barriers between neighborhoods—the notion at the beginning was that these roads would bring people together, both between and within cities. Roadways were a salve for the isolation that had prevailed in America's past. They were imagined as nothing less than a revelation—until, that is, progressivism's cultural aversion to power began to reframe the movement's understanding of its once great triumph.

THE FREEWAY WARS

Progressivism's subsequent turn against the interstate system—Buttigieg's more recent comments about the system's racist moorings reflect a standard critique—did not emerge overnight.[50] As early as the late 1950s, the prominent critic Lewis Mumford, complaining that the highway program had been conceived more for the benefit of the "motorcar" than society, argued that "in many parts of the country the building of a highway has about the same result upon vegetation and human structures as the passage of a tornado or the blast of an atom bomb." But to account for that destructive tendency, he didn't propose to thwart the system's expansion, as Jane Jacobs, Anona Stoner, and their acolytes would later demand. Rather, he wanted to perfect the new system, to better balance these major "arteries" with the "elaborate network of minor blood vessels and capillaries" that allowed humanity to circulate within cities.

Mumford's peevishness may not have been entirely on the level. He was likely angry that the aesthetic vision he'd proposed for the nation's expressways had been rejected in favor of a more affordable, utilitarian alternative. He had proposed, for example, that Massachusetts's Route 128, the interstate that winds itself around Boston's outskirts, be built with enormous parks *between* the lanes of traffic, thereby creating a "green belt" for public recreation. This, of course, would have required the government to seize even more land—to purchase or condemn more homes and businesses, driving an even more impenetrable barrier between those on either side of the now-widened roadway. But in the aftermath of Eisenhower signing the 1956 bill, Mumford's frustration typified the core of progressivism's complaint: the centralized planning was not sufficiently robust.[51] Government was failing to think bigger—to be bolder.

Democrats in Washington responded to this criticism by mandating a new *process*. Kennedy administration officials worried less that expressway construction was doing damage than that highways, transit, and housing construction weren't being sufficiently coordinated—that highway engineers were making decisions that failed to account for all the other changes happening simultaneously around them. They reacted by inserting into a 1962 bill a provision known as Section 134, which mandated that any urbanized area of at least fifty thousand people create and maintain, by the summer of 1965, a planning process that was continuing, cooperative, and comprehensive—the so-called three C's.[52] Here again, the administration's primary intention wasn't to give citizens greater voice; it was to give "experts" even more authority to manipulate the urban landscape. Progressivism's Hamiltonian impulse remained at the wheel.[53]

Nevertheless, it was at this moment, as the New Left was beginning to come into its own, that the Jeffersonian impulse began seeking its level. Cracks began to emerge in the coalition that had initially supported the highway program. For one, cities and states began bickering among themselves. In most rural and suburban parts of America, county and municipal governments were not technically equipped to make the sorts of routing and engineering decisions that were integral to building an expressway, thus leaving it to state highway officials to do so from on high. But cities were more typically replete with their own engineers, and mayors often had their own ideas about where expressways should be sited.[54] At the same time, corruption began to sour public perceptions of the broader endeavor. Any program of this size, scope, and expense was bound to be a target for corruption—and the schemes trickled out into public view. The chairman of Indiana's state highway commission was caught tipping off friends who, on several occasions, purchased parcels slated for condemnation only to flip them to the government at a profit.[55] Perhaps, many reformers would conclude upon closer inspection, the Establishment wasn't quite so unimpeachable.

Washington responded—but, again, less by trying to devolve power than by attempting to perfect its Hamiltonian approach. The Bureau of Public Roads (BPR) peeled its right-of-way experts out of its engineering division, believing the shift would free these more conservation-minded lawyers and wonks to push back against engineers who were more singularly driven to keep costs down. Here was pluralism's theory of balance in practice: if people divergently concerned about money and environmental impacts were put around a table together, Hamiltonians figured they would eventually come to a mutually agreeable solution. In 1964, BPR created a list of twenty economic, environmental, and social concerns that needed to be considered in any planning process, thus, again, trying to fix the program from on high.[56]

Here, the context really matters. In the immediate aftermath of the Second World War, citizens had been more inclined to bend to the Establishment's wisdom—and engineers came to expect that audiences would react to their official presentations with oohs and aahs. But as public skepticism grew, the questions became more pointed. Community members became less pliant, and engineers became more abrasive in turn, taking umbrage when their hard work was called into question.[57] It wasn't exactly that the planners disputed that some communities would be inconvenienced by their projects; they simply took for granted that *they* spoke for the public interest, and that those voicing objections were selfish and small-minded. Asked about public opposition to one of his projects, Robert Moses explained: "The individual has to yield in matters of this kind to the entire country, to the advantages and needs of the majority of people."[58] Here, in mundane meetings about expressway routes and access roads, was a microcosm of the growing cultural divide pitting the Establishment against a new way of thinking. And it quickly turned nasty.

At meetings in San Francisco, protestors booed and hissed whenever anyone spoke in favor of plans to construct what would become the Embarcadero Freeway. Similar freeway revolts emerged up and down what many considered crunchier parts of the Pacific coast—Los Angeles, Seattle, Marin County.[59] But the second-guessing wasn't limited to liberal corners of the country. Iowans complained that 710 miles of interstate had devoured 26,000 acres of arable cropland. A report out of Kentucky noted that "severance"—namely the process of splitting a parcel to accommodate a road—was forcing 75 percent of affected farmers to sell stray areas of their own lots for lack of access. And residents of big cities across the country—Boston, Cleveland, Miami, and Indianapolis among them—were up in arms when confronted with plans made by imperious planners and engineers to bifurcate vibrant sections of their various metropolises.[60] Perhaps, many began to believe, the nation had been naive when Eisenhower signed the Interstate Act into law in 1956. Perhaps the upside wasn't worth the upheaval.

These new roads had been bound to be disruptive. But somehow, the toll began to be colored in a different light. A century earlier, when railroads had demanded new rights-of-way in order to run soot-belching trains through congested cities, corporations had been sensitive to the people they were inconveniencing if only because those same people were soon to become their regular customers. That wasn't true for most highway engineers. Once they'd built their expressway, local citizens were un-likely ever to see them again. The Establishment, claiming wisdom of the greater good, was functionally removed from the citizenry—a plane above—and had no incentive to bargain.[61] By 1966, Verdelle Smith's song "Tar and Cement," ruing what highways destroyed, rose to 38 on the Bill-board chart.[62] And that reflected the broader contemporaneous cultural shift. Planning, sprawl, and growth were becoming a broader menace even as the Establishment was being questioned in other contexts at the same time (see Chapter 3).[63] The hostile meetings about expressway routes were not convened in a vacuum.

Unsurprisingly, many beacons of the Establishment interpreted the blowback as evidence that they needed to centralize power even further. *Better* planning. *Wiser* decisions. *Savvier* engineering. If experts were given *greater* authority to fashion their plans with fewer hurdles—if they were liberated to deliver utopia more expeditiously—the doubters could finally be made to see. So the same 1966 bill establishing the Yarbor-ough rule rechristened the Bureau of Public Roads as the Federal High-way Administration and merged that singular bureaucracy with other transportation-related agencies under the aegis of the newly established federal Department of Transportation. This new behemoth was conceived to be a more coordinated emanation of public power. If the engineers in the bowels of these various federal agencies had, by the mid-1960s, developed a reputation for deafness to public frustration, old-school reformers imag-ined that putting everyone under a single roof could tamp down popular discontent. A Hamiltonian solution to a distinctly Hamiltonian problem.

The temptation to tighten the Establishment's grip extended down to states and communities as well.[64] A year before establishing the Urban Development Corporation (see Chapter 6), New York's governor Nel-son Rockefeller, frustrated that the state's Department of Transportation wasn't performing to his or the public's satisfaction, directed a large por-tion of a $2.5 billion transportation bond to the new Metropolitan Trans-portation Authority. This new public authority, to be run by his loyal

262 | WHY NOTHING WORKS

lieutenant, William Ronan, was established in part to make it possible for Rockefeller to build an airport north of New York City and a bridge spanning the Long Island Sound between Rye and Oyster Bay. He similarly assigned the Thruway Authority responsibility for finishing an expressway paralleling the Hudson River.[65] And the subtext of *all* these moves was that these public authorities, purportedly more responsive to the governor, would be able to get their jobs done more expeditiously.

Perhaps, in theory, this "up and in" approach could have worked, even in the face of intensifying public frustration. But, as in other realms of public policy, the cultural aversion to power found its voice not only in community meetings but also in the courts. Vocal public opposition surely played a role in ensuring that Rockefeller's airport and bridge were never built. But the issue wasn't just that those whose homes stood where the runways and ramps might be laid attended forums to complain. It wasn't just that those who worried that bridge traffic would gridlock their secluded suburbs organized rallies on the town square. Rather, by the mid-1960s, people threatened by Rockefeller's bridge and airport schemes had new ways to leverage the power of the judiciary to stop the governor and his lieutenants from moving forward. In much the same way critics of housing developments managed to weaponize the law in service of lassoing the Establishment's grand designs, opponents of new public works employed the same tactics. And in so doing, they illustrated how Jeffersonianism was snapping back into shape.

An early front in this battle centered on Rockefeller's plan to build a new Hudson Valley expressway. In 1966, the same year Senator Ralph Yarborough schemed to kill San Antonio's North Expressway, New York's engineers were plotting the route for what would, for a time, become I-87, an interstate splicing up from New York City through affluent Westchester County. Residents of the county's well-to-do towns were of scattered (and often self-serving) opinions about where the new highway could best be routed, some preferring an option a bit farther to the east, others the west. But no matter which route highway engineers ended up selecting, some number of New York's toniest suburban communities were bound to be unhappy. And so, when the engineers chose their route, the suburbanites did what has subsequently become de rigueur among those united in opposition to a perceived slight from a group of outsiders: they formed an interest group. A few years earlier, even the residents of Westchester County might have been more pliant—more accepting of the government's plans. But in 1966, residents who believed that engineers should have chosen a different route established the Road Review League. And the Road Review League then filed a lawsuit.

The core of the League's complaint was simple: the state's highway engineers had chosen the wrong route. And if their justification was self-interested, the group's concerns were real enough. The chosen route *would* destroy a bunch of high-value property. Construction *would* be noisy and dirty. The finished highway *was* likely to bifurcate several nice neighborhoods. And perhaps most important, the engineers *had* been presented with other options. So the lawsuit asked the federal judge hearing the case to direct the bureaucrats to select an alternative route—to substitute his judgment for that of the engineers'. The government responded in court in the most Hamiltonian way possible, arguing essentially that ordinary citizens had no standing even to bring suit—that the legislature had endowed the executive branch with the authority to make these sorts of decisions, and that allowing citizens (and, for that matter, judges) into the process would just invite chaos.

Perhaps surprising the Establishment's ardent defenders, Judge Edward C. McLean, a Republican who had been appointed to Manhattan's federal district court by President Kennedy, rejected most of the government's arguments. There was nothing in the law that precluded ordinary citizens from challenging expert decisions—they were affected by a government decision, and therefore had standing to bring suit. That said, McLean noted that no provision in the law permitted a judge to substitute his or her judgment for the experts' determination. If a highway department took all the proper factors into consideration and reached a conclusion someone didn't like, courts could not unilaterally substitute their judgment. Route choices were the prerogatives of the lawmaking and policymaking branches of the government, not the branch charged with interpretation. And in McLean's estimation, New York State and the Bureau of Public Roads *had*, in fact, followed a reasonable process in selecting I-87's route, so he had no grounds to set it aside.[66]

But in rejecting the citizens' lawsuit, McLean's ruling also pointed the way for aggrieved parties like the Road Review League to utilize the courts more effectively. If the government *hadn't* followed the proper procedures—if, in exercising their discretion, policymakers had failed to weigh the relevant concerns properly, or had neglected to investigate the potentially adverse consequences, or had looked past impacts that should have been considered before making a decision—then a purportedly expert decision *could* be struck down. That sort of procedural oversight could well deem the government's decision "arbitrary and capricious," to use the phrase from 1946's Administrative Procedure Act. In other words, ordinary citizens couldn't question an expert's discretion, but they could challenge the *process* the experts had used to come to their decisions.[67] And that proved to be a revelation—a sliver of opportunity that opponents of various government decisions could use to wedge open closed Establishment-dominated decision-making.

By the late 1960s, highway construction was claiming 62,000 housing units nationwide each year, with the most significant impacts falling on Black neighborhoods.[68] And while Hamiltonian voices were promising to build *more* housing to replace what had been lost through programs ranging from urban renewal to Rockefeller's prized Urban Development Corporation (see Chapter 6), reformers were more drawn to an alternative strategy.[69] Far from wanting to transfer more power *up* to the likes of Lyndon Johnson or Nelson Rockefeller, progressives were driven to cut the nation's power brokers *down*.[70] And suing over flaws in process proved to be a mechanism to do exactly that. Best yet, this particular Jeffersonian strategy did not require reformers to hatch grand schemes to repeal the programs big government was employing, or even to divine alternative ways to accomplish the big problems those big programs had been designed to allay. Using the courts, they could simply argue that even minor elements of the processes the big bureaucracies used to make even minor decisions were, for example, "arbitrary and capricious."[71] That was all the leverage they would need; here was a way to align the movement's agenda with its cultural aversion to power.

Just a few years earlier, progressives might have chosen to address the range of complaints now before them with more purely Hamiltonian approaches. Historic buildings were being demolished; many reformers might have imagined then that the best way to preserve them was to assign a centralized bureaucracy the task of deciding when they could be demolished. Various species were seeing their habitats ruined by changes in the physical landscape—the development of new housing, of new factories, and of new infrastructure, including highways. Progressives might previously have fought primarily to create a bureaucratic star chamber sworn to decide which parcels of land could and could not be changed for fear of species extinction. Many progressives became increasingly concerned about the noise that washed over areas bisected by expressways—they might have created a centralized institution to determine when noise pollution was too much to allow a project, and how much road builders should be required to spend in order to mitigate impacts on any given neighborhood. Or, they might have created a single bureaucracy to take *all* these and many other issues under consideration, weigh the trade-offs, and render final decisions.

But by the latter part of the Johnson administration, this Hamiltonian approach had lost its purchase. Reformers no longer trusted centralized bureaucracies with massive grants of authority. The figures appointed to such august positions appeared inevitably prone to capture, if they weren't crooks in and of themselves. Even if they held themselves to a higher standard, few would have imagined them giving sufficient weight to the interests of the historic buildings, or the endangered species, or the victims of noise pollution—they would have appeared more poised to rubber-stamp whatever Robert Moses or Richard Daley wanted. Even if they received the testimony of potential victims, they might set it aside, as highway engineers had been so prone to do when compelled to convene public meetings about new expressways. The salve for all these problems, many knew almost instinctually by this point, wasn't going to be found in centralizing power, but in *de*centralizing it. By following the light shown by Judge McLean. By empowering individuals to challenge the *process* by which any given bureaucracy came to a decision.

Not that Hamiltonian strategies were excised *entirely* from the progressive agenda—new bureaucracies *were* created, and in some cases they were granted various fiats of authority. Planning boards. Landmarks commissions. Community councils. Yet the real action wasn't in the new power now wielded by those on top, but rather in the ways that the public now could push around those with that power. The National Historic Preservation Act (1966), for example, established two seemingly centralized nodes of power: the president's Advisory Council on Historic Preservation and the National Register of Historic Places. But the real teeth of the act were found in the requirement that any project using federal funding undergo what's known as a Section 106 review—namely a process designed to determine whether any given change would impact a historic site, and if it would, what was being done to minimize the impact.[72] And there, in that last element, was the invitation to a Jeffersonian fix: if a citizen believed that the project sponsor was *not* taking a historic site into proper account, or that the mitigation strategy had been cobbled together in some way that a court might view as arbitrary, capricious, or otherwise insufficient, they could now bring suit. And then a judge, rather than any centralized bureaucracy, would make a determination.

That mix of Hamiltonian and Jeffersonian reform was typical. The 1966 bill creating the Department of Transportation was designed, in theory, to centralize power—to give the president and his political appointees more direct control over the planners and engineers who had previously worked so imperiously to impose their will on defenseless communities. But that same law included the original version of the Yarborough rule. The reauthorization of highway and interstate construction in 1970 added noise to the list of issues engineers had to address, thereby opening administrative decisions to more expansive judicial scrutiny. The Endangered Species Act of 1973 purported to add authority to bureaucrats within the Fish and Wildlife Service and the National Marine Fisheries Service. But the bill simultaneously required highway engineers to minimize the impact their decisions might have on the habitats of species at risk of extinction.[73] In each case, provisions that appeared to empower the bureaucracy, or to focus its mandate, served more directly to open discretionary decisions to new examination through the courts. Historic buildings, green spaces, neighborhood tranquility, endangered species—these would all be protected less by powerful figures at the top of the food chain than by outside interests holding an enfeebled bureaucracy's feet to a judicial fire. The Establishment's discretion was being curtailed.

Reformers could be forgiven for failing to see the significance of the shift. If you were determined simply to ensure that the gleaming old buildings in your hometown were protected from a developer's wrecking ball—if you just wanted to prevent condos from replacing the beautiful art deco theater situated at the heart of your neighborhood's quaint little commercial strip—you might not have had any occasion to think through any broader political implication; you would have simply just wanted to stop the Establishment in its tracks. And even those who were on the front lines of the broader debate about which sorts of policies to pursue were, at the outset, dubious about whether the Jeffersonian approach could really prevail over the long run. Joseph Sax, a committed environmental activist, referred to the whole strategy of attacking the Establishment on procedural grounds with derision as late as 1973: "I know of no solid evidence to support the belief that requiring articulation, detailed findings or reasoned opinions enhances the integrity or propriety of administrative decisions. I think the emphasis on the redemptive quality of procedural reform is about nine parts myth and one part coconut oil."[74]

But Justice Thurgood Marshall's opinion in *Overton Park*, taken in combination with a whole range of opinions written by, among others, two judges on the DC Circuit Court of Appeals, J. Skelly Wright and David Bazelon, fundamentally altered the dynamic. Not long after the *Overton Park* ruling, the Center for Science in the Public Interest published an analysis of seventy-six NEPA-mandated environmental impact statements. More than a dozen hadn't mentioned air pollution. Nearly a fifth made no mention of noise pollution. Almost every report had failed to consider alternatives like mass transit.[75] And while these oversights may have been due to nothing more than a bureaucrat wanting to get a project done with a minimum of delay, the nation's judiciary made clear that they were grounds for upending the projects altogether.[76] Passed with the best of intentions, laws designed to require that decision-makers account for consequences beyond the scope of their original intention became tools in any opponent's toolbox.

Here, the National Environmental Policy Act of 1970 became a procedural lynchpin. Planners and engineers began to weave the full panoply of protections into the singular process of environmental review. That then streamlined the way government weighed the impacts of any project on water quality, on noise, on historic buildings, on air quality, on endangered species, on recreation, on waterway navigability, on racial dynamics—the list went on. A project that might impact electricity transmission lines *and* an endangered species *and* the fishing industry *and* a river's navigability would be brought under a single rubric, with experts from all the various responsible bureaucracies working through their separate concerns. The government would then come to a decision, mitigating those concerns to the maximum extent possible, but arriving at the public interest. But then the kicker: if the process used to reach that decision was in any way defective or deficient, outsiders were entitled now to sue on the grounds that the review had been insufficient, and courts were willing in certain circumstances to shut them down.

The shift that occurred in the 1970s and 1980s is often described as *cultural*. In the wake of *The Power Broker*'s publication, Jane Jacobs–type admonitions had eclipsed the public's tendency to accept Establishment wisdom. But perhaps more important, and certainly more everlasting, the *process* for doing, well, almost anything also changed.[77] The old authorizations for highway planning and construction remained largely the same—state highway engineers persevered the same prerogatives to plan, erect, and maintain new roads, and the federal government still reimbursed states at much the same rate. But the underlying power dynamic had been turned on its head. Bureaucrats had once acted with impunity—now the people boasting of those same positions operated under the novel scrutiny of every detractor, almost any one of whom could bring suit on the basis of the bureaucrat's failure to consider this or that concern with sufficient detail or scope.

Even if judges *did* rule in a project's favor—and in many cases, still to this day, planners and engineers *do* prevail—the sheer avalanche of rigmarole narrowed the scope of what once powerful bureaucracies could ever hope to accomplish. And that was the underlying point. The once powerful bureaucrat's burden under the new regime wasn't to engineer a road, or a rail line, or whatever else—it was to navigate the requirements and obstacles, to create a record of each factor contributing to a decision, and to anticipate the lawsuits that were sure to be filed against any decision.[78] Environmental impact statements, initially imagined at NEPA's birth to be 150-page documents, eventually came to be volumes long, the length born of a bureaucratic desire to insulate any given decision from criticism that a concern had not been sufficiently considered. And that pushed many projects, both good and bad, beyond the pale of consideration. The old Hamiltonian approach had, of course, provided no real mechanism for community input. But the new Jeffersonian regime belabored the process beyond what many initially imagined. All the legal technicalities aside, the underlying dynamic was clear: power once wielded by the Establishment had been diffused, pushed down and out to those who might well have objected. And the open question was whether the public was well served by either extreme.

NO SUCH THING AS SHOVEL-READY PROJECTS

The American economy was still sluggish when *New York Times* reporter Peter Baker was granted an interview with President Barack Obama in the fall of 2010.[79] Two months before the shellacking Democrats would sustain in the midterm elections, Baker asked the president to explain why massive federal investments he'd pushed through Congress hadn't yet sparked a more robust economic recovery. In a seemingly contemplative mood, Obama wondered aloud how he might have handled things differently. He acknowledged that funding poured into the nation's dilapidated infrastructure hadn't yet pulled the country out of the economic doldrums. But, the president argued, that wasn't for lack of effort or money. Rather, he explained, the problem was that "there's no such thing as shovel-ready projects."[80]

At the time, Obama's complaint was interpreted as a commentary on government incompetence—the administration had provided billions for infrastructure, but the planners and engineers who would spend it hadn't been ready to go. No one disputed that America's infrastructure was in rough shape coming out of the Great Recession. But the problems predated the mortgage bubble's collapse two years earlier. While other countries—most specifically China—were racing ahead with modern new roads, rails, wires, ports, and more, America seemed stuck.[81] White House advisors might have imagined, upon Obama's signing the $787 billion American Recovery and Reinvestment Act in early 2009, that the president would spend the next two years traveling the country posing for pictures with ceremonial shovels at various groundbreaking ceremonies. But it hadn't happened.

The frustration wasn't new. For years, progressives had fulminated that the country lacked the *political will* to get big projects going.[82] And they'd adopted a range of theories to explain that lack of gumption. Some postulated that elected officials were too preoccupied with their next campaign to champion projects that might be completed only after they were out of office. Others theorized that elected officials were cowed by the wealthy property owners who might object, not to mention the community groups that would demand public concessions. Or perhaps the problem was just a lack of salience: public works don't tear at the heartstrings like abortion rights and school shootings, and so progressives trained their focus elsewhere. Whatever the problem, the lack of progress had left the country lagging—and would continue to do so. China has erected more than 23,000 miles of high-speed rail. As of 2025, the United States still does not boast a single operational line, unless you count the drastically slower Acela, which runs a mere 457 miles from Boston through New York to Washington, DC.

But for all that progressives tend, still today, to ascribe their frustration to a lack of political will, the bulk of culpability clearly rests elsewhere. Robert Moses managed to remake New York's physical landscape not just because he was determined, or manipulative, or unyielding; he succeeded because he operated during an era without nearly so many roadblocks. With power pulled up and in, Establishment power brokers had been able to work their will with relative ease. But the movement had subsequently awoken to the attendant abuses with horror, and that revulsion steered reformers back into a Jeffersonian crouch. The cultural aversion to power had driven policymakers to erect new checks, balances, and hurdles. In short, Obama's dreams of an infrastructure bonanza weren't spoiled by incompetence, but by design. It was impossible to get *good* projects going in the 2000s explicitly because it had been so easy to pursue *bad* projects in the decades before.

The effects of progressivism's turn against power are evident today not just in the projects that haven't happened but in the price paid for those that receive the green light. The cost of an average mile of interstate tripled from the 1960s to the 1980s.[83] And while some of that can be ascribed to rising prices for concrete, steel, and labor, recent research suggests as much as a quarter of the increased costs had been driven explicitly by the cost of litigation.[84] When Citizens to Preserve Overton Park sued to stop I-40, Anona Stoner had appeared like a judicial pioneer; now, her approach is standard fare. And while project opponents don't always win, the new rigmarole almost invariably adds expense and time, precluding government bureaucracies and others interested in erecting or improving infrastructure from spending those dollars on other projects.[85] Delay, in short, has become project opponents' most powerful weapon.

California's ongoing struggle to build a high-speed rail line between San Francisco and Los Angeles is a case in point.[86] The route appears like a no-brainer—two large cities, a lot of traffic between them, with most travelers forced to either fly or drive. But whether or not the state's leaders have been willing to stand behind any given route or plan, no surfeit of tenacity has proven capable of pushing through the process reforms (the California Environmental Quality Act, for example) that render stick-to-itiveness almost inconsequential. It's simply too easy to raise objections to a route decision over environmental concerns, or whatever else. Each study, lawsuit, and adjustment drives up the cost. No one has the power to push the plan forward. And the same story prevails almost everywhere. Governors and bureaucrats today wield less power in their respective states than Robert Moses did in New York alone—and that's not because they aren't as driven as Moses was. It's that reformers have purposefully clipped their wings.[87]

Moreover, many of the guardrails had been erected *inside* the bureaucracy. Environmental reviews have typically been assigned to single agencies—the Federal Transit Administration might be tasked, for example, with overseeing the evolution of a proposed new light-rail line. But other agencies within the federal government are responsible for approving the final report. The Army Corps of Engineers might have to sign off on whether a proposed bridge would interfere with ferries traversing the water below. The US Fish and Wildlife Service might have to sign off on the impact new forest track might have on an endangered species. The EPA might have to sign off on any potential impact on the local water supply. No matter how committed the executive branch as a whole might be to enhancing transit accessibility, that particular public-policy goal would be viewed as entirely secondary to bureaucracies charged with preserving navigability, wildlife, or water quality.[88] And each might be subject to public-interest litigation if they failed to upend the approval.

In an era where Hamiltonianism prevailed, a single figure could have sliced through all those concerns. But in an era defined by a more Jeffersonian ethos, government is hamstrung by the process. The federal bureaucracy has tried in various incarnations to craft mechanisms for weighing competing concerns—for deciding how many homes should be taken in lieu of cutting through a public park, or how many fishing boats could lose access to a lake in service of preserving local water quality. Disagreements between the Federal Highway Administration and the Fish and Wildlife Service over a new bridge can be resolved by the Council on Environmental Quality, or the federal Permitting Council, or even the president.[89] Congress can demand expedited reviews, as it did in the Fiscal Responsibility Act that President Biden signed in 2023.[90] But in an environment where an increasingly beleaguered universe of bureaucrats is worried that courts will excoriate them for failing to take proper account of any among a seemingly unending list of concerns, the greater good gets lost in minutiae. Set aside the abuse wrung by Robert Moses–type figures; today, no figure is empowered to ratify a trade-off.[91]

Many of these guardrails have been erected for the good—the rise of various Jeffersonian protections has managed to smother a handful of bad expressway projects in the crib. Yet the new system guarantees not only that less will get done but that when projects *do* come to fruition they will be much more expensive. Environmental impact statements completed from 2013 to 2017 averaged nearly six hundred pages.[92] In 2020, the White House Council on Environmental Quality released statistics suggesting that the average environmental impact statement takes more than four years to complete and is nearly seven hundred pages long.[93] And the problem isn't only federal. If a property owner in New York City contests a condemnation, the ensuing legal fight can today last ten years.[94] The environmental assessments for Seattle's East Link light-rail system were compelled to analyze twenty-four separate routes in great detail; in Canada, that sort of intensive study is not necessary because the environmental review process presumes that the government has determined the most effective alternative and simply seeks to minimize impact.[95]

These heightened costs aren't on the margins. Recent studies have found that infrastructure costs in the United States aren't twice what they are in South Korea—they're more than *six times* as expensive.[96] That disparity was particularly stark due in part to the costs of building in New York City, where the recent Second Avenue Subway demanded twenty times as much as similar projects in other global cities.[97] But projects in other American cities cost on average 50 percent more than projects elsewhere. A 9.3-mile line requiring construction of a tunnel in Toulouse cost the same as a 3.2-mile project constructed at grade in Houston.[98] And so no one should be perplexed as to why China has built so much more high-speed rail. Even with more money, Amtrak would need new rights-of-way to straighten its track. And all too often, the deluge of protections drives costs beyond the point of feasibility.

If the "absence of political will" is a red herring, the oft-proposed salve for the problem of community opposition may be even more invidious. As in the realm of regulation, where NegReg became a siren song for those hoping to herd stray interest groups into alignment (see Chapter 5), opponents often complain that the problems are born of bad sequencing—that ideas are sprung on stakeholders too late in the process. They imagine, somehow, that notifying people who stand to lose something important to them might have cleared the way to consensus. Infrastructure white papers often imagine that if the planners had just engaged citizens *from the outset*—that if the communications plan had been more thorough, or the plans had been subject to widespread scrutiny, or the engineers had engaged in a grassroots strategy to weave the community together—the process might have been smooth.[99]

But when the stakes are high—when, for example, a new high-speed train track is going to be installed a few blocks from someone's home—no "give" is realistically capable of placating the opposition. A region *as a whole* may benefit from a new rail line—less pollution, fewer traffic jams, improved mobility, a surge in economic growth. But as is true in any tragedy of the commons, the individual neighborhoods and hamlets inconvenienced by a new line are almost sure to be worse off. No tax break, no promise of a new community center, no noise-controlling barrier is going to convince them that they should bear the burden of the broader region's progress. Robert Moses didn't keep his plans secret simply because he relished springing a surprise—he shrouded his intentions so as to thwart the opposition. And the same dynamic prevails today, except that those who object to a project have many more levers to pull to prevent it from moving forward.

In 1978, when Memphis mayor Wyeth Chandler testified before the Senate subcommittee on transportation about the barriers to completing I-40 through Overton Park, he made his frustration clear. Like nearly every other powerful figure in Tennessee, he worried that downtown Memphis was going to suffer without expedited access to the suburbs. But even more than his exasperation with the result, he was angry with the process. The opposition's calls for the state to investigate alternative routes—routes, everyone knew, that would invariably require additional homes and businesses to be taken—appeared to Chandler to be little more than delaying tactics. "We need no more study," the mayor argued. "We need no referendum. We need the legislative bodies of this Nation to review the record of unbelievable Alice-in-Wonderland-like series of planning studies, administrative hearings, public hearings . . . court hearings, on and on, and draft a law that gives due credence to the proposal."[100]

Say what you will about that particular expressway; America's infrastructure troubles today aren't born primarily from the government's failure to invest.[101] The problem hasn't been born from a lack of will, or a failure to accommodate detractors. Rather, the foundation of progressivism's frustration, and the genesis of America's general skepticism of government, is the reality that there are too many hurdles to clear, crosses to bear, and vetoes to avoid. Obama's Recovery Act, for example, spawned a full 192,705 NEPA reviews.[102] Is it any wonder why he couldn't find any "shovel-ready" projects? Or that voters have been losing faith in government? Who would want to give *more* authority to a bureaucracy that is so utterly conflicted against itself?

Here is progressivism's self-contained dilemma distilled to its essence. Reformers want both to build great infrastructure *and* to protect communities from coercive power. We want fast trains without having to cut straight rights-of-way. We want the benefits of Robert Moses without the drawbacks. We are willing to throw money at improvements, but we fear unleashing the Establishment. And rather than seek to balance these two impulses, progressivism has, through the decades, toggled between the two, letting Robert Moses–like figures run amok during one period, and then overcorrecting in the decades that follow.

From time to time through the last several decades, clear-eyed reformers have recognized that the process has become too pockmarked with veto points. And they have, on occasion, managed to strike some good blows against "red tape."[103] A bill passed in 2005 made it possible for government to pursue projects in public green spaces that had a "de minimus" impact.[104] Environmental suits must now be filed in shorter order. Highway administrators have imposed new guidelines with catchy phrases like "Every Day Counts" or "One Federal Decision" in the hopes that officials will be spurred to work more expeditiously.[105] Perhaps most hopefully, President Biden signed a reform in 2023 that directs bureaucracies to complete their permit reviews within two years.[106] But the problem today is not born from any one law. It's in the water—endemic to the process, to the jurisprudence, and to inertia. Most of all, it's born from a lack of perspective.

No one who has read *The Power Broker* can reasonably argue for a return to the era when Hamiltonian dogma was left unchecked. But today's Jeffersonian predicament is an oppression of its own. Rather than toggle interminably between the two impulses, progressives need now to put them in harmony. Beyond merely reforming one law because it serves as obstruction for one tranche of projects, and repealing another law because it's a barrier to a separate set, the movement needs to grapple with the uncomfortable reality that girds policymaking: there is no process, no protection, no approach that will obviate the burdens of progress. Government should be open and transparent in seeking to understand every angle and concern. Policymakers should seek to mitigate the attendant harm. But, in the end, *someone* responsible to the greater good needs to be imbued with the discretion to point the way forward. A movement born in the late 1800s from a frustration that government couldn't deliver has spent the last half century correcting for the grievous errors of centralized authority. The correction has itself become oppressive. Now, the movement needs to come full circle.

8

A Tragedy of the Commons in Reverse

PROLOGUE: A BONANZA FOR VACATIONLAND

On a bright, sunny Monday in the summer of 2016, Massachusetts governor Charlie Baker sat outside the Bay State's gold-domed statehouse to sign a bill designed to ensure that "Massachusetts and New England can remain a leader in clean and renewable energy production."[1] The bill, passed after a year of wrangling among the state's overwhelmingly Democratic legislators, sought to curtail the region's carbon emissions without driving up electricity bills. To that end, the Baker administration was authorized to coordinate the purchase of clean electricity generated from, among other potential sources, wind turbines planned for the shallow water off the state's southern coast, and from hydropower generated by dammed rivers in Canada.[2] But because Massachusetts did not share a border with Canada, the new hydropower would have to travel through a neighboring state. And that, many quickly realized, would add several complications.

Climate change was a particularly potent political issue in New England, a region then, as now, dominated by progressive legislators. The nation as a whole had seen energy prices drop dramatically after fracking enabled nearby states to tap new stores of domestic natural gas. But if consumers elsewhere were happily taking advantage of the new bounty, New England was loath to embrace yet another fossil fuel—while it was cleaner than coal, burning gas still emitted carbon.[3] And so Massachusetts, the largest and most powerful of New England's six states, had been eager to identify affordable clean energy alternatives. Quebec's government-owned power company, Hydro-Québec, had been using a fleet of sixty-three hydropower plants to produce almost all of the province's electricity for decades.[4] Now, Bay Staters wanted to draw from Canada's surplus—reformers proposed purchasing enough to cut 3.5 million metric tons of greenhouse emissions, the rough equivalent of taking 700,000 cars off the road each year.[5]

To do that, someone would need to build an enormous transmission line—something the functional equivalent of a giant extension cord— from north of the Canadian border, across New York, Vermont, New Hampshire, or Maine, and into the power grid serving Massachusetts.[6] A whole range of companies submitted proposed routes, each bidding for Baker's support. And after evaluating the proposals, Baker's administration decided in 2018 to move forward with a plan submitted by the enormous energy company Eversource. "Northern Pass," as the proposal was named, would build a 192-mile transmission line south from Canada, through New Hampshire, and into Massachusetts.[7] The challenge would be to get the Granite State to agree.

Eversource had actually proposed much the same project before Baker signed his 2016 climate bill.[8] But without the newly authorized incentives, utilities would have had to raise consumer rates more than regulators were inclined to approve. Now, with Massachusetts offering to subsidize the expense, the project seemed financially viable. Unfortunately, as details became subject to greater public scrutiny, New Hampshire began to balk. Northern Pass was slated to cut through the iconic White Mountain National Forest. Interest groups, perhaps most boldly the Society for the Protection of New Hampshire Forests, began to raise environmental concerns. Residents of the Granite State, famous for both their independence and simmering resentment of their haughty neighbor to the south, eventually concluded that their natural landscape was being sacrificed to serve the Bay State's thirst for clean power. Late in 2018, an obscure New Hampshire siting board killed the project by declining to authorize its construction.[9] And that was it—Massachusetts would have to look elsewhere.

Baker quickly pivoted to see if Maine might step up. Situated right across a long border from New Hampshire, the state that styled itself as America's "Vacationland" was led at the time by a bombastic Republican who governed in much the same mold as Donald Trump. Governor Paul LePage viewed Massachusetts's thirst for Canadian hydropower less as a scourge than as a point of leverage. If the Bay State was willing to pay the cost, he could demand concessions. The line was poised, after all, to be constructed by Mainers. The line's owner would pay Maine in perpetuity to lease the land. Maine might even be able to purchase and divert some of the Canadian power on the cheap. And so LePage was supportive when Central Maine Power, a subsidiary of the Spanish-owned Avangrid, proposed to step in for Eversource with an alternative to Northern Pass, this project to be called New England Clean Energy Connect (NECEC).

Slated to cost a mere $950 million—a bargain when compared to Northern Pass's $1.6 billion—NECEC turned out to be more than a big extension cord. Engineers proposed that the new infrastructure also connect to several additional wind farm projects in western Maine.[10] Avangrid, estimating that the new infrastructure would create 1,700 jobs, promised LePage that cheap power imported from Canada could act as a check on rising prices for traditional fuel, taking roughly $40 million off Maine's utility bills. The communities touched by the new lines, Avangrid proposed, would harvest more than $18 million in new local tax revenue— payments made essentially as rent for the utility poles set up nearby.[11] And perhaps best of all, as LePage and Avangrid were keen to remind Mainers, Massachusetts would foot the entire bill. By almost any standard, this was poised to be a bonanza for Vacationland.

But like their neighbors in New Hampshire, Mainers soon came to worry that they were being "used" by the Bay State. Early on, a group concerned about those proposed wind farms—a purported threat to western Maine's natural beauty—formed an advocacy group, Saving Maine, to fight the new connection.[12] Initially dismissed as self-serving, their concerns began to have real purchase when a collection of more reputable environmental groups began expressing similar reservations—the North Woods demanded protection.[13] And that wasn't the only complaint. The new line not only threatened to gash through beautiful woodland, it would cross the Appalachian Trail three separate times. It was slated to run over the region's purported crown jewel, the Kennebec River Gorge.[14] Vacationland was a draw for its natural beauty, and NECEC appeared increasingly like a scourge to the state's tourism industry.

There were financial complications as well. Avangrid was proposing to supply as much as a sixth of Massachusetts's electricity—enough to power 1.2 million homes. That new supply promised to claim market share from the older, dirtier, less efficient power plants that had long served many of the same consumers. The president of a trade group representing the incumbent generation plants complained that his members had invested more than $13 billion in various facilities on the presumption that they would be able to recover those costs over future years of service.[15] And that prompted an archetypical "politics makes strange bedfellows" moment: those wanting to preserve the beauty of Maine's North Woods were aligned with advocates wanting to protect the fossil fuel industry. Both viewed the roughly one thousand steel structures Avangrid would erect through western Maine as a serious threat.

Initially, NECEC's supporters appeared to have a leg up, having proactively nurtured relationships with the communities slated to host the line. Setting aside the global benefits of bringing more clean power online, Avangrid's representatives had gone town by town, carefully delineating all the benefits that would accrue to each municipality. Enhanced reliability. Portions of a $50 million fund established to offset electricity bills. Tax revenue to renovate schools, or improve roads, or even cut local levies. Details in hand, town boards in twenty-nine separate communities adopted resolutions proactively supporting the line.[16] And to some outsiders, that made the venture appear like a slam dunk: if a Trump-like populist like Governor Paul LePage and the host of climate-focused interest groups were *both* supportive of a proposal that promised to be both a financial boon to Maine and a powerful blow against carbon emissions, could it realistically be defeated?

As it turned out, quite possibly yes. Once the motley crew of conservationists, not-in-my-back-yard localists, and entrenched oil, coal, and natural gas–burning electricity generators organized themselves, they emerged with a series of well-articulated counterpoints that echoed the same complaints that had scuttled New Hampshire's Northern Pass.[17] NECEC's development hinged on approvals from a whole range of government bureaucracies. Maine's Public Utilities Commission would have to determine whether there was sufficient demand for the new line. The state's Department of Environmental Protection would have to ensure the wilderness was properly preserved. The Army Corps of Engineers would have to ensure that the project would not unduly impact navigable waterways. Even the Department of State in Washington would have to approve because the wires crossed an international border.[18] If opponents could get *any* of these various bureaucracies to reject the project—any single one—they might prevail. The race was on to find a veto.

Admittedly, the line was going to exact real costs. Some portion of Maine's vast wilderness was going to be affected. So, to head off public frustration, Avangrid began making additional concessions. Executives agreed to invest $22 million in conservation projects to compensate the state's tourism industry.[19] Responding to concerns that the power line would somehow ruin the grand vista of the Kennebec River Gorge, the company abandoned its plan to build the line *over* the river, promising to bury the wires below—a shift that would cost $37 million.[20] And when opponents began complaining that the package of compensation Maine would receive was paltry compared to what New Hampshire had been promised through Northern Pass, Avangrid offered to sweeten the pot even further.[21] Nevertheless, it wasn't clear that these additional concessions would suffice. And as Governor LePage was set to end his second term, Democratic attorney general Janet Mills, poised to be installed as his successor, began to criticize the project on the campaign trail.[22] Perhaps this was going to end up like Northern Pass.

As it was, Mills came around after her inauguration. Soon thereafter, her administration negotiated and signed what became known as "the stipulation," a new pot sweetener that saw Avangrid agree to invest $140 million in "rate relief" for ordinary Mainers, with an additional $50 million for low-income families. Avangrid promised also to invest $15 million to subsidize the installation of heat-pump furnaces—alternatives to the gas- and oil-burning boilers that prevailed throughout Maine. The company threw in $15 million to enhance the facilities required to accommodate electric cars, like charging stations.[23] And executives agreed to specific concessions targeting the economically strained areas of western Maine touched by the new line. In total, the package came to $258 million—$17 million more than had been offered to New Hampshire. For a state that had long struggled economically, the infusion of capital appeared to represent a true lifeline.

The concessions had a powerful political impact, inducing the Conservation Law Foundation and the Acadia Center, both leading environmental groups, to endorse the venture.[24] It gave Governor Mills cover to come out publicly in support as well, her endorsement helping to convince the state's Public Utility Commission to grant the project a certificate of public convenience and necessity in April.[25] By then it seemed as though the whole thing was settled. But, again, the notion that Maine was being hoodwinked, as opponents would argue with heightened fervor, proved effective in stirring up public opposition. Various environmental groups and competing energy companies had no incentive to wave the white flag. And so, by some measure, the battle had just begun.

NECEC's detractors came to understand that convincing any government body to exercise a veto would depend primarily on their ability to turn public opinion. So they organized what turned out to be a very sophisticated public relations campaign. Funded largely by a series of fossil fuel–burning energy companies concerned about losing market share—Calpine Corporation, Vistra Energy, and NextEra Energy, among them—local conservation groups served as the mouthpieces for what became known as "Stop the Corridor." The coalition published reports detailing the potential impacts of the new transmission line, arguing that it would gash through wetlands and cross streams, and bisect globally significant bird-breeding habitats with a clearance "as wide as the New Jersey Turnpike."[26] They managed to get Patagonia, the environmentally focused clothing company, to encourage its customers to sign a petition opposing approval.[27] And they paid particular attention to the towns along the corridor, hoping to spark anger among the Mainers most likely to have vistas interrupted by the towers and lines.

This last move was particularly audacious because many of these same towns had endorsed the project just a few months earlier. Local officials had in many cases spent significant time weighing the pros and cons of Avangrid's proposal, concluding that the localized benefits would outweigh the costs even before Governor Mills had negotiated the stipulation. But now, in the summer of 2019, with many of their constituents and neighbors mobilized by the Stop the Corridor campaign, some changed their minds.[28] Those withdrawals then put pressure on the state's Department of Environmental Protection and Land Use Planning Commission to look anew at whether the line violated the state's Natural Resources Protection Act and land use standards.[29]

By the end of 2019, NECEC's opponents had settled on what was essentially a two-pronged strategy. The first centered on the regulatory bodies that would have to issue permits and approvals for the project—Stop the Corridor would aim to compel regulators to question whether approving the project would amount to their dereliction of duty. The second, however, was further afield and, ironically, a vestige of early progressivism. More than a century earlier, the movement had fought to reform government so that citizens would have a new mechanism for legislating over the heads of captured machines—reformers being of the mind that robber barons and corporate interests had too powerful a hand among elected officials. Now, NECEC opponents hatched a plan to have the legislature pass a bill giving every bisected community an opportunity to kill the project via *local* referendum.[30] And while that idea did not gain a foothold, it laid the seed for another obstructive strategy: upending the project via a *statewide* referendum.

Stop the Corridor strategists remained hopeful it wouldn't come to that—that regulators would kill NECEC without their having to put the project up for a popular vote. The corporation running a gas-burning plant in Yarmouth, Maine, argued before the Public Utilities Commission that the alternatives to NECEC had not been sufficiently vetted, and that previous reviews had been "replete with errors."[31] An ecologist with the Maine Natural Areas Program voiced concerns that the chosen route might impact terrain serving as a home to the small whorled pogonias, orchids considered "threatened" by the federal government.[32] A member of the state's congressional delegation berated the Army Corps of Engineers for failing to be more transparent about its study of the route.[33]

Eventually it came time for Maine's ten-member Land Use Planning Commission to pass judgment on Avangrid's efforts to avoid spoiling three natural treasures: the Kennebec River Gorge, the Appalachian Trail, and the little-known Beattie Pond. The company's vow to dig below the gorge had eliminated that issue of contention.[34] Commissioners then accepted, however grudgingly, that there was no alternative to crossing the Appalachian Trail. But when it came to Beattie Pond, the commission deadlocked, frustrated that there *was* a better alternative but that Avangrid had refused to accede to a local property owner's demand that the company pay fifty times market value for land in a way that would reduce sight lines from the pond. After further search, Avangrid discovered a way to snake the wires over a strip of land nearer to the Canadian border owned by Yale University. For the cost of a single dollar (and other considerations kept hidden from the public), Yale granted Avangrid permission to erect towers through their property. And with that, the Land Use Planning Commission certified that the project met Maine's standards.[35]

Approvals in hand, Avangrid began making the investments necessary to break ground.[36] The company contracted for $12 million in wooden mats that would be used to ferry heavy equipment through the North Woods.[37] But opponents, still holding the threat of referendum in their back pocket, now endeavored to take the project to court. Several towns along the corridor joined a lawsuit to overturn the Department of Environmental Protection's decision-making process. Several environmental groups claimed that the wrong state bureaucracy had granted the project's approval. And NextEra Energy, still operating both an oil-burning power plant in Yarmouth and a nuclear plant nearby in New Hampshire, filed suit claiming that the state's approvals had been granted without substantial evidence.[38] But none of these cases went anywhere. And so, as a last-ditch effort, NECEC's opponents turned to what seemed almost like a nuclear option.

In early 2020, opponents submitted a petition with seventy-five thousand signatures in support of holding a referendum to demand that the state's Public Utility Commission withdraw the new line's certificate of public convenience and necessity.[39] Avangrid objected in court, claiming that Maine's constitution did not allow for a public voice to overturn a regulatory decision—that the proposed referendum "exceed[ed] the scope of the legislative powers reserved to the people" under the state's constitution.[40] In a remarkable turn, the state's Supreme Court ruled that the referendum could *not* go before the voters. "What is proposed here is not legislation," the ruling decreed. "Directing an agency to reach findings diametrically opposite to those it reached based on extensive adjudicatory hearings and a voluminous evidentiary record, affirmed on appeal, is not 'making' and 'establishing' a law."[41] It seemed, for a moment, as though Avangrid had finally run the gauntlet. But, again, no.

A continuing flurry of abortive legal efforts won opponents some continued delays. They argued, for one, that the Army Corps of Engineers had not been sufficiently thorough when evaluating the project's environmental impact. But when these various process-oriented objections faltered, opponents were left to focus again on the public referendum.[42] This time, rather than force a regulatory agency to reverse its own determination, they designed an initiative that would erect new political hurdles. If passed, this second referendum would require any proposed high-power transmission line to earn the support of two-thirds of the state legislature, and would furthermore ban wires through the remote portions of northern Maine. The language was *explicitly* legislative. And so, when a petition in support of the referendum was submitted with sufficient backing, the new statewide vote was deemed appropriate for the November 2021 ballot.[43] Finally, an advantage for NECEC's detractors.

The battle over what became known as "Question 1" became an almost all-consuming political affair through 2021, with $70 million spent on campaigns for and against passage.[44] Opponents of the proposition—those campaigning to see the new transmission line through—pulled out all the stops. Governors Mills and Baker, a Maine Democrat and a Massachusetts Republican, respectively, both endorsed the plan. Biden administration secretary of energy Jennifer Granholm made a public pitch. Both of the state's major daily papers wrote editorials dismissing the opponents' objections. And the nation's broader clean energy community—those bent on bringing more renewable energy sources online—weighed in, fearful that passage would chill clean energy efforts across the country. Advocates were nervous about the precedent.

This last part was particularly profound. There were, at that point in 2021, at least twenty-one high-voltage transmission lines nearing approval throughout the United States—enough to grow solar and wind power by 50 percent. But if regulatory approvals like the one in Maine weren't considered ironclad—if this one project could be overruled post hoc by referenda—lenders might think twice about making loans to companies proposing similar projects elsewhere. Alternatively, to account for the risk, they might raise interest rates, putting promising projects beyond financial reach. And that could set back the transition to green by years, if not decades. NECEC, was, in essence, a test case. Those interested in building out the nation's clean energy grid were watching the doings in Vacationland with studied concern.[45]

The project's opponents almost inarguably had the more compelling pitch. As in New Hampshire, resentment toward Massachusetts was woven deep into Maine politics—the supposition was that the Bay State was somehow trying to take advantage of its provincial neighbors. Vacationers who drove up the Maine turnpike each summer in their Land Rovers and BMWs were now attempting to exploit Maine's natural assets for their benefit. And so, in the end, by a wide margin—nearly 60 percent in favor—Mainers passed the referendum.[46] Suddenly, and for the first time since the campaign had begun a half decade earlier, opponents of bringing hydro to New England seemed to have the upper hand.

In the immediate aftermath, Avangrid issued a statement refusing to abandon the project, and the company quickly filed suit arguing that the referendum had violated Maine's constitution by reneging on a valid lease. The company's chief executive, noting that Avangrid had already spent $450 million on the project, cleared 80 percent of the right-of-way, and erected more than 120 electrical towers, vowed to complete the project by the end of 2023.[47] But executives nevertheless agreed to halt construction until the litigation played out. Despite Avangrid's contention that they could find an alternative route to avoid the Upper Kennebec Valley, the Department of Environmental Protection suspended the company's license.[48] Opponents were, by this point, elated. It appeared like their Hail Mary strategy had paid off.

The better part of a year later, in August 2022, the Maine Supreme Court weighed in. The justices wanted a lower court to decide whether the work Avangrid had done *before* their license was suspended was sufficient to protect the endeavor from being upended retroactively by the referendum. The case was tried in April 2023, nearly a year and a half after the opponents' victory at the ballot box.[49] Avangrid's lawyers argued that the company had "vested rights" to finish the line. The state of Maine, now litigating against a project it had once championed, argued that Avangrid had sped up its construction explicitly to rob Maine voters of the opportunity to work their will.[50] At the end of a seven-day trial, nine jurors took a mere three hours to return with a unanimous verdict: Avangrid, they determined, *did* in fact have a vested interest in completing the approved route. The company could proceed with NECEC despite the referendum.[51]

By then, however, another problem had emerged. The line, when initially approved, had been slated to cost $950 million—an amount that ratepayers in Massachusetts had agreed to cover. Now, however, Avangrid estimated that inflation and delay had driven the costs up to $1.5 billion.[52] It had by then been seven years since former governor Charlie Baker had signed the climate law promising to finance the project, and Massachusetts was now halfway through the period it had given itself to reduce its carbon emissions to 50 percent below its 1990 levels. It wasn't clear, even then, that this cornerstone of the most ecologically progressive state's plan to address climate change was actually viable.

By the point that NECEC's financing became the subject of renewed debate, the project had been the focus of no fewer than thirty-eight reviews.

The trial in April 2023 had generated two million documents.[53] Vegetation had begun to grow in parts of the corridor that had previously been cleared.[54] And despite all that, not a single watt of additional clean Canadian power had flowed into the American grid.[55] To further cloud the picture, a Connecticut-based company filed suit to stop the project because, in their view, the line was not available for use by other small energy projects. The new governor of Massachusetts wanted to review whether Bay Staters were getting a fair deal.[56] And it was anyone's guess what further obstacles opponents might throw in the project's way. As of March 2024, the project was not slated for completion before late 2025.[57]

NECEC is just one project, running through just one state, tucked into one corner of an enormous country. Its fate, by itself, will not determine whether America can stem the global threat of climate change. But the barriers thwarting construction of this one high-voltage transmission line aren't unique—they were, and are, indicative of a more typical rigmarole. Not all transmission lines are worthwhile. Not all efforts at conservation—of neighborhoods, of forests, of species—are self-interested. Preposterous as some of NECEC's opponents may have been, others presented legitimate gripes. That said, the system's inability to metabolize concerns, let alone come to an expeditious decision on whether to build the new line, poses what is perhaps the most important cut against efforts to stem climate change. Even if we have the *will* to overcome our addiction to fossil fuels, is there actually a way?

THE POWER OVER POWER

If the process for approving new transmission lines appears almost entirely inscrutable today, the initial build-out of the nation's electricity grid must have appeared to many Americans like some zany plot out of a science fiction novel. Here, at the turn of the twentieth century, was a newfangled technology, operating almost akin to magic, transporting some invisible force into people's homes by dint of nothing but metal wire. In the early days, this magic was delivered almost haphazardly by competing companies, each having to string or bury wires along public routes and between private properties. These companies weren't endeavoring to build out the nation's electrical grid for the greater good; they were sending electricity across publicly owned spaces, through private technology, in ways that were notoriously dangerous, all in efforts to turn a profit. And, in many cases, enfeebled government was cowed by them—public authority wasn't sophisticated enough to ensure against private-sector abuse.

The results were largely predictable—electricity's emergence sparked public anger. And while some of that fury was directed at the electric companies themselves, a great deal focused on public-sector incompetence. What if an electricity company wanted to build a little power plant on a block adjacent to your house? What if executives wanted to string wires across your backyard? What if they were preparing to bring electricity to the house attached to yours—one that, if it caught fire, might spread an inferno? What if a local power company refused to serve your block? What if they charged an unreasonable fee? Who would ensure that the two competing power producers didn't collude to drive prices up? No bureaucracy existed capable of imposing order on the prevailing chaos.

In an age when the entire electrical marketplace was immature— when, in many cases, little companies were setting up their own little plants, importing the raw materials required to manufacture power, and then serving that "load" through largely unregulated networks of wire— these sorts of disputes were rampant. In 1889, the mayor of New York City was so incensed by rooftop wires that he dispatched city employees to chop them down with axes. One journalist, describing the "copper and steel wire octopus that has so encircled our streets," reported that crowds cheered on Broadway when electrical poles fell.[58] And the growing tension between the private and public interests presented a classic Progressive Era dilemma. Reformers began to ask how the miracle of electricity might be deployed to the masses without trampling the rights of individuals.

And in an age of rising Hamiltonianism, many were drawn to the same potential salve: centralizing power in the hands of disinterested experts.

In the first decades of the twentieth century, progressivism's centralizing impulse spurred many reformers to recommend public ownership of the entire industry.[59] Referenda favoring arrangements authorizing municipalities to assume control of private infrastructure were so pervasive that private companies often became the most vociferous advocates of regulation—they viewed public oversight as the less radical alternative to municipal ownership. Electricity investors worried about suffering the same fate that had befallen many trolley (or "traction") companies— Chicago's 1906 municipal election had been won by the candidate promising to take ownership from the private corporations running various routes. Amid the uncertainty rife within the early electricity marketplace, it wasn't clear which approach—municipal ownership or public regulation— was more likely to prevail.

Fortunately for private industrialists, support for public takeovers flagged when the bottom fell out of the municipal bond market in 1907. To that point, small towns and cities had found it fairly affordable to borrow capital at low rates, with that easy money enticing mayors and city councils to buy out private interests (sometimes forcibly) on the presumption that they could then expand and improve the various grids put under City Hall's control. In many cases, these had proven to be shrewd investments: a city that purchased a couple of small and inefficient generators located near bustling neighborhoods could replace them with more efficient facilities set further away—a win-win-win for consumers, residents, and investors alike. But when, in 1907, lenders began to worry more acutely that cities were investing those borrowed funds haphazardly—that elected officials weren't astute enough to avoid municipal bankruptcy—higher interest rates induced many city officials to back off that strategy altogether. Reformers, in turn, began to seek alternative ways to exert control. Public oversight presented itself as the obvious solution.[60]

The stampede to *regulate* the electricity industry did not, of course, emerge in a vacuum. This was the same moment that standard-issue Hamiltonian progressivism was coming into full bloom, with Wisconsin, New York, and Massachusetts imbuing new public-sector regulatory commissions, staffed by expert professionals, with the authority to establish standards across a range of industries. These commissions will, to the contemporary ear, sound like incarnations of the sort that corporate interests openly revile—the kinds of bureaucracies subjected to regular broadsides from organizations ranging from the US Chamber of Commerce to the American Enterprise Institute. But, in fact, not only were these explicitly progressive institutions often welcomed by many in the private sector—they were, at the outset, celebrated as a way to pry private industry from the tentacles of machine-controlled legislatures.[61]

Perhaps most profoundly, many reformers came to believe that professionalized commissions were better positioned to balance the competing interests of profit-seeking investors and a price-sensitive public.[62] Experts frequently appeared open to experimentation—to modifying regulatory regimes as conditions changed in the marketplace. And that was the essence of their public value proposition: in exchange for allowing a private company the opportunity to provide some utility—electricity, telephone service, sewers, and more—regulators could demand certain concessions.[63] They could benchmark reasonable rates of return for investors. They could set reasonable rules limiting the company's license to install, say, electrical poles on the edge of a citizen's private property. They provided a venue for warring parties to air their disputes and have them resolved.[64]

These arrangements had their critics, but the potential upside was clear for the private and public sectors alike. Absent the power yielded by regulatory commissions, early electricity providers might have chosen to serve only the better-off neighborhoods equipped to purchase the service. They might have provided poor customer service without any fear of sanction. But if, in the case of regulated electricity providers, a utility agreed to work within a public commission's regulatory regime, and often to serve every potential customer within a limited geography, they were granted in exchange an exclusive franchise. In other words, if the company promised to connect wires to all the homes and businesses in a certain region, executives could be freed from the concern that a competing venture would cut into their revenue.

The public return from these sinecures was substantial. Perhaps most important, progressive regulation opened the door for private money and public power to work in harmony. The nation's electrical grid expanded in ways that would have been much less likely if private companies had been incapable of leaning on public authority—if there had been no way for a utility to put up a pole when a recalcitrant property owner was determined to keep a lot pristine. Commissions could expeditiously bless a utility's claim on that private property. On the other hand, municipally owned systems might have been unable to tap private capital to expand service to poorer or more remote corners of their various jurisdictions. Here, in the end, was a compromise arrangement where everyone had something to gain.

Take, as an example, the story of Samuel Insull, a British immigrant who arrived in the United States to serve as Thomas Edison's secretary and subsequently rose to lead Chicago Edison. Insull noted at one point that Lake County, Illinois, located just south of the Wisconsin border, was dotted with a whole phalanx of inefficient power plants, each serving a small, localized grid. The county's patchwork system even included a small plant run by a "gentleman farmer" who sold power to his immediate neighbors. Insull proposed to replace the jerry-rigged network with a top-down system powered by a single, efficient plant sited along Lake Michigan. It was an audacious suggestion—one that, most notably, promised to benefit the consuming public by providing cheaper, more reliable electricity. But seizing the opportunity required business and government to work in harmony. A company alone would not have had sufficient authority to impose its network across public and private interests alike; a government alone might not have had access to the huge sums of money required to get the project constructed. Working with the government, however, Insull's new operation managed to turn a profit even while lowering the consumer's price of electricity from 7 cents per kilowatt-hour to 2.9 cents.[65]

Insull's success was a near-perfect distillation of Hamiltonian progressivism's great promise—professional expertise and public authority combined to do for ordinary people what neither the market nor the government was capable of doing on its own.[66] By 1930, every state but Delaware had established some sort of public utility commission regime—each charging some group of experts with overseeing water, gas, or electricity systems, among other large enterprises serving the public.[67] And while they varied on the specifics—some were elected, others appointed, some with huge staffs (940 in California), others much smaller (15 in Utah)—the core of the proposition remained the same everywhere. Independently powerful government bureaucrats maintained the power to grant private industry sufficient runway to operate at a reasonable profit, assuming they provided good service to everyone within a designated geography.[68] This represented order from chaos in a way that served the greater good.

Beyond marrying government and industry in common purpose, Hamiltonian regulatory schemes worked because they were malleable. Progressive theorists presumed that, as technology changed, the commissions would evolve with it—that as new, more efficient power plants, wires, and appliances became available, these public bodies would abandon old arrangements and, in an orderly way, improve service.[69] That malleability was crucial because the electricity marketplace remained immature. What might happen, for example, if a company wanted to sell power across state lines—namely, that is, from a market regulated by one commission into a market regulated by another?

The issue came to a head in the 1920s when the Narragansett Electric Lighting Company, based in Rhode Island, reached an agreement to supply power to the customers of Massachusetts's Attleboro Steam and

Electric Company. When Narragansett subsequently asked Rhode Island's public utility commission for permission to charge a higher rate, officials in Providence agreed. But Massachusetts objected, arguing that Rhode Island regulators had no authority to approve a rate change in a neighboring jurisdiction. In a key 1927 decision, the Supreme Court ruled that *neither* state had proper authority—that interstate commerce was exclusively a federal responsibility. But the federal government had not, to that point, made any provision for exercising federal authority in this arena. And despite the progressive answer to this problem being almost blindingly obvious—a federal agency—conservatives in the Coolidge administration had no real interest in growing the federal bureaucracy.

Only amid the horrors of the Great Depression was Washington finally propelled to grant regulators more control over the energy marketplace. And here, as in other realms, the Establishment took hold. Together, the New Deal–era Federal Power Act of 1935 and the Natural Gas Act of 1938 established fairly bright lines between what states could regulate and what was the domain of the federal government. But the two laws were different in at least one key respect. Because natural gas, once extracted, had to be transported across state lines for burning, the executive branch was granted pipeline siting authority. Federal legislators made no similar provision for transmission lines because electrical current wasn't being sent vast distances, meaning that the siting of electrical equipment would remain the province of state and local regulators.[70] And that, then, established a foundation for a complex but largely centralized regime that would guide the electricity industry during the postwar era. Few would argue that the system was perfect—but it was *balanced*.

Over the course of the following several decades, federal and state regulators would often tangle over who was authorized to control various elements of the system, and everyone had their gripes. Consumers sometimes complained that the system was "captured"—that various regulators were too wedded to the interests of the companies they oversaw. Private industry griped that the regulators were too strict—that they prevented innovation and experimentation.[71] But through the 1970s, the nation enjoyed what some termed the "utility consensus." In service of growth, the government encouraged the consumption of *more* energy. In service of expanding prosperity, reformers wanted that bounty of cheap energy to be distributed to the farthest corners of the nation.[72] For all the hiccups and complaints, the downsides were a far cry from what might have prevailed had progressives *not* divined an architecture of shared authority. Progressivism had crafted a system capable of wielding power over power. The country was happy enough to rely on that balance—until, that is, circumstances changed once again.

THE CONSENSUS BREAKS APART

During the immediate postwar era, electricity had typically been generated near the places it was used—coal would be shipped from, say, West Virginia to Massachusetts, and then burned at a generating plant near the homes and businesses it powered around Boston. But alternative models seemed within grasp. In response to Soviet innovation, Eisenhower administration officials endeavored to construct a new American transmission system that would enable energy companies to send the electricity itself vast distances—allowing, for example, coal burned in West Virginia to power homes and businesses in Massachusetts directly. They proposed, as a demonstration, to erect this sort of transmission line between the Pacific Northwest and Southern California, allowing underutilized hydropower generated by the Columbia River to keep air conditioners humming around Los Angeles during the hot summer.

For years, logistical and political questions kept the proposal in check—the natural gas suppliers who traditionally supplied utilities in and around Los Angeles weren't keen to compete with hydroelectric power wired in from Oregon. But the Johnson administration worked through the details, and when an 865-mile transmission line known as the Pacific Intertie finally opened in 1970, the *Los Angeles Times* declared that the $700 million project "ranks with the pyramids as an engineering feat."[73] More consequential, the line offered a window into an entirely different way of organizing the nation's electricity infrastructure. During the consensus era, most of the nation's electrical marketplace had been "vertically integrated"—that is, responsibility for generating the power (burning the gas, coal, or oil) and then distributing that electricity to homes and businesses fell within the purview of a single institution. Now, it appeared, the electricity could come in from the outside, and that might open the door to more competition.

The Pacific Intertie represented one among a broad array of cuts against the old consensus. The fees regulated utilities were permitted to charge local ratepayers had typically been determined in some part by the cost of importing coal, oil, or gas and maintaining the plant that burned that fuel. If electricity could be brought in directly—and if that electricity was cheaper to generate—the local utility would no longer be able to justify the same rates. Having been outcompeted for the business of *generating* electricity, long-staid utilities risked being incapable of eliciting the same profits. And that created a novel problem: utility executives had largely cheered public regulation when it served to protect them from the threat of municipal ownership. But now those same regulatory commissions were poised to compel utilities to purchase cheaper electricity in the name of lowering rates.

The upheaval extended beyond the relationship between utilities and their local regulators. Through part of the 1960s, the industry had been focused almost exclusively on exploiting economies of scale—making improvements along the lines Samuel Insull had instituted in Lake County decades earlier. Consumers, regulators, and energy companies had all benefited when electricity prices fell and the market demanded ever more load. But now two things changed that: First, absent finding entirely new sources of power, America was beset with fewer small, inefficient generating plants to replace. Second, and perhaps, more important, during the

1970s, the market for fuel changed. In the wake of the Yom Kippur War, America faced an oil crisis. Supply shocks sent utility bills up, and consumers began to cut back.[74]

This was yet another reflection of the nation's increasingly cynical view of the power brokers who controlled the often shrouded institutions governing American life. In 1969, nine days after Richard Nixon had been sworn into office, a privately owned oil platform off the coast of Santa Barbara exploded, leaving muck to leak across eight hundred square miles of the Pacific Ocean. Less than a half year later, the chemical film sitting atop Ohio's putrid Cuyahoga River erupted into flames.[75] These two events, having preceded the oil crises that would define much of the following decade, burnished the growing notion that the nation's economic growth was coming at too high an ecological cost—that consumerism was denuding the nation's natural bounty. Put another way: the people who had been put in charge appeared not to be holding a torch for the greater good after all.

These various indignities worked to a variety of effects. For one, a slew of academic studies delineating the tendency of utility commissions to rubber-stamp industry requests for rate hikes spurred broad-based skepticism that they were seen in earnest as guardians of the public interest. Separately, reformers began to wonder more pointedly whether the fee-for-service model that had served to incentivize energy consumption perversely cut against designs on reducing energy use. Finally, during and after the oil crisis, many critics began to express concern that the country's thirst for cheap power had fed a national dependence on foreign countries that did not share America's best interests.[76] While progressives began to consider the wisdom of steering more generally in a new direction, it wasn't immediately clear where that new direction might point. No *new* consensus seemed right at hand.

The problem was that the nation's new priorities all cut against each other. Energy "independence"—that is, weaning the nation from its reliance on foreign oil—was bound to require either more drilling at home or else replacing cheap foreign oil with more expensive sources of clean power. The first option appeared sure to denude the environment, the second to worsen inflation. Unsure of the top priority, well-intentioned reformers often found themselves at odds. But perhaps even more frustrating for progressives was their inability to determine *how* to address the potpourri of problems. Would solutions emerge from centralizing power so that clean energy projects like the Pacific Intertie could overcome pushback? Or, alternatively, were they better advised to hack at the dynamics that had allowed the incumbent cabal of energy executives and regulators to lead the country down a primrose path? Who, in the end, should be assigned the difficult task of choosing how America would refashion the electricity marketplace: regulators, market forces, or some new amalgamation of the two?

As in other realms, the impulse to *de*centralize proved more appealing. By the 1970s, reformers were embracing an almost reflexive notion that the Establishment was prone to put profit above everything else. Some among the same coterie of federal judges then putting guardrails around highway engineers (see Chapter 7) began tightening the screws on the energy companies and the associated regulatory bureaucracies. A 1971 opinion drafted by DC Circuit Court of Appeals judge J. Skelly Wright criticized the Atomic Energy Commission's "crabbed interpretation" of environmental law. And his criticism of the lax manner in which expert bureaucrats oversaw a nuclear power plant in Maryland compelled the energy industry to engage in many of the same analyses that highway departments were now obligated to complete before starting new projects. Building new energy infrastructure became subject to many of the same process-centered limitations.[77] The guardrails being built for highway engineers were coming for energy executives too.

By some measure, this shift happened at the most inopportune moment: The infrastructure required to keep the old vertically integrated system in operation—the rail lines required to ship coal across the country so that it could be burned in plants located near the homes and businesses— had already been built. But the transmission lines that would be required for clean electricity to be sent long distances had yet to be constructed.

And that bifurcation had profound implications. With oil prices on the rise, Minnesota utility executives began looking for alternative sources of power; they eventually keyed in on coal being mined in North Dakota. But mining that coal and shipping it to be burned near the Twin Cities made less economic sense than burning the coal near the mine and sending the electricity by wire. As with the Pacific Intertie, they proposed a plan, subsidized by the federal government, to have consumers nearer Minneapolis and St. Paul pay for the 1,650 towers that would connect the 430 miles by wire.

The same dynamics that would later emerge in Maine quickly now came to the fore. Engineers assigned an algorithm to determine the course, lest anyone complain that the routing had been clandestinely manipulated by political insiders. But before any algorithm could set a path, planners had to assign values to different categories of terrain. Residential neighborhoods, for example, were assigned a value that would induce the algorithm to avoid them. So were unspoiled forests. The land that was deemed least valuable, and therefore most likely to be utilized, or even seized, was agricultural. The result was a route that claimed farmers' livelihoods much more readily than it impacted animal habitats. Unsurprisingly, residents of rural Minnesota were incensed, with one farmer noting wryly, "I guess a skunk is worth more than a farmer." Here was yet another instance where the Establishment appeared to be up to its old tricks.

What emerged in the subsequent months amounted to a cultural battle between Twin City suburbanites, many of whom prized the wilds of the state's parks and forests, and the farmers of rural western Minnesota. The ensuing unrest—what future liberal senator Paul Wellstone would call "America's energy war"—eventually turned violent. After the farmers sabotaging the poles were eventually compelled by state police to relent, the underlying tensions remained. Here, as in other venues, the old narrative emerged: Establishment figures had imposed their will over the protests of communities that were helpless to defend themselves—this population being one that was largely white and rural.[78] And for many progressives watching the story unfold, the inescapable conclusion was that the transmission line *could* have been erected along some less obtrusive route. Here, as in the story of Robert Moses, progressives could grasp the David-versus-Goliath dynamics. And so, much as they had done in the realm of highway construction, they determined to establish for potential victims a new set of Jeffersonian protections.

The Carter administration was, once again, caught in the middle. Even if the president might have *wanted* to upend the old regime, it wasn't always clear that hacking at the Establishment would guarantee an effective result. In the market for natural gas, for example, a crazy quilt of tax privileges and subsidies protected non-gas-producing states in the Midwest and Northeast from suffering under the weight of high prices. As a result, energy companies tapping reserves in Texas and Louisiana could sell the gas at higher local prices than if they sent it elsewhere via pipeline. When OPEC curtailed America's oil supply, leaving much of the country desperate for additional gas, Washington was in a bind: *deregulating* would subject various markets to much higher prices; but keeping prices low, or imposing *more* regulation, seemed likely to disincentivize the pipeline expansions.[79]

What emerged, per Carter's impulse to marry progressivism's Jeffersonian and Hamiltonian impulses, was a hodgepodge that satisfied almost no one. The president signed a bill allowing federal regulators, once limited to manipulating *inter*state gas markets, to control *intra*state pricing as well—an archetypical Hamiltonian effort to place more power in the hands of centralized figures.[80] But he also signed into law a little-known but influential law designed to empower the small-time energy producers to bring alternative sources of electricity online. Wind and solar energy were, at that point, expensive and unreliable—neither appeared capable of producing power at the scale the nation required. Given that technological reality, rate-conscious state and local utility commissioners had been loath to build out the sorts of lines and substations required to let these operations serve the grid. The 1978 Public Utility Regulatory Policies Act, or PURPA, required utilities to purchase energy from "qualifying facilities" at a benchmarked price.[81] Here, Carter was pushing power down.

The better part of a half century later, the energy battles of the 1970s can be hard to decipher. But the underlying dynamics in this realm resembled those in other areas of progressive thinking. What few questioned by 1980 was that the old regime had failed—that America's faith in the Establishment that had crafted the energy consensus had been misplaced. All the ideological lodestones of the incumbent model—the drive to induce the public to consume more electricity, for companies to exploit economies of scale, for regulators to nurture vertical integration—appeared suspect. Reformers, eager for something new, simply wanted to liberate the nation's energy policy from the energy octopus that had sold out the nation's natural resources in the name of profit. And as the movement's abiding concerns continued to evolve—environmental and climate-centered concerns were rising up the progressive agenda—the desire to pull power away from the Establishment rose more decisively to the fore.

FROM DEREGULATION TO PARALYSIS

By the 1990s, environmental concerns had emerged as the beating heart of progressivism's energy agenda. Not that costs weren't of any residual concern—they were. But the underlying presumption was that high prices were born less from market conditions than from a conspiracy of deep-pocketed corporate interests and captured regulators. It had been one thing to centralize power during the 1930s such that the TVA could extend service to impoverished pockets of the Upper South. But most every community was, six decades later, entirely wired up. So, amid concerns about pollution and global warming, progressives began thinking more expansively about how to get electricity providers to adopt cleaner forms of generation. The technology required to create power from wind and solar wasn't what it would become, but reformers were willing to pay some premium to begin "greening" the energy sector. The challenge was to speed up that transition.

Once again, progressives, faced with a variety of options, might have proposed to do for electricity what the federal government had done with retirement savings in the 1930s: establish a bureaucracy that would take responsibility from incumbent actors much as the Social Security Administration had assumed some share of the burden for guaranteeing Americans' income in old age. Rather than permit local utilities to choose the manner to generate electricity, or allow state public utility commissioners to decide where to invest, the Federal Energy Regulatory Commission (FERC) might have been given authority to dictate how Americans would get their electricity, and what they might be charged for it. That approach, however, was anathema to a whole range of interests, many of which were explicitly progressive.

To be sure, few among the power companies themselves were eager to embrace new rules that might imperil the returns they owed their investors. And state regulators had no real interest in being bigfooted by their federal counterparts. But the innate instinct among progressives wasn't to use command-and-control regulation to drive environmentally friendly reforms; it was to incentivize everyone in the sector to make these decisions on their own. To nudge them. To make dirty energy more expensive and cheaper energy more affordable. To set targets that states and utilities could strive to meet, potentially with sticks to punish those who fell short. To make it economically attractive to be environmentally responsible.

This alternative strategy, a desire to green the energy sector from the bottom up, was not only aspirational—it made intuitive sense. During the peak of the consensus era, when the energy sector had been vertically integrated nearly everywhere across the United States—that is, when a single company generated power and distributed it to the homes and businesses in its coverage area—incentives issued from on high were metabolized by utility executives who wielded real power over all aspects of their regional monopoly. A government mandate might compel an energy company to shut down a dirty coal-burning plant, but the regulator overseeing that transition might then allow the utility to charge its customers to cover the costs of the switch. In a system composed of centrally administered fiefdoms, there was a clear path to reform.

But the cultural aversion to power had spurred progressives not only to want to green the energy sector, but to strip the energy establishment of its traditional sinecure. The same impulse that had induced Jimmy Carter and Ted Kennedy to deregulate the airline and trucking industries in the 1970s now informed a progressive desire to give alternative energy producers opportunities to compete with the old guard. Here, reformers weren't eager to take control of the market; they wanted instead to force the old guard to compete in ways that would serve the greater good. And so, with the support of a whole phalanx of conservative voices eager to hack at government almost wherever its tentacles extended, progressives began angling to create a competitive, deregulated marketplace among those *generating* electricity.[82] The first trick would be to find leverage sufficient to steer utilities away from exploiting their own old, cheap, fossil-burning power plants. The second would be to convince those same utilities to spend the resources required to build *transmission* lines accessing that newly generated electricity. From a policymaker's perspective, that was no easy task.

Energy "deregulation" took off in the 1990s, with a bill signed by President George H. W. Bush giving independent power generators new access to the grid, and FERC moving to create markets for wholesale electricity. And while the nature of deregulation varied from place to place—in some cases, ordinary consumers were given the power to choose between energy suppliers; in others, local utilities were simply compelled to consider purchasing power from different power generators—by the late 1990s, nearly half the states had initiated some effort to create some competition. Then, however, when a crisis hit recently deregulated California in 2000 and 2001—Pacific Gas and Electric found itself unable to pay for the electricity required to meet demand, leaving the state mired temporarily in blackouts—the transition began to trail off.[83] And this created an odd dynamic. Everyone wanted to green the economy, but no one had sufficient leverage to drive the transition.

The ensuing paralysis reflected a unique dynamic within the nation's electricity system. If the officials running a state highway department want to build a new road, they may face steep public resistance, but they are empowered, in theory, to push their project forward. In the realm of electricity, however, no similar figure exists. Utilities in the 1990s had few incentives to build transmission lines to new generation facilities likely to put their generating plants out of business. Government, in the main, did not have the planners or engineers required to construct or maintain the electrical superhighways needed to transport the power created by, say, a new wind farm. In the old vertically integrated model, a regulator might have had the leverage to lean on that utility to build the required transmission line—promising, most likely, to allow that utility to charge customers higher fees to cover the costs. But in a deregulated marketplace, that leverage was gone.

In some cases, energy companies *did* want to build transmission lines—and they were blocked from doing so by the same barriers erected to stop government from razing whole neighborhoods while preparing to site a new expressway. At one point in the early 2000s, a private utility proposed to build a transmission line between Connecticut and Long Island. But local utilities threatened by the transfer of energy from one market to the other raised a whole host of environmental objections. Where exactly would the line come ashore? What impact would the wires have on the shellfish beds in Long Island Sound? How might the whole project impact New Haven's harbor? Arizonans raised similar objections when Southern California Edison proposed building a transmission line across state lines.[84] For every proposal to green the grid, or make it more resilient, there were interests who stood opposed. But those eager to build transmission lines suffered from more than a bevy of ordinary veto points. They were hampered by the reality that so many people could say no—and no one, ultimately, could push through to yes.

Remarkably, this problem was significantly less vexing in other realms of the energy industry. In 1999, FERC set a policy of approving nearly any gas pipeline for which there was market demand, meaning that if a natural gas company could demonstrate that a power plant was prepared to buy more natural gas, FERC would (with the exception of one project) not only approve the plan but also bequeath to the gas company the federal government's power of eminent domain. As such, if a farmer did not willingly offer to let a gas company erect the pipeline across his field, the gas company could "take" the property for what was deemed fair-market value.[85] But because the Federal Power Act, passed during the 1930s, had not anticipated the demise of vertical integration, a company proposing to site a new transmission line could *not* turn to the federal government for siting authority. And so when it came to greening the economy, the onus fell on the states, few of which wanted to impose transmission lines on their own residents simply to serve populations across the border.

Unfortunately for those eager to build up the renewable side of the industry, not every state was eager to set policy based on environmental concerns. Governors and legislators in coal-exporting states saw very little upside to siting new transmission lines carrying wind-powered energy from one neighboring state to another. Even if they believed that the new transmission line promised to strike a blow against climate change, it simultaneously threatened to undermine their local economies. And absent another figure powerful enough to drive the new line through the inevitable political opposition, many worthwhile proposals died on the vine. Deregulating the energy marketplace *sounded* good to progressives averse to coercive political power—and so did the idea of investing in the nation's electrical grid. But the two goals cut against each other in ways that often left the green economy wallowing in good intentions.

During the George W. Bush presidency, Republicans at both ends of Pennsylvania Avenue acted largely to protect the incumbent players. Conservatives stood in the way of efforts to make it easier to build new, cleaner electricity infrastructure. And that wasn't just a frustration for progressives; it was an irritation for many energy executives as well. At one point, the chief executive of American Electric Power, a conglomerate operating power plants in seven states, noted that, between 1966 and 1986, his company had built and begun operating huge facilities in West Virginia to burn locally mined coal that created power that reached all the way to Indiana. Now, he explained, new sources of power were coming online, but it was almost impossible to get that power from one place to another.[86] For all that the private sector bristled at regulation, the absence of public authority was also a big problem.

In 2005, reformers tried again. Sections of a massive energy bill passed that year created what were called National Interest Electric Transmission Corridors. Under the new provision, if the Department of Energy determined that there was good reason for energy to flow across state lines, FERC was now empowered to use eminent domain to site the line if any given state failed to accommodate a right-of-way—insiders termed this "backstop authority." But soon after that energy bill was passed into law, a ruling by the Fourth Circuit Court of Appeals seated in Richmond determined that backstop authority only applied if a state failed to come to a decision; if a state affirmatively rejected a transmission line, Washington was powerless to intervene. And so, yet again, those proposing to build transmission lines across noncooperative states were without any real leverage.[87]

Frustrating as it might have been, most reformers would have had to acknowledge by the mid-2000s that there was no realistic way to green the grid from the bottom up. Market forces could potentially play a role speeding the transition from fossil fuels—that was the impulse behind a policy called cap-and-trade, which sought to induce dirtier forms of electricity *generation* to subsidize cleaner alternatives. But the nut was harder to crack in the realm of electricity *transmission*. In a deregulated environment, the chain connecting those who harvested clean energy and those who used it was simply too complex.[88] As in the realm of infrastructure, no single entity had the leverage required to force the changes needed to bring clean power into the nation's convoluted energy system. And unfortunately, progressivism's Jeffersonian orientation was fundamentally allergic to establishing the Hamiltonian authority required to push the system toward environmental sustainability.

A FAILURE OF PROCESS

In December 2008, with the economy in the throes of the Great Recession, President-elect Barack Obama convened his senior aides for a meeting at his transition office in Chicago. They were, together, wrestling with the question of what the new president should propose as a stimulus. Soon-to-be chief of staff Rahm Emanuel was arguing, famously, that "you should never let a crisis go to waste." And in that vein, Obama was eager to entertain bold ideas that might have seemed outlandish before the crisis. A longtime resident of Illinois, the president-elect noted almost in passing that the administration could help connect the plentiful supply of wind power available in the Dakotas to the almost limitless demand in Chicago. What if the federal government proposed to build a big new clean transmission line? Vice President–elect Joe Biden liked the idea. Construction jobs. Clean energy. A way to integrate America's blue and red economies. A proposal that seemed to have something for everyone.

But Carol Browner quickly interjected. A Washington veteran who was poised to be the incoming administration's climate czar, she argued that it would be difficult to acquire the right-of-way—the line, she noted, would have to run through Iowa, Minnesota, and rural Illinois. Sure, Chicago would get power and the Dakotas would get jobs—but what would the in-between states get for hosting the wires? Moreover, Browner argued, the line would take years to build, offering few benefits until after all the requisite environmental studies and siting issues were resolved. The stimulus was supposed to get money out into the economy in the short term. Building a smart grid was all well and good, but it would take time.

Her points were well-taken, and by the time the meeting had adjourned, Obama had abandoned the idea. On to more promising proposals.[89]

It was at roughly this same time that an energy industry entrepreneur named Michael Skelly alighted on a similar idea elsewhere in the country. Skelly believed that the barren and wind-swept panhandle of Oklahoma was poised to be a fount of clean energy. He also presumed that the incoming Obama administration was going to be on the lookout for ways to green the grid. So he sketched out a plan to build wind farms in the Sooner State and deliver the power those turbines generated to the (federally owned) Tennessee Valley Authority. His Clean Line would cross Oklahoma, Arkansas, and finally the Mississippi River, connecting at its endpoint to the TVA's grid near Memphis. The whole operation would deliver power at $40 per megawatt—competitive with natural gas, and only slightly more expensive than coal.[90] To Skelly's mind, the project appeared to be a win-win-win. The Tennessee Valley would get cheap, clean energy. The United States would take another step toward reducing its emissions. And per Skelly's intentions, those who gave right-of-way to the new transmission line would get a slice of the project's earnings.

But if the project appeared promising to some, others saw it as a threat. For one, the legions of blue-collar workers employed at various fossil fuel–burning generation plants in and around the Tennessee Valley viewed wind power as unwelcome competition. To that same end, much as the Clean Line might eventually represent cost savings to the TVA and its customers, the whole endeavor threatened to undermine the government-owned utility's solvency—the TVA made a bundle running existing power plants. And of course there were implications for the communities in Oklahoma and Arkansas that would host the hulking towers lining the hundred-foot cut traversing intervening farms and forests alike. These same communities were, in many cases, hosts to coal-fired and nuclear power plants that served the TVA, meaning that they were being asked to give right-of-way to a project poised to put locals out of work.

At the outset, Skelly thought he could amicably work out these various concerns. He was prepared to cut deals with property owners who were reluctant to let him site towers on property they controlled. What he found, however, was that many of Clean Line's opponents were entirely intractable—there was no deal to be done. In Arkansas, only utilities could erect transmission lines, and only companies serving customers could be considered utilities. As a result, Clean Line, which planned purely to pass electricity *through* Arkansas, needed a regulatory exception. But the state's regulators had no real incentive to provide one. And that left the project in a kind of catch-22. In the absence of regulatory approval, investors viewed Skelly's ideas with skepticism; absent the stated interest of those investors, regulators were loath to consider an exception. Clean Line had made so much sense on paper, but the process of making it happen seemed fanciful.

Skelly kept working at it nevertheless. In the spring of 2012, Obama administration Energy Department officials agreed to let Clean Line use the federal government's siting authority, so long as Clean Line reimbursed the federal government for any expenses and used eminent domain as sparingly as possible. And by 2015, Skelly had managed to prevail on the powers that be in both Oklahoma and Tennessee to buy in. But even with federal siting authority, Arkansas remained an obstacle. Early in 2015, Arkansas's two conservative senators, John Boozman and Tom Cotton, jointly introduced a bill designed explicitly to curtail the backstop authority that Congress had given FERC in 2005, scaring off at least one of Skelly's investors. Obama's energy secretary, Ernest Moniz, backed Skelly up, brokering a deal that exacted additional concessions. Subject to the new agreement, construction was scheduled to commence by 2018. But then, as Obama's presidency came to a close, the whole thing unraveled.

The Trump administration, once in office, showed no real interest in Skelly's project. And without support from Washington, Skelly was almost entirely without leverage. The project's opponents pounced: Senator Lamar Alexander, an influential Tennessee Republican closely aligned with the fossil fuel interests selling power to the TVA, resolved to put the whole matter to bed. Taking to the Senate floor, he brazenly threatened the TVA's leaders with investigations and recriminations if the utility refused to relent—and the TVA almost immediately caved. After working to make the project a reality for nearly a decade Skelly abandoned the whole endeavor.

Blame for the downfall typically centered on climate-denying conservatives. Donald Trump, Lamar Alexander, John Boozman, and Tom Cotton were, and are, after all, hardly at the vanguard of efforts to save the planet from the scourge of fossil fuel.[91] But Republican intransigence hadn't been the sole root of the problem. If, in eight years of Obama's presidency, a project to replace carbon-emitting generation with wind power couldn't prevail, the system was more fundamentally broken. This was, at root, a failure of *process*. The succession of hurdles a proposal like Skelly's had to clear, and the absence of any centralized authority capable of pushing past entrenched resistance, made it practically impossible to pursue. In a system full of vetoes, no one has sufficient power to push through a worthwhile endeavor. And Clean Line's failure was more the rule than the exception.

The hit parade of potentially worthwhile clean energy projects undermined explicitly or implicitly by the legacy of progressivism's Jeffersonian impulse is too long to list in full. But the most blatant examples make clear that the problem isn't just climate denialism. Progressives mobilized, for example, to fight a developer's plan to build a 690-megawatt solar plant northeast of Las Vegas, with the detractors claiming the new facility would imperil a desert tortoise habitat.[92] The Audubon Society sued to block wind farms in California.[93] The Sunrise Movement, a youth-oriented project whose tagline is "We *are* the climate revolution," mobilized to fight solar projects in Amherst, Massachusetts, for fear that new paneling might lead to deforestation.[94] And the local chapter of the Sierra Club would play a crucial role in the fight against NECEC in Maine.

The problem, at root, isn't that these groups are mobilizing against phantom concerns—the costs born from renewable energy and transmission are real. Moreover, the spirit of conservation, which many of these groups were established to promote, is legitimately at odds with what would be worthwhile efforts to reduce carbon emissions.[95] But if progressives might once have had faith that government officials could be trusted to weigh the pros and cons, Jeffersonianism's cultural aversion to power has denuded the system's capacity to make tough calls. The movement had very purposefully granted various countervailing concerns with what amounted to vetoes. And while each veto may serve to protect a worthwhile interest, piled together they almost inevitably foment paralysis. Almost worse, the contemporary impulse to limit creativity has had the perverse effect of incentivizing projects less likely to take climate concern into account.

For years, for example, Florida Power and Light (FPL) harbored designs on building a high-voltage transmission line from the state's northwestern panhandle, near its border with Alabama, south toward Orlando, Tampa, and Miami. The utility's ability to move power around the state would allow executives to purchase energy from a broader range of generating plants—and perhaps some would eventually be greener than others. But the Sunshine State's Transmission Line Siting Act, passed years earlier to prevent utilities from erecting unsightly metal towers in neighborhoods that might otherwise be powerless to fight back, stood in the way. The law hadn't been intended to preclude new lines entirely; it simply required that any proposed high-voltage line be approved not just by the state's Department of Environmental Protection and Public Service Commission, but by the state's cabinet as well, a body that included several independently elected officials.[96] And, in this instance, FPL hadn't been able to clear that hurdle.

To be sure, the process had been designed to be politically treacherous, to impede any governor inclined to rubber-stamp a utility's requests to seize land or erect unsightly or unwelcome infrastructure. And FPL had earned a reputation for being insensitive to local concerns. The result was gridlock: much as it might have made economic and environmental sense to connect power available in Florida's panhandle to consumers further south, interests opposed to the line were always able to pick off members of the cabinet inclined to heed an objection. Having given veto power to many political figures eager to play the hero to communities worried about new towers, the law made it impossible for the state's electricity utility to move forward.

Eventually, however, the utility alighted on a loophole. The Transmission Line Siting Act, FPL lawyers realized, only applied to high-voltage lines—the bill did not preclude utilities from erecting the sorts of ordinary distribution lines that customarily connect buildings. As such, FPL was permitted to build a transmission line to a lesser voltage—161 kilovolts instead of 230—along the same proposed route without having to seek approval from the cabinet. The new lower-voltage line would bisect most communities in the same disruptive way, but it would not boast nearly so many of the benefits: it would be less efficient, losing more electricity mile upon mile thereby forcing the company to purchase more power to get the same load to customers. Perhaps most galling, ratepayers would be forced to cover the cost of that lost electricity, in addition to the $692 million required to build the line.[97]

The Transmission Line Siting Act hadn't been passed with bad intentions—legislators had wanted to protect communities from FPL's penchant for imperiousness. The loophole for lower-transmission lines had been included for good reason as well—to allow energy companies some flexibility to move energy around with less obtrusive poles. But the combination had left progressives with the worst of several outcomes. As it was, everyone lost. The line was built with nearly all the attendant disruptions but few of the benefits.

THE LEASH TO BE COMPETENT

If some conservatives have spent decades questioning climate science, few who have studied the evidence harbor any real doubt. The facts are clear: Temperatures are rising. Polar ice caps are melting. Melted ice caps will drive up sea levels, imperiling coastal communities, changing weather patterns, and sparking more destructive storms. The deluge of effects will spread more famine and disease. The movie *Don't Look Up* set the right analogy: climate change is an asteroid speeding straight toward Earth—but it's one that we're capable of avoiding if we act in time. And yet, to this point, humanity hasn't proven capable of making the sacrifices necessary to save what Al Gore once famously termed "our only home."[98] Too many disagreements in the ranks. Too much confusion and chaos. For all the tools at our disposal, we're struggling to mobilize in our own defense.

If, as some believe, conservative denialism is the primary barrier to action, it might be sufficient to continue raising alarms. To throw paint at precious artwork. To post pleas on social media. To publish more reports and studies delineating what will happen if temperatures continue to surge. But if, as recent history appears to demonstrate, the essence of the problem stems from something else—if, no matter how panicked we are, government is too hamstrung to steer humanity toward a solution—then banging the drum louder isn't really sufficient. Put another way: if all progressives needed to do was convince the others that the planet was in peril, it might be worthwhile to spread more panic. But as we've seen, that's *not* the core problem. Even absent denialism, government today would thwart the progress the planet demands.

Progressives should honor those who have invested their careers in building coalitions to set the ambitious goals required to reduce carbon emissions. But beyond establishing aspirations, progressivism needs to work on building governing structures capable of making the hard, expensive, painful, inconvenient, and often politically unpalatable choices required to steer humanity in a new direction. We can build all the solar, wind, and hydro facilities we want, but if we can't get that power to the places where people are currently utilizing coal, oil, and gas, we're no better off. The coal industry is so keenly aware that a more integrated transmission grid threatens their business model that the Trump administration angrily stifled a government study making that point.[99] And yet the regulatory regime born from progressivism's cultural aversion to power worked just as effectively to thwart progress on Clean Line when a Democrat sat inside the White House.

The good news is that, if given the license to act, we have at hand the tools required to address the challenge. Technological innovation is bringing to scale humanity's ability to turn sunlight, wind, and water currents into electricity at scale. Battery technology is evolving to make it possible for us to store power for use even when the sun is hidden and the wind is still. Even better, other forms of energy may soon be on the way—fusion, for example, could end up creating vast quantities of power without imposing severe environmental impacts.[100] But that's also what's so frustrating: without a modernized transmission system, all of these advances in electricity generation may prove to be something of a useless bounty. Absent public authority's ability to clear ways for newly tapped sources of clean power to travel, it's of almost no value at all.

As of late 2022, the United States boasted roughly 400,000 miles of transmission wire. According to the National Academies, to get to net zero emissions, the US will have to build 120,000 more miles of high-voltage line. In 2021, a mere 386 were added to the grid. In 2022, the lack of transmission capacity kept the delay for new projects requesting connection to roughly four years long, a duration twice as long as in 2005.[101] And a recent study by researchers at Princeton estimated that, absent a vast acceleration of grid development, four-fifths of electrification's environmental benefit—our growing ability to replace polluting technologies with clean alternatives—will be squandered.[102] The problem here isn't a lack of awareness. Nor is it that the movement's leaders aren't motivated to get things moving. The issue is *procedural*.[103] Progressives, fearful of centralized power, have inserted so many checks that building the grid is an exercise in futility.

The South Fork Wind project was, for example, designed to construct wind turbines in ocean waters near New York, Rhode Island, and Massachusetts, subject to sign-off from nine separate federal agencies. Those bureaucracies are, in the main, chartered to protect the natural environment, to preserve fisheries, navigability, bird migratory patterns, and more. Many of the bureaucrats working inside those agencies may want to reduce carbon emissions, but they are hired to pursue separate concerns.[104] They frequently worked in partnership with state and local agencies, and maintain collaborative relationships with various interest groups. Their studies had to meet certain standards of rigor or else they were almost sure to be subject to lawsuits that they might well lose (see Chapter 7).

These reviews are not, in and of themselves, beyond the pale; they were all created for good reason. But together, they create gauntlets that are simply too difficult to clear expeditiously, if at all. The reviews have the effect of creating redlines, rather than informing deliberative and discretionary decision-making processes. As Michael Skelly complained after his decade of work on Clean Line collapsed: "You could have Robert Moses come back from the dead and he wouldn't be able to do shit."[105] And that's the problem. For those determined to thwart climate change, the central challenge isn't simply to castigate the climate deniers who aren't inclined to move on climate solutions. It's to restore the government's ability to ratify trade-offs—to accept that saving the planet requires sacrifices that impose real costs.

Cognizant of this broader challenge, reformers through the Obama years made sustained, but limited, progress speeding the construction of transmission lines. The backstop siting authority created in 2005 may have been undermined by results of subsequent litigation, but the White House pressed on several fronts, including $4.5 billion for smart grid development as a part of the Recovery Act, and creating an Interagency Rapid Response Team for Transmission to help coordinate efforts and quickly respond to challenges between federal agencies.[106] FERC adopted a general framework, Order 1000, that encouraged utilities to share the costs of transmission lines.[107] In 2015, as part of a highway reauthorization, Democrats created a Federal Permitting Improvement Council to help site transmission lines across federally owned property.[108]

But the underlying frictions remain because so many players who, in theory, want to help on climate are conflicted not only because of disagreements within the federal government, but also by power wielded outside it. Utilities decline to pursue projects that threaten to eat into their profit margins. State regulators refuse to issue certificates of public convenience and necessity to controversial transmission lines.[109] Localities reject requests to site electrical infrastructure because they will have deleterious impacts on nearly all property values. These barriers are born less of denialism than intersecting priorities. The executives running energy companies have a fiduciary responsibility to their shareholders. State regulators have a legal obligation to protect ratepayers. Town councils have a political mandate to represent those who vote them into office. It's a tragedy of the commons in reverse. Everyone is boxed into pursuing their own interests even as the proverbial asteroid speeds toward Earth.[110]

It's worth remembering that the federal government has, in fact, dispatched this sort of problem before. The Natural Gas Act of 1938, passed just three years after the Federal Power Act of 1935, gave the bureaucracy that has since morphed into FERC the explicit authority to site pipelines, with Washington bigfooting states out of the regulatory frame almost by default. Today, if a company wants to build a new natural gas pipeline, planners simply need to provide evidence that there's someone willing to burn the gas at the tail end, and *federal* siting authority can be used to override local concerns.[111] Put another way, the interests that maintain veto leverage over transmission lines—property concerns, existing utilities, state objections—have much less bearing. And for that reason, the permitting time for gas pipelines is less than half what it is for transmission lines, though that too has become more difficult.[112]

As many progressive advocates will argue, the power granted to the federal government under the Natural Gas Act is *too* comprehensive. Often, FERC simply transfers its power of eminent domain to the private company looking to build a pipeline, and work begins on sections so quickly that the worst damage is done before landowners can mobilize a defense. The expeditious siting of new pipelines explains, in no small part, why the United States was able to take such quick advantage of the shale gas boom: companies quickly constructed new means of getting fracked gas to power plants around the country. Had these pipelines been subject to the same rigmarole as a new high-voltage transmission line, many fewer would have been constructed.

Recognizing this disparity, members of Congress more recently worked in concert with the Biden administration to level the playing field. Included, for example, in the bipartisan infrastructure bill passed in 2021 was a provision that ensures that the federal government's backstop siting authority can be used if a state rejects a transmission project—not just when the relevant bureaucracy fails to come to a decision. The Inflation Reduction Act established a new regime of federal financing for transmission lines: money developers could claim up front and pay back at reduced interest.[113] Senator Sheldon Whitehouse (D-RI) had introduced the SITE Act, which would give FERC primary siting authority over interstate transmission lines.[114] And the Biden administration pushed for expedited NEPA reviews of certain climate-friendly projects both as part of the Inflation Reduction Act and in subsequent rulemaking.[115]

Many of these proposed reforms would be welcome—some are almost inarguably crucial. But if some often appear like mere tweaks to the system, each solution actually addresses just a corner of a much broader challenge. At root, America's inability to steer clear of the asteroid centers on government's inability to make expeditious decisions. Perhaps policymakers *should* maintain some redlines—some "rights" considered inviolable no matter the benefits to humanity as a whole. But the globe can no longer abide a system in which any potential objection can delay every potential project. We need to empower figures to take all relevant factors into consideration, weigh them against one another, and green-light the best options. We need, in short, to give government the leash required to permit public authority to prove itself competent.

CONCLUSION

Full-Circle Progressivism

ORNAMENTS OF DOUBTFUL BEAUTY

In January 1911, Henry Stimson, the blueblood aristocrat who would go on to serve in cabinets of Presidents William Howard Taft, Franklin Delano Roosevelt, and Harry Truman, addressed a Republican confab in Cleveland. Still young at the time, Stimson was, back then, a beacon of the GOP's progressive wing. In his view, a corrupt bargain aligning machine bosses and corporate interests was undermining the public interest. The solution, Stimson argued, wasn't to keep steering into laissez-faire economics. It was to empower executive branch officials to rise above the morass. The future luminary argued that America faced then something similar to what the Founding Generation had confronted in the years immediately following the American Revolution. And, given the relatable circumstances, he prescribed a similar tonic.

The analogy appeared clear enough. The figures who ruled the colonies at the behest of the English crown had been, in the prevailing view of eighteenth-century patriots, utter tyrants, men accountable only to a parliament sitting across a vast ocean. They had been abusive to their subjects, imposing their will without accounting for popular sentiment, subjecting them, most famously, to "taxation without representation." Upon declaring independence, the Founding Generation had crafted a system of government that was purposefully, and explicitly, weak.[1] As Stimson explained: "They cut the Executive down to a term too short to carry through any constructive policy; they took away his chiefs of department, and made them either elective or otherwise independent of him; they separated him as far as possible from the representative lawmaking body with which he must work; and in every way they reduced him to a mere ornament of doubtful beauty."[2]

But the results of what we might call America's *original* cultural aversion to power had been an out-and-out disaster.[3] The pitifully inept government created by the Articles of Confederation was too ham-handed to hold a burgeoning society together. No national law could be passed without the support of nine of the thirteen states. The national government could not tax citizens directly, provide for a standing military, or establish a national currency. When foreign creditors began to demand that the United States begin repaying debts from the Revolutionary War, some in the Confederation Congress proposed a 5 percent tax on imported goods, and nearly all thirteen original states agreed. But the small state of Rhode Island held out, undermining the entire effort. The national government, in short, couldn't deliver.

Perhaps of even more concern to James Madison and many of the other well-heeled men who had led the campaign for independence, the states were themselves falling into chaos. State legislators came from different stock than the men who had by and large signed the Declaration of Independence. Many were beacons of the working class who, by the standards of the aristocracy, appeared shortsighted and dim-witted. These new workaday legislators championed laws designed to serve their own constituencies, even when those interests cut against the broader public interest. A French minister complained that the new class of legislator was too tethered "to the vulgar and sordid notions of the populace." Perhaps most pointedly, many supported schemes to issue new, looser currency that benefited those paying off debts but cut against the interest of men who, like George Washington, had originally extended various credits.[4]

It was the national government's incompetent response to what became known as Shays's Rebellion in western Massachusetts that finally propelled a whole band of founders, including Washington, to pursue a course correction. That's what the Constitution of 1787 was designed to be: a form of government less tyrannical than the colonial governors, but more competent (or, put less delicately, less democratic) than what existed under the Articles.[5] It rebalanced America's competing desires for more and less centralized power.[6] Even the Bill of Rights, viewed today as an addendum intended to protect individuals *against* coercive public authority, was seen at the time as protecting the government against popular opinion. The Founding Generation was more worried about, say, Catholics making government a tool of the papacy than they were about ensuring everyone could worship using the liturgy of their choice.[7]

During the century that followed, Americans adjusted this balance several times. If George Washington, James Madison, and Alexander Hamilton had burnished centralized power for fear of chaos, the Jacksonians of the 1820s worked to peel power away from the nation's capital for want of protecting their little hamlets from far-off authority. The Civil War spelled that counterimpulse, with Abraham Lincoln building up the national government to put down a rebellion over the institution of slavery. But then, as Stimson argued a half century later, Americans had sought a return, again, to more limited government. During the Gilded Age, government had been so entirely corrupted by trusts, machines, and courts—legislatures answered to bosses and judges to corporations—that the teeter-totter had tipped the other way.[8] As Stimson exclaimed to the

Republicans in Cleveland: "The boss and his power is the direct out-growth of depriving the public officer of his power."[9]

It was from this core dynamic that Herbert Croly, founding editor of the *New Republic*, had derived his famous phrase to define progressivism: "Jeffersonian ends by Hamiltonian means." Recognizing that the government was too hamstrung to deliver, he wanted to re-enliven the thrust that had spurred Washington to support the Constitution in the wake of Shays's Rebellion and that had driven Abraham Lincoln to protect the Union in the wake of the South's secession. He wanted to steal power away from machines and judges not simply because he believed that some band of well-educated, upper-crust bureaucrats would be better at leading the country—though that surely informed his thinking. He and his fellow progressives believed that, in the great American tradition of perfecting the balance between two well-intentioned impulses, the country had edged too far in one direction.

Croly's view prevailed, even as the impulse to centralize power seeped out of Stimson's GOP and into Woodrow Wilson's Democratic Party.[10] And for more than the half century that followed—really until the late 1960s and early 1970s—progressivism's Hamiltonian impulse carried greater weight. The narrative that framed the movement's understanding of government was one that argued public authority was the only salve for the big societal problems. Professional bureaucrats were deemed beacons of the only institution capable of corralling the selfish interests of corporations, political machines, and special-interest groups. As Franklin Roosevelt declared during his first presidential campaign: "When the interests of the many are concerned, the interests of the few must yield."[11] And while Jeffersonian notions still hovered in the background, the movement's impulse to centralize power reigned supreme.

But then, in keeping with America's long history of sailing in one direction and then later tacking back in the other, the Jeffersonian impulse reemerged. Echoing America's eighteenth-century revulsion for colonial tyrants, and the country's Jacksonian rejection of federal power, progressivism began to spurn its Hamiltonian bent. Reformers began to realize that the bureaucracies born out of Herbert Croly's vision had become imperious to the point of being authentically tyrannical. Robert Moses wasn't some benevolent public figure by the end—he had morphed into a scourge. And he represented just one of the octopus's many tentacles. By the 1970s, progressivism undoubtedly needed a course correction. Centralized power had to be brought to heel.

Over the course of the last half century, that explicitly Jeffersonian project has succeeded—and, in many cases, beyond what its original champions might have thought possible. To that very point, we've now reached the other inflection point in the cycle, a moment not unlike when the Articles of Confederation proved unworkable, and when Henry Stimson addressed some of his fellow Republicans in 1911. In the latter instance, the culprits were machines and courts, institutions that answered to different constituencies but whose collective influence prevented government from serving the public interest. Today, by contrast, the underlying dysfunction is born from different sources—from laws, and precedents, and various other machinations. But the effect is largely the same. Progressivism, born more than a century ago, has come full circle.

A VOICE BUT NOT A VETO

If America faces today another Articles of Confederation moment—if, as this book has argued, public power has been diffused too thoroughly for government to deliver—progressivism will need to shift course yet again.[12] But rather than perpetuate the cycle, or open the door to another age defined by Robert Moses–style Hamiltonianism, reformers need now to seek a more balanced approach, one that puts centralized power and individualized safeguards in proper harmony. First and foremost, that will require a change in the progressive mindset. It will mean pursuing policies that give public officials more room to maneuver, even while guarding against unlimited mandates. It will mean shaving back but not eviscerating some of the reforms that have defined the last half century. In a phrase, it will mean giving communities a voice but not a veto.

This new approach will play differently in distinct contexts.[13] In the realm of housing, for example, the shift may take a lighter touch simply because reformers have found a Jeffersonian approach to expanding supply. The YIMBY (Yes In My Back Yard) movement that has emerged to counter the rampant NIMBYism isn't Hamiltonian at all—it agitates for pushing power down past neighborhood opponents of new development to property owners eager to develop their underutilized lots. YIMBYs, in many instances, would allow otherwise frustrated developers to build multifamily homes near transit stops *as of right*—that is, no matter whether the neighbors object. No zoning restrictions. No noise standards. No environmental protections. Worries about local "character" notwithstanding. If someone purchases that lot, YIMBY reformers would build housing supply up by pushing power down.

But if Jeffersonianism may work effectively to enhance the nation's housing supply, the same approach will likely come up short when applied to other challenges. You can't coalesce the right-of-way to build a high-speed rail track or a high-voltage transmission line by pushing power down. Some centralized authority needs to clear the path. And that centralized authority will need the wisdom and discretion to render judgment. Not every proposed mass transit line will meet the standard of a wise public investment, nor does every new roadway threaten a pernicious scheme to marginalize a minority community. Not every transmission line is worthwhile, but neither is every new pipeline a step toward the apocalypse. Citizens of all stripes can disagree in good faith on the merits— progressives will inevitably disagree among themselves. But, in the end, someone needs to be empowered to choose.[14]

The question is, how? Not every stakeholder should have the wherewithal to stand in the way. No single figure should be able to impose their will with impunity. Not every decision should be made by a court bound by the limits of judicial precedent. Government "by the people, and for the people," as Abraham Lincoln once described American democracy, needs today to develop more expeditious ways to weigh competing interests against one another. It needs to be able to metabolize opposition without an excess of delay. We can't forever endure the false choice of tyranny or nothing—of either letting Robert Moses tear up the South Bronx or allowing a fetid Penn Station to fester for decades. We need a process that considers broad public interests *and* that provides everyone a voice but not a veto.

This is not a new idea. In the early Progressive Era, those worried about the unfettered power of executive branch agencies proposed molding the judiciary to oversee their decisions—a Commerce Court, for example, to rule on decisions made by the Interstate Commerce Commission charged with regulating the railroads.[15] In 1977, DC Circuit Court judge David Bazelon, pushing back against colleagues agitating for new depths of judicial oversight of regulatory decisions, argued that the courts should instead ensure that decisions were "ventilated in a public forum and with public input and participation."[16] Then, in his view, the responsible expert would make a decision. He extolled, for example, Carter administration transportation secretary William Coleman's efforts to solicit input as to whether the loud and potentially cancer-inducing supersonic passenger jet, the Concorde SST, should be permitted to land in the United States. Coleman, having been careful to demonstrate that he understood the trade-offs, was empowered to make the decision.[17]

We've seen that sort of process work. Recall, for example, that a single figure was given authority to divvy up the compensation provided to victims of the September 11 attacks. President George W. Bush appointed a former counsel to Ted Kennedy, Ken Feinberg, as the fund's special master, and he alone had the power to determine what each affected family should receive. Feinberg didn't have an entirely free hand—and families had the option of rejecting his recommendation and bringing separate suits to court. But in most cases, Feinberg's judgment was satisfactory, however subjective it appeared to be. A single figure, with singular power, limited within certain bounds, to shape the final outcome.

328 | WHY NOTHING WORKS

The same basic premise prevails in the realm of criminal justice. Designed as a diversionary program for drug offenders, drug courts offer individuals charged with minor offenses an opportunity to avoid indictment. To be diverted, the accused must take responsibility for their crime and agree to certain conditions established by a combination of lawyers, social workers, and addiction specialists. During the course of the program, offenders are often required to submit to drug tests, attend counseling sessions, keep a job, and more. But in return for allowing these government officials to play a strong hand, the offender is spared a criminal sentencing. When executed well, the program can offer someone whose life is spiraling a way forward that prison might forestall.

So-called immigration courts provide another example—even if the system has more recently been overwhelmed. Since 1940, the Department of Justice has maintained an often overwhelmed system for making adjudicative decisions about who can and cannot come and stay in the United States almost entirely within its own purview. Decisions made by presidentially appointed "judges" who report to the attorney general are frequently final. Indeed, they are explicitly exempt from the procedures required by the Administrative Procedure Act.[18] But decision-making processes need not cut the judiciary out altogether. Colorado, for example, has created a special water court to deal with disputes over water consumption, and Utah has begun to experiment with a similar, if more limited, model. Colorado cases are subjected to a mediation process before coming to trial—a process designed to head off further litigation using a "referee." The hope is that having a clear expert figure sitting in judgment will expedite decision-making.[19]

The analogies aren't perfect. But these programs are birds of a feather in that they offer substantive but not unlimited discretion to specific government figures—more decision-making power than, say, highway engineers and housing officials generally have over new construction, but less than the Federal Reserve has over interest rates and the Pentagon has over troop deployments. And while mechanisms for determining family compensation and diverting criminals from incarceration are fundamentally different than the process for siting a transmission line or clearing a train track's right-of-way, the balance of public authority and individual rights points to a broad sort of precedent.[20] Progressives need not make a Manichaean choice between coercion and paralysis.

In some cases, progressives can look overseas for promising models. Spain, for example, has embraced an alternative approach to infrastructure construction. Rather than assign the public bureaucracies that *operate* the transit system responsibility for building new lines, the Spanish empower an expert *national* agency to plan and construct new infrastructure that, once complete, is bequeathed to local authorities to operate and maintain. As a result, those making the decisions about routes and station sitings are less beholden than the operating authority might be to locals with self-interested concerns.[21] America could adapt this system to provide a process by which local objections were given a forum, or even weighted consideration.

But it's not just the *structure* of decision-making that needs to change. Even if the judicial system was too deferential to figures like Robert Moses in the early postwar era, administrative jurisprudence has since overcorrected. The challenge now isn't to find a way back to the norms of the previous era. It's to carve a jurisprudence that allows, once again, for government to parse conflicting interests expeditiously.[22] The judiciary today, for example, maintains a whole separate system of patent law designed to balance the rights of those who create new things against the rights of those who would seek to utilize that intellectual property.[23] The executive branch has created a whole bureaucracy to deal with tax disputes: the United States Tax Court.[24] A similar sort of system could be erected to settle disputes in realms of housing, infrastructure, and more. Already, some have proposed that all challenges to the National Environmental Policy Act be funneled directly past federal district courts to be considered at first instance by the DC Circuit Court of Appeals.

All that said, if the details of these changes are important, they are downstream of how progressives understand the nature of their dilemma.

The last major progressive pivot was born not from some technical epiphany or ideological breakthrough. Fundamentally, reformers beginning in the 1960s and 1970s shifted their policy agenda in response to a change in culture—in the progressive zeitgeist. The movement was reacting viscerally to evidence that the Establishment was rotten, as demonstrated by the carnage of war, the scourge of pesticides, the injustice of institutional racism, the corruption of Watergate, and more. It was only after the zeitgeist changed that reformers began to hammer out the Jeffersonian thrust that has prevailed over the last several decades. The movement had to behold the octopus before it could seek to manacle its tentacles.

This book was written not to prescribe the specific changes that should be made in every realm of public policy, but to argue for a shift in narrative. Solutions are at hand to nearly all the movement's grievances. America *can* address climate change. We *can* build more housing. We *can* make communities more equitable, expand opportunity, redress old bigotries, and more. But reformers are bound to face unnecessary frustration if they refuse to allow some measure of additional power to flow into the hands of responsible public officials. The movement faces an Articles of Confederation moment, and the only way out is to recognize the problem, and pivot.

ACROSS THE GREAT DIVIDE

Which brings us back to politics. It likely goes without saying that rendering government incompetent is a lousy way to draw voters into an ideological movement bent on employing government to solve big problems. Ordinary people who experience the morass of inept bureaucracy will, like New Yorkers frustrated with Mayor Ed Koch's inability to restore Wollman Rink, be tempted to turn to someone with the individual moxie to get the job done. That was Donald Trump's appeal in the mid-1980s, and he employed the same basic rationale as an iconoclastic politician on the national stage. But it's not just that unrepentant Jeffersonianism doesn't work. Ordinary people aren't monolithically averse to power. They don't want public authority abused, but they know that progress is impossible without leadership. And insofar as the subtext of contemporary progressive ideology is that anyone wielding power is in the wrong, the movement alienates itself from voters who might otherwise support its agenda.

Some will retort that progressive ideology isn't the problem. Right-wingers, the argument goes, purposefully distort what progressives really aim to do. And their dishonesty metastasizes in right-wing echo chambers, with Fox News, conservative talk radio, and various voices on social media manipulating an impressionable electorate into believing, erroneously, that progressives hate America and want to upend every vestige of "traditional" American life. Well, fair enough. Some of progressivism's detractors are bound to take that angle—and there's not much we can do to stop them.

But even if progressives aren't actually bent on tearing down every manifestation of public and private authority, the conservative criticism that progressives hate America draws strength from the naked reality of our cultural aversion to power. Conservative critiques may *seem* to those inside the movement as something close to preposterous—progressives typically bill themselves as beacons of *more* government. But the public's recoil when Barack Obama suggested that red America was "cling[ing] to guns or religion" and when Hillary Clinton labeled some Trump supporters "deplorables" didn't emerge from thin air.[25] It was rooted in public perceptions that progressivism wants to upend any vestige of tradition and . . . power.

This is the crux of the *political* argument for rebalancing progressivism's Hamiltonian and Jeffersonian impulses. The movement purports to support growing government so that public authority can take a stronger hand protecting the vulnerable. But then progressives excoriate government as a captured tool of the patriarchy. Those of us who style ourselves progressive typically gloss over that nuance for a simple reason: it's awkward and confusing. Most progressives want both to empower government to combat climate change and to curtail government's authority

over a woman's right to choose. And squaring that circle is more intellectually difficult than standing strong against Trumpism, or calling out
conservative bigotry, or excoriating the shadowy figures eager to steer the
country toward fascism. There's no storming the barricades in support of
a healthy balance between contradictory impulses. And so progressives
typically retreat into reflexive anticonservatism.

Criticizing your adversaries is not, of and by itself, a terrible political strategy. When the other side supports truly terrible and unpopular ideas—separating children from their parents at the border, limiting
women's bodily autonomy, stripping away environmental protections, cutting Social Security and Medicare—there's little downside to drawing the
public's attention to their retrograde agenda. But, for progressives, there's
danger in that appeal. A movement consumed by exasperation over how
so many people could have voted for Trump, or supported his agenda, or
turned a blind eye to his conduct after losing in 2020, will be less inclined
to correct for its own errors. If progressives put making government work
not on the periphery of the movement's agenda but at the heart of its
zeitgeist, voters might be less vulnerable to the sirens of the populist right.

There is, of course, one authentic and powerful reason progressives
should worry about making government hum. A government that op-
erates expeditiously—a public authority with fewer guardrails—will inevitably be utilized not only to serve progressive desires but to pursue
conservative ends as well. Any change that would have made it easier
for the Obama administration to identify well-intentioned "shovel-ready"
projects in 2009 and 2010, or for clean energy companies to build transmission lines through Arkansas or Maine, or for developers to build new
affordable housing in New York and California, might well have opened
the door for someone else to build a legion of new coal-fired power plants,
or to gentrify minority neighborhoods.

But that's a risk progressives today need to take, a bargain they need
to accept. A government too hamstrung to serve the public good will fuel
future waves of conservative populism. Voters are drawn to figures like

Donald Trump not because public authority is too pervasive, but because government can't deliver. His refrain claiming that the "deep state" has sold the ordinary citizen out—that insiders are constantly making "bad deals" on the nation's behalf—lands, in no small part, because voters have witnessed the incompetence firsthand. Lionizing government and then ensuring it fails is, in the end, among the worst of bad political strategies.[26] The movement needs to change course not only because it's bad policy, but because it's bad politics as well.

That, in the end, is the best argument for full-circle progressivism. The movement has been justified to erect protections against Robert Moses–era abuse—to manacle the octopus. But that Jeffersonian retrenchment, now more than fifty years old, has run its course. Now, the core obstacle to the movement's substantive success—to greater economic equality and prosperity, to more social justice and responsibility, to a more robust response to climate change, to more housing, to greater mobility—isn't centralized power. It's the *absence* of centralized power. Populism takes hold not when democracy works well, but rather when it doesn't deliver. No amount of righteous sanctimony can substitute for the political benefits of making public authority serve the public interest. Moving forward, that should be the progressive movement's north star.

ACKNOWLEDGMENTS

For the longest time, I doubted the wisdom of writing this book. More than a decade ago, when I was rereading *The Power Broker* on my commute to New York, I had some notion that something peculiar was going on inside progressivism—something I didn't yet understand. But when I hesitantly suggested to a handful of friends that I wanted to write about the morass at Penn Station, most tried, however gently, to wave me off. Sure, there existed great books about the construction of the Brooklyn Bridge and the Verrazano-Narrows, among other famous engineering triumphs. But who would want to read hundreds of pages about an ambitious project that *hadn't* happened? Moreover, almost no one needed convincing that New York's front door was a rat's nest; they'd been subjected to it firsthand.

To that end, the people most deserving of acknowledgment are those who insisted that there was, in fact, some "there" here. My indefatigable agent, Bridget Wagner Matzie, never let up. Chris Suellentrop, the editor, and now friend, who helped shape my 2019 article on Penn Station, was another. Daniel Kurtz-Phelan insisted that I push past any lingering doubts. Patrick Collison reached out to encourage further research. Carlye Adler, Jeff Nussbaum, and Jeff Shesol, each writers themselves, dismissed various recitations of my self-doubt. Ezra Klein and Steve Teles ushered me into a community of similarly minded scholars. Whether they *actually* believed the toil would be worthwhile, they never wavered. I thank them.

Early in the journey—during the period when I'd yet to develop a theory of why New York had allowed the western hemisphere's most-trafficked transit hub to deteriorate into an international embarrassment—a whole host of people with firsthand experience walked me through the story from their various perspectives. Hilary Ballon, Christopher Boylan, David Brodsky, Tonio Burgos, Vishaan Chakrabarti, John Connorton, Anthony Coscia, Bill Cunningham, Tim Gilchrist, Andy Goldman, Peter Goldmark, Susan Heilbron, Peter Henry, Richard Kahan, Jay Kriegel, Justin Lapatine, Janno Lieber, Andrew Lynn, Norman McGrath, Juliette Michaelson, Jim Millstein, Mitchell Moss, Charles O'Byrne, Richard Ravitch, Don Rice, Marc Ricks, Justin Rivers, Paul Romer, Eric Rothman, Lynne Sagalyn, Elliot Sander, Joshua Sirefman, Eliot Spitzer, Chris Ward, Alex Washburn, Iris Weinshall, Carl Weisbrod, Warren Wheat, Kay Sarlin Wright, and Tom Wright were particularly generous with their time. Bill Wachtel was both insightful and supportive. Without them, I would never have stumbled onto the notion that our shared collective frustration wasn't specific to Penn Station, or to New York, or even to the development of transportation infrastructure.

As any author exploring whether one example is indicative of a broader phenomenon will likely testify, my challenge at that point was to see if something similar was happening in other realms. The problem is that it's the rare expert who becomes expert in more than one realm. Academics tend to go deep rather than wide—but so do lawyers, and engineers, and political aides. My charge was to do the opposite: develop some preliminary grounding in realms that typically require years of study—anti-trust, clean energy, criminal justice, housing, regulation, social welfare, and more—to see if similar patterns prevailed throughout. I sought out a whole range of scholars, many of whom were very generous in letting me prod and poke before offering some recommended reading. Cary Coglianese, Franklin Foer, Sam Gill, David Greenberg, Jeff Grybowski, Robert Kagan, Darrin McMahon, Jonathan Rauch, Andy Rotherham, James Sanders, Michael

Tolhurst, Mark K. Updegrove, Jacob Weisberg, Darrell West, and Howard Wolfson were sometimes skeptical of my argument, but they nevertheless pointed me to research that then came to shape my broader understanding.

I wish I could list all the people who contributed to my thinking on the broad range of subjects in this book—and the many who spoke to me about subjects I ended up having to abandon for lack of space. Several were kind enough to look over drafts of discrete sections and chapters. Joe Birbiglia, Dave Buchanan, Matt Burriesci, Lizabeth Cohen, Chris Elmendorf, Mark Gammon, Eric Goldwyn, Rick Kahlenberg, Bradley Katz, Ira Katznelson, Toby Lester, Will Marshall, Macky McCleary, Susan Moffitt, Dustin Palmer, Ari Peskoe, Vincent Ragosta, Liza Reed, Reuel Schiller, David Schleicher, Bruce Schulman, Seth Schulman, David Shribman, Jeff Solomon, Mark Steinmeyer, Daniel Stid, Sean Sweeney, Fred Wagner, Paul Weinstein, and Gordon Wood each critiqued and improved early drafts; any remaining errors are entirely mine.

An army of friends, colleagues, and thoughtful acquaintances supported me through the writing, offering both to be sounding boards and to help me think through issues and topics that were often unfamiliar. Among them were Dean Aguillen, Valerie Alexander, Gabe Amo, Yoni Appelbaum, Ben Armstrong, Nick Bagley, Matt Bai, Frank Barry, Victoria Bassetti, Debbie Berger, Jenn Bramley, Matt Bucci, Debbie Cox Bultan, Dan Carol, Buff Chace, Reid Cherlin, Ryan Clancy, Ben Cooper, John Davis, Todd DeLorenzo, Jerusalem Demsas, Stuart Eizenstat, Rahm Emanuel, Randy Ford, Tom Freedman, Bill Galston, Dan Gerstein, Ken Girardin, Russell Gold, Robert Gordon, Mark Halperin, Risa Heller, Philip Howard, Josh Hurvitz, Eric Jaffe, Edward Kussy, Cheryl LaFleur, Lindsay Lewis, Zachary Liscow, Stu Loeser, Dylan Loewe, Jenny Mayfield, Matt McKenna, EJ McMahon, Craig Minassian, Jim Morone, Ted Nesi, Steve Neuman, Jen Pahlka, Clay Risen, Tim Roberts, Wendy Schiller, Judith Shulevitz, Harry Siegel, Richard Norton Smith, Brad Snyder, Daniel Squadron, Edward Steinfeld, Alex Stern, Eileen Sullivan, George Tagg, Mike Tomasky, Tevi Troy, Tux Turkel, Angel Urena,

Melvin Urofsky, Tracy Van Grack, Nicole Verdi, Richard Weingroff, Laura Weinrib, Jason Willick, and Alisa Amarosa Wood.

The team at PublicAffairs has been supportive throughout. My editor, John Mahaney, has been a wise counsel from the beginning, and the book would never have come together without many of his peers at Hachette, including Clive Priddle, Melissa Veronesi, Shena Redmond, Liz Wetzel, Jenny Lee, and the superb copyeditor Susie Pitzen. Elizabeth Shreve of Shreve Williams has been an invaluable partner thinking through the audience that might be receptive to these ideas. It takes a village to write a book, and I couldn't have had better neighbors.

Finally, a whole host of friends have traveled this journey with me. Three cheers for Artie, the dog we had when I was commuting to Penn Station, and to Franklin, the puppy we have now. Thanks to the whole Scher/Gong clan, who have seen me through lots of ups and downs. Luke Anderson, Arthur Baraf, Gabe Bernstein, Jan Groblewski, Tony Hitchman, Mike Herzlinger, and Matt Whiteley have asked great questions throughout my research, typically over a beer. Jon Lemire, a buddy from college, brought to my thinking a perspective unique to someone in the middle of the action. Table 8 from Zoe's bat mitzvah deserves credit (or blame) for the choice of cover design. My parents, Martha and David Dunkelman; my sister, Anna Gallagher; and my in-laws, Pat and John Prael, have been supportive throughout.

The most profound acknowledgment is reserved for those who have suffered the most during this project. Having children is, without any doubt, the most profound reason for wanting the future to be brighter than the past—that, ultimately, is why I wrote this book. But as high-minded as that may be, its truth does not cancel the sacrifice born from having an author for a father. Along with my wife, Kathryn, my daughters Emilia and Helen endured my various moods, frustrations, and panics. They've done so with a rare degree of grace and magnanimity. I would never have been able to come through without their support, and I would never have finished this manuscript had I given them the attention they deserve. I love them—and I'm sorry for all the time burrowed in my office.

NOTES

Introduction

1. Robert A. Caro, *The Power Broker: Robert Moses and the Fall of New York* (New York: Vintage Books, 1975), 850–894.

2. Remarks of Governor Kathy Hochul, November 3, 2021.

3. *New York: A Documentary Film*, episode 4, "The Power and the People (1898–1914)," directed by Ric Burns, aired November 17, 1999, on PBS, www.amazon.com/gp/video/detail/B006CCOIZI/ref=msx_wn_av. Jill Jonnes, *Conquering Gotham: Building Penn Station and Its Tunnels* (New York: Penguin, 2007), 308–315.

4. This is not to say that New York had not built *any* infrastructure. William Finnegan, "The Fight Over Penn Station and Madison Square Garden," *New Yorker*, March 6, 2023.

5. David W. Dunlap, "With Many Modifications, Penn Station Project Is 'Go,'" *New York Times*, July 21, 2005. For a rendering of David Childs's proposed design, see www.pbs.org/wgbh/pages/frontline/shows/sacred/deconstruction/c6.html.

6. Ronald Brownstein, "Biden's 'Big Build,'" *Atlantic*, July 6, 2023.

7. Bruce Bartlett, "'Starve the Beast': Origins and Development of a Budgetary Metaphor," *The Independent Review* 12, no. 1 (Summer 2007): 5–26.

8. Thomas Frank, *What's the Matter with Kansas? How Conservatives Won the Heart of America* (New York: Henry Holt, 2004).

9. Bill Clinton, "First Inaugural Address of William J. Clinton; January 20, 1993," via the Avalon Project at Yale Law School, https://avalon.law.yale.edu/20th_century/clinton1.asp.

10. Melvin I. Urofsky, *Louis D. Brandeis: A Life* (New York: Schocken Books, 2009), 330–332.

11. Jazmine Ulloa and Lisa Lerer, "For Progressive Democrats, New Momentum Clashes with Old Debates," *New York Times*, April 19, 2023.

12. Jonathan Rauch, *Demosclerosis: The Silent Killer of American Government* (New York: Times Books, 1994), 229. George Packer, *Last Best Hope: America in Crisis and Renewal* (New York: Picador, 2021), 66.

13. Matthew Yglesias, "Chuck Schumer Should Call the Baileys," *Slow Boring*, January 25, 2022, www.slowboring.com/p/chuck-schumer-should-call-the-baileys.

14. John Sides, Chris Tausanovitch, and Lynn Vavreck, *The Bitter End: The 2020 Presidential Campaign and the Challenge to American Democracy* (Princeton, NJ: Princeton University Press, 2022), 19–23, 115. Humans tend to weight their fears of loss more than their hopes of seeing gains. Daniel Kahneman, *Thinking, Fast and Slow* (New York: Farrar, Straus and Giroux, 2011).

15. Packer, *Last Best Hope*, 65.

16. Walter Lippmann, *Public Opinion* (New York: Harcourt, Brace and Company, 1922; Overland Park, KS: Digireads.com, 2020), 12–13, 18–20, 48–49, 52, 55–56, 72–73, 89–90. Citations refer to the Digireads.com edition.

17. This is broadly derivative of Isaiah Berlin's "positive" definition of freedom—freedom to climb to some "higher nature." Isaiah Berlin, "Two Concepts of Liberty," in *Four Essays on Liberty* (New York: Oxford University Press, 1969).

18. Hamiltonianism might also be described as a "high-modernist ideology." James C. Scott, *Seeing Like a State: How Certain Schemes to Improve the Human Condition Have Failed* (New Haven, CT: Yale University Press, 1998).

19. This is more in line with Isaiah Berlin's "negative" definition of freedom—freedom *from* coercion. Berlin, "Two Concepts of Liberty."

20. Jennifer Medina, "Across the Echo Chamber, a Quiet Conversation About War and Race," *New York Times*, November 5, 2023.

21. See Ernest Gellner, "The Struggle to Catch Up," *Times Literary Supplement*, December 9, 1994, cited in Scott, *Seeing Like a State*, 193.

22. Letter from Alexander Hamilton to George Washington, April 14, 1794. Founders Online, National Archives, https://founders.archives.gov/documents/Hamilton/01-17-02-0497.

23. This is the essence of the challenge undermining efforts to combat climate change. Deb Chachra, *How Infrastructure Works: Inside the Systems That Shape Our World* (New York: Riverhead, 2023), 191.

24. Urofsky, *Louis D. Brandeis*, 359–360. Herbert Croly on Jefferson in *The Promise of American Life*, cited in David K. Nichols, "The Promise of Progressivism: Herbert Croly and the Rejection of Individual Rights," *Publius: The Journal of Federalism* 17, no. 2 (Spring 1987): 29.

25. Scott, *Seeing Like a State*, 355.

26. As quoted in "The Permanence of Jefferson," a speech delivered by Supreme Court justice Felix Frankfurter at the opening of the Thomas Jefferson bicentennial at the Library of Congress, April 13, 1943, www.loc.gov/resource/mff.003028.

27. See, as an example, Josh Kraushaar, "Left Loses Momentum," *Axios*, July 31, 2022, www.axios.com/2022/07/31/moderate-progressives-democratic-primaries. See also Tony Romm and Marianna Sotomayor, "Standoff Between Liberal and Moderate Democrats Looms over Biden Economic Agenda Ahead of Key House Vote," *Washington Post*, September 21, 2021.

28. Congressional Progressive Caucus, "21st Century New Deal for Jobs," accessed January 2024, https://progressives.house.gov/21st-century-new-deal-for-jobs. On Roosevelt, see first section of Chapter 1.

29. Todd Gitlin, *The Sixties: Years of Hope, Days of Rage* (New York: Bantam, 1993).

30. Lionel Trilling coins the phrase "the cultural assumptions that make politics." Louis Menand, "Regrets Only," *New Yorker*, September 22, 2008.

31. Acton-Creighton Correspondence (1887). John Emerich Edward Dalberg-Acton's suspicion of power was born from a tradition that viewed the French Revolution as an object lesson in the perils of power. Samuel Moyn, *Liberalism Against Itself: Cold War Intellectuals and the Making of Our Times* (New Haven, CT: Yale University Press, 2023), 22–23.

32. Martin Gottlieb, "Who Can Fix the Wollman Rink Faster? City and Trump Agree It's Trump," *New York Times*, June 6, 1986. Joyce Purnick, "City to Use Old Way to Rebuild Ice Rink After New Way Fails," *New York Times*, May 22, 1986. Alan Finder, "Wollman Rink: 6 Years of Errors and Delays," *New York Times*, June 17, 1986.

33. Finder, "Wollman Rink."

34. Joyce Purnick, "City Optimistic on Trump Offer," *New York Times*, June 4, 1986. Finder, "Wollman Rink." "Lessons of the Wollman Rink," *New York Times*, November 13, 1986. Purnick, "City to Use Old Way to Rebuild Ice Rink." Suzanne Daley, "Trump to Rebuild Wollman Rink at the City's Expense by Dec. 15," *New York Times*, June 7, 1986.

35. "Lessons of the Wollman Rink."

36. Dorothy Samuels, "From Donald Trump to Eliot Spitzer: Still Battling over a Wasteful Law," *New York Times*, May 29, 2007.

37. Gottlieb, "Who Can Fix the Wollman Rink Faster?" Deputy Mayor Robert Esnard: "The pleasure of hiring contractors and firing contractors on the basis of performance . . . in government, you don't always have that pleasure." Oral history interview with Robert Esnard 1995, part 3, Columbia University, https://dlc.library.columbia.edu/catalog/cul:stqjq2bxk0.

38. Alan Finder, "New York Hopes to Learn from Rink Trump Fixed," *New York Times*, November 21, 1986.

39. "Lessons of the Wollman Rink."

40. Eleanor Blau, "A New Ice Age Starts at Wollman Rink," *New York Times*, November 14, 1986. William E. Geist, "Psst, Here's a Secret: Trump Rebuilds Ice Rink," *New York Times*, November 15, 1986.

41. "The President's News Conference," August 12, 1986, Ronald Reagan Presidential Library and Museum, www.reaganlibrary.gov/archives/speech/presidents-news-conference-23#:~:text=I%20think%20you%20all%20know,I'm%20here%20to%20help.

42. Geist, "Psst, Here's a Secret."

43. This is a paraphrase of *New York Times* columnist Ezra Klein's oft-cited notion that we need to erect a "progressivism that builds." Ezra Klein, "What America Needs Is a Liberalism That Builds," *New York Times*, May 29, 2022.

44. Nicholas Lemann, "The Myth of Community Development," *New York Times*, January 9, 1994.

45. Heather Knight, "San Francisco Tried to Build a $1.7 Million Toilet. It's Still Not Done," *New York Times*, January 24, 2024.

46. As quoted in Terry Teachout, *The Skeptic: A Life of H. L. Mencken* (New York: Harper, 2002), 30.

47. Stephen Skowronek, *Building a New American State: The Expansion of National Administrative Capacities, 1877–1920* (New York: Cambridge University Press, 1982), 41. Teachout, *The Skeptic*, 98.

48. "Public Trust in Government: 1938–2023," Pew Research Center, September 19, 2023, www.pewresearch.org/politics/2023/09/19/public-trust-in-government-1958-2023/.

49. Daniel Bell, *The Cultural Contradictions of Capitalism* (New York: Basic Books, 1978), 176.

50. Even when faith in government was nearing record lows in 2016, Donald Trump garnered less than half the nation's support.

Chapter 1: Servant or Master of the Public?

1. Sidney M. Milkis, *Theodore Roosevelt, the Progressive Party, and the Transformation of American Democracy* (Lawrence: University Press of Kansas, 2009), 16. President McKinley's most important patron, Ohio senator Mark Hanna, vowed during the 1896 campaign that a GOP administration would never disrupt the efficiencies born of monopoly power. Ron Chernow, *Titan: The Life of John D. Rockefeller, Sr.* (New York: Vintage Books, 1998), 388.

2. Milkis, *Theodore Roosevelt*, 178. Taken from "Amos Pinchot to Theodore Roosevelt, December 3, 1912," Roosevelt Papers, available from Jane Addams Project, https://digital.janeaddams.ramapo.edu/items/show/5515.

3. Charles McCarthy, "Memorandum for the Future," August 12, 1912, Charles McCarthy Papers (microfilm edition, 1982), State Historical Society of Wisconsin. Richard Fairchild, interview with Charles McCarthy, *American Record Herald*, November 21, 1912, Charles McCarthy Papers (microfilm edition, 1982), State Historical Society of Wisconsin.

4. John A. Garraty, *Right-Hand Man: The Life of George W. Perkins* (New York: Harper and Brothers, 1960), 48–49, 216. Melvin I. Urofsky, *Louis D. Brandeis: A Life* (New York: Schocken Books, 2009), 303. Inspiration for the Chapter 1 title came from Urofsky's *Louis D. Brandeis*, 138.

5. Milkis, *Theodore Roosevelt*, 178. Taken from Garraty, *Right-Hand Man*, 270.

6. Garraty, *Right-Hand Man*, 265, 303. Milkis, *Theodore Roosevelt*, 208. Taken from Louis Brandeis, "Labor and the New Party Trust Program," September 18, 1912, Brandeis Papers, Reel 28.

7. Arthur M. Schlesinger Jr., *The Crisis of the Old Order, 1919–1933*, The Age of Roosevelt, Volume I (New York: Mariner, 2003), 33.

8. Walter Lippmann, *Public Opinion* (Overland Park, KS: Digireads.com, 2020), 6–8.

9. The impulse to strengthen the Sherman Act was aligned with reforms designed to break up the institutions that monopolized political power. They proposed the direct election of the president, for example, and supported creation of a mechanism to recall senators.

10. Milkis, *Theodore Roosevelt*, 210–211.

11. Charles McCarthy Papers (microfilm edition, 1982), State Historical Society of Wisconsin.

12. Urofsky, *Louis D. Brandeis*, 341–342.

13. Garraty, *Right-Hand Man*, 279.

14. The Civil War, fought primarily over the question of slavery, presented a rare case in which federal authority prevailed over local concerns.

15. Michael Kazin, *What It Took to Win: A History of the Democratic Party* (New York: Farrar, Straus and Giroux, 2022), 33–36. James T. Kloppenberg, *Uncertain Victory: Social Democracy and Progressivism in European and American Thought, 1870–1920* (New York: Oxford University Press, 1986), 356. Urofsky, *Louis D. Brandeis*, 350. Daniel P. Carpenter, *The Forging of Bureaucratic Autonomy: Reputations, Networks, and Policy Innovation in Executive Agencies, 1862–1928* (Princeton, NJ: Princeton University Press, 2001), 60–62.

16. Richard White, *The Republic for Which It Stands: The United States During Reconstruction and the Gilded Age, 1865–1896* (New York: Oxford University Press, 2017), 229–230.

17. Stephen Skowronek, *Building a New American State: The Expansion of National Administrative Capacities, 1877–1920* (New York: Cambridge University Press, 1982), 122–123.

18. Slavery, the preeminent political issue of the nineteenth century, was the most prominent exception to this rule.

19. The Week Staff, "The Demise of Local News," *The Week*, January 24, 2023, https://theweek.com/briefing/1020220/the-demise-of-local-news.

20. Daniel Bell, *The Cultural Contradictions of Capitalism* (New York: Basic Books, 1978), 66.

21. Robert H. Wiebe, *The Search for Order: 1877–1920* (New York: Hill and Wang, 1967), xiii.

22. Milkis, *Theodore Roosevelt*, 40. From Martha Derthick, "Federalism," in *Understanding America: The Anatomy of an Exceptional Nation*, ed. Peter H. Schuck and James Q. Wilson (New York: PublicAffairs, 2008), 123–127. For a contrast, see George Packer, *Last Best Hope: America in Crisis and Renewal* (New York: Picador, 2021), 205–206.

23. Skowronek, *Building a New American State*, 24–42.

24. H. L. Mencken, *A Mencken Chrestomathy: His Own Selection of His Choicest Writings* (New York: Vintage Books, 1982), 250.

25. Nikolas Bowie and Daphna Renan, "The Supreme Court Is Not Supposed to Have This Much Power," *Atlantic*, June 8, 2022. Robert A. Kagan, *Adversarial Legalism: The American Way of Law*, 2nd ed. (Cambridge, MA: Harvard University Press, 2019), 17–19. Theodore J. Lowi, *The End of Liberalism: The Second Republic of the United States*, 2nd ed. (New York: W. W. Norton, 1979), 3–21.

26. Not everyone was represented by the party machines—the concerns of women and minorities, for example, were explicitly excluded. Richard Rothstein, *The Color of Law: A Forgotten History of How Our Government Segregated America* (New York: Liveright, 2017), 39–41.

27. Eldon J. Eisenach, *The Lost Promise of Progressivism* (Lawrence: University Press of Kansas, 1994), 104–108. William L. Riordan, *Plunkitt of Tammany Hall: A Series of Very Plain Talks on Very Practical Politics* (New York: Signet, 2015). Urofsky, *Louis D. Brandeis*, 433.

28. Kagan, *Adversarial Legalism*, 50–51. Wiebe, *The Search for Order*, 2–4.

29. Samuel P. Hays, "The Politics of Reform in Municipal Government in the Progressive Era," *Pacific Northwest Quarterly* 55, no. 4 (October 1964): 166.

30. Thomas K. McCraw, *Prophets of Regulation* (Cambridge, MA: Belknap, 1986), 4–5. Urofsky, *Louis D. Brandeis*, 277–278.

31. Alfred D. Chandler Jr., *The Visible Hand* (Cambridge, MA: Belknap, 1977), 88. By 1890, the country would have 2,600 miles of track for every million inhabitants—up from 162 miles forty years earlier. Earl Swift, *The Big Roads: The Untold Story of the Engineers, Visionaries, and Trailblazers Who Created the American Superhighways* (New York: Houghton Mifflin Harcourt, 2011), 39.

32. Skowronek, *Building a New American State*, 98–103. Stephen Jay Gould, *Punctuated Equilibrium* (Cambridge, MA: Harvard University Press, 2007).

33. Brandeis speech to the Chicago Bar Association, January 3, 1916. Quoted in Urofsky, *Louis D. Brandeis*, 432.

34. Skowronek, *Building a New American State*, 123–125.

35. McCraw, *Prophets of Regulation*, 65–68. Henry L. Stimson and McGeorge Bundy, *On Active Service in Peace and War* (New York: Harper, 1948), 60.

36. Lippmann, *Public Opinion*, 63.

37. Chandler, *The Visible Hand*, 88. By another estimate, the tracks grew from 30,000 in 1860 to 254,000 in 1916. Urofsky, *Louis D. Brandeis*, 183.

38. Urofsky, *Louis D. Brandeis*, 183.

39. Richard Hofstadter, *The Age of Reform* (New York: Vintage Books, 1955), 169. Lewis Mumford, foreword to *Planned Society: Yesterday, Today, Tomorrow*, ed. Findlay MacKenzie (New York: Prentice Hall, 1937), v. Urofsky, *Louis D. Brandeis*, 350. Chernow, *Titan*, 129.

40. Packer, *Last Best Hope*, 172. Urofsky, *Louis D. Brandeis*, 168–169, 308. Lionel Trilling, *The Liberal Imagination* (New York: NYRB, 1978), 113–114.

41. Forrest McDonald, "Samuel Insull and the Movement for State Utility Regulatory Commissions," *Business History Review* 32, no. 3 (Autumn 1958): 243–244. Max Weber, *The Protestant Ethic and the "Spirit" of Capitalism and Other Writings*, trans. and ed. Peter Baehr and Gordon C. Wells (New York: Penguin, 2002). Urofsky, *Louis D. Brandeis*, 301.

42. Wiebe, *The Search for Order*, 78–79.

43. Hofstadter, *The Age of Reform*, 230–231.

44. On substantive due process: Jeff Shesol, *Supreme Power: Franklin Roosevelt vs. the Supreme Court* (New York: W. W. Norton, 2010), 30. Urofsky, *Louis D. Brandeis*, 208. Skowronek, *Building a New American State*, 41–42, 151–154. Peter S. Canellos, *The Great Dissenter: The Story of John Marshall Harlan, America's Judicial Hero* (New York: Simon and Schuster, 2021), 400.

45. George Packer, *The Unwinding* (New York: Farrar, Straus and Giroux, 2014).

46. Packer, *Last Best Hope*, 173. Bruce J. Schulman, "Modern American Liberalism: A Story in Four Acts," excerpted from Bruce J. Schulman, *Lyndon B. Johnson and American Liberalism: A Brief Biography with Documents* (New York: Bedford/St. Martin's, 2007).

47. Kloppenberg, *Uncertain Victory*, 312.

48. Lowi, *The End of Liberalism*, 3–21. James C. Scott, *Seeing Like a State: How Certain Schemes to Improve the Human Condition Have Failed* (New Haven, CT: Yale University Press, 1998), 77. Urofsky, *Louis D. Brandeis*, 306, 339. Herbert Croly in *The Promise of American Life*: cited in David K. Nichols, "The Promise of Progressivism: Herbert Croly and the Progressive Rejection of Individual Rights," *Publius: The Journal of Federalism* 17, no. 2 (Spring 1987): 30.

49. Milkis, *Theodore Roosevelt*, 22–23. Hofstadter, *The Age of Reform*, 58–59.

50. Kazin, *What It Took to Win*, 11–82.

51. Urofsky, *Louis D. Brandeis*, 186–188.

52. Urofsky, *Louis D. Brandeis*, 302, 319–325.

53. Wiebe, *The Search for Order*, 44–52.

54. Chernow, *Titan*, 298.

55. Urofsky, *Louis D. Brandeis*, 161.

56. Philippa Strum, "The Legacy of Louis Dembitz Brandeis, People's Attorney," *American Jewish History* 81, no. 3/4 (Spring/Summer 1994): 406–427. Urofsky, *Louis D. Brandeis*, 201–206.

57. Urofsky, *Louis D. Brandeis*, 20, 164, 307. Shesol, *Supreme Power*, 62.

58. Hofstadter, *The Age of Reform*, 5–6. Urofsky, *Louis D. Brandeis*, 384.

59. Wiebe, *The Search for Order*, 81–84.

60. Brad Snyder, *The House of Truth: A Washington Political Salon and the Foundations of American Liberalism* (New York: Oxford University Press, 2017), 40–41. Chandler, *The Visible Hand*, 333.

61. Urofsky, *Louis D. Brandeis*, 390.

62. Canellos, *The Great Dissenter*, 307, 436–437. Snyder, *The House of Truth*, 13. Urofsky, *Louis D. Brandeis*, 317, 390–391, 610–611.

63. A Hamiltonian wrinkle here: many reformers wanted to grant children new rights, and to place them in the custody of school officials, believing that immigrant parents would exploit them. Christopher Lasch, *The Culture of Narcissism: American Life in an Age of Diminishing Expectations* (New York: W. W. Norton, 1979), 186–187.

64. Snyder, *The House of Truth*, 14–15.

65. Urofsky, *Louis D. Brandeis*, 482–485.

66. Urofsky, *Louis D. Brandeis*, 211–212.

67. Milkis, *Theodore Roosevelt*, 59–60. In 1922, Progressive Republican senator Robert La Follette would propose a constitutional amendment providing Congress an opportunity to overturn Supreme Court decisions rejecting legislation based on its constitutionality. Urofsky, *Louis D. Brandeis*, 581.

68. Snyder, *The House of Truth*, 350–353. In 1923, the "Four Horsemen" of conservatism on the court—Justices Van Devanter, McReynolds, Butler, and Sutherland—would join Justice McKenna in striking down a minimum wage enacted for women in the District of Columbia in *Adkins v. Children's Hospital*. Urofsky, *Louis D. Brandeis*, 594–596. "These were nineteenth century men": Shesol, *Supreme Power*, 38.

69. Conor Dougherty, *Golden Gates: Fighting for Housing in America* (New York: Penguin, 2020), 76.

70. Urofsky, *Louis D. Brandeis*, 332–336.

71. Urofsky, *Louis D. Brandeis*, 181–184, 191, 277–281, 300–305.

72. McCraw, *Prophets of Regulation*, 14–15.

73. Daniel T. Rodgers, "In Search of Progressivism," *Reviews in American History* 10, no. 4 (December 1982): 113–132. Chandler, *The Visible Hand*, 334–335. Hofstadter, *The Age of Reform*, 203.

74. A report commissioned by President Grover Cleveland made clear that America was uniquely terrorized by the new industrial behemoths. From Simon Sterne, "Relations of the Governments," as quoted in Skowronek, *Building a New American State*, 135.

75. Skowronek, *Building a New American State*, chapters 3 and 4. Carpenter, *The Forging of Bureaucratic Autonomy*, 30.

76. Carpenter, *The Forging of Bureaucratic Autonomy*, 59–60, 63.

77. Eisenach, *The Lost Promise of Progressivism*, 152–155. Carpenter, *The Forging of Bureaucratic Autonomy*, 50.

78. Stimson and Bundy, *On Active Service in Peace and War*, 57–58.

79. Carpenter, *The Forging of Bureaucratic Autonomy*, 56.

80. Scott, *Seeing Like a State*, 94.

81. Urofsky, *Louis D. Brandeis*, 87.

82. See "Part 1: State Projects of Legibility and Simplification" in Scott, *Seeing Like a State*, 76–83. See also Scott, *Seeing Like a State*, 286–287. Lasch, *The Culture of Narcissism*, 159–160.

83. From Herbert Croly in *The Promise of American Life*. Cited in Nichols, "The Promise of Progressivism," 31.

84. Carpenter, *The Forging of Bureaucratic Autonomy*, 41.

85. Wiebe, *The Search for Order*, 61. Philip K. Howard, "From Progressivism to Paralysis," *Yale Law Journal Forum* (January 6, 2021): 376–377. Carpenter, *The Forging of Bureaucratic Autonomy*, 26, 42–43, 45–46.

86. A mere 15,000 civilian employees in the early 1870s. McCraw, *Prophets of Regulation*, 65–68. Other sources, presumably counting postal workers, contend it was 53,000 civilian employees in 1871, growing to 256,000 in 1901. Skowronek, *Building a New American State*, 49.

87. Skowronek, *Building a New American State*, 52–55.

88. Eisenach, *The Lost Promise of Progressivism*, 114.

89. Hays, "The Politics of Reform," 160.

90. Wiebe, *The Search for Order*, 176–177. Eisenach, *The Lost Promise of Progressivism*, 8–9.

91. McCraw, *Prophets of Regulation*, 15.

92. Urofsky, *Louis D. Brandeis*, 94.

93. Hays, "The Politics of Reform," 162.

94. Lippmann, *Public Opinion*, 137.

95. Stimson and Bundy, *On Active Service in Peace and War*, 58.

96. The Gilded Age and Progressive Era spanned forty years (1877–1917), from the end of Reconstruction into the First World War.

97. Scott, *Seeing Like a State*, 92–93. Wiebe, *The Search for Order*, 109–110. Skowronek, *Building a New American State*, 165.

98. Hofstadter, *The Age of Reform*, 131–134.

99. Brandeis did not share Bryan's populism. The jurist would react quite negatively to Bryan's "Cross of Gold" speech in 1896. Urofsky, *Louis D. Brandeis*, 92–93.

100. Wiebe, *The Search for Order*, 8.

101. Chandler, *The Visible Hand*, 130. Deb Chachra, *How Infrastructure Works: Inside the Systems That Shape Our World* (New York: Riverhead, 2023), 57.

102. McCraw, *Prophets of Regulation*, 57–61. Skowronek, *Building a New American State*, 144–150.

103. Note that the ICC's mandate wasn't to break the railroads up, but rather to impose regulations from the top down—to do for national railroads what the Granger Laws had empowered states to do within their own borders. Edward V. A. Kussy, "Surface Transportation and Administrative Law: Growing Up Together in the 20th Century," *Transportation Research Record* 1527, no. 1 (January 1996): 4.

104. Chernow, *Titan*, 292–293.

105. McCraw, *Prophets of Regulation*, 61–62. Skowronek, *Building a New American State*, 150–160.

106. Schulman, "Modern American Liberalism."

107. Garraty, *Right-Hand Man*, 223.

108. David Greenberg, *Republic of Spin: An Inside History of the American Presidency* (New York: W. W. Norton, 2016), 21.

109. Hanna himself would quietly seek ways to push the Colonel off the GOP ticket in 1904. "Mark Hanna and the 1896 Election," United States Senate, accessed June 1, 2024, www.senate.gov/artandhistory/history/minute/Hanna_1896Election.htm.

110. Chernow, *Titan*, 434.

111. Skowronek, *Building a New American State*, 250–251. Urofsky, *Louis D. Brandeis*, 287.

112. Hofstadter, *The Age of Reform*, 235–238. Chandler, *The Visible Hand*, 333–334.

113. McCraw, *Prophets of Regulation*, 62–63.

114. Skowronek, *Building a New American State*, 256–259.

115. Greenberg, *Republic of Spin*, 65.

116. Canellos, *The Great Dissenter*, 448.

117. J. P. Morgan's efforts to "organize" the economy amounted to a private-sector effort to stabilize the economy—a role that would be assumed by the Federal Reserve.

118. Canellos, *The Great Dissenter*, 437, 447–448.

119. Skowronek, *Building a New American State*, 172, 254–255, 259–263, 266. Milkis, *Theodore Roosevelt*, xvi, 55–56, 75–76. Snyder, *The House of Truth*, 40. Shesol, *Supreme Power*, 223, 501.

120. Urofsky, *Louis D. Brandeis*, 347.

121. McCraw, *Prophets of Regulation*, 101–108.

122. Charles McCarthy letter to Norman Hapgood of *Collier's Weekly*, September 4, 1912, Charles McCarthy Papers (microfilm edition, 1982), State Historical Society of Wisconsin. Urofsky, *Louis D. Brandeis*, 344–346.

123. Woodrow Wilson, "The Study of Administration," *Political Science Quarterly* 2, no. 2 (June 1887): 197–222. Milkis, *Theodore Roosevelt*, 134. Urofsky, *Louis D. Brandeis*, 348, 385.

124. David K. Nichols, "The Promise of Progressivism: Herbert Croly and the Rejection of Individual Rights," *Publius: The Journal of Federalism* 17, no. 2 (Spring 1987).

125. Christopher Lasch, *The True and Only Heaven: Progress and Its Critics* (New York: W. W. Norton, 1991), 342–344.

126. William J. Novak, "The Legal Origins of the Modern American State," in *Looking Back at Law's Century*, ed. Austin Sarat, Bryant Garth, and Robert A. Kagan (Ithaca, NY: Cornell University Press, 2002), 271.

127. Chernow, *Titan*, 617. Urofsky, *Louis D. Brandeis*, 384–398.

128. Urofsky, *Louis D. Brandeis*, 225.

129. Schlesinger, *The Crisis of the Old Order*, 34–35. Interview with David Greenberg, November 3, 2020.

130. Urofsky, *Louis D. Brandeis*, 381–384, 435.

131. Wiebe, *The Search for Order*, 219–220. Urofsky, *Louis D. Brandeis*, 394.

132. Henry Steele Commager, *The American Mind: An Interpretation of American Thought and Character Since the 1880's* (New Haven, CT: Yale University Press, 1950). Skowronek, *Building a New American State*, 271–274.

133. Urofsky, *Louis D. Brandeis*, 435. Milkis, *Theodore Roosevelt*, 272–273.

134. Urofsky, *Louis D. Brandeis*, 545–548.

135. Snyder, *The House of Truth*, 209–213, 216–225. Urofsky, *Louis D. Brandeis*, 500–501.

136. Milkis, *Theodore Roosevelt*, 277.

137. Skowronek, *Building a New American State*, 279–284. Urofsky, *Louis D. Brandeis*, 547–548.

138. Snyder, *The House of Truth*, 209–213, 216–225.

139. Edward J. Larson, *Summer for the Gods: The Scopes Trial and America's Continuing Debate Over Science and Religion* (New York: Basic Books, 2000), 61. Terry Teachout, *The Skeptic: A Life of H. L. Mencken* (New York: Harper, 2002), 144–145. Snyder, *The House of Truth*, 413–414.

140. Snyder, *The House of Truth*, 178–180.

141. David Cole, "Who's Canceling Whom?" *New York Review*, February 8, 2024. Urofsky, *Louis D. Brandeis*, 554.

142. Urofsky, *Louis D. Brandeis*, 554–555.

143. Skowronek, *Building a New American State*, 176. Shesol, *Supreme Power*, 24.

Chapter 2: The Price of Progress

1. Stuart Chase, "TVA: The New Deal's Best Asset, Planning by Consent," *The Nation*, June 17, 1936. Ira Katznelson, *Fear Itself: The New Deal and the Origins of Our Time* (New York: Liveright, 2013), 253–255.

2. Stuart Chase, "TVA: The New Deal's Best Asset, Broadening the Exchange Base," *The Nation*, June 10, 1936. The two million figure comes from this article. The income level is from Schlesinger in Note 3 below.

3. Arthur M. Schlesinger Jr., *The Coming of the New Deal: 1933–1935*, The Age of Roosevelt, Volume II (New York: Mariner, 2003), 320–321.

4. Jordan A. Schwarz, *The New Dealers* (New York: Knopf, 1993), 39. Jeff Shesol, *Supreme Power: Franklin Roosevelt vs. the Supreme Court* (New York: W. W. Norton, 2010), 271.

5. Schlesinger, *The Coming of the New Deal*, 321–323.

6. Schwarz, *The New Dealers*, 210–211.

7. Interview with energy policy expert, November 18, 2022. Separately, some object to the notion of this being described as an exchange or compact. See Ari Peskoe, Senior Fellow in Electricity Law, Harvard Environmental Policy Initiative, to Quadrennial Energy Review Task Force, Office of Energy Policy and Systems Analysis, U.S. Department of Energy, http://eelp.law.harvard.edu/wp-content/uploads/Harvard-Environmental-Policy-Initiative-QER-Comment-There-Is-No-Regulatory-Compact.pdf. Deb Chachra, *How Infrastructure Works: Inside the Systems That Shape Our World* (New York: Riverhead, 2023), 118.

8. Interview with energy policy expert, November 18, 2022.

9. Arthur M. Schlesinger Jr., *The Crisis of the Old Order, 1919–1933*, The Age of Roosevelt, Volume I (New York: Mariner, 2003), 453–455.

10. Interview with energy policy expert, November 18, 2022.

11. Avigail Sachs, *The Garden in the Machine* (Charlottesville: University of Virginia Press, 2023), 2–5.

12. Schlesinger, *The Coming of the New Deal*, 323–325.

13. Marion Elizabeth Rodgers, *Mencken: The American Iconoclast* (New York: Oxford University Press, 2005), 282.

14. Schlesinger, *Crisis of the Old Order*, 117–124.

15. David Levering Lewis, *The Improbable Wendell Willkie* (New York: Liveright, 2018), 86–88.

16. This is a clear distillation of what James C. Scott calls "high modernism." James C. Scott, *Seeing Like a State: How Certain Schemes to Improve the Human Condition Have Failed* (New Haven, CT: Yale University Press, 1998), 5.

17. Schlesinger, *The Coming of the New Deal*, 329–333.

18. Only one of every twenty-five farms in Tennessee and Alabama, merely one farm for every thirty-six in Georgia, and a measly one of one hundred Mississippi farms were powered up. Lewis, *The Improbable Wendell Willkie*, 72–73.

19. Arthur M. Schlesinger Jr., *The Politics of Upheaval: 1935–1936*, The Age of Roosevelt, Volume III (New York: Houghton Mifflin Harcourt, 1960), 362–376.

20. Sachs, *The Garden in the Machine*, 7–8. Morgan wanted planners to upend the physical infrastructure of the region such that locals could make the most of their own ingenuity. Lilienthal wanted the TVA to wield more disruptive power from its own perch.

21. Lewis, *The Improbable Wendell Willkie*, 91–92.

22. David Ekbladh, "'Mr. TVA': Grass-Roots Development, David Lilienthal, and the Rise and Fall of the Tennessee Valley Authority as a Symbol for U.S. Overseas Development, 1933–1973," *Diplomatic History* 26, no. 3 (Summer 2002): 335–374. Melvin I. Urofsky, *Louis D. Brandeis: A Life* (New York: Schocken Books, 2009), 707–708. Schwarz, *The New Dealers*, 236.

23. Lewis, *The Improbable Wendell Willkie*, 80–81.

24. Schlesinger, *The Coming of the New Deal*, 325–334. Schlesinger, *The Politics of Upheaval*, 362–376. Eric Rauchway, *The Great Depression and the New Deal: A Very Short Introduction* (New York: Oxford University Press, 2008), 91.

25. Ekbladh, "'Mr. TVA,'" 345.

26. Schlesinger, *The Politics of Upheaval*, 362–376. Henry Steele Commager, *The American Mind: An Interpretation of American Thought and Character Since the 1880's* (New Haven, CT: Yale University Press, 1950), 344–345.

27. Katznelson, *Fear Itself*, 254–255. See also Philip Selznick's *TVA and the Grass Roots: A Study of Politics and Organization* and Nancy Grant's *TVA and Black Americans: Planning for the Status Quo*, as cited in Sachs, *The Garden in the Machine*, 49–50.

28. Lewis, *The Improbable Wendell Willkie*, 82.

29. Schlesinger, *The Crisis of the Old Order*, 454–455.

30. Scott, *Seeing Like a State*, 224–227, 270.

31. James T. Patterson, *Grand Expectations: The United States, 1945–1974* (New York: Oxford University Press, 1996), 131.

32. Anthony J. Badger, *The New Deal: The Depression Years, 1933–1940* (Chicago: Ivan R. Dee, 2002), 3. Ekbladh, "'Mr. TVA.'"

33. Civil rights leader Whitney Young and Jacob Javits (R-NY) among them. Gareth Davies, *From Opportunity to Entitlement: The Transformation and Decline of Great Society Liberalism* (Lawrence: University Press of Kansas, 1996), 62–68, 127, 132, 186.

34. Paul Sabin, *Public Citizens: The Attack on Big Government and the Remaking of American Liberalism* (New York: W. W. Norton, 2021), 5–6.

35. Commager, *The American Mind*, 342–343.

36. Having seen how centralized power could be abused during and after the war, Frankfurter turned through the 1920s into a more vocal advocate for the civil liberties. Brad Snyder, *The House of Truth: A Washington Political Salon and the Foundations of American Liberalism* (New York: Oxford University Press, 2017), 413–414.

37. Laura M. Weinrib, "From Left to Rights: Civil Liberties Lawyering Between the World Wars," *Law, Culture, and the Humanities* 15, no. 3 (2019): 624.

38. Schlesinger, *The Crisis of the Old Order*, 40–43. Glenda Elizabeth Gilmore, "'Somewhere' in the Nadir of African American History, 1890–1920," National Humanities Center, accessed June 2024, https://nationalhumanitiescenter.org/tserve/freedom/1865-1917/essays/nadir.htm.

39. As quoted in Daniel P. Carpenter, *The Forging of Bureaucratic Autonomy: Reputations, Networks, and Policy Innovation in Executive Agencies, 1862–1928* (Princeton, NJ: Princeton University Press, 2001), 44.

40. Natasha Geiling, "The Real Johnny Appleseed Brought Apples—and Booze—to the American Frontier," *Smithsonian Magazine*, November 10, 2014.

41. Christopher Lasch, *The Culture of Narcissism: American Life in an Age of Diminishing Expectations* (New York: W. W. Norton, 1979), 265.

42. Rodgers, *Mencken*, 123.

43. Reuel Schiller, "Regulation and the Collapse of the New Deal Order, or How I Learned to Stop Worrying and Love the Market," in *Beyond the New Deal Order*, ed. Gary Gerstle, Nelson Lichtenstein, and Alice O'Connor (Philadelphia: University of Pennsylvania Press, 2019), 170.

44. Alfred D. Chandler Jr., *The Visible Hand* (Cambridge, MA: Belknap, 1977), 275–277. Scott, *Seeing Like a State*, 336–337.

45. Ira Katznelson, *Desolation and Enlightenment: Political Knowledge After Total War, Totalitarianism, and the Holocaust* (New York: Columbia University Press, 2003), 137.

46. Melvin I. Urofsky, *Louis D. Brandeis*, 240–243, 293–294. Walter Lippmann, *Public Opinion* (Overland Park, KS: Digireads.com, 2020), 197–198. Lizabeth Cohen, *Making a New Deal: Industrial Workers in Chicago, 1919–1939* (New York: Cambridge University Press, 1998), 167–176.

47. Chandler, *The Visible Hand*, 280.

48. Theodore J. Lowi, *The End of Liberalism: The Second Republic of the United States*, 2nd ed. (New York: W. W. Norton, 1979), 24–31. Scott, *Seeing Like a State*, 99.

49. Stephen Skowronek, *Building a New American State: The Expansion of National Administrative Capacities, 1877–1920* (New York: Cambridge University Press, 1982), 42–45.

50. Robert H. Wiebe, *The Search for Order: 1877–1920* (New York: Hill and Wang, 1967), 114–118, 123–127, 293–295.

51. Christopher Lasch, *The True and Only Heaven: Progress and Its Critics* (New York: W. W. Norton, 1991), 424–429.

52. Comte was a beacon of a rationalist approach to discerning truth and putting it into use. Isaiah Berlin, "Two Concepts of Liberty," in *Four Essays on Liberty* (New York: Oxford University Press, 1969). Skowronek, *Building a New American State*, 269–271. Eldon J. Eisenach, *The Lost Promise of Progressivism* (Lawrence: University Press of Kansas, 1994), 111.

53. Schiller, "Regulation and the Collapse of the New Deal Order," 170.

54. Henry L. Stimson and McGeorge Bundy, *On Active Service in Peace and War* (New York: Harper, 1948), 61–62. Shesol, *Supreme Power*, 47.

55. Walter Weyl, *The New Democracy*, 1912, as quoted in Skowronek, *Building a New American State*, 177. See also pp. 135–138, 165–166. Elisabeth S. Clemens, "Lineages of the Rube Goldberg State: Building and Blurring Public Programs, 1900–1940," in *Rethinking Political Institutions: The Art of the State*, ed. Ian Shapiro, Stephen Skowronek, and Daniel Galvin (New York: NYU Press, 2006), 201–208.

56. Brandeis was a great believer in scientific management, but was suspicious of experts. Urofsky, *Louis D. Brandeis*, 349.

57. Annmarie Hauck Walsh, *The Public's Business: The Politics and Practice of Government Corporations* (Cambridge, MA: MIT Press, 1978), 173.

58. Schlesinger, *The Crisis of the Old Order*, 377–378.

59. Lewis, *The Improbable Wendell Willkie*, 69. Chachra, *How Infrastructure Works*, 124–127.

60. Weinrib, "From Left to Rights," 630.

61. Schlesinger, *The Crisis of the Old Order*, 130–134.

62. Daniel R. Ernst, "Ernst Freund, Felix Frankfurter and the American Rechtsstaat: A Transatlantic Shipwreck, 1894–1932," *Studies in American Political Development* 23 (October 2009): 171–188.

63. S. J. Woolf, "A Friend of the Brain Trust Speaks Up," *New York Times Magazine*, September 30, 1934.

64. Wiebe, *The Search for Order*, 159–163.

65. Schwarz, *The New Dealers*, 135–136.

66. Thomas K. McCraw, *Prophets of Regulation* (Cambridge, MA: Belknap, 1986), 105. Urofsky, *Louis D. Brandeis*, 524.

67. Schlesinger, *The Crisis of the Old Order*, 147–149. Walter Lippmann, "H. L. Mencken," *Saturday Review of Literature*, December 11, 1926, www.mencken.org/text/txt001/lippman.walter.1926.h-l-mencken.htm. David Greenberg, *Republic of Spin: An Inside History of the American Presidency* (New York: W. W. Norton, 2016), 146. Rodgers, *Mencken*, 99.

68. James T. Kloppenberg, *Uncertain Victory: Social Democracy and Progressivism in European and American Thought, 1870–1920* (New York: Oxford University Press, 1986), 350–352. Eisenach, *The Lost Promise of Progressivism*, 117–118.

69. Greenberg, *Republic of Spin*, 36–39.

70. Kloppenberg, *Uncertain Victory*, 381–383.

71. Shesol, *Supreme Power*, 2, 239.

72. John B. Judis and Ruy Teixeira, *The Emerging Democratic Majority* (New York: Scribner, 2004).

73. Shesol, *Supreme Power*, 20, 466.

74. Walsh, *The Public's Business*, 27–28.

75. Schlesinger, *The Crisis of the Old Order*, 202–203.

76. Urofsky, *Louis D. Brandeis*, 694–695. Lewis Mumford, foreword to *Planned Society: Yesterday, Today, Tomorrow*, ed. Findlay MacKenzie (New York: Prentice Hall, 1937), v–x.

77. Franklin D. Roosevelt, "Inaugural Address," January 20, 1937, American Presidency Project, www.presidency.ucsb.edu/node/209135.

78. Alan Brinkley, *The End of Reform: New Deal Liberalism in Recession and War* (New York: Vintage Books, 1996), 5.

79. Katznelson, *Fear Itself*, 229–235. Shesol, *Supreme Power*, 20.

80. Schlesinger, *The Crisis of the Old Order*, 194–195, 400–401, 420.

81. Shesol, *Supreme Power*, 43–44, 174. Findlay MacKenzie, introduction to *Planned Society*, xx–xxi. Katznelson, *Fear Itself*, 53–54, 93–94.

82. Schlesinger, *The Coming of the New Deal*, 167–169. Brad Snyder, *Democratic Justice: Felix Frankfurter, the Supreme Court, and the Making of the Liberal Establishment* (New York: W. W. Norton, 2022), 239. Badger, *The New Deal*, 74–77, 159, 168–169. Shesol, *Supreme Power*, 13.

83. Schlesinger, *The Coming of the New Deal*, 179–181.

84. Badger, *The New Deal*, 84–94. Schlesinger, *The Coming of the New Deal*, 121, 132–134.

85. Shesol, *Supreme Power*, 127–146.

86. *A. L. A. Schechter Poultry Corp. v. United States*, 295 U.S. 495 (1935). Shesol, *Supreme Power*, 147–152.

87. Schwarz, *The New Dealers*, 113. Brinkley, *The End of Reform*, 18. Snyder, *Democratic Justice*, 249–250. Urofsky, *Louis D. Brandeis*, 705. Shesol, *Supreme Power*, 136–137.

88. Badger, *The New Deal*, 78.

89. Schlesinger, *The Crisis of the Old Order*, 113.

90. Shesol, *Supreme Power*, 113–116, 162. David M. Kennedy, *Freedom from Fear: The American People in Depression and War, 1929–1945* (New York: Oxford University Press, 1999), 238.

91. Brinkley, *The End of Reform*, 109–110.

92. Shesol, *Supreme Power*, 70–73. William Boyd, "Public Utility and the Low-Carbon Future," *UCLA Law Review* 61, no. 6 (May 2014): 1637–1639.

93. Lasch, *The True and Only Heaven*, 429–435.

94. McCraw, *Prophets of Regulation*, 210.

95. Brinkley, *The End of Reform*, 16.

96. Badger, *The New Deal*, 94–108.

97. Brinkley, *The End of Reform*, 48–58.

98. Snyder, *Democratic Justice*, 250–253.

99. Brinkley, *The End of Reform*, 48–58.

100. "The Communications Act of 1934," Bureau of Justice Assistance, https://bja.ojp.gov/program/it/privacy-civil-liberties/authorities/statutes/1288.

101. Brinkley, *The End of Reform*, 62–64.

102. Franklin D. Roosevelt, "Address on Constitution Day, Washington, D.C.," September 17, 1937, American Presidency Project, www.presidency.ucsb.edu/documents/address-constitution-day-washington-dc.

103. McCraw, *Prophets of Regulation*, 213–214.

104. Shesol, *Supreme Power*, 429–454. Peter S. Canellos, *The Great Dissenter: The Story of John Marshall Harlan, America's Judicial Hero* (New York: Simon and Schuster, 2021), 453–457. In 1944, the court went yet another step further, ruling that judges should largely leave the intricacies of ratemaking to the bureaucrats. Boyd, "Public Utility and the Low-Carbon Future," 1644–1645.

105. Walsh, *The Public's Business*, 26–29.

106. Shesol, *Supreme Power*.

107. Badger, *The New Deal*, 306.

108. Schwarz, *The New Dealers*, 290–292.

109. Schlesinger, *The Coming of the New Deal*, 100–103.

110. Brinkley, *The End of Reform*, 87, 140–141.

111. J. M. Balkin, "The Footnote," *Northwestern University Law Review* 83, nos. 1 and 2 (1989). Shesol, *Supreme Power*, 392–415.

112. Katznelson, *Fear Itself*, 342–346.

113. Brinkley, *The End of Reform*, 140–148, 230–233. Schwarz, *The New Dealers*, 281. Reuel Schiller, *Forging Rivals: Race, Class, Law, and the Collapse of Postwar Liberalism* (New York: Cambridge University Press, 2015), 13, 18. Katznelson, *Fear Itself*, 382–388. Bruce J. Schulman, *The Seventies: The Great Shift in American Culture, Society, and Politics* (New York: Da Capo Press, 2001), 4–5. Allen J. Matusow, *The Unraveling of America: A History of Liberalism in the 1960s* (Athens: University of Georgia Press, 2003), 20. Todd Gitlin, *The Sixties: Years of Hope, Days of Rage* (New York: Bantam, 1993), 61.

114. Gitlin, *The Sixties*, 17–18.

115. Katznelson, *Fear Itself*, 319–320. Reviewing Sigmund Freud's last book for the *New York Times*, Lionel Trilling argued that progress was predicated on a kind of self-control. Samuel Moyn, "Liberalism in Mourning," *Boston Review*, August 30, 2023. In the immediate postwar era, there emerged a much stricter divide between those who identified as "liberals" and those who identified as "progressives." Gitlin, *The Sixties*, 61–64. Patterson, *Grand Expectations*, 98–104.

116. As E. J. Dionne points out, the Establishment was, in some way, an emanation of what Arthur Schlesinger had deemed the "Vital Center" of American politics. E. J. Dionne Jr., *Why Americans Hate Politics* (New York: Touchstone, 1991), 116–118.

117. Samuel Moyn, *Liberalism Against Itself: Cold War Intellectuals and the Making of Our Times* (New Haven, CT: Yale University Press, 2023), 147.

118. Scott, *Seeing Like a State*, 82, 241.

119. Louis Menand, "Regrets Only," *New Yorker*, September 22, 2008.

120. Harry McPherson, *A Political Education: A Washington Memoir* (Austin: University of Texas Press, 1995), 206.

121. Betty Friedan, *The Feminine Mystique* (New York: W. W. Norton, 1963).

122. Laura Kalman, *The Strange Career of Legal Liberalism* (New Haven, CT: Yale University Press, 1996), 25.

123. Scott, *Seeing Like a State*, 88. Schiller, *Forging Rivals*, 15–16.

124. Patterson, *Grand Expectations*, 131, 167.

125. Urofsky, *Louis D. Brandeis*, 611–616.

126. David L. Bazelon, "Coping with Technology Through the Legal Process," *Cornell Law Review* 62, no. 5 (June 1977).

127. Scott, *Seeing Like a State*, 94–95.

128. Schiller, *Forging Rivals*, 139–148.

129. McPherson, *A Political Education*, 160–163.

130. "Remarks of Senator John F. Kennedy at Harvard University, Cambridge, Massachusetts, June 14, 1956," John F. Kennedy Presidential Library, www.jfklibrary.org/archives/other-resources/john-f-kennedy-speeches/harvard-university-19560614.

131. Lasch, *The Culture of Narcissism*, 96.

132. Gitlin, *The Sixties*, 59.

133. Walsh, *The Public's Business*, 118–119. Charles M. Haar, "In Accordance with a Comprehensive Plan," *Harvard Law Review* 68, no. 7 (May 1955).

134. *American Experience: New York*, season 1, episode 7, "New York: The City and the World (1945–2000)," directed by Ric Burns, aired October 7, 2001, on PBS, www.amazon.com/American-Experience-New-York-Season/dp/B006CAKNA4.

135. Walsh, *The Public's Business*, 240–241.

Chapter 3: Bodies on the Machine

1. Isabel Wilkerson, *The Warmth of Other Suns: The Epic Story of America's Great Migration* (New York: Random House, 2010). Daniel Bell, *The Cultural Contradictions of Capitalism* (New York: Basic Books, 1978), 184–185.

2. Robert Park, "The City: Suggestions for the Investigation of Human Behavior in the Urban Environment," *American Journal of Sociology* (1915), in *Classic Essays on the Culture of Cities*, ed. Richard Sennett (New York: Appleton-Century-Crofts, 1969). Daniel Okrent, *Last Call: The Rise and Fall of Prohibition* (New York: Scribner, 2010).

3. Some may take offense at my use of the term "ghetto." But as Richard Rothstein argues, the term accurately reflects America's purposeful strategy of relegating certain populations to circumspect locales, just as happened in Europe. Richard Rothstein, *The Color of Law: A Forgotten History of How Our Government Segregated America* (New York: Liveright, 2017), xvi.

4. David Halberstam, *The Best and the Brightest* (New York: Random House, 1973).

5. Joshua Zeitz, *Building the Great Society: Inside Lyndon Johnson's White House* (New York: Viking, 2018), 46–47.

6. Dennis Hevesi, "David L. Hackett, Led Efforts on Poverty and Juvenile Crime, Dies at 84," *New York Times*, April 30, 2011. Daniel P. Moynihan, *Maximum Feasible Misunderstanding: Community Action in the War on Poverty* (New York: Free Press, 1969), 61–66.

7. James T. Patterson, *Grand Expectations: The United States, 1945–1974* (New York: Oxford University Press, 1996), 464. This point of view was most pointedly argued by Walter Heller, who is often credited with convincing President Lyndon Johnson to pursue a war on poverty in the wake of Kennedy's assassination. Nicholas Lemann, "The Politics of Poverty," *Atlantic*, September 18, 2013.

8. Nicholas Lemann, "The Myth of Community Development," *New York Times*, January 9, 1994.

9. Moynihan, *Maximum Feasible Misunderstanding*, 15–19.

10. "Participation of the Poor: Section 202(a)(3) Organizations under the Economic Opportunity Act of 1964," *Yale Law Journal* 75, no. 4 (March 1966): 602–605. Allen J. Matusow, *The Unraveling of America: A History of Liberalism in the 1960s* (Athens: University of Georgia Press, 2003), 244–245. Zeitz, *Building the Great Society*, 82.

11. Matusow, *The Unraveling of America*, 107–119.

12. Moynihan, *Maximum Feasible Misunderstanding*, 35–36, 67–68.

13. Moynihan, *Maximum Feasible Misunderstanding*, 38–40. Emphasis added.

14. Taken from Lyndon B. Johnson, *Public Papers of the President: 1964*, vol. 1, 377. Quoted in Gareth Davies, *From Opportunity to Entitlement: The Transformation and Decline of Great Society Liberalism* (Lawrence: University Press of Kansas, 1996), 35.

15. Harry McPherson, *A Political Education: A Washington Memoir* (Austin: Texas University Press, 1995), 177–178.

16. Zeitz, *Building the Great Society*, 50–53.

17. Moynihan, *Maximum Feasible Misunderstanding*, 75–101.

18. Patterson, *Grand Expectations*, 590.

19. Moynihan, *Maximum Feasible Misunderstanding*, 143.

20. Davies, *From Opportunity to Entitlement*, 35.

21. Matusow, *The Unraveling of America*, 119–127.

22. Theodore J. Lowi, *The End of Liberalism: The Second Republic of the United States*, 2nd ed. (New York: W. W. Norton, 1979), 212–219.

23. Matusow, *The Unraveling of America*, 245–246.

24. Moynihan, *Maximum Feasible Misunderstanding*, 132–135. Zeitz, *Building the Great Society*, 84–89. A similar controversy emerged with the Child Development Group of Mississippi. McPherson, *A Political Education*, 353–355. Matusow, *The Unraveling of America*, 246–247. Davies, *From Opportunity to Entitlement*, 91, 195.

25. Matusow, *The Unraveling of America*, 246–271.

26. Zeitz, *Building the Great Society*, 84–87.

27. Bell, *The Cultural Contradictions of Capitalism*, 179.

28. The early interwar era was suffused with market speculation, Jazz Age flappers, urban unrest, and America letting its hair down after the horrors of the First World War.

29. David E. Lilienthal, *Big Business: A New Era* (New York: Pocket Books, 2006).

30. Interview with Bruce Schulman, January 13, 2021.

31. Lowi, *The End of Liberalism*, 52–61.

32. Thomas K. McCraw, *Prophets of Regulation* (Cambridge, MA: Belknap, 1986), 230.

33. Bruce J. Schulman, "Modern American Liberalism: A Story in Four Acts," excerpted from Bruce J. Schulman, *Lyndon B. Johnson and American Liberalism: A Brief Biography with Documents* (New York: Bedford/St. Martin's, 2007).

34. Lowi, *The End of Liberalism*, 34–39. Reuel E. Schiller, "Enlarging the Administrative Polity: Administrative Law and the Changing Definition of Pluralism, 1945–1970," *Vanderbilt Law Review* 53, no. 5 (2000): 1399–4010. Ira Katznelson, *Desolation and Enlightenment: Political Knowledge After Total War, Totalitarianism, and the Holocaust* (New York: Columbia University Press, 2003), 133. "Participation of the Poor," 601n5.

35. Quote from Lyndon Johnson. Davies, *From Opportunity to Entitlement*, 38, 69.

36. Patterson, *Grand Expectations*, 369–370.

37. Christopher Lasch, *The True and Only Heaven: Progress and Its Critics* (New York: W. W. Norton, 1991), 445–459.

38. Zeitz, *Building the Great Society*, 62–70.

39. Todd Gitlin, *The Sixties: Years of Hope, Days of Rage* (New York: Bantam, 1993), 56–66.

40. David Truman, *The Governmental Process: Political Interests and Public Opinion* (New York: Alfred A. Knopf, 1951), 524, as quoted in Katznelson, *Desolation and Enlightenment*, 131–132. Emphasis added.

41. "Participation of the Poor," 606.

42. Patterson, *Grand Expectations*, 369–370.

43. "Sherman Adams Dies at 87 in N.H.: Forced Out as Top Eisenhower Aide in Vicuna Coat Scandal," *Los Angeles Times*, October 28, 1986.

44. Katznelson, *Fear Itself*, 373–374.

45. Earl Swift, *The Big Roads: The Untold Story of the Engineers, Visionaries, and Trailblazers Who Created the American Superhighways* (New York: Houghton Mifflin Harcourt, 2011), 241–243.

46. Lewis Mumford, "The Highway and the City," *Architectural Record*, April 1958. Reprinted in Lewis Mumford, *The Urban Prospect* (New York: Harcourt, Brace and World, 1968).

47. McPherson, *A Political Education*, 246.

48. Matusow, *The Unraveling of America*, 98–107.

49. "USAID and PL-480, 1961–1969," Office of the Historian, United States Department of State, accessed January 2024, https://history.state.gov/milestones/1961-1968/pl-480. James C. Scott, *Seeing Like a State: How Certain Schemes to Improve the Human Condition Have Failed* (New Haven, CT: Yale University Press, 1998), 237.

50. Gitlin, *The Sixties*, 91. See also Chester J. Pach Jr., "Dwight D. Eisenhower: Foreign Affairs," Miller Center at UVA, https://millercenter.org/president/eisenhower/foreign-affairs.

51. Paul Sabin did a very thoughtful and thorough examination of this intellectual transformation. Paul Sabin, *Public Citizens* (New York: W. W. Norton), 2021.

52. Interview with Bruce Schulman, January 13, 2021. Reuel Schiller, "The Curious Origins of Airline Deregulation: Economic Deregulation and the American Left," *Business History Review* 93 (Winter 2019): 732–739.

53. Alexander Stern, "Critical Theory and the Newest Left: What the Frankfurt School Has to Say About Bureaucratic Progressivism," *Hedgehog Review*, June 25, 2021. In 1960, the political scientist E. E. Schattschneider wrote: "The flaw in the pluralist heaven is that the heavenly chorus sings with a strong upper-class accent." As quoted in Katznelson, *Fear Itself*, 402.

54. Judith Shklar, Isaiah Berlin, Karl Popper, and Lionel Trilling, among them. Samuel Moyn, *Liberalism Against Itself: Cold War Intellectuals and the Making of Our Times* (New Haven, CT: Yale University Press, 2023).

55. Reuel Schiller, *Forging Rivals: Race, Class, Law, and the Collapse of Postwar Liberalism* (New York: Cambridge University Press, 2015), 143–145. Gitlin, *The Sixties*, 19. Sean Illing, "If You Want to Understand the Age of Trump, Read the Frankfurt School," *Vox*, January 27, 2019, www.vox.com/conversations/2016/12/27/14038406/donald-trump-frankfurt -school-brexit-critical-theory. Schiller, "Enlarging the Administrative Polity," 1410–1416.

56. Gitlin, *The Sixties*, 96, 81–85.

57. Moynihan, *Maximum Feasible Misunderstanding*, 111–113. Bell, *The Cultural Contradictions of Capitalism*, 182–191. E. J. Dionne Jr., *Why Americans Hate Politics* (New York: Touchstone, 1991), 23–28. Irving Howe, "New Styles in 'Leftism,'" in *A Voice Still Heard: Selected Essays of Irving Howe*, ed. Nina Howe (New Haven, CT: Yale University Press, 2014), 47–50.

58. Francois Cusset, *French Theory: How Foucault, Derrida, Deleuze, & Co. Transformed the Intellectual Life of the United States*, trans. Jeff Fort (Minneapolis: University of Minnesota Press, 2008), 55–57. Gitlin, *The Sixties*, 97–109. Dionne, *Why Americans Hate Politics*, 31–45. Matusow, *The Unraveling of America*, 308–321. Schiller, "The Curious Origins of Airline Deregulation."

59. Bruce J. Schulman, *The Seventies: The Great Shift in American Culture, Society, and Politics* (New York: Da Capo Press, 2001), 8–14. Matusow, *The Unraveling of America*, 32–42.

60. Mario Savio, "Sit-in Address on the Steps of Sprout Hall, Delivered 2 December 1964, The University of California at Berkeley," American Rhetoric, updated January 3, 2021, www.americanrhetoric.com/speeches/mariosaviosproulhallsitin.htm.

61. In 1963's *America and the New Era*, SDS argued Kennedy "was tinkering with the corporate economy in order to maintain it." Gitlin, *The Sixties*, 130–133.

62. Jeff Shesol, *Supreme Power: Franklin Roosevelt vs. the Supreme Court* (New York: W. W. Norton, 2010), 374.

63. Gitlin, *The Sixties*, 134. Carl Oglesby would argue in 1965 that the New Left was driven by a belief that there were two different liberalisms: "one authentically humanist; the other not so human at all." "Statement of Carl Oglesby, President of Students for a Democratic Society, March on Washington, November 27, 1965 ["Let Us Shape the Future"]," https://freedom archives.org/Documents/Finder/DOC30_scans/30.sds.carloglesbyspeech.pdf.

64. Howe, "New Styles in 'Leftism,'" 57–59. "Participation of the Poor," 608–609. One SDS leader described it as "moral dislike for [the] administrative process." Gitlin, *The Sixties*, 134.

65. Howe, "New Styles in 'Leftism,'" 62–68.

66. Lyndon B. Johnson, "Commencement Address at Howard University: 'To Fulfill These Rights,'" June 4, 1965, American Presidency Project, www.presidency.ucsb.edu/documents /commencement-address-howard-university-fulfill-these-rights.

67. Davies, *From Opportunity to Entitlement*, 32–34, 62–68.

68. "Thomas Jefferson and Sally Hemings: A Brief Account," Thomas Jefferson Foundation, www.monticello.org/thomas-jefferson/jefferson-slavery/thomas-jefferson-and-sally -hemings-a-brief-account/.

69. "Civil Rights Act (1964)," U.S. National Archives and Records Administration, www .archives.gov/milestone-documents/civil-rights-act. In subsequent years, equal employment opportunity offices and divisions proliferated throughout public bureaucracies at various levels of government.

70. Davies, *From Opportunity to Entitlement*, 77.

71. The Report of the White House Conference "To Fulfill These Rights." McPherson, *A Political Education*, 344–364. Vincent J. Cannato, *The Ungovernable City: John Lindsay and His Struggle to Save New York* (New York: Basic Books, 2001), 267–352.

72. Daniel Geary, "The Moynihan Report: An Annotated Edition," *Atlantic*, September 14, 2015.

73. McPherson, *A Political Education*, 334–345.

74. Zeitz, *Building the Great Society*, 255–262. *The Negro Family* stated: "Three centuries of injustice have brought about deep-seated structural distortions in the life of the Negro American. . . . The cycle can be broken only if these distortions are set right." McPherson, *A Political Education*, 337.

75. Geary, "The Moynihan Report."

76. McPherson, *A Political Education*, 339.

77. Matusow, *The Unraveling of America*, 194–198.

78. "Statement of Carl Oglesby."

79. Gitlin, *The Sixties*, 239–241.

80. Michael Kazin, *What It Took to Win: A History of the Democratic Party* (New York: Farrar, Straus and Giroux, 2022), 237.

81. Thomas Frank, *What's the Matter with Kansas? How Conservatives Won the Heart of America* (New York: Henry Holt, 2004), 229.

82. Christopher B. Daly, *Covering America: A Narrative History of the Nation's Journalism* (Boston: University of Massachusetts Press, 2012), 334–335.

83. Daly, *Covering America*, 357–360.

84. Daly, *Covering America*, 378–380.

85. Gitlin, *The Sixties*, 302.

86. Rachel Carson, *Silent Spring* (New York: Houghton Mifflin, 1962).

87. Kim Phillips-Fein, "The Liberals Who Weakened Trust in Government," *New Republic*, August 2, 2021.

88. Phillips-Fein, "The Liberals Who Weakened Trust in Government."

89. Bill Kauffman, "When the Left Was Right," *American Conservative*, May 19, 2008.

90. Gitlin, *The Sixties*, 243.

91. Sentiment against the old guard was so pervasive that Senator Robert Kennedy (D-NY), considering a run for president, was reluctant to address ADA (Americans for Democratic Action), which was a beacon of the old liberal order. Quoted in Davies, *From Opportunity to Entitlement*, 141. See also pp. 165–166, 174–178, 201–203. Gitlin, *The Sixties*, 256–260, 285–288.

92. Patterson, *Grand Expectations*, 712–713.

93. To lean on Tolstoy's iconic dichotomy: the Establishment represented the hedgehog that knew one thing well. But America's cultural vanguard turned instead to the fox, who knew many things. Scott, *Seeing Like a State*, 45–47.

94. Gitlin, *The Sixties*, 256–260, 285–287.

95. "Ribicoff Protests 'Gestapo Tactics' at 1968 Chicago Convention," History channel video, www.history.com/speeches/ribicoff-protests-gestapo-tactics-at-1968-chicago-convention.

96. Matusow, *The Unraveling of America*, 422.

97. "Anti-busing in the North," Equal Justice Initiative, July 26, 2019, https://eji.org/news/history-racial-injustice-anti-busing-in-the-north/.

98. Christopher Lasch, *The Culture of Narcissism: American Life in an Age of Diminishing Expectations* (New York: W. W. Norton, 1979).

99. Paul Potter speech at March on Washington, April 1965, as quoted in Gitlin, *The Sixties*, 184.

100. Davies, *From Opportunity to Entitlement*, 137. Gitlin, *The Sixties*, 391–395.

101. Davies, *From Opportunity to Entitlement*, 110.

102. Patterson, *Grand Expectations*, 714.

103. Gitlin, *The Sixties*, 341.

104. Davies, *From Opportunity to Entitlement*, 212–219. Gitlin, *The Sixties*, 377–380.

105. Dionne, *Why Americans Hate Politics*, 66–73.

106. Todd S. Purdum, "Three Decades Later, 'Woodstein' Takes a Victory Lap," *New York Times*, June 3, 2005.

107. Daly, *Covering America*, 391–396.

108. Moyn, *Liberalism Against Itself*.

109. Cusset, *French Theory*, 27–28.

110. Scott, *Seeing Like a State*, 23, 97–102.

111. Cusset, *French Theory*, 108–118, 277–286.

112. Gitlin, *The Sixties*, 344. George Packer, *Last Best Hope: America in Crisis and Renewal* (New York: Picador, 2021), 118–125.

113. *1971: The Year That Music Changed Everything*, season 1, episode 6, "Exile," aired May 20, 2021, on Apple+, https://tv.apple.com/us/episode/exile/umc.cmc.3rq0gmi1y6c41vaho1xcss5cs.

114. Chris Morris, "Hunter S. Thompson Brings 'Fear and Loathing' to Island," *Billboard* 108, no. 43 (October 26, 1996): 10. Further evidence: Lasch, *The Culture of Narcissism*, 11–15.

115. Gitlin, *The Sixties*, xix.

116. Lasch, *The True and Only Heaven*, 31–34. Lasch, *The Culture of Narcissism*.

117. Seyla Benhabib, "Thinking Without Banisters," *New York Review*, February 24, 2022.

118. Bell, *The Cultural Contradictions of Capitalism*, 37. Matusow, *The Unraveling of America*, 305–307.

119. Gitlin, *The Sixties*, 341–345.

120. "Q&A: Susannah Cahalan," C-SPAN, November 7, 2019, www.c-span.org/video/?466007-1/qa-susannah-cahalan.

121. Schulman, *The Seventies*, 48–52, 146–150.

122. Lasch, *The True and Only Heaven*, 369–370.

Chapter 4: Manacling the Octopus

1 Interview with Vincent Ragosta, July 15, 2022.

2. Several years earlier, the Academy Award–winning film *Patton* had depicted the mercurial general, George S. Patton, slapping a shell-shocked soldier across the face. Here was the chief of the Providence Police Department treating his officer in much the same way.

3. Katherine J. Bies, "Let the Sunshine In: Illuminating the Powerful Role Police Unions Play in Shielding Officer Misconduct," *Stanford Law and Policy Review* 29 (May 1, 2017): 121–123.

4. Todd Gitlin, *The Sixties: Years of Hope, Days of Rage* (New York: Bantam, 1993), 326.

5. "Mandel Orders Report on Police Spying," *Baltimore Sun*, December 31, 1974.

6. Michael Olesker, "Why So Long to Get Pomerleau Out of Office?" *Baltimore Sun*, May 12, 1981.

7. Roger Twigg, "The Commissioner and Me," *Baltimore Sun*, January 26, 1992.

8. Roger Twigg, "Pomerleau Said to Learn Jury Secrets," *Baltimore Sun*, February 21, 1973.

9. "Police Bill of Rights Pushed," *Capital* (Annapolis, MD), March 9, 1973.

10. "Policemen, Wives Demand Rights Bill," *Baltimore Sun*, March 9, 1973. "House Panel Passes Police 'Rights,'" *Baltimore Sun*, March 24, 1973.

11. "A Cloud over the Police Department," *Baltimore Sun*, January 23, 1973.

12. Even labor leaders had been inclined to sanction Franklin Roosevelt's view that taxpayer-paid employees should not be permitted to organize. During the early 1960s, President Kennedy opened the door to public-sector collective bargaining at the federal level. New York and California green-lit public employee unionization in 1967 and 1968, respectively. Kevin M. Keenan and Samuel Walker, "An Impediment to Police Accountability? An Analysis of Statutory Law Enforcement Officers' Bills of Rights," *Boston University Public Interest Law*

Journal 14, no. 2 (Spring 2005): 196–201. Philip K. Howard, "From Progressivism to Paralysis," *Yale Law Journal Forum* (January 6, 2021): 378–379.

13. Interview with Vincent Ragosta, July 15, 2022.

14. The first federal LEOBOR was introduced in the 1970s. Florida and Maryland adopted officer protections in 1974. California and Rhode Island passed versions in 1978. Ten more followed over the next sixteen years. Keenan and Walker, "An Impediment to Police Accountability?" 196–197.

15. Interview with Vincent Ragosta, July 15, 2022.

16. Ethan Shorey, "Chief: No Issues During Feeley's First Weeks Back on the Job," *Valley Breeze*, April 6, 2022.

17. Jim Hummel, "A Pivot on Police Discipline in Rhode Island? How Officers' Bill of Rights Might Change," *Providence Journal*, March 10, 2022.

18. In the spring of 2024, Rhode Island enacted a LEOBOR reform that modified several provisions, permitting chiefs to comment publicly on cases, diversifying the panels charged with arbitrating disputes, and lengthening the time that chiefs could suspend officers absent a review. Melanie DaSilva, "McKee Signs LEOBOR Reform Bill into Law," WPRI.com, June 11, 2024. Similar reform efforts were under way elsewhere in the country. Rachel Sawicki, "Senate Unanimously Passes LEOBOR Reform, Internal Investigation Guidance," Delaware Public Media, July 2, 2023.

19. Kim Barker and Serge F. Kovaleski, "Officer Who Pressed His Knee on George Floyd's Neck Drew Scrutiny Long Before," *New York Times*, July 18, 2020.

20. Brad Snyder, *Democratic Justice: Felix Frankfurter, the Supreme Court, and the Making of the Liberal Establishment* (New York: W. W. Norton, 2022), 334, 340.

21. Snyder, *Democratic Justice*, 351–362. Melvin I. Urofsky, *Louis D. Brandeis: A Life* (New York: Schocken Books, 2009), 219–220. This was in part an extension of the logic Stone had used in his dissent in *United States v. Butler* (1936). Jeff Shesol, *Supreme Power: Franklin Roosevelt vs. the Supreme Court* (New York: W. W. Norton, 2010), 184–186.

22. Shesol, *Supreme Power*, 520.

23. Philip K. Howard and Geoff Kabaservice, "Can America Untangle Itself from Red Tape? (With Philip K. Howard)," September 1, 2021, in *Vital Center*, podcast, www.niskanen center.org/can-america-untangle-itself-from-red-tape-with-phillip-k-howard/. Reuel E. Schiller, "Enlarging the Administrative Polity: Administrative Law and the Changing Definition of Pluralism, 1945–1970," *Vanderbilt Law Review* 53, no. 5 (2000): 1401–1430. Laura Kalman, *The Strange Career of Legal Liberalism* (New Haven, CT: Yale University Press, 1996), 41–42. William N. Eskridge Jr., and Philip P. Frickey, "The Making of *The Legal Process*," *Harvard Law Review* 107, no. 8 (June 1994): 2040–2045.

24. The APA served to guarantee that executives could not act like star chambers. The APA required that the processes regulators used to make determinations also be subject to scrutiny. Edward Rubin, "It's Time to Make the Administrative Procedure Act Administrative," *Cornell Law Review* 89, no. 1 (November 2003): 110–112.

25. Laura M. Weinrib, "From Left to Rights: Civil Liberties Lawyering Between the World Wars," *Law, Culture, and the Humanities* 15, no. 3 (2019): 640–647. Daniel P. Carpenter, *The Forging of Bureaucratic Autonomy: Reputations, Networks, and Policy Innovation in Executive Agencies, 1862–1928* (Princeton, NJ: Princeton University Press, 2001), 356–357.

Edward V. A. Kussy, "Surface Transportation and Administrative Law: Growing Up Together in the 20th Century," *Transportation Research Record* 1527, no. 1 (January 1996): 7–8.

26. Thomas O. McGarity, "Some Thoughts on 'Deossifying' the Rulemaking Process," *Duke Law Journal* 41, no. 6 (1992): 1396–1398. The law established some norms of adjudication. Adam B. Cox and Emma Kaufman, "The Adjudicative State," *Yale Law Journal* 132, no. 6 (April 2023): 1785–1786.

27. Rubin, "It's Time to Make the Administrative Procedure Act Administrative," 137–146.

28. As quoted in Reuel Schiller, "Reining in the Administrative State: World War II and the Decline of Expert Administration," in *Total War and the Law*, ed. Daniel R. Ernst and Victor Jew (Westport: Praeger, 2002), 201.

29. Paul Sabin, *Public Citizens: The Attack on Big Government and the Remaking of American Liberalism* (New York: W. W. Norton, 2021), 6–9.

30. Charles A. Reich, "The New Property," *Yale Law Journal* 73, no. 5 (April 1964).

31. Reuel Schiller, "The Ideological Origins of Deregulation," *Regulatory Review*, March 18, 2019.

32. Kussy, "Surface Transportation and Administrative Law," 9.

33. James T. Patterson, *Grand Expectations: The United States, 1945–1974* (New York: Oxford University Press, 1996), 639–642.

34. Francis X. Clines, "Clinton Signs Bill Cutting Welfare; States in New Role," *New York Times*, August 23, 1996.

35. Christopher Lasch, *The Culture of Narcissism: American Life in an Age of Diminishing Expectations* (New York: W. W. Norton, 1979), 188–191.

36. Gareth Davies, *From Opportunity to Entitlement: The Transformation and Decline of Great Society Liberalism* (Lawrence: University Press of Kansas, 1996), 10–13.

37. Lizabeth Cohen, *Making a New Deal: Industrial Workers in Chicago, 1919–1939* (New York: Cambridge University Press, 1998). Many reformers at this time wanted to educate parents to do a better job. Lasch, *The Culture of Narcissism*, 191–193.

38. Davies, *From Opportunity to Entitlement*, 23–27.

39. These values were not exclusively designed to be imposed from the middle classes onto those struggling at the base of the ladder. They were extensions of the nineteenth century's embrace of the Protestant ethic. Lasch, *The Culture of Narcissism*, 71–75.

40. William H. Simon, "Legality, Bureaucracy, and Class in the Welfare System," *Yale Law Journal* 92, no. 7 (June 1983). Davies, *From Opportunity to Entitlement*, 23–27.

41. Simon, "Legality, Bureaucracy, and Class in the Welfare System."

42. Davies, *From Opportunity to Entitlement*, 158–161.

43. Nicholas Lemann, "The Myth of Community Development," *New York Times*, January 9, 1994. Davies, *From Opportunity to Entitlement*, 87–99.

44. Civil rights luminary Bayard Rustin on the thinking behind this approach. Davies, *From Opportunity to Entitlement*, 170–173.

45. Schiller, "Enlarging the Administrative Polity," 1433–1434.

46. Howard, "From Progressivism to Paralysis," 374–376.

47. Simon, "Legality, Bureaucracy, and Class in the Welfare System."

48. Theodore J. Lowi, *The End of Liberalism: The Second Republic of the United States*, 2nd ed. (New York: W. W. Norton, 1979), 229.

49. Daniel Bell, *The Cultural Contradictions of Capitalism* (New York: Basic Books, 1978), 194–196. Fred Siegel, *The Future Once Happened Here: New York, D.C., L.A., and the Fate of America's Big Cities* (New York: Encounter Books, 1997), 56.

50. Simon, "Legality, Bureaucracy, and Class in the Welfare System."

51. Jason Deparle, "Whose Welfare?" *New York Times*, January 7, 1996. Simon, "Legality, Bureaucracy, and Class in the Welfare System," 1203–1204.

52. Simon, "Legality, Bureaucracy, and Class in the Welfare System," 1198–1199.

53. Davies, *From Opportunity to Entitlement*, 115–124.

54. The same bill that established the war on poverty's community action programs also created the Legal Services Program, hiring lawyers at federal expense to litigate against state agencies refusing to dispense federal welfare dollars as generously as applicants desired. Lowi, *The End of Liberalism*, 220–226.

55. Siegel, *The Future Once Happened Here*, 70.

56. Bruce J. Schulman, *The Seventies: The Great Shift in American Culture, Society, and Politics* (New York: Da Capo Press, 2001), 24–35.

57. Howard, "From Progressivism to Paralysis," 384.

58. Despite the failures of community action programs, successive progressive efforts embraced the same underlying bottom-up approach. Lemann, "The Myth of Community Development."

59. As Frederick Jackson Turner would argue in his Frontier Thesis, the nation's self-perception had hinged on a sense that the North American continent was an endless expanse. Frederick Jackson Turner, "The Significance of the Frontier in American History," a paper read at the meeting of the American Historical Association in Chicago, July 12, 1893, https://nationalhumanitiescenter.org/pds/gilded/empire/text1/turner.pdf.

60. "How the Highway Beautification Act Became a Law," Federal Highway Administration, updated June 27, 2017, www.fhwa.dot.gov/infrastructure/beauty.cfm.

61. Sabin, *Public Citizens*, 15–23.

62. Harry McPherson, *A Political Education: A Washington Memoir* (Austin: University of Texas Press, 1995), 223–226.

63. Eisenhower is often credited with building the highway system. But as we'll see in Chapter 7, the program had been conceived at Roosevelt's behest.

64. Nader's broader thrust was typified by a 1969 report he released blasting the Federal Trade Commission as a backwater that did much too little to protect American citizens from private interests. Sabin, *Public Citizens*, 24, 41, 63.

65. Louis L. Jaffe, *Judiciary Control of Administrative Action* (Boston: Little, Brown, 1965), 344. As quoted in Reuel Schiller, "Regulation and the Collapse of the New Deal Order, or How I Learned to Stop Worrying and Love the Market," in *Beyond the New Deal Order*, ed. Gary Gerstle, Nelson Lichtenstein, and Alice O'Connor (Philadelphia: University of Pennsylvania Press, 2019), 168–185.

66. George Packer, *Last Best Hope: America in Crisis and Renewal* (New York: Picador, 2021), 66–70.

67. In a commencement address at Yale in 1962, President Kennedy had argued explicitly for more and bigger government to "research for sophisticated solutions to complex and obstinate issues" that were "more subtle and less simple." John Gardner, who had served as Lyndon Johnson's secretary of health, education, and welfare, echoed a very different creed. Richard

Pearson, "John Gardner, HEW Secretary, Common Cause Founder, Dies," *Washington Post*, February 17, 2002. Sabin, *Public Citizens*, 165–166.

68. Robert A. Kagan, *Adversarial Legalism: The American Way of Law*, 2nd ed. (Cambridge, MA: Harvard University Press, 2019), 19.

69. Richard Stewart, "Madison's Nightmare," *University of Chicago Law Review* 57, no. 2 (Spring 1990): 337. Sabin, *Public Citizens*, 81–85.

70. Richard J. Lazarus, "The National Environmental Policy Act in the U.S. Supreme Court: A Reappraisal and a Peek Behind the Curtains," *Georgetown Law Journal* 100, no. 5 (June 2012): 1509–1510. The House passed the bill 372–15; the Senate passed it without objection. Aaron Gordon, "Why Doesn't America Build Things?" *Vice News*, August 22, 2022, www.vice.com/en/article/93a39e/why-doesnt-america-build-things.

71. Richard F. Weingroff, "Addressing the Quiet Crisis: Origins of the National Environmental Policy Act of 1969," Federal Highway Administration, updated June 27, 2017, www.fhwa.dot.gov/highwayhistory/nepa/index.cfm.

72. Kussy, "Surface Transportation and Administrative Law," 12.

73. Lazarus, "The National Environmental Policy Act in the U.S. Supreme Court," 1515–1521.

74. Sabin, *Public Citizens*, 103.

75. Weingroff, "Addressing the Quiet Crisis."

76. Robert B. Ditton and Thomas L. Goodale, eds., *Environmental Impact Analysis: Philosophy and Methods: Proceedings, Conference on Environmental Impact Analysis, Green Bay, Wisconsin, January 4–5, 1972* (Madison, WI: Sea Grant Publications Office, 1972), 45–52.

77. Lazarus, "The National Environmental Policy Act in the U.S. Supreme Court," 1520.

78. Hillel Aron, "The Last Freeway," *Slate*, July 2011, https://longreads.com/2015/03/23/the-last-freeway-2/.

79. Richard J. Lazarus, "The Tragedy of Distrust in the Implementation of Federal Environmental Law," *Law and Contemporary Problems* 54, no. 4 (Autumn 1991): 334.

80. Schulman, *The Seventies*, 35–42.

81. Michael Kazin, *What It Took to Win: A History of the Democratic Party* (New York: Farrar, Straus and Giroux, 2022), 252.

82. Martha Derthick and Paul J. Quirk, *The Politics of Deregulation* (Washington, DC: Brookings, 1985), 8–13.

83. Joshua Zeitz, *Building the Great Society: Inside Lyndon Johnson's White House* (New York: Viking, 2018), 312.

84. David French, "The Wisdom and Prophecy of Jimmy Carter's 'Malaise' Speech," *New York Times*, February 23, 2023.

85. Schulman, *The Seventies*, 47–48.

86. Kazin, *What It Took to Win*, 257–263. The TVA's own David Lilienthal, who had been preaching the potential of planning and development around the world since his success in the Upper South four decades earlier, was dismissed in favor of a development ethos centered on the notion that "small is beautiful." David Ekbladh, "'Mr. TVA': Grass-Roots Development, David Lilienthal, and the Rise and Fall of the Tennessee Valley Authority as a Symbol for U.S. Overseas Development, 1933–1973," *Diplomatic History* 26, no. 3 (Summer 2002): 371–372.

87. Anika Singh Lemar, "The Role of States in Liberalizing Land Use Regulations," *North Carolina Law Review* 97, no. 2 (January 2019): 332. Kagan, *Adversarial Legalism*, 56–59, 184–190. Schulman, *The Seventies*, 48.

88. Annmarie Hauck Walsh, *The Public's Business: The Politics and Practice of Government Corporations* (Cambridge, MA: MIT Press, 1978), 24–26, 241–243.

89. Walsh, *The Public's Business*, 156–162, 175–178, 332–351.

90. Robert A. Caro, *The Power Broker: Robert Moses and the Fall of New York* (New York: Vintage Books, 1975).

91. Jameson W. Doig, *Empire on the Hudson* (New York: Columbia University Press, 2001). Walsh, *The Public's Business*. Remarkably, the consensus during the late 1960s and 1970s was not entirely that the problem was born from too much centralized authority. In *The End of Liberalism*, Theodore Lowi complained that power was too decentralized.

92. Walsh, *The Public's Business*, 234–241.

93. Nicholas Bagley, "The Procedure Fetish," Niskanen Center, December 7, 2021, www.niskanencenter.org/the-procedure-fetish/.

94. Judges would, on occasion, take on a quasi-executive function if they determined that a bureaucracy ordered to reduce crowding at a jail was dragging its feet or that a segregated school system was failing to integrate with "all deliberate speed." Abram Chayes, "The Role of the Judge in Public Law Litigation," *Harvard Law Review* 89, no. 7 (May 1976): 1281–1316.

95. Kagan, *Adversarial Legalism*, 56–60, 184–190.

96. Jonathan Rauch, *Demosclerosis: The Silent Killer of American Government* (New York: Times Books, 1995), 141–142.

97. Ezra Klein and Alex Tabarrok, "A Critique of Government That Progressives—Myself Included—Need to Hear," February 18, 2022, in *The Ezra Klein Show*, podcast, www.nytimes.com/2022/02/18/opinion/ezra-klein-podcast-alex-tabarrok.html.

98. Popular impressions are that the war on poverty failed, but many of the Hamiltonian programs worked to great effect. McPherson, *A Political Education*, 449–451. See also Christopher Jencks, "The War on Poverty: Was It Lost?" *New York Review*, April 2, 2015.

99. Lisa Mascaro and the Associated Press, "Trump White House Vets Have Far-Reaching Plans to Dismantle Federal Government: 'We Have a Democracy That Is at Risk of Suicide,'" *Fortune*, August 29, 2023.

100. Howard, "From Progressivism to Paralysis," 385.

Chapter 5: More Harm Than Good

1. Stuart E. Eizenstat, *President Carter: The White House Years* (New York: St. Martin's, 2018), 358–360.

2. T. J. Stiles, *The First Tycoon: The Epic Life of Cornelius Vanderbilt* (New York: Vintage Books, 2009). Michael E. Levine, "Why Weren't the Airlines Reregulated?" *Yale Journal on Regulation* 23, no. 269 (2006): 275.

3. Eizenstat, *President Carter*, 359–360. Reuel Schiller, "The Curious Origins of Airline Deregulation: Economic Deregulation and the American Left," *Business History Review* 93 (Winter 2019).

4. Levine, "Why Weren't the Airlines Reregulated?," 276.

5. Eizenstat, *President Carter*, 358–360.

6. Schiller, "The Curious Origins of Airline Deregulation." Thomas K. McCraw, *Prophets of Regulation* (Cambridge, MA: Belknap, 1986).

7. Martha Derthick and Paul J. Quirk, *The Politics of Deregulation* (Washington, DC: Brookings, 1985), 39–53. Schiller, "The Curious Origins of Airline Deregulation."

8. McCraw, *Prophets of Regulation*, 265–270.

9. Derthick and Quirk, *The Politics of Deregulation*, 5. Schiller, "The Curious Origins of Airline Deregulation."

10. "United Airlines Receives Court Approval to Terminate Workers' Pension Plans," PBS News Hour, May 11, 2005, www.pbs.org/newshour/show/united-airlines-receives-court-approval -to-terminate-workers-pension-plans.

11. United States Government Accountability Office, "Airline Deregulation: Reregulating the Airline Industry Would Likely Reverse Consumer Benefits and Not Save Airline Pensions," June 2006, www.gao.gov/assets/gao-06-630.pdf.

12. Debbie Aiken, "Remembering FDR's Commencement Address at Oglethorpe," *Source*, May 22, 2012, https://source.oglethorpe.edu/2012/05/22/remembering-fdrs -commencement-speech-at-oglethorpe/.

13. Richard Stewart, "Madison's Nightmare," *University of Chicago Law Review* 57, no. 2 (Spring 1990): 335–342.

14. Richard Stewart, "The Reformation of American Administrative Law," *Harvard Law Review* 88, no. 8 (June 1975): 1676–1681.

15. Reuel E. Schiller, "Enlarging the Administrative Polity: Administrative Law and the Changing Definition of Pluralism, 1945–1970," *Vanderbilt Law Review* 53, no. 5 (2000): 1405–1417.

16. Brock Adams, "The Shameful State of Transport," *Reader's Digest* 106 (February 1975).

17. John S. Steinhart and Henry Steele, "Reviewed Work: Limiting Oil Imports: An Economic History and Analysis by Douglas R. Bohi and Milton Russell," *Land Economics* 55, no. 4 (November 1979): 553–554.

18. Theodore J. Lowi, *The End of Liberalism: The Second Republic of the United States*, 2nd ed. (New York: W. W. Norton, 1979), 113, 124–126. In 2008, the annual document totaled nearly eighty thousand. "Federal Register Facts," Office of the Federal Register, revised July 15, 2010, www.federalregister.gov/uploads/2011/01/fr_facts.pdf.

19. Steinhart and Steele, "Reviewed Work: Limiting Oil Imports."

20. George J. Stigler, "The Theory of Economic Regulation," *Bell Journal of Economics and Management* 2, no. 1 (Spring 1971): 4.

21. Ronald Reagan and Johnny Carson, "Ronald Reagan Government Is the Problem Johnny Carson Interview 1975," from the *Johnny Carson Show*, January 1975, YouTube video posted October 18, 2020, www.youtube.com/watch?v=8IWY6uLaxKE.

22. Reuel E. Schiller, "Rulemaking's Promise: Administrative Law and Legal Culture in the 1960s and 1970s," *Administrative Law Review* 53, no. 4 (Fall 2001).

23. Derthick and Quirk, *The Politics of Deregulation*, 56–57. Schiller, "Enlarging the Administrative Polity," 1417–1428.

24. William Boyd, "Public Utility and the Low-Carbon Future," *UCLA Law Review* 61, no. 6 (May 2014): 1651–1656. Lina M. Khan, "Amazon's Antitrust Paradox," *Yale Law Journal* 126, no. 3 (January 2017): 710, 723, 800.

25. H. D. Lloyd, "The Story of a Great Monopoly," *Atlantic*, March 1881.

26. Stewart, "The Reformation of American Administrative Law," 1717–1722.

27. Schiller, "Enlarging the Administrative Polity," 1417–1428.

28. Schiller, "Enlarging the Administrative Polity," 1435–1442.

29. Stewart, "The Reformation of American Administrative Law," 1723–1748.

30. Schiller, "Enlarging the Administrative Polity," 1437–1439.

31. *Office of Communication United Church of Christ, Petitioner, v. Federal Communications Commission and United States of America, Respondents*, 425 F.2d 543 (D.C. Cir. 1969).

32. Schiller, "Enlarging the Administrative Polity," 1440–1442.

33. Sidney A. Shapiro, "*United Church of Christ v. FCC*: Private Attorneys General and the Rule of Law," *Administrative Law Review* 58, no. 4 (Fall 2006): 939–960. Paul Sabin, *Public Citizens: The Attack on Big Government and the Remaking of American Liberalism* (New York: W. W. Norton, 2021), 94–96.

34. Sabin, *Public Citizens*, xv.

35. Schiller, "Rulemaking's Promise," 1159–1160, 1166–1170.

36. Richard B. Stewart, "The Discontents of Legalism: Interest Group Relations in Administrative Regulation," *Wisconsin Law Review* 1985, no. 3 (1985): 659–660.

37. Peter L. Strauss, "*Citizens to Preserve Overton Park v. Volpe*—Of Politics and Law, Young Lawyers and the Highway Goliath," in *Administrative Law Stories*, ed. Peter L. Strauss (New York: Foundation Press, 2006), 260–261.

38. Sabin, *Public Citizens*, 66.

39. Eizenstat, *President Carter*, 243–266. Harry McPherson, *A Political Education: A Washington Memoir* (Austin: University of Texas Press, 1995), 223–226.

40. Jimmy Carter, "Georgia Law Day Address," May 4, 1976, American Rhetoric, www.americanrhetoric.com/speeches/jimmycarterlawday1974.htm.

41. Schiller, "Rulemaking's Promise," 1148.

42. Stigler, "The Theory of Economic Regulation," 5–6.

43. Eizenstat, *President Carter*, 376–381.

44. "Interstate Commerce Act (1887)," U.S. National Archives and Records Administration, www.archives.gov/milestone-documents/interstate-commerce-act.

45. Note: Adams would later be run out of office for sexual predation. Adams, "The Shameful State of Transport," 65–66.

46. Eizenstat, *President Carter*, 376–381. Derthick and Quirk, *The Politics of Deregulation*, 5–8.

47. Eizenstat, *President Carter*, 153–169.

48. Steinhart and Steele, "Reviewed Work: Limiting Oil Imports."

49. Eizenstat, *President Carter*, 354–359. Derthick and Quirk, *The Politics of Deregulation*, 8–19.

50. Dan Aykroyd as President Jimmy Carter, "Ask President Carter—SNL," *Saturday Night Live*, season 2, 1977, YouTube video posted February 15, 2018, www.youtube.com/watch?v=-68iTvhWNB0.

51. Eizenstat, *President Carter*, 11–13.

52. Derthick and Quirk, *The Politics of Deregulation*, 31. Bruce J. Schulman, *The Seventies: The Great Shift in American Culture, Society, and Politics* (New York: Da Capo Press, 2001), 121–124.

53. Sabin, *Public Citizens*, 150–161.

54. During the First World War, the Wilson administration lobbied Congress for a version of this authority, and it was provided in the Overman Act. Stephen Skowronek, *Building a New American State: The Expansion of National Administrative Capacities, 1877–1920* (New York: Cambridge University Press, 1982), 198–200.

55. Bruce Reed and Paul Weinstein, "Reform Authority: How to Turn the Page of 20th Century Bureaucracy," Democratic Leadership Council, January 2010. Hogue, "Executive Branch Reorganization," https://crsreports.congress.gov/product/pdf/R/R44909.

56. McCraw, *Prophets of Regulation*, 300–309.

57. Stewart, "Discontents of Legalism," 659–660.

58. Schiller, "Rulemaking's Promise," 1166–1170.

59. Schiller, "Rulemaking's Promise," 1175–1178.

60. In many cases, administrative agencies decided for the most part to abandon informal rulemaking in favor of simply adjudicating cases, if only because the process of making a rule was deemed so laborious as to be impossible. Richard J. Pierce Jr., "The Unintended Effects of Judicial Review of Agency Rules: How Federal Courts Have Contributed to the Electricity Crisis of the 1990s," *Administrative Law Review* 43, no. 1 (Winter 1991): 7–29.

61. Jeremy A. Rabkin and Neal E. Devins, "Averting Government by Consent Decree: Constitutional Limits on the Enforcement of Settlements with the Federal Government," *Stanford Law Review* 40, no. 1 (November 1987): 203.

62. Stewart, "Discontents of Legalism," 655–656.

63. Some conservatives would come to embrace the judiciary's greater involvement in decision-making, believing that executive branch officials could not be trusted. Adam B. Cox and Emma Kaufman, "The Adjudicative State," *Yale Law Journal* 132, no. 6 (April 2023): 1789–1796, 1809.

64. Joseph A. Califano Jr., *Governing America* (New York: Simon and Schuster, 1981), 217–219.

65. Rabkin and Devins, "Averting Government by Consent Decree," 273–276.

66. Thomas O. McGarity, "Some Thoughts on 'Deossifying' the Rulemaking Process," *Duke Law Journal* 41, no. 6 (1992): 1385–1462.

67. Edward V. A. Kussy, "Surface Transportation and Administrative Law: Growing Up Together in the 20th Century," *Transportation Research Record* 1527, no. 1 (January 1996): 8. McGarity, "Some Thoughts on 'Deossifying' the Rulemaking Process," 1387.

68. See the Clean Water Act of 1977 and a revision of the Clean Air Act in 1990, among other bills. Robert A. Kagan, *Adversarial Legalism: The American Way of Law*, 2nd ed. (Cambridge, MA: Harvard University Press, 2019), 254–258.

69. Richard J. Lazarus, "The Tragedy of Distrust in the Implementation of Federal Environmental Law," *Law and Contemporary Problems* 54, no. 4 (Autumn 1991).

70. For more on regulatory oversight and, in particular, the Reagan administration's efforts to layer more red tape through additional White House oversight, see McGarity, "Some Thoughts on 'Deossifying' the Rulemaking Process," 1428–1436.

71. Lazarus, "The Tragedy of Distrust."

72. Jerry L. Mashaw, "Is Administrative Law at War with Itself?" *N.Y.U. Environmental Law Journal* 29 (2021): 421.

73. Jerry L. Mashaw and David L. Harfst, "Regulation and Legal Culture: The Case of Motor Vehicle Safety," *Yale Journal on Regulation* 4 (1987): 257–316.

74. Stewart, "Madison's Nightmare."

75. McGarity, "Some Thoughts on 'Deossifying' the Rulemaking Process," 1426.

76. Francis X. Clines and Bernard Weinraub, "Washington Talk: Briefing," *New York Times*, September 28, 1981.

77. Reuel Schiller, "Regulation and the Collapse of the New Deal Order, or How I Learned to Stop Worrying and Love the Market," in *Beyond the New Deal Order*, ed. Gary Gerstle, Nelson Lichtenstein, and Alice O'Connor (Philadelphia: University of Pennsylvania Press, 2019).

78. Philip K. Howard and Geoff Kabaservice, "Can America Untangle Itself from Red Tape? (With Philip K. Howard)," September 1, 2021, in *Vital Center*, podcast, www.niskanen center.org/can-america-untangle-itself-from-red-tape-with-phillip-k-howard/.

79. Stewart, "The Reformation of American Administrative Law," 1704–1706.

80. An example of a report extolling the virtues of greater voice and earlier notification: Romic Aevaz, Brianne Eby, Paul Lewis, and Robert Puentes, "Saving Time and Making Cents: A Blueprint for Building Transit Better," Eno Center for Transportation, July 29, 2021, https://enotrans.org/eno-resources/saving-time-and-making-cents-a-blueprint-for-building-transit-better/.

81. Cary Coglianese, "Assessing Consensus: The Promise and Performance of Negotiated Rulemaking," *Duke Law Journal* 46, no. 6 (April 1997): 1255–1349. Cary Coglianese, "Is Consensus an Appropriate Basis for Regulatory Policy?" in *Environmental Contracts: Comparative Approaches to Regulatory Innovation in the United States and Europe*, ed. Eric W. Orts and Kurt Deketelaere (London, UK: Kluwer Law, 2001), 93–113. Schiller, "Regulation and the Collapse of the New Deal Order," 173. Cary Coglianese and Laurie K. Allen, "Does Consensus Make Common Sense? An Analysis of EPA's Common Sense Initiative," *Environment* 46 (January/February 2004): 10–25. Charles Mohr, "Opposing Sides Agree on Ways to Shift to Coal," *New York Times*, February 10, 1978. McGarity, "Some Thoughts on 'Deossifying' the Rulemaking Process," 1438–1440.

82. For more on NegReg's subsequent evolution, see Peter H. Schuck and Steven Kochevar, "Reg Neg Redux: The Career of a Procedural Reform," *Theoretical Inquiries in Law* 15, no. 2 (2014): 441–442.

83. Stewart, "Discontents of Legalism," 678–682.

84. Kagan, *Adversarial Legalism*, 216–218.

85. McGarity, "Some Thoughts on 'Deossifying' the Rulemaking Process," 1396–1398.

86. Kagan, *Adversarial Legalism*, 233–235.

Chapter 6: No Place to Call Home

1. E. J. Dionne Jr., *Why Americans Hate Politics* (New York: Touchstone, 1991), 88. Harry McPherson, *A Political Education: A Washington Memoir* (Austin: University of Texas Press, 1995), 376. The Commission's recommendations were quintessentially Hamiltonian, with "the creation of 2 million jobs over the next three years, a massive school desegregation program, 600,000 housing starts" among them. Gareth Davies, *From Opportunity to Entitlement: The Transformation and Decline of Great Society Liberalism* (Lawrence: University Press of Kansas, 1996), 203–206.

2. Annmarie Hauck Walsh, *The Public's Business: The Politics and Practice of Government Corporations* (Cambridge, MA: MIT Press, 1978), 266. President Johnson and his staff also believed that the nation's grief over King would spur Congress, at long last, to invest in the

range of Great Society programs that Johnson believed had been underfunded. But Congress balked at the White House's efforts, much as New York's legislature initially rejected Rockefeller's. McPherson, *A Political Education*, 366–376.

3. Mark Bynes, "Don't Forget About Ed Logue," *Bloomberg CityLab*, March 15, 2017, www.bloomberg.com/news/articles/2017-03-15/don-t-forget-about-ed-logue.

4. Interview with real estate attorney, October 4, 2018.

5. Interview with planning official, October 11, 2018.

6. "Legislators Vote Own Pension Aid; Improve Benefits and Then Recess, Ignoring Budget," *New York Times*, April 11, 1968.

7. Richard Norton Smith, *On His Own Terms: A Life of Nelson Rockefeller* (New York: Random House, 2014), 521–526. Sydney H. Schanberg, "How to Twist Arms: The Rockefeller Way; Governor Shows Arm-Twisting Art," *New York Times*, April 11, 1968.

8. Richard Ravitch, *So Much to Do: A Full Life of Business, Politics, and Confronting Fiscal Crises* (New York: PublicAffairs, 2014), 50.

9. Lizabeth Cohen, *Saving America's Cities* (New York: Farrar, Straus and Giroux, 2019), 2019. Moreland Act Commission, *Restoring Credit and Confidence: A Reform Program for New York State and Its Public Authorities—A Report to the Governor by the New York State Moreland Act Commission on the Urban Development Corporation and Other State Financing Agencies*, March 31, 1976, 116–120, https://publicauthority.org/wp-content/uploads/2014/05/restoring_credit__confidence_part1.pdf.

10. Interview with real estate attorney, October 4, 2018.

11. Bynes, "Don't Forget About Ed Logue." Interview with real estate attorney, December 13, 2018.

12. Joseph P. Fried, "Logue Offers 5-Point Plan to Improve Urban Agency," *New York Times*, December 26, 1974.

13. Interview with former public authority executive, August 31, 2018.

14. Walsh, *The Public's Business*, 3–13, 220–222, 332–337.

15. Interview with former state official, October 13, 2017.

16. Interview with former public authority executive, August 31, 2018.

17. Richard Ravitch, *So Much to Do*, 62–65.

18. Arkansas had declared bankruptcy. Interview with former state official, December 11, 2018. E. Bruce Hallett, "Good Money After Bad?: The Urban Development Corporation Is Wheeling and Dealing Again," *Barron's National Business and Financial Weekly*, August 20, 1979. David Schleicher, *In a Bad State: Responding to State and Local Budget Crises* (New York: Oxford, 2023).

19. Interview with former public authority executive, October 29, 2018.

20. It was during the City's quest for a federal bailout that the *New York Daily News* published its famous headline, "Ford to City: Drop Dead," October 30, 1975.

21. Interview with litigator, September 7, 2018.

22. Paul Goldberger, "Architecture View: A Commission That Has Itself Become a Landmark," *New York Times*, April 15, 1990. Interview with architectural historian via email, September 7, 2018. David W. Dunlap, "The Quest for a New Zoning Plan," *New York Times*, April 12, 1992.

23. Charles V. Bagli, "New Idea for Penn Station Entails Relocating a College," *New York Times*, February 4, 2013.

24. Katie Honan and Joshua Jamerson, "Half of Jobs at Amazon's Two New Headquarters Won't Be Tech Positions," *Wall Street Journal*, November 21, 2018.

25. Mike Pesca, "I'm Really Upset About Losing Amazon's HQ2," *Slate*, February 15, 2019.

26. Nathaly Pesantez, "Residents, Activists Demand CB2 Reject Amazon with 'No Negotiations, No Concession,'" *Sunnyside Post*, December 7, 2018.

27. Dana Rubinstein, "Ocasio-Cortez Takes on the Amazon Fight in New York," *Politico*, November 22, 2018.

28. Jessica Trounstine, *Segregation by Design: Local Politics and Inequality in American Cities* (New York: Cambridge University Press, 2018), 1–3. Nicholas Lemann, "The Myth of Community Development," *New York Times*, January 9, 1994.

29. William A. Fischel, "The Rise of the Homevoters: How the Growth Machine Was Subverted by OPEC and Earth Day," presented at the Kreisman Initiative conference "Bringing It All Back Home: Evidence and Innovation in Housing Law & Policy," University of Chicago, June 2016.

30. Perhaps the greatest champion of modern, professionalized, central planning, Le Corbusier, was quite explicit about plans being imposed from above, with the opinions of the ordinary person subordinated to expertise. James C. Scott, *Seeing Like a State: How Certain Schemes to Improve the Human Condition Have Failed* (New Haven, CT: Yale University Press, 1998), 111–114.

31. Fred Bosselman and David Callies, *The Quiet Revolution in Land Use Control*, Council on Environmental Quality, Washington, DC, December 1971, 12–15.

32. Sara C. Bronin, "The Quiet Revolution Revived: Sustainable Design, Land Use Regulation, and the States," *Minnesota Law Review* 93 (2008): 236–238.

33. Bosselman and Callies, *The Quiet Revolution*, 2. Fischel, "The Rise of the Homevoters," 12–15. Robert C. Ellickson, "Zoning and the Cost of Housing: Evidence from Silicon Valley, Greater New Haven, and Greater Austin" (Yale Law School paper, January 13, 2020), https://ssrn.com/abstract=3472145.

34. Richard Rothstein, *The Color of Law: A Forgotten History of How Our Government Segregated America* (New York: Liveright, 2017), 43–48.

35. Trounstine, *Segregation by Design*, 73–85. This strategy was struck down in *Buchanan v. Wiley* (1917).

36. Richard D. Kahlenberg, "How Minneapolis Ended Single-Family Zoning," Century Foundation, October 24, 2019, https://tcf.org/content/report/minneapolis-ended-single-family-zoning/. Conor Dougherty, *Golden Gates: Fighting for Housing in America* (New York: Penguin, 2020), 9. Trounstine, *Segregation by Design*, 25–38, 92–96.

37. *Village of Euclid v. Ambler Realty Company*, decided November 22, 1926, accessed July 6, 2024, www.oyez.org/cases/1900-1940/272us365.

38. Bosselman and Callies, *The Quiet Revolution*.

39. Bronin, "The Quiet Revolution Revived," 236–238. Rothstein, *The Color of Law*, 51–54.

40. Anika Singh Lemar, "The Role of States in Liberalizing Land Use Regulations," *North Carolina Law Review* 97, no. 2 (January 2019): 300–301. Trounstine, *Segregation by Design*, 73–85.

41. Trounstine, *Segregation by Design*, 1.

42. Rothstein, *The Color of Law*, chapter 4, particularly p. 75.

43. Trounstine, *Segregation by Design*, 23–38.

44. Rosalind Tough, "Land Planning and Housing in the Urban Community," in *Planned Society: Yesterday, Today, Tomorrow*, ed. Findlay MacKenzie (New York: Prentice Hall, 1937), 253–260.

45. In some cases, that meant paving over tenements and slums to make way for roads and highways. In others, it meant razing old buildings so that developers could be given opportunities to erect new, modern buildings. Trounstine, *Segregation by Design*, 13–19.

46. More than four of every five homes constructed between 1946 and 1958 were located outside central cities. Todd Gitlin, *The Sixties: Years of Hope, Days of Rage* (New York: Bantam, 1993), 14.

47. Robert A. Dahl, *Who Governs? Democracy and Power in an American City* (New Haven, CT: Yale University Press, 2005), 115–122. Trounstine, *Segregation by Design*, 120–136. Rothstein, *The Color of Law*, 30–34. Dougherty, *Golden Gates*, 63–74.

48. Dahl, *Who Governs?*, 120.

49. Allen J. Matusow, *The Unraveling of America: A History of Liberalism in the 1960s* (Athens: University of Georgia Press, 2003), 97–107.

50. Before moving forward on any project, he made it a practice to build support through a Citizens Action Council that included all the important players in town. And here was the Establishment at work: to be a part of the cabal, you needed to support the mayor, who would, in turn, do his best to work around your concerns.

51. Dahl, *Who Governs?*

52. Theodore J. Lowi, *The End of Liberalism: The Second Republic of the United States*, 2nd ed. (New York: W. W. Norton, 1979), 169–177.

53. Trounstine, *Segregation by Design*, 169–172.

54. Many projects came to be viewed as dangerous, crime-ridden, decrepit, and forlorn. James T. Patterson, *Grand Expectations: The United States, 1945–1974* (New York: Oxford University Press, 1996), 333–342. Lowi, *The End of Liberalism*, 180.

55. Jerusalem Demsas, "Community Impact Is Bad, Actually," *Atlantic*, April 22, 2002. Digital Scholarship Lab, "Renewing Inequality," *American Panorama*, ed. Robert K. Nelson and Edward L. Ayers, accessed June 14, 2024, https://dsl.richmond.edu/panorama/renewal/#view=0/0/1&viz=cartogram.

56. Rothstein, *The Color of Law*, 126–131.

57. Jacob Anbinder, "The Pandemic Disproved Urban Progressives' Theory About Gentrification," *Atlantic*, January 2, 2021.

58. Lowi, *The End of Liberalism*, 247.

59. Scott, *Seeing Like a State*, 132.

60. Dionne, *Why Americans Hate Politics*, 66–73. Bronin, "The Quiet Revolution Revived," 262–263. Jayne E. Daly, "A Glimpse of the Past—A Vision for the Future: Senator Henry M. Jackson and National Land-Use Legislation." *Urban Lawyer* 28, no. 1 (Winter 1996): 7–9.

61. Fischel, "The Rise of the Homevoters."

62. Carol M. Rose, "Planning and Dealing: Piecemeal Land Controls as a Problem of Local Legitimacy," *California Law Review* 71, no. 3 (May 1983): 857–863.

63. Salim Furth, "The Two-Board Knot: Zoning, Schools, and Inequality," *American Affairs* 1, no. 4 (Winter 2017).

64. "New York's original 1916 [zoning] code was about 14 pages. Today, it is nearly 3,500 pages." Emily Badger, "American Cities Have a Conversion Problem, and It's Not Just Offices," *New York Times*, July 4, 2023.

65. Rose, "Planning and Dealing," 841–846.

66. Ellickson, "Zoning and the Cost of Housing."

67. Bernard J. Frieden, "The New Regulation Comes to Suburbia," *Public Interest* (Spring 1979): 18–20.

68. David Schleicher, "Exclusionary Zoning's Confused Defenders," September 4, 2021, *Wisconsin Law Review*, https://ssrn.com/abstract=3917621.

69. Ellickson, "Zoning and the Cost of Housing." In the Bay Area, for example, 29,000 prospective housing units faced environmentally oriented lawsuits from 1971 to 1975, a figure that represented well more than half of the total units constructed on average during any single year. Frieden, "The New Regulation Comes to Suburbia," 21–22.

70. Robert H. Freilich, "Editor's Comments: *Fasano v. Board of County Commissioners of Washington County*: Is Rezoning an Administrative or Legislative Function?" *Urban Lawyer* 6, no. 1 (Winter 1974): vii–xiii.

71. Rose, "Planning and Dealing," 851–853.

72. Stewart E. Sterk, "Structural Obstacles to Settlement of Land Use Disputes," *Boston College Law Review* 91 (March 2011): 228–234.

73. Schleicher, "Exclusionary Zoning's Confused Defenders."

74. Sara Bronin, "Houston: Still Zoning's Last Frontier?" *SLoGLaw*, September 14, 2021, www.sloglaw.org/post/houston-still-zoning-s-last-frontier.

75. Schleicher, "Exclusionary Zoning's Confused Defenders." Frieden, "New Regulation," 16.

76. M. Nolan Gray, "How Californians Are Weaponizing Environmental Law," *Atlantic*, March 12, 2021.

77. Dougherty, *Golden Gates*, 81–82.

78. Maybe most important, the law was not designed to be policed by a government agency, but rather it was "self-enforcing," meaning that citizens were directed to file lawsuits when they objected to a project. Remarkably, they could file the lawsuits anonymously. Gray, "How Californians Are Weaponizing Environmental Law."

79. Fischel, "The Rise of the Homevoters," 5–7. Frieden, "New Regulation," 23–25.

80. Dougherty, *Golden Gates*, 78–86.

81. Frieden, "New Regulation," 16–19.

82. David Schleicher, "City Unplanning," *Yale Law Journal* 122, no. 7 (May 2013): 1704–1717.

83. Ellickson, "Zoning and the Cost of Housing," 59–62.

84. "Population of Connecticut Towns 1900–1960," Office of the Secretary of the State of Connecticut, https://portal.ct.gov/sots/register-manual/section-vii/population-1900-1960. "Population of Connecticut Towns 1970–2010," Office of the Secretary of the State of Connecticut, https://portal.ct.gov/sots/register-manual/section-vii/population-1970-2010.

85. Jacobs was, at root, a Jeffersonian battling against the Hamiltonian Moses. Scott, *Seeing Like a State*, 142–146.

86. Samuel J. LeFrak, "Of Planners, Head-Bopping and Mountain Goats," *New York Times*, January 18, 1974.

87. Jessie Scanlon, "Success Is Killing San Francisco. Is Boston Next?" *Boston Globe Magazine*, January 29, 2020. Frieden, "New Regulation," 26.

88. Governor Hiram Johnson, a classic progressive in the early twentieth century, championed the Jeffersonian tools of direct democracy—most notably the referendum—to protect against big trusts that would try to control the state legislature.

89. Adjusting for inflation, the $16,000 would have been $150,000 in 2019. Ellickson, "Zoning and the Cost of Housing," 4–5.

90. Scanlon, "Success Is Killing San Francisco."

91. Jennifer Hernandez, David Friedman, and Stephanie DeHerrera, "In the Name of the Environment," Holland & Knight, 2015, 79–80.

92. "Editorial: Antiabortion Group Exploiting Environmental Law to Halt Clinic," *San Francisco Chronicle*, April 13, 2015.

93. Times Editorial Board, "Editorial: Using California's Signature Environmental Law to Shut Down Homeless Housing Is NIMBYism at Its Worst," *Los Angeles Times*, April 21, 2018.

94. Ezra Klein, "California Is Making Liberals Squirm," *New York Times*, February 11, 2021.

95. John Infranca, "The New State Zoning: Land Use Preemption Amid a Housing Crisis," *Boston College Law Review* 60, no. 3 (March 2019): 825–830. Dougherty, *Golden Gates*, 188–195, 227–231. Times Editorial Board, "Editorial: SB 50 Is Dead. Again. L.A. Lawmakers Need to Stop Stonewalling and Come Up with a Housing Solution," *Los Angeles Times*, January 31, 2020.

96. Conor Dougherty, "After Years of Failure, California Lawmakers Pave the Way for More Housing," *New York Times*, September 20, 2021. Timothy B. Lee, "How California Plans to Turn the Screws on NIMBY Cities," Full Stack Economics, September 24, 2021.

97. Conor Dougherty, "Twilight of the NIMBY," *New York Times*, June 5, 2022.

98. Richard Kahlenberg, "Taking on Class and Racial Discrimination in Housing," *American Prospect*, August 2, 2018.

99. Conor Dougherty, "The Californians Are Coming. So Is Their Housing Crisis," *New York Times*, February 12, 2021.

100. Ira Glass, "Human Resources," February 29, 2008, episode 350 in *This American Life*, podcast, www.thisamericanlife.org/350/transcript.

101. Infranca, "The New State Zoning," 837–844. Trounstine, *Segregation by Design*, 1–13.

102. Bosselman and Callies, *The Quiet Revolution*, 1.

103. "In Brief," *Advisory Commission on Intergovernmental Relations*, August 1979, 7–8, https://digital.library.unt.edu/ark:/67531/metadc1293/.

104. Infranca, "The New State Zoning," 836–837.

105. Dougherty, "The Californians Are Coming."

106. Nolan Gray, "When the Federal Government Takes on Local Zoning," *Bloomberg CityLab*, August 20, 2018, www.bloomberg.com/news/articles/2018-08-20/a-bipartisan-push-against-exclusionary-zoning-is-overdue.

107. Dougherty, *Golden Gates*, 24–38.

108. Sterk, "Structural Obstacles," 253–255.

109. Infranca, "The New State Zoning," 879–881.

110. Sarah Mervosh, "Minneapolis, Tackling Housing Crisis and Inequality, Votes to End Single-Family Zoning," *New York Times*, December 13, 2018.

111. Kahlenberg, "How Minneapolis Ended Single-Family Zoning."

112. The Housing, Opportunity, Mobility, and Equity [HOME] Act of 2018 introduced by Senator Cory Booker (D-NJ). Gray, "When the Federal Government Takes on Local Zoning."

113. Jon Chesto, "Housing Choice Brings the Biggest Changes to Massachusetts Zoning Laws in Decades," *Boston Globe*, February 8, 2021.

Chapter 7: The Bridge to Nowhere

1. Herbert Molloy Mason Jr., "The Second Battle for San Antonio," *Texas Monthly*, April 1973. Raymond A. Mohl, "Citizen Activism and Freeway Revolts in Memphis and Nashville: The Road to Litigation," *Journal of Urban History* 40, no. 5 (2014): 870–893.

2. Tennessee had done exactly that when building I-40 through Nashville several years earlier. Martin Waldron, "Memphis Debates Road Through a Park," *New York Times*, January 18, 1970.

3. Mohl, "Citizen Activism and Freeway Revolts in Memphis and Nashville," 870–893.

4. Interview with George Tagg, October 6, 2022. Peter L. Strauss, "*Citizens to Preserve Overton Park v. Volpe*—Of Politics and Law, Young Lawyers and the Highway Goliath," in *Administrative Law Stories*, ed. Peter L. Strauss (New York: Foundation Press, 2006), 262–268. "Proposed Highway Construction Through Overton Park, Memphis, Tenn.: Hearing before the Subcommittee on Transportation of the Committee on Environment and Public Works, United States Congress, Ninety-fifth Congress, Second Session, April 19, 1978," 11–12.

5. Waldron, "Memphis Debates Road Through a Park." E. W. Kenworthy, "Court Orders Review of a Plan for Road to Cut Through Park," *New York Times*, March 3, 1971.

6. "San Antonio Area Freeway System: US Highway 281 North (Walter McAllister Freeway)," Texas Highway Man, updated February 5, 2024, www.texashighwayman.com/us281n.shtml. "Proposed Highway Construction Through Overton Park, Memphis, Tenn.," 9.

7. Mason, "The Second Battle for San Antonio."

8. "Proposed Highway Construction Through Overton Park, Memphis, Tenn.," 78.

9. Mohl, "Citizen Activism and Freeway Revolts."

10. Helen Leavitt, *Superhighway-Superhoax* (Garden City, NY: Doubleday, 1970), 17.

11. Strauss, "*Citizens to Preserve Overton Park v. Volpe*," 264–268.

12. "Proposed Highway Construction Through Overton Park, Memphis, Tenn.," 58–59.

13. *America's Highways, 1776–1976: A History of the Federal-Aid Program* (U.S. Department of Transportation, Federal Highway Administration, 1977), 373–374, https://library.si.edu/digital-library/book/americashighways00unit.

14. Richard F. Weingroff, "Addressing the Quiet Crisis: Origins of the National Environmental Policy Act of 1969," Federal Highway Administration, updated June 27, 2017, www.fhwa.dot.gov/highwayhistory/nepa/index.cfm. "San Antonio Area Freeway System."

15. Melvin I. Urofsky, *Louis D. Brandeis: A Life* (New York: Schocken Books, 2009), 617.

16. Mohl, "Citizen Activism and Freeway Revolts," 870–893.

17. Justice William O. Douglas shared the same perspective. William O. Douglas, "The Public Be Damned," *Playboy*, July 1969, 182.

18. "Proposed Highway Construction Through Overton Park, Memphis, Tenn.," 50.

19. Edward V. A. Kussy, "Surface Transportation and Administrative Law: Growing Up Together in the 20th Century," *Transportation Research Record* 1527, no. 1 (January 1996): 11.

20. "Proposed Highway Construction Through Overton Park, Memphis, Tenn.," 101.

21. "A Defeat for the Bulldozer," *New York Times*, March 25, 1971. Far from being a mere nudge toward considering other alternatives, Marshall had turned the "feasible and prudent" standard into a formidable obstacle. Kussy, "Surface Transportation and Administrative Law," 11.

22. William V. Shannon, "Keep 'Em Moving," *New York Times*, August 3, 1972.

23. CPI Inflation Calculator, US Bureau of Labor Statistics, https://data.bls.gov/cgi-bin /cpicalc.pl.

24. "Proposed Highway Construction Through Overton Park, Memphis, Tenn.," 9.

25. Strauss, "*Citizens to Preserve Overton Park v. Volpe.*"

26. *Named Individual Members of the San Antonio Conservation Society v. Texas Highway Dept.*, No. 30915 (5th Cir., August 5, 1971). William V. Shannon, "The Highwaymen," *New York Times*, September 17, 1972.

27. Mason, "The Second Battle for San Antonio."

28. "San Antonio Area Freeway System."

29. "Cracks in the Cement," *New Republic* 167, no. 12 (September 30, 1972): 10–11.

30. "San Antonio Area Freeway System." "4.5-Mile Section of Texas Freeway Opens After Long and Bitter Fight," *New York Times*, February 13, 1978.

31. Kathleen McCormick, "Deconstruction Ahead," *Lincoln Institute of Land Policy*, April 14, 2020.

32. Steven Malanga, "The Agenda Behind Buttigieg's Claim That Highways Are 'Racist'," *Wall Street Journal*, April 19, 2021. Alabama officials chose, for example, to run a highway through Rosa Parks's home in the 1950s. Ryan Reft, "We Mythologize Highways, but They've Damaged Communities of Color," *Washington Post*, January 19, 2023.

33. Nate Rawlings, "Joe Biden Says NYC Airport Like 'Some 3rd-World Country,'" *Time*, February 7, 2014.

34. Urofsky, *Louis D. Brandeis*, 181–184.

35. This bureaucracy would later become the Federal Highway Administration.

36. Earl Swift, *The Big Roads: The Untold Story of the Engineers, Visionaries, and Trailblazers Who Created the American Superhighways* (New York: Houghton Mifflin Harcourt, 2011), 45–75.

37. Kussy, "Surface Transportation and Administrative Law," 5–6.

38. Raymond A. Mohl, "Stop the Road: Freeway Revolts in American Cities," *Journal of Urban History* 30, no. 5 (July 2004): 676–678.

39. *America's Highways*, 154–158, 357–358. Richard F. Weingroff, "President Franklin D. Roosevelt and Excess Condemnation," Federal Highway Administration, updated June 30, 2023, https://highways.dot.gov/highway-history/general-highway-history/president -franklin-d-roosevelt-and-excess-condemnation.

40. Swift, *The Big Roads*, 144–145.

41. Legislators left aside some mileage to accommodate the delicacy of selecting where exactly various interstates would be cut through dense urban terrain. Daniel P. Moynihan, "New Roads and Urban Chaos," *Reporter*, April 14, 1960.

42. Weingroff, "President Franklin D. Roosevelt and Excess Condemnation."

43. Swift, *The Big Roads*, 177–189.

44. William V. Shannon, "The Untrustworthy Highway Fund: Road to Ruin?," *New York Times*, October 15, 1972.

45. Leah Brooks and Zachary Liscow, "Infrastructure Costs," *American Economic Journal: Applied Economics* 15, no. 2 (April 2023): 5.

46. Shannon, "The Untrustworthy Highway Fund."

47. Sidney Goldstein, James Rice, and William Lavelle, "The Discovery Process in Highway Land Acquisition," *Public Roads* 33, no. 2 (June 1964): 36.

48. Norman Ritter, "Interstate 87," *Atlantic*, September 1967, 104.

49. *America's Highways*, 370–371. That wasn't entirely for reasons of mobility. In the early days, properties set near interstates saw their values soar. Moynihan, "New Roads and Urban Chaos."

50. Richard Rothstein, *The Color of Law: A Forgotten History of How Our Government Segregated America* (New York: Liveright, 2017), 126–131. Reft, "We Mythologize Highways, but They've Damaged Communities of Color."

51. Lewis Mumford, "The Highway and the City," *Architectural Record,* April 1958. Reprinted in Lewis Mumford, *The Urban Prospect* (New York: Harcourt, Brace and World, 1968).

52. Kussy, "Surface Transportation and Administrative Law," 9. Richard F. Weingroff, "Busting the Trust," *Public Roads* 77, no. 1 (July/August 2013), https://highways.dot.gov/public-roads/julyaugust-2013/busting-trust. Swift, *The Big Roads*, 268.

53. As late as the 1970s, those responding to criticisms of the interstate system, and of the nation's automobile-centric transportation system more generally, continued to argue that the salve was greater central planning. Weingroff, "Busting the Trust."

54. Strauss, "*Citizens to Preserve Overton Park v. Volpe*," 272.

55. Swift, *The Big Roads*, 220–221.

56. Weingroff, "Addressing the Quiet Crisis," *America's Highways*, 372. Conor Dougherty, *Golden Gates: Fighting for Housing in America* (New York: Penguin, 2020), 79.

57. Reft, "We Mythologize Highways, but They've Damaged Communities of Color."

58. *American Experience: New York*, season 1, episode 7, "New York: The City and the World (1945–2000)," directed by Ric Burns, aired October 7, 2001, on PBS, www.amazon.com/American-Experience-New-York-Season/dp/B006CAKNA4.

59. Dougherty, *Golden Gates*, 79.

60. Swift, *The Big Roads*, 267–268.

61. William A. Fischel, "The Rise of the Homevoters: How the Growth Machine Was Subverted by OPEC and Earth Day," presented at the Kreisman Initiative conference "Bringing It All Back Home: Evidence and Innovation in Housing Law & Policy," University of Chicago, June 2016, 11.

62. Strauss, "*Citizens to Preserve Overton Park v. Volpe*," 260.

63. Dougherty, *Golden Gates*, 80–81.

64. Mohl, "Stop the Road."

65. "Transportation Bond Issue," *New York Times*, May 2, 1967. Annmarie Hauck Walsh, *The Public's Business: The Politics and Practice of Government Corporations* (Cambridge, MA: MIT Press, 1978), 267–275.

66. *Road Review League, Town of Bedford v. Boyd*, 207 F. Supp. 650 (S.D.N.Y., 1967), as cited in John Barry Kelly II, "Challenging Highways: Widening the Access to Judicial Review," *Catholic University Law Review* 20, no. 1 (Fall 1970): article 11, 147–148.

67. Ritter, "Interstate 87," 108–109.

68. Mohl, "Citizen Activism and Freeway Revolts," 680.

69. Wally Nowinski, "America's Top Environmental Groups Have Lost the Plot on Climate Change," *Noahpinion*, January 15, 2022, www.noahpinion.blog/p/americas-top -environmental-groups.

70. Strauss, *"Citizens to Preserve Overton Park v. Volpe,"* 307–311.

71. Kussy, "Surface Transportation and Administrative Law," 8.

72. "National Historic Preservation Act," National Park Service, updated November 1, 2023, www.nps.gov/subjects/historicpreservation/national-historic-preservation-act.htm.

73. Brooks and Liscow, "Infrastructure Costs," 27.

74. Joseph L. Sax, "The (Unhappy) Truth About NEPA," *Oklahoma Law Review* 26 (1973). Quoted in Richard Stewart, "The Reformation of American Administrative Law," *Harvard Law Review* 88, no. 8 (June 1975): 1701–1702.

75. Weingroff, "Addressing the Quiet Crisis," 50.

76. Strauss, *"Citizens to Preserve Overton Park v. Volpe."*

77. Isabel Hibbard and Ian Coss, "Part 4: The Double Cross," in *The Big Dig*, podcast, www.wgbh.org/podcasts/the-big-dig/part-4-the-double-cross.

78. Strauss, *"Citizens to Preserve Overton Park v. Volpe."* Weingroff, "Addressing the Quiet Crisis."

79. Two months later, Democrats would lose sixty-three seats and control of the House in 2010's midterm elections.

80. Peter Baker, "Education of a President," *New York Times Magazine*, October 12, 2010.

81. Vice President Joe Biden would later complain that "if I took you and blindfolded you and took you to LaGuardia Airport in New York you must think, 'I must be in some third world country.'" Rawlings, "Joe Biden Says NYC Airport Like 'Some 3rd-World Country.'"

82. Jill Cowan, "California's Ambitious High-Speed Rail at a Crossroads," *New York Times*, March 13, 2022.

83. Leah Brooks and Zachary Liscow, "Can America Reduce Highway Spending? Evidence from the States," in *Economic Analysis and Infrastructure Investment*, ed. Edward L. Glaeser and James M. Poterba (Chicago: University of Chicago Press, 2021): 109.

84. Brooks and Liscow, "Infrastructure Costs."

85. Robert A. Kagan, *Adversarial Legalism: The American Way of Law*, 1st ed. (Cambridge, MA: Harvard University Press, 2001), 248–254.

86. Luz Lazo, "The 5 Higher-Speed Rail Projects Taking Shape in the U.S.," *Washington Post*, August 30, 2023. Ezra Klein, "What the Hell Happened to the California of the '50s and '60s?," *New York Times*, June 18, 2023.

87. The reforms of the last half century, if not longer, have inserted more and more vetoes into the system: the Clean Air Act, the Clean Water Act, the Endangered Species Act, and the National Historic Preservation Act, among others.

88. "Highway and Transit Projects: Evaluation Guidance Needed for States with National Environmental Policy Act Authority," U.S. Government Accountability Office, GAO-18-222, published January 30, 2018, www.gao.gov/products/gao-18-222.

89. Interview with administrative law attorney, January 26, 2024.

90. "Fiscal Responsibility Act of 2023," public law no. 118-5, June 3, 2023, www.congress .gov/118/plaws/publ5/PLAW-118publ5.pdf.

91. By "no figure," I mean that no one is so empowered. But fewer people are so employed as well. Zachary Liscow, Will Nober, and Cailin Slattery, "Procurement and Infrastructure Costs," working paper, September 2023, www.nber.org/papers/w31705. Philip K. Howard and Geoff Kabaservice, "Can America Untangle Itself from Red Tape? (With Philip K. Howard)," September 1, 2021, in *Vital Center*, podcast, www.niskanencenter.org /can-america-untangle-itself-from-red-tape-with-phillip-k-howard/.

92. Eli Dourado, "Much More Than You Ever Wanted to Know About NEPA," Center for Growth and Opportunity at Utah State University, October 20, 2022, www.thecgo.org /benchmark/much-more-than-you-ever-wanted-to-know-about-nepa/.

93. Jeremiah Johnson, "The Case for Abolishing the National Environmental Policy Act," *Liberal Currents*, September 6, 2022. In fairness, some believe the figure is overblown. Aaron Gordon, "Why Doesn't America Build Things?" *Vice News*, August 22, 2022, www.vice.com /en/article/93a39e/why-doesnt-america-build-things.

94. "Eminent Domain: Information About Its Uses and Effect on Property Owners and Communities Is Limited," Government Accounting Office, GAO-07-28, November 30, 2006, www.gao.gov/products/gao-07-28.

95. Romic Aevaz, Brianne Eby, Paul Lewis, and Robert Puentes, "Saving Time and Making Cents: A Blueprint for Building Transit Better," Eno Center for Transportation, July 29, 2021, https://enotrans.org/eno-resources/saving-time-and-making-cents-a-blueprint-for-building -transit-better/. Henry Grabar, "The Perverse Reason It's Easier to Build New Highways Than New Subways," *Slate*, August 19, 2021.

96. Transit Costs Project, "What the Data Is Telling Us," Marron Institute, accessed June 2, 2023, https://transitcosts.com/new-data/.

97. Eric Goldwyn, Alon Levy, and Elif Ensari, "Transit Costs Project: Lessons from the MBTA's Green Line Extension," NYU Marron Institute of Urban Management, YouTube video posted December 9, 2020, www.youtube.com/watch?v=gJ0BbJjE9cM.

98. Aevaz, Eby, Lewis, and Puentes, "Saving Time and Making Cents," 5.

99. Klein, "What the Hell Happened to the California of the '50s and '60s?"

100. "Proposed Highway Construction Through Overton Park, Memphis, Tenn."

101. The Clinton administration added money to transportation coffers by raising the gas tax. The Obama administration passed the Recovery Act. The Biden administration championed a massive bipartisan investment in the nation's infrastructure, not to mention billions in clean energy.

102. Eli Dourado, "We Need to Build Our Way Out of This Mess," *New York Times*, August 11, 2021.

103. "Highway and Transit Projects."

104. Interview with Ed Kussy, November 11, 2022. "Highway Projects: Some Federal and State Practices to Expedite Completion Show Promise," General Accounting Office, GAO-12-593, June 2012, 17–18, www.gao.gov/assets/gao-12-593.pdf.

105. Aevaz, Eby, Lewis, and Puentes, "Saving Time and Making Cents," 66–69.

106. Chris Megerian and Matthew Daly, "Debt Ceiling Deal Advances Pipeline and Tweaks Environmental Rules. But More Work Remains," *Associated Press*, June 1, 2023.

Chapter 8: A Tragedy of the Commons in Reverse

1. Shira Schoenberg, "Gov. Charlie Baker Signs Hydropower, Wind Energy Bill into Law," *MassLive.com*, August 8, 2016, www.masslive.com/politics/2016/08/gov_charlie_baker_signs_hydrop.html.

2. Shira Schoenberg, "Massachusetts Legislature Passes Renewable Energy Compromise Bill," *MassLive.com*, August 1, 2016, www.masslive.com/politics/2016/08/massachusetts_legislature_vote_1.html. Coal was almost entirely off the system by 2016. Today, it's gone. Per interview with Ari Peskoe, August 2023.

3. Tux Turkel, "Transmission Lines Over Kennebec Gorge? That May Be a Choke Point for Renewable Energy Advocates," *Portland Press Herald*, June 24, 2018. For example: www.bard.edu/cep/blog/?p=6888.

4. Josh Keefe, "What You Need to Know About the CMP Transmission Line Proposed for Maine," *Bangor Daily News*, January 29, 2019.

5. David Gelles, "A Border Clash Over a Project for U.S. Energy," *New York Times*, May 7, 2022. William Reilly, "This Maine Power Struggle Could Portend Trouble for Energy Projects Nationwide," *Washington Post*, October 6, 2021.

6. Tux Turkel, "CMP Wants to Build 145-Mile Transmission Line Through Western Maine," *Portland Press Herald*, July 27, 2017.

7. Tux Turkel, "$1 Billion CMP Proposal Fails to Win Bay State Energy Competition," *Portland Press Herald*, January 26, 2018, www.pressherald.com/2018/01/25/1-billion-cmp-proposal-fails-to-win-massachusetts-energy-competition/. Tux Turkel, "Prospects Improve for CMP's $950 Million Power Line Plan," *Portland Press Herald*, March 13, 2018.

8. David Brooks, "N. Pass Project Off the Table," *Concord Monitor*, July 27, 2019.

9. Turkel, "Prospects Improve for CMP's $950 Million Power Line Plan."

10. Turkel, "Transmission Lines Over Kennebec Gorge?" Turkel, "$1 Billion CMP Proposal Fails to Win Bay State Energy Competition."

11. Turkel, "CMP Wants to Build 145-Mile Transmission Line Through Western Maine."

12. Tux Turkel, "CMP Touts Its Bid to Build Transmission Line Through Maine," *Portland Press Herald*, December 6, 2017.

13. Matt Hongoltz-Hetling, "In Maine's North Woods, Some Worry a Fragile Ideal of Untouched Wilderness Could Be Lost Forever with a Changing Landscape and Risks for a Critical Species," *Portland Press Herald*, January 13, 2020.

14. David Abel, "Project Would Bring Renewable Energy to Mass. by Cutting Through Wilderness in Maine," *Boston Globe*, April 22, 2018.

15. Staff report, "CMP's $1 Billion Project to Deliver Renewable Power to Massachusetts Gets Second Chance," CentralMaine.com, February 16, 2018, www.centralmaine.com/2018/02/16/cmps-1-billion-project-to-deliver-renewable-power-to-massachusetts-gets-a-second-chance/.

16. Abel, "Project Would Bring Renewable Energy to Mass." Jon Chesto, "Enemies Line Up to Fight Power-Line Project Through Maine," *Boston Globe*, July 16, 2018.

17. Tux Turkel, "Unexpected Foes Emerge to CMP's Plan to Build Transmission Line to Canada," *Portland Press Herald*, March 25, 2018.

18. Turkel, "Prospects Improve for CMP's $950 Million Power Line Plan."

19. "CMP to Invest $22M in Western Maine Conservation, Tourism Projects," Mainebiz, June 7, 2018, www.mainebiz.biz/article/cmp-to-invest-22m-in-western-maine-conservation-tourism-projects.

20. Peter McGuire, "In Concession to Critics, CMP Says It Would Run Power Line Under Scenic Kennebec Gorge," *Portland Press Herald*, October 18, 2018.

21. Jon Chesto, "Delays in Maine Power Line Review Embolden Its Critics," *Boston Globe*, November 2, 2018.

22. Tux Turkel, "Issues in the Governor's Race: Energy Policy," *Portland Press Herald*, October 21, 2018.

23. "Maine Gov Boosts Power Line Project," *Lowell Sun*, February 22, 2019, www.lowellsun.com/2019/02/22/maine-gov-boosts-power-line-project/.

24. Tux Turkel, "CMP Sweetens Its Offer for Approval of Transmission Corridor, to $258 Million," *Portland Press Herald*, February 6, 2019.

25. "Governor Mills Statement Regarding NECEC Stipulation Before the PUC," *Targeted News Service*, February 21, 2019.

26. Doug Harlow, "High Profile Supporters Talk Up Virtues of CMP Power Line Project," *Morning Sentinel*, December 5, 2018. Tux Turkel, "Dark Money and Blurred Alliances Drum Up Resistance to CMP Power Line Project," *Portland Press Herald*, September 13, 2018. Benjamin Storrow, "Inside a Clean Energy Titan's Fight to Kill a Climate Project," *E&E News*, February 21, 2024, www.eenews.net/articles/inside-a-clean-energy-titans-fight-to-kill-a-climate-project/. Eliza Donoghue, "Maine Audubon Comments on the Proposed NECEC Transmission Line," Maine Audubon, April 4, 2019, https://maineaudubon.org/news/maine-audubon-comments-on-the-proposed-necec-transmission-line/.

27. Tux Turkel, "Patagonia Joins Fight Against CMP Transmission Line Through Maine," *Portland Press Herald*, June 7, 2018.

28. Christopher Burns, "Franklin County Town Overwhelmingly Rejects CMP's Proposed Transmission Line," *Bangor Daily News*, September 5, 2019. Edward D. Murphy, "List of Maine Towns Opposing CMP Transmission Corridor Grows," *Portland Press Herald*, September 1, 2019. Andrew Rice, "Growing Number of Towns Revolt Against CMP Transmission Line," *Sun Journal*, June 2, 2019.

29. Lori Valigra, "How and When Maine Will Decide Whether to Approve Permits for CMP's $1B Transmission Line," *Bangor Daily News*, April 5, 2019.

30. Opinion Contributor, "In CMP Corridor Debate, Process Matters," *Bangor Daily News*, April 15, 2019.

31. David Sharp, "CMP Power Line Approval 'Replete with Errors,' Energy Supplier Says in Appeal," *Portland Press Herald*, August 6, 2019.

32. Lori Valigra, "Feds Want CMP to Look Again at Ways to Reduce Environmental Impact of Proposed Hydro Project," *Bangor Daily News*, May 3, 2019.

33. Christopher Burns, "Jared Golden Concerned About 'Lack of Transparency' in Federal Permitting of CMP Corridor," *Bangor Daily News*, October 16, 2019.

34. Peter McGuire, "CMP Transmission Line Faces Critical Vote by State Land-Use Panel," *Portland Press Herald*, September 11, 2019.

35. Peter McGuire, "CMP Submits Last-Minute Change to Power Line Plan to Avoid Protected Pond," *Portland Press Herald*, September 19, 2019. Peter McGuire, "Revised Route for CMP Transmission Corridor Provides New Point of Contention," *Portland Press Herald*, September 27, 2019. Hongoltz-Hetling, "In Maine's North Woods, Some Worry a Fragile Ideal of Untouched Wilderness Could Be Lost Forever."

36. Tux Turkel, "Despite Its Foes, CMP Corridor Effort Well Underway," *Portland Press Herald*, March 8, 2020.

37. Edward D. Murphy, "CMP Shrugs Off Referendum," *Portland Press Herald*, February 15, 2020.

38. Lori Valigra, "Maine Towns, Environmental Group Challenge One of CMP Corridor's Key Permits," *Bangor Daily News*, June 10, 2020.

39. Lori Valigra, "Opponents Take First Formal Step to Bring CMP's Transmission Project to a Statewide Vote," *Bangor Daily News*, August 30, 2019. Peter McGuire, "Opponents of CMP Power Line Submit Signatures for Referendum," *Portland Press Herald*, February 3, 2020. Caitlin Andrews, "CMP Corridor Opponents Say They Have Signatures to Put Western Maine Project to a Vote," *Bangor Daily News*, February 3, 2020. Edward D. Murphy, "Referendum Effort on CMP Corridor Has Qualified for Ballot," *Portland Press Herald*, March 5, 2020.

40. Steve Collins, "Avangrid Sues to Block Fall Referendum on CMP Corridor," *Portland Press Herald*, May 14, 2020.

41. Editorial Board, "Our View: Maine Supreme Court Upholds Rule of Law in NECEC Case," *Portland Press Herald*, August 16, 2020.

42. Edward D. Murphy, "Groups File Lawsuit Against Army Corps of Engineers over CMP Corridor Analysis," *Portland Press Herald*, October 28, 2020. Jon Chesto, "Controversial Maine Power Line Gets Final Federal Permit, but Suffers Setback in Court," *Boston Globe*, January 16, 2021. "Controversial Power Project Gets Final Permit," *Sun Journal*, January 15, 2021. Edward D. Murphy, "Court Denies Injunction to Stop Work on CMP Corridor," *Portland Press Herald*, May 14, 2021. Edward D. Murphy, "Transmission Corridor in Jeopardy After Judge Vacates Lease of Public Land to CMP," *Portland Press Herald*, August 10, 2021. Edward D. Murphy, "Judge's Ruling May Jeopardize CMP Corridor," *Portland Press Herald*, August 11, 2021. Tux Turkel, "One Crucial Mile Creates Wide Gap for Power Project," *Portland Press Herald*, October 17, 2021.

43. Greg Kesich, "The View from Here: Western Maine Corridor Vote Would Add New Ways to Say 'No,'" *Morning Sentinel*, February 28, 2021.

44. Editorial Board, "Our Endorsement: Vote 'No' on Question 1 to Fight Climate Change," *Portland Press Herald*, October 24, 2021.

45. Sabrina Shankman, "Maine Vote Imperils Climate Bid by Mass.," *Boston Globe*, November 1, 2021.

46. Sabrina Shankman, "Maine Voters Reject Transmission Line That Would Bring Clean Energy to Mass.," *Boston Globe*, November 3, 2021. "Avangrid Statement on Results of Maine Referendum," *Business Wire*, November 3, 2021.

47. Jon Chesto, "Despite Loss in Maine, Avangrid CEO Vows to Press Forward with Power Line for Massachusetts," *Boston Globe*, November 5, 2021.

48. Megan Gray, "At Mills' Request, Work on Corridor Suspended," *Portland Press Herald*, November 20, 2021. Edward D. Murphy and Tux Turkel, "Maine DEP Suspends Construction License for $1 Billion Power Line," *Portland Press Herald*, November 23, 2021. Peter McGuire, "Judge Allows Ban on Power Line to Take Effect," *Portland Press Herald*, December 17, 2021. Colin A. Young, "Maine Suspends N.E. Hydro Project's License," *Boston Globe*, November 25, 2021.

49. Sabrina Shankman, "Maine Court Finds Part of Referendum Blocking Transmission Line to Massachusetts Unconstitutional," *Boston Globe*, August 30, 2022. Tux Turkel, "CMP Corridor Case Sent Back to Lower Court," *Portland Press Herald*, August 31, 2022. "Editorial: Maine Supreme Court Left Big Questions Unanswered in CMP Corridor Ruling," *TCA Regional News*, August 31, 2022. Richard Barringer, "Insight: Defeat by Delay: A Tale of Clean Energy and Dirty Money," *Portland Press Herald*, October 9, 2022.

50. Sabrina Shankman, "A Maine Jury Will Decide the Fate of the Embattled CMP Transmission Line," *Boston Globe*, April 7, 2023.

51. Tux Turkel, "Work Can Resume on CMP Power-Line Project, Jury Rules," *Portland Press Herald*, April 20, 2023.

52. Colin A. Young, "As Construction Costs Balloon, Mass. Hydro Transmission Project Set to Restart in August," *WBUR*, July 28, 2023.

53. Turkel, "Work Can Resume." Mika Damiano, "Maine Jury Rules Clean Energy Transmission Line from Canada to New England Can Proceed," *Boston Globe*, April 30, 2023.

54. Lori Valigra, "Work on the CMP Corridor Is Restarting but You Won't See It," *Bangor Daily News*, August 1, 2023.

55. Benjamin Storrow, "Maine Transmission Line Is Stalled Despite Court Victories," *E&E News*, April 27, 2023, www.eenews.net/articles/maine-transmission-line-is-stalled-despite-court-victories/.

56. Valigra, "Work on the CMP Corridor Is Restarting but You Won't See It."

57. Marissa Bodnar, "Ask the I-Team: What's Going on with the CMP Corridor?," WGME.com, March 19, 2024, https://wgme.com/news/i-team/ask-the-i-team-whats-going-on-with-the-cmp-corridor-maine-central-maine-power-new-england-clean-energy-connect-canadian-hydropower-avangrid-hydro-quebec.

58. Russell Gold, *Superpower: One Man's Quest to Transform American Energy* (New York: Simon and Schuster, 2019), 20.

59. Melvin I. Urofsky, *Louis D. Brandeis: A Life* (New York: Schocken Books, 2009), 140, 150.

60. Forrest McDonald, "Samuel Insull and the Movement for State Utility Regulatory Commissions," *Business History Review* 32, no. 3 (Autumn 1958): 249–250.

61. William Boyd and Ann E. Carlson, "Accidents of Federalism: Ratemaking and Policy Innovation in Public Utility Law," *UCLA Law Review* 63, no. 4 (May 2016): 822.

62. McDonald, "Samuel Insull and the Movement for State Utility Regulatory Commissions," 251.

63. The "exchange" was not legally binding. See Ari Peskoe, Senior Fellow in Electricity Law, Harvard Environmental Policy Initiative, to Quadrennial Energy Review Task Force, Office of Energy Policy and Systems Analysis, U.S. Department of Energy, http://eelp.law .harvard.edu/wp-content/uploads/Harvard-Environmental-Policy-Initiative-QER-Comment -There-Is-No-Regulatory-Compact.pdf.

64. William Boyd, "Public Utility and the Low-Carbon Future," *UCLA Law Review* 61, no. 6 (May 2014): 1641–1644.

65. Gold, *Superpower*, 21.

66. Lina M. Khan, "Amazon's Antitrust Paradox," *Yale Law Journal* 126, no. 3 (January 2017): 797–798.

67. Boyd, "Public Utility and the Low-Carbon Future," 1640.

68. Boyd and Carlson, "Accidents of Federalism," 823–825.

69. Boyd, "Public Utility and the Low-Carbon Future," 1635.

70. Jim Rossi, "The Brave New Path of Energy Federalism," *Texas Law Review* 95, no. 2 (2016). Boyd and Carlson, "Accidents of Federalism," 823–826. Interview with Ari Peskoe, December 14, 2021. Eric Holmes, "This Land Is Your Land? Eminent Domain Under the Natural Gas Act and State Sovereign Immunity," Congressional Research Service, October 30, 2019.

71. Annmarie Hauck Walsh, *The Public's Business: The Politics and Practice of Government Corporations* (Cambridge, MA: MIT Press, 1978), 3–13.

72. Boyd and Carlson, "Accidents of Federalism," 829–830.

73. Gold, *Superpower*, 168–173.

74. Boyd, "Public Utility and the Low-Carbon Future," 1658–1659.

75. Richard F. Weingroff, "Addressing the Quiet Crisis: Origins of the National Environmental Policy Act of 1969," Federal Highway Administration, updated June 27, 2017, www .fhwa.dot.gov/highwayhistory/nepa/index.cfm. Lorraine Boissoneault, "The Cuyahoga River Caught Fire at Least a Dozen Times, but No One Cared Until 1969," *Smithsonian Magazine*, June 19, 2019.

76. Stuart E. Eizenstat, *President Carter: The White House Years* (New York: St. Martin's, 2018), 137–141.

77. Weingroff, "Addressing the Quiet Crisis."

78. Gold, *Superpower*, 187–195.

79. Eizenstat, *President Carter*, 141–147.

80. Lawrence Kumins, "National Gas Policy Act," Congressional Research Service, May 1983.

81. Interview with energy policy expert, November 18, 2022. Alexandra B. Klass and Elizabeth J. Wilson, "Interstate Transmission Challenges for Renewable Energy: A Federalism Mismatch," *Vanderbilt Law Review* 65, no. 6 (2012): 1806. Boyd, "Public Utility and the Low-Carbon Future," 1653–1661.

82. Boyd, "Public Utility and the Low-Carbon Future," 1661–1662.

83. Boyd and Carlson, "Accidents of Federalism," 830–834.

84. Jim Rossi, "The Trojan Horse of Electric Power Transmission Line Siting Authority," *Environmental Law* 39 (2009): 1021–1022.

85. Interview with Ari Peskoe, December 14, 2021.

86. Gold, *Superpower*, 30–31.

87. Interview with energy policy expert, November 18, 2022.

88. Klass and Wilson, "Interstate Transmission Challenges for Renewable Energy," 1817–1821.

89. Gold, *Superpower*, 129–130.

90. Gold, *Superpower*, 157–159, 197–201.

91. Gold, *Superpower*, 157–227, 202–204.

92. Jim Carlton, "Solar Power's Land Grab Hits a Snag: Environmentalists," *Wall Street Journal*, June 4, 2021.

93. Wally Nowinski, "America's Top Environmental Groups Have Lost the Plot on Climate Change," *Noahpinion*, January 15, 2022, www.noahpinion.blog/p/americas-top -environmental-groups.

94. Scott Merzbach, "Amherst Residents Voice Support for Moratorium on Large-Scale Solar Projects," *Daily Hampshire Gazette*, January 11, 2022.

95. Nowinski, "America's Top Environmental Groups Have Lost the Plot on Climate Change."

96. Email from Ivan Penn of the *New York Times*, June 9, 2022.

97. Ivan Penn, "How a Florida Power Project Flew Under the Regulatory Radar," *New York Times*, May 31, 2022.

98. *An Inconvenient Truth*, directed by David Guggenheim (Paramount, 2006), www .amazon.com/gp/video/detail/amzn1.dv.gti.eea9f730-cc03-4407-e866-aa4a9ee893d5.

99. Peter Fairley, "How a Plan to Save the Power System Disappeared," *Atlantic*, August 20, 2020.

100. Tom Wilson, "Fusion Energy Breakthrough by US Scientists Boosts Clean Power Hopes," *Financial Times*, December 11, 2022.

101. The number of miles of existing line is in seemingly perpetual dispute. See, among other possible sources, Lara Pierpoint and Liza Reed, "Getting More Energy on the Wires," November 3, 2022, in *Catalyst with Shayle Kann*, podcast, www.canarymedia.com/podcasts /catalyst-with-shayle-kann/getting-more-energy-on-the-wires. Liza Reed, "Transmission Stalled: Siting Challenges for Interregional Transmission," Niskanen Center, April 14, 2021, www .niskanencenter.org/transmission-stalled-siting-challenges-for-interregional-transmission/.

102. Editorial Board, "We Desperately Need a New Electrical Grid. Here's How to Make It Happen," *New York Times*, May 4, 2023.

103. Jerusalem Demsas, "Why America Doesn't Build," *Atlantic*, October 27, 2023.

104. Rayan Sud, Sanjay Patnaik, and Robert Glicksman, "How to Reform Federal Permitting to Accelerate Clean Energy Infrastructure: A Nonpartisan Way Forward," Center on Regulation and Markets at Brookings, February 14, 2023, 13, www.brookings.edu/wp-content /uploads/2023/02/20230213_CRM_Patnaik_Permitting_FINAL.pdf.

105. Gold, *Superpower*, 252.

106. Interview with Ari Peskoe, December 14, 2021. Klass and Wilson, "Interstate Transmission Challenges for Renewable Energy," 1813.

107. Interview with Liza Reed, November 30, 2021.

108. Joseph H. Eto, "Building Electric Transmission Lines: A Review of Recent Transmission Projects," Lawrence Berkeley National Laboratory, September 2016, 26, https://live -etabiblio.pantheonsite.io/sites/default/files/lbnl-1006330.pdf.

109. Rossi, "The Trojan Horse of Electric Power Transmission Line Siting Authority."

110. Liza Reed, "The Exploding Federal Role in Electricity Transmission," www.youtube.com/watch?v=VS_FjMwiCI8.

111. Klass and Wilson, "Interstate Transmission Challenges for Renewable Energy," 1859–1860.

112. Sud, Patnaik, and Glicksman, "How to Reform Federal Permitting." Reed, "Transmission Stalled," 9. Joe Weisenthal and Tracy Alloway, "John Arnold on Why It's So Hard to Build Things in America," June 20, 2024, in *Odd Lots*, podcast, www.bloomberg.com/news/articles/2024-06-20/john-arnold-on-why-it-s-so-hard-to-build-things-in-america.

113. Reed, "Transmission Stalled," 9. Reed, "The Exploding Federal Role in Electricity Transmission." Interview with Liza Reed, November 8, 2022.

114. Reed, "The Exploding Federal Role in Electricity Transmission."

115. Brad Plummer, "Energy Dept. Aims to Speed Up Permits for Power Lines," *New York Times*, April 25, 2024. Coral Davenport, "Biden Administration Moves to Speed Up Permits for Clean Energy," *New York Times*, April 30, 2024.

Conclusion: Full-Circle Progressivism

1. Daniel P. Carpenter, *The Forging of Bureaucratic Autonomy: Reputations, Networks, and Policy Innovation in Executive Agencies, 1862–1928* (Princeton, NJ: Princeton University Press, 2001), 37.

2. Henry L. Stimson and McGeorge Bundy, *On Active Service in Peace and War* (New York: Harper, 1948), 59.

3. Stephen Skowronek, *Building a New American State: The Expansion of National Administrative Capacities, 1877–1920* (New York: Cambridge University Press, 1982), 20–21.

4. Gordon S. Wood, *Power and Liberty: Constitutionalism in the American Revolution* (New York: Oxford University Press, 2021), 54–73. Mary Sarah Bilder, *Madison's Hand: Revising the Constitutional Convention* (Cambridge, MA: Harvard University Press, 2015), 29.

5. Those who went to Philadelphia to write the Constitution wanted "to restore government as against democracy." Walter Lippmann, *Public Opinion* (Overland Park, KS: Digireads.com, 2020), 151–153.

6. Skowronek, *Building a New American State*, 21–23.

7. Jamal Greene, *How Rights Went Wrong: Why Our Obsession with Rights Is Tearing America Apart* (New York: Houghton Mifflin Harcourt, 2021), xxii.

8. Skowronek, *Building a New American State*, 160.

9. Stimson and Bundy, *On Active Service in Peace and War*, 59.

10. Skowronek, *Building a New American State*, 165–166.

11. David Levering Lewis, *The Improbable Wendell Willkie* (New York: Liveright, 2018), 68–69.

12. Ezra Klein, "Two Theories of What I'm Getting Wrong," *New York Times*, July 16, 2023.

13. Even the fiercest critics of Hamiltonianism or, using a different label, "high modernism" can see its value when applied in the right contexts: James C. Scott, *Seeing Like a State: How Certain Schemes to Improve the Human Condition Have Failed* (New Haven, CT: Yale University Press, 1998), 221.

14. Ezra Klein, "The Problem with Everything-Bagel Liberalism," *New York Times*, April 2, 2023.

15. Skowronek, *Building a New American State*, 259–263.

16. As quoted in Reuel E. Schiller, "Rulemaking's Promise: Administrative Law and Legal Culture in the 1960s and 1970s," *Administrative Law Review* 53, no. 4 (Fall 2001): 1165–1166.

17. David L. Bazelon, "Coping with Technology Through the Legal Process," *Cornell Law Review* 62, no. 5 (June 1977): 824.

18. Adam B. Cox and Emma Kaufman, "The Adjudicative State," *Yale Law Journal* 132, no. 6 (April 2023): 1798–1803, 1811.

19. Saige Miller, "Utah Will Soon Have Water Judges. This Is What They'll Do and Why It Matters," *Salt Lake Tribune*, June 29, 2022.

20. Herbert Croly, at the dawn of the progressive movement, spoke explicitly to the desire not to let "rights" become too powerful a force—as the confluence of various intersecting rights had upended efforts to end slavery until Lincoln pushed through. David K. Nichols, "The Promise of Progressivism: Herbert Croly and the Rejection of Individual Rights," *Publius: The Journal of Federalism* 17, no. 2 (Spring 1987): 31.

21. Romic Aevaz, Brianne Eby, Paul Lewis, and Robert Puentes, "Saving Time and Making Cents: A Blueprint for Building Transit Better," Eno Center for Transportation, July 29, 2021, 172–174, https://enotrans.org/eno-resources/saving-time-and-making-cents-a-blueprint-for-building-transit-better/.

22. Because this book has focused on progressivism, conservative political doctrine has not received a great deal of scrutiny. But it's worth noting here that the conservative majority on the Roberts court is actively working against this sort of outcome. Cox and Kaufman, "The Adjudicative State," 1774–1778. Amy Howe, "Supreme Court to Hear Major Case on Power of Federal Agencies," SCOTUSblog, January 16, 2024, www.scotusblog.com/2024/01/supreme-court-to-hear-major-case-on-power-of-federal-agencies/.

23. Edward Rubin, "It's Time to Make the Administrative Procedure Act Administrative," *Cornell Law Review* 89, no. 1 (November 2003): 137.

24. Richard J. Pierce Jr., "The Unintended Effects of Judicial Review of Agency Rules: How Federal Courts Have Contributed to the Electricity Crisis of the 1990s," *Administrative Law Review* 43, no. 1 (Winter 1991). Harold Dubroff and Brant J. Hellwig, *The United States Tax Court: An Historical Analysis* (Government Printing Office, 2014), www.ustaxcourt.gov/resources/book/Dubroff_Hellwig.pdf.

25. Ed Rogers, "The Consequences of Clinton's 'Deplorables' and Obama's 'Clingers,'" *Washington Post*, September 12, 2016, www.washingtonpost.com/blogs/post-partisan/wp/2016/09/12/the-consequences-of-clintons-deplorables-and-obamas-clingers/.

26. Nicholas Lemann, "The Myth of Community Development," *New York Times*, January 9, 1994.

INDEX

timber industry, 60
Tobin, Austin, 157
Tonight Show (television), 176
totalitarianism, 14, 121
Tower, John, 250
trans-Alaska oil pipeline, 152–153
transmission lines, 280–291, 297–299, 301–303,
    306–309
  Clean Line, 311–313, 317–318
  federal government supporting, 310–311,
    318–320
  fracking compared to, 320
  TPL, 314–315
Transmission Line Siting Act, Florida, 314–315
Triborough Bridge Authority, 157
Trilling, Lionel, 88
trucking industry, 183–184
Truman, David, 104–105
Truman, Harry S., 67, 85, 87, 89, 106, 109
  APA by, 138, 173, 192
  Roosevelt, F., and, 102
  "slum clearing" under, 218
Trump, Donald, 7, 19–20, 34, 312–313, 316,
    330–333
tuberculosis, 60, 69
Tugwell, Rexford, 75–76
TVA. *See* Tennessee Valley Authority
typhoid fever, 21, 69

UCLA. *See* University of California, Los Angeles
UDC. *See* Urban Development Corporation
ULURP. *See* Uniform Land Use Review
    Procedure
unemployment, 98
Uniform Land Use Review Procedure (ULURP),
    New York, 227–228
unionization, unions and, 79, 90, 98, 131, 165,
    169–170, 183
United States (US). *See specific topics*
United States v. E. C. Knight Co., 39
University of California, Los Angeles (UCLA), 8
Unsafe at Any Speed (Nader), 116
Urban Development Corporation (UDC),
    202–209, 220, 264
urban planning, 214–223, 229, 232–233,
    239–249, 266–267
US. *See* United States (US)
Utah, 328

Vanderbilt University, 8
Vanzetti, Bartolomeo, 72
Vermont Yankee Nuclear Power Corp. v. NRDC,
    188
Verrazzano-Narrows Bridge, New York City, 3

vertical integration, energy industry, 299, 301,
    304, 308
Vietnam War, 2, 14, 67, 114–115, 118, 128
violence, 35, 94, 104, 117–118, 127
Virginia, 309
voice but not a veto approach, 325–330
voters, 8, 11, 32, 331
  rights of, 33, 54, 78, 111–113
  Trump attracting, 332–333
Voting Rights Act (1965), US, 111–113

*Wabash, St. Louis & Pacific Railway Company v.
    Illinois*, 51
wages, 40, 44
  minimum, 8, 79, 82, 84
  poverty, 41, 96
Wagner Act, US, 81
War Industries Board, US, 56, 60, 76, 84
War Powers Act, US, 155
Washington, George, 323–324
Washington Post (newspaper), 121, 166
water courts, 328
Watergate scandal, 14, 120–121, 123, 160, 182
welfare programs, 7, 139–148, 154, 158–159
Wellstone, Paul, 302
Wendell, Oliver, 79
Wertham, Fredric, 104
West Coast Hotel Co. v. Parrish, 82
West Virginia, 298, 309
Wheeler, Burton, 83, 90
white flight, 220, 251
Whitehouse, Sheldon, 320
white supremacy, 66, 87–88, 116
Wicks Law, New York, 18, 20
widows, 141
Willkie, Wendell, 63–64, 179
Wilson, Sloan, 86
Wilson, Woodrow, 13, 27, 29, 79–81, 108, 324
  Hamiltonianism of, 55–56
  Roosevelt, T., and, 50, 54–56
wind turbines, wind powers and, 279, 281–282,
    289, 303, 307–308
  Obama on, 310–313
  South Fork Wind project, 317–318
Wisconsin, 64, 295
the Wisemen (Georgetown Set), 87, 105, 150
Wollman Rink, Central Park, 16–20,
    330
women, 181
  African American, 113
  bodily autonomy and, 8, 331–332
  minimum wages for, 41–42
  voting rights for, 33, 54, 78
  welfare programs and, 141–148

MARC J. DUNKELMAN is a fellow at Brown University's Watson Institute for International and Public Affairs, and a former fellow at NYU's Marron Institute of Urban Management. During more than a decade working in politics, he worked for Democratic members of both the Senate and the House of Representatives, and as a senior fellow at the Clinton Foundation. He is the author of *The Vanishing Neighbor: The Transformation of American Community*, and his work has also appeared in the *New York Times, Atlantic, Politico, Washington Post*, and the *Wall Street Journal*. He lives in Providence, Rhode Island.

PublicAffairs is a publishing house founded in 1997. It is a tribute to the standards, values, and flair of three persons who have served as mentors to countless reporters, writers, editors, and book people of all kinds, including me.

I. F. STONE, proprietor of *I. F. Stone's Weekly*, combined a commitment to the First Amendment with entrepreneurial zeal and reporting skill and became one of the great independent journalists in American history. At the age of eighty, Izzy published *The Trial of Socrates*, which was a national bestseller. He wrote the book after he taught himself ancient Greek.

BENJAMIN C. BRADLEE was for nearly thirty years the charismatic editorial leader of *The Washington Post*. It was Ben who gave the *Post* the range and courage to pursue such historic issues as Watergate. He supported his reporters with a tenacity that made them fearless and it is no accident that so many became authors of influential, best-selling books.

ROBERT L. BERNSTEIN, the chief executive of Random House for more than a quarter century, guided one of the nation's premier publishing houses. Bob was personally responsible for many books of political dissent and argument that challenged tyranny around the globe. He is also the founder and longtime chair of Human Rights Watch, one of the most respected human rights organizations in the world.

· · ·

For fifty years, the banner of Public Affairs Press was carried by its owner Morris B. Schnapper, who published Gandhi, Nasser, Toynbee, Truman, and about 1,500 other authors. In 1983, Schnapper was described by *The Washington Post* as "a redoubtable gadfly." His legacy will endure in the books to come.

Peter Osnos, *Founder*